Preparation
for the
Gospel

Eusebius
TRANSLATED BY
Edwin Hamilton Gifford

2 PARTS

Part 2
Books 10-15

Baker Book House
Grand Rapids, Michigan 49506

Reprinted 1981 by Baker Book House Company

ISBN: 0-8010-3369-1 (paper)
ISBN: 0-8010-3370-5 (cloth)

This edition is a reproduction of the 1903 edition
issued by The Clarendon Press (Oxford). Reproduction copy was supplied by The University of Texas
at Austin General Libraries.

Printed in the United States of America

Contents

EUSEBIUS

THE PREPARATION FOR THE GOSPEL

BOOK X

CHAPTER I

WE have previously explained for what reasons we p. 460
(Christians) have preferred the philosophy of the Hebrews
to that of the Greeks, and on what kind of considerations b
we accepted the sacred Books current among the former
people ; and then afterwards we proved that the Greeks
themselves were not ignorant of that people, but men-

tioned them by name, and greatly admired their mode
of life, and have given a long account both of their royal
capital, and other matters of their history. Now then let
us go on to observe how they not only deemed the record of
these things worthy to be written, but also became zealous
imitators of the like teaching and instruction in some
c of the doctrines pertaining to the improvement of the
soul.

I shall show then almost immediately how, from various
sources, one and another of these wonderful Greeks, by
going about among the Barbarians, collected the other
branches of learning, geometry, arithmetic, music, astronomy, medicine, and the very first elements of grammar,
and numberless other artistic and profitable studies.

d   In the previous part of my discourse I proved that
they had received from Barbarians their opinion concerning a multitude of gods, and their mysteries and initia-
tions, and moreover their histories, and their fabulous
stories about gods, and their physical explanations of the
fables as expressed in allegory, and the rest of their
superstitious error. This, I say, was proved at the time
when we convicted the Greeks of having wandered
over much of the earth, and then set up their own
theology on all points, not indeed without labour and care,
but by contributions from the learning current among
Barbarians : and soon it shall be proved that from no
other source than from Hebrews only could they have
procured the knowledge of the worship of the One
Supreme God, and of the doctrines most ,in request
for the benefit of the soul, which of course would also
be most conclusive of their discussions on philosophy.

p. 461   Or otherwise, if any one should say that they were
moved to the same conclusions by innate conceptions,
even this would be in our favour, that we preferred to be zealous followers of the doctrines delivered
not only to Hebrews from the earliest ages by prophets
who spake of God, but also, if not to all, yet to some, and

those certainly the very men who were greatly renowned in Greece, doctrines carefully examined also in the discussions of the philosophers.

Now these men you would find to be few in number, because all excellence is proverbially difficult to attain; but nevertheless they have been honoured with the first place among the philosophers of Greece, so that through **b** their great fame they overshadow the reputation of their fellows.

But you must not be surprised if we say that possibly the doctrines of the Hebrews have been plagiarised by them, since they are not only proved to have stolen the other branches of learning from Egyptians and Chaldees and the rest of the barbarous nations, but even to the present day are detected in robbing one another of the honours gained in their own writings.

At all events one after another they surreptitiously steal the phrases of their neighbours together with the thoughts **c** and whole arrangement of treatises, and pride themselves as if upon their own labours. And do not suppose that this is my statement, for you shall again hear the very wisest of them convicting one another of theft in their writings.

And this very fact, since we have once mentioned it, we must consider as evidence before all else of the character of the said persons. Our Clement then, in his sixth *Miscellany*, has arranged the proof of this point at full **d** length: so take and read me his words first, such as the following:

Chapter II

' Now after having shown that the significance of Greek CLEMENT thought was illumined on all sides from the truth bestowed on us through the Scriptures, according to the sense which we took in proving that the theft of the truth (if it be not offensive to say so)

---

461 d 4 Clement, *Miscellanies*, vi. c. 2, § 4

CLEMENT came home to them ; let us proceed to bring forward the Greeks as witnesses of the theft against themselves.

p. 462   ' For they who so openly filch their own works one from another establish the fact that they are thieves, and betray, however unwillingly, that they are secretly appropriating to their own countrymen the truth borrowed from us. For if they do not keep their hands off even from one another, it is not likely that they will from our writers.

' Now of their philosophical doctrines I shall say nothing, since the very men who have divided themselves into sects, confess in writing, in order that they may not be convicted of ingratitude, **b** that they have received the most important of their doctrines from Socrates.   But after employing a few testimonies of men familiarly known and renowned among the Greeks, and exposing their style of plagiarism, by dealing with various periods, I shall turn to the subjects next in order.'

After these statements by way of preface, he brings forward his proofs in order, using all kinds of evidence, and calls the poets first to account as having stolen the thoughts from other poets, by a comparison of their respective utterances.

c   Then next he adds the following :

' In order that we may not allow philosophy, nor history, nor even rhetoric to pass free from the same charge, it is reasonable to bring forward a few passages from them also.'

Then he successively compares passages of Orpheus, Heracleitus, Plato, Pythagoras, Herodotus, Theopompus, Thucydides, Demosthenes, Aeschines, Lysias, Isocrates, and ten thousand others, of whose sayings it is superfluous for me to make a catalogue, as the author's work is ready **d** at hand, in which, after the evidences concerning the said authors, he again speaks as follows :

' Let then these specimens of Greek plagiarism in thought suffice, being such as they are, for a clear example to one who has any power of discernment.   But further they have been detected not

---

462 c 2 Clement, *Miscellanies*, vi. c. 2, § 16   d 3 ibid. § 25

only in filching and paraphrasing the thoughts and the expres- CLEMENT
sions, but, as shall be shown, they have stolen the works of others
wholesale, and brought them out as their own; as Eugamon of
Cyrene stole the entire book *Concerning the Thesprotians* from
Musaeus.'

Clement having afterwards added to these very many
proofs of his argument, again at the end makes this
addition:

'Life would fail me, should I attempt to go over in particular
detail the proof of the selfish plagiarism of the Greeks, and how
they claim as their own the discovery of the noblest doctrines
current among them, which they have taken from us.

'But now they are convicted not only of stealing their doctrines **p. 463**
from the Barbarians, but also of copying our records of deeds so
wonderfully wrought of old by the divine power through men of
holy lives for our study, and exhibiting them in the marvellous
stories of Greek mythology.

'And so we shall inquire of them whether these stories which
they relate are true or false. False they would not say; for they
would not willingly convict themselves of the great folly of
recording falsehoods; but they would of necessity confess that they **b**
are true.

'But how then do the deeds miraculously exhibited by Moses
and the other prophets any longer appear incredible to them?
For the Almighty God in His care for all men tries to convert
them to salvation, some by commandments, some by threatenings,
some by miraculous signs, and some by gentle promises.

'Moreover, once when a drought was for a long time ruining
Greece, and a dearth of food prevailed, the Greeks, those of them
who were left, it is said, because of the famine came as suppliants **c**
to Delphi, and asked the Pythoness how they might be delivered
from the danger. And she answered them that there was only
one way of escape from the calamity, that they should employ the
prayer of Aeacus. So Aeacus was persuaded by them, and went
up to the Hellenic Mount, and, stretching out his pure hands to
heaven, called upon God as the common Father, and prayed Him
to have pity upon Hellas in her distress.

---

d 14 Clement, *Miscellanies*, vi. c. 2, § 27   463 a 1 ibid. c. 3, § 28

CLEMENT   'And while he was yet praying there was a portentous
d sound of thunder, and all the surrounding air grew clouded, and
violent and continuous rains burst forth and filled the whole
country. Thence an abundant and rich harvest, produced by the
husbandry of the prayers of Aeacus, is brought to perfection.

'" *And Samuel* (says the Scripture) *called upon the Lord, and
the Lord gave thunder and rain in the day of harvest.* Seest thou
that there is One God, who *sendeth rain upon the just and unjust*
by means of the powers subject to Him? "'   And the rest.

To this Clement subjoined countless instances, and
convicted the Greeks of having been plagiarists by indisputable proofs. But if you do not think him trustworthy,
inasmuch as he, like us, has himself preferred the philosophy of the Barbarians to that of Greece, well then let
him be dismissed, although he conducted his argument
not in words of his own, but in those of Greeks themselves. But what would you say, if you should learn the
like facts even from your noble philosophers themselves?
Listen then to their testimonies also.

CHAPTER III

p. 464   'WHEN Longinus was entertaining us in Athens at the banquet
PORPHYRY in memory of Plato, he had invited among many others Nicagoras
the Sophist, and Major, and Apollonius the Grammarian, and
b Demetrius the Geometer, and Prosenes the Peripatetic, and
Callietes the Stoic.

'With these reclined the host himself making seven, and while
supper was going on, and some question about Ephorus had
arisen among the others, he said, Let us hear what is this
clamour about Ephorus? Now the disputants were Caÿstrius
and Maximus : for the latter was for preferring him to Theopompus, while Caÿstrius called him a plagiarist.

---

463 d 5 1 Sam. xi. 18   d 7 Matt. v. 45   464 a 1 Porphyry, *Lecture
on Literature*, Bk. i, Fragment preserved by Eusebius

' " For what," said he, " belongs properly to Ephorus, who PORPHYRY transfers from the writings of Daïmachus, and Callisthenes, and Anaximenes word for word sometimes as much as three thousand whole lines ? "

' In answer to whom Apollonius the Grammarian said, " Yes, **c** for you are not aware that even Theopompus, whom you prefer, is infected with the same fault, as having in the eleventh book of his *History of Philip* copied word for word from the *Areopagiticus* of Isocrates that famous passage, " that nothing good and nothing evil comes to men quite of itself," and the rest.

' And yet he despises Isocrates, and says that his master was defeated by himself in the contest in honour of Mausolus. Then he has committed a theft of facts, by transferring what he found told of some men to others, that in this way he might also be convicted of falsehood. **d**

' For whereas Andron in *The Tripod*, writing of the philosopher Pythagoras, had narrated the story of his predictions, and said that once at Metapontium having been thirsty, and having drawn up and drunk water from a certain well, he foretold that on the third day there would be an earthquake. And after adding some other remarks to these, he proceeds :

' " So whereas Andron had told this story concerning Pythagoras, Theopompus filched it all. If he had mentioned Pythagoras, perhaps others also would have known about it, and said, The Master also said that. But now the change of the name has made the plagiarism manifest ; for he has made use **p. 465** of the same facts, but substituted another name : and he has represented Pherecydes of Syros as uttering this prediction.

' And not only by this name does he try to conceal the theft, but also by a change of localities : for the prophecy of the earthquake narrated by Andron as spoken in Metapontium, Theopompus says was uttered in Syria. And the incident about the ship was observed, he says, not from Megara in Sicily, but from Samos : and the capture of Sybaris he has transferred to that of Messene.

' But in order that he might seem to say something more than **b** common, he has also added the name of the stranger, saying that

---

c 5 Isocrates, *Areopagiticus*, p. 140   d   465 a 3 Or ' Pherecydes the Syrian '

PORPHYRY he was called Perilaus." "I too," says Nicagoras, "in reading his *Hellenics* and Xenophon's, have detected him in transferring many things from Xenophon; and the mischief is that he has changed them for the worse.

'"For instance, the account of the conference of Pharnabazus with Agesilaus through the mediation of Apollophanes of Cyzicus, and their conversations with each other under a truce, which Xenophon in his fourth Book recorded very gracefully and in a c manner becoming to both, Theopompus has transferred into the eleventh Book of his *Hellenics*, and deprived of all vigour, and movement, and effect.

'"For while, in order to hide his theft, he strives to throw in and to display forcible and elaborate language, he appears slow, and hesitating, and procrastinating, and destroys the animation and vigour of Xenophon."

'After Nicagoras had thus spoken, Apollonius said, But what wonder that the vice of plagiarism infected Theopompus and Ephorus, who were merely very dull men, when even Menander was full of this infirmity, though in censuring him Aristophanes the d Grammarian, because of his excessive friendship for him, dealt gently in his parallel extracts from him and from those whom he plagiarised. But Latinus in six books, which he entitled *Of Menander's Appropriations*, exposed the multitude of his plagiarisms.

'In the same way Philostratus of Alexandria began a treatise *On the Plagiarism of Sophocles*. And Caecilius, thinking that he has discovered something of great importance, says that Menander transcribed a whole drama, *The Augur* of Antiphanes, from beginning to end, into *The Superstitious Man*.

'But since, says he, it has seemed good to you, I know not how, p. 466 to bring forward the plagiarists, I myself also inform against the charming Hyperides as having stolen many things from Demosthenes, both in the speech *Against Diondas* and in the one *Concerning the bribes of Eubulus*.

'And that one of them has borrowed from the other is manifest : but as they were contemporaries it must be your task, Apollonius, says he, to track the plagiarist from the dates. Now I suspect that the one who has stolen is Hyperides : but as it is uncertain b which it was, I admire Demosthenes, if he borrowed from Hyperides and made appropriate corrections; but I blame Hyperides if he Porphyry borrowed from Demosthenes, and perverted it for the worse.'

And soon after he says :

'Why need I tell you, how the *Barbarian Customs* of Hellanicus is a compilation out of the works of Herodotus and Damastes? Or how Herodotus in his second Book has transferred many passages of Hecataeus of Miletus from the *Geography,* verbally with slight falsifications, as the account of the bird Phoenix, and of the hippopotamus, and of the hunting of crocodiles?

'Or how the statements in Isaeus concerning torture, in his **c** oration *Concerning the inheritance of Cylon,* are found also in the *Trapeziticus* of Isocrates, and in the oration of Demosthenes *Against Onetor on an action of ejectment* are expressed almost in the same words?

'Or how Dinarchus in his first speech *Against Cleomedon in an action for assault* has transferred many things word for word from the speech of Demosthenes *Against Conon for assault?*

'Or how this sentiment of Hesiod's,

"Nought can man better than a good wife win,
  Nor find a worse bane than a vicious shrew,"

was borrowed by Simonides in his eleventh Book, who took it **d** thus :
    "Of all the prizes man can win, a wife
    If good is best, if evil far the worst."

'And by Euripides in *Melanippe the Captive* :

"For than a bad wife nought can e'er be worse,
  Nor aught excel a virtuous woman's worth ;
  But of their natures there is difference great."

'And whereas Euripides said :

"A race most wretched we poor women are,"

Theodectes says in the *Alcmaeon* :

"'Tis a true proverb in the mouths of men,
  Than woman nought more wretched e'er was born."

---

466 c 10 Hesiod,*Works and Days*, 702   d 3 Simonides, *Fr.* 6 (Bergk),
224 (Gaisf.)   d 6 Euripides, *Fr.* 29 (511)   d 10 Euripides, *Medea*, 231
d 12 Theodectes, *Fr.* 2 (Wagner)

497

p. 467   This author has not only taken the suggestion from that passage, but
PORPHYRY   has also employed the very words ; and he craftily preferred to give
it a proverbial character, and to employ it as a saying used by
many, rather than to seem to have taken it from its original author.

'Antimachus too steals Homer's verse, and blunders in correct-
ing it. For Homer having said :

> "Idas was strongest born of men on earth,"

Antimachus says :

b   "Idas was strongest of all men on earth."

And Lycophron praises the alteration on the ground that the line
is thereby strengthened.

'As to Homer's

> "Τὸν δ' ἀπαμειβόμενος προσέφη κρείων Διομήδης"

I say nothing, since Homer has been ridiculed in comedy by
Cratinus because of his frequent repetition of

> "Τὸν δ' ἀπαμειβόμενος"

which, though so trite, Antimachus did not hesitate to borrow.

c   'The line,

> "The tribes he ruled with mild paternal sway,"

is Homer's : and again in another place it is written,

> "They on either side
> In closer ranks the deep battalions ranged."

But Antimachus, by transferring half-lines, has made the verse

> "Of all the tribes they ruled
> In closer ranks the deep battalions ranged."

d   'But lest while charging others with plagiarism I should be
convicted as a plagiarist myself, I will indicate those who have
treated this subject.   There are two books of Lysimachus *Concerning the Plagiarism of Ephorus*.   Alcaeus also, the poet of the
vituperative Iambics and Epigrams, has detected and parodied
the plagiarisms of Ephorus : then there is an epistle of Pollio
to Soteridas *Concerning the Plagiarism of Ctesias*, and a book of
the same author *Concerning the Plagiarism of Herodotus*, and in the

---

467 a 7 Hom. *Il.* i. 558   b 1 Antimachus, *Fr.* 34 (Dübner)   c 2
Hom. *Od.* ii. 234   c 4 Hom. *Il.* xvi. 563   c 7 Antimachus, *Fr.* 34

book entitled *The Searchers* there are many statements concerning PORPHYRY Theopompus, and there is a treatise of Aretades *Concerning Coincidence*, from which works one may learn many examples of this kind.'

After other passages he adds:

'Prosenes also said, The other plagiarists you have detected: but that even this hero Plato himself, after whom the feast which **p. 468** we are celebrating to-day is named, makes use of many works of his predecessors (for in his case I feel too much respect to use the term "plagiarism"), this you have not proceeded to discover.

'What say you? said Callietes. I not only say, replied Prosenes, but I also offer the proof of my statement. Now the books of Plato's predecessors are rare: else perhaps one might have detected more of the philosopher's plagiarisms. As to one, however, which I myself lighted upon by chance, in reading the discourse of Protagoras *Concerning Being* against those who represent "Being" as one, I find him employing answers of the **b** following kind; for I was careful to remember what he said in his very words.'

And after this preface he sets out the proofs at large.

But I think that out of numberless examples those which have been mentioned are sufficient to show what was the character of the Greek writers, and that they did not spare even the exposure one of another. Yet in further preparation for showing the benefit which has overflowed to the Greeks from the Hebrew Scriptures, I think it will be right and necessary for me to prove generally that all the celebrated learning and philosophy of the Greeks, both their elementary studies, and their grand system **c** of logical science, have been collected by them from Barbarians, so that none of them may any longer lay blame upon us, because forsooth we have preferred the religion and philosophy of the Barbarians to their grand doctrines.

---

d 14 Porphyry, *Lecture on Literature*, Bk. i

CHAPTER IV

d   YOU may judge that not without sound reason have we given a secondary place to the doctrines of the Greek philosophy, and preferred the theology of the Hebrews, when you learn that even among the Greeks themselves those who have most of all treated philosophy correctly, and thought out something more and better than the vulgar talk about the gods, have discovered no other true doctrines than those which had received a previous sanction among the Hebrews.

For some of them, being carried away hither and thither by various false opinions, were driven about into an abyss of idle prating ; while others, who have in some p.469 degree employed candid reasoning, have shown themselves partakers in the teaching of the Hebrews in those points wherein they attained to the conception of the truth.

It is probable at all events that having become very learned, and having curiously investigated both the customs and the learning of the nations, they were not unacquainted with the philosophy of the people just mentioned, being younger in time, so to speak, than all men, not Hebrews only, nor yet Phoenicians and Egyptians only, but also than the ancient Greeks themselves.

b   For these ancients some doctrines derived from Phoenicia were arranged by Cadmus son of Agenor ; and others concerning the gods from Egypt or elsewhere, mysteries and rites, the setting up of statues, and hymns, odes, and epodes, either by the Thracian Orpheus, or some other Greek or Barbarian, who became their leaders in error : for the Greeks themselves would acknowledge that they know no men more ancient than these.

They say at least that Orpheus flourished first of all, then Linus, and afterwards Musaeus about the time

of the Trojan war, or a little before. But certainly in
their time nothing more than the theology of the c
Phoenicians and Egyptians, with its manifold errors, had
a home among the Greeks.

Moreover, among the other nations, in all countries
and cities, these very doctrines and others similar to
them were carefully observed in sacrifices and mysteries.
At all events, the aforesaid doctrine concerning the gods
largely prevailed among all mankind : and very beautiful
shrines were everywhere furnished and adorned with all
kinds of statues and offerings : moreover, images of all
kinds of material were moulded into every form of mortal
animals and tastefully finished.

And further, there was among them all a manifold and d
profuse abundance of oracles. Indeed a certain god
especially revered and mighty among the Greeks was at
that time most flourishing, the Pythian, Clarian, and
Dodonaean god : and then Amphiaraus, and Amphi-
lochus, and after these flowed on a countless multitude
of soothsayers rather than of poets and rhapsodists.

But at length, long ages after them, philosophy arrived
among the Greeks, and found among their forefathers
nothing that properly belonged to herself, but discovered
that the sanctities and antiquities of the theology which
had come to them from their fathers, and even the
marvellous and universally famous divinities and oracles,
were in reality superfluous and unprofitable.

Wherefore she proceeded to put these back into a p. 470
secondary place, as they could not be of any use to her
for the discovery of things necessary and true : and
thenceforth, as one naked and destitute of any reasonings
or learning of her own, she went about examining the
foreign and barbarous systems, and providing, collecting,
and borrowing what was useful to her from all sides,
whatever she found among the several nations.

For indeed she began to discover that not only the
true theology was lacking to the Greeks, but also the

b most useful in daily life of all the other arts and sciences.
Indeed the Greeks themselves confess that it was after
Orpheus, Linus, and Musaeus, the most ancient of all
their theologians and the first to introduce among them
the error of polytheism, that their seven men whom they
surnamed Sages were celebrated for wisdom. And these
flourished about the time of Cyrus king of Persia.

Now this was the time in which the very latest of the
c Hebrew prophets were prophesying, who lived more than
six hundred years after the Trojan war, and not less than
fifteen hundred years after the age of Moses: and this
will be manifest to you when presently going through
the records of the chronology.

Born somewhere about this recent period the Seven
Sages are remembered for a reform of moral conduct, but
nothing more is recorded of them than their celebrated
maxims. But somewhat late, and lower down in time,
the philosophers of the Greeks are reported to have
flourished.

d   First among these Pythagoras the pupil of Pherecydes,
who invented the name ' philosophy,' was a native, as
some say, of Samos, but according to others of Tyrrhenia;
while some say that he was a Syrian or Tyrian, so that
you must admit that the first of the philosophers,
celebrated in the mouth of all Greeks, was not a Greek
but a Barbarian.

Pherecydes also is recorded to have been a Syrian, and
Pythagoras they say was his disciple. He is not, however,
the only teacher with whom, as it is said, Pythagoras was
associated, but he spent some time also with the Persian
Magi, and became a disciple of the Egyptian prophets, at
the time when some of the Hebrews appear to have made
their settlement in Egypt, and some in Babylon.

p. 471   In fact the said Pythagoras, while busily studying the
wisdom of each nation, visited Babylon, and Egypt, and
all Persia, being instructed by the Magi and the priests:
and in addition to these he is related to have studied

under the Brahmans (these are Indian philosophers); and from some he gathered astrology, from others geometry, and arithmetic and music from others, and different things from different nations, and only from the wise men of Greece did he get nothing, wedded as they were to a poverty and dearth of wisdom: so on the contrary he himself became the author of instruc- b tion to the Greeks in the learning which he had procured from abroad.

Such then was Pythagoras. And first in succession from him the so-called Italian philosophy was formed, which derived its title to the name from its abode in Italy: after this came the Ionic school, so called from Thales, one of the seven Sages: and then the Eleatic, which claimed as its founder Xenophanes of Colophon.

Even Thales, however, as some relate, was a Phoenician, but as others have supposed, a Milesian: and he too c is said to have conferred with the prophets of the Egyptians.

Solon also who was himself one of the Seven Sages, and is said to have legislated for the Athenians, is stated by Plato to have resorted in like manner to the Egyptians, at the time when Hebrews were again dwelling in Egypt. At least he introduces him in the *Timaeus* as receiving instruction from the Barbarian, in the passage where the Egyptian says to him, 'O Solon, Solon, you Greeks are always children, and there is not one old man among the Greeks, ... nor is there among you any learning grown hoary with time.'

This same Plato, too, after having attended the teaching d of the Pythagoreans in Italy, was not contented with his studying with them only, but is said to have sailed to Egypt and devoted a very long time to their philosophy. This testimony indeed he himself bears to the Barbarians

---

471 c 10 Plato, *Timaeus*, 22 B; cf. Clement, *Miscellanies*, i. c. 15

in many passages of his own discourses, and therein, I think, does well, and candidly confesses that the noblest doctrines are imported into philosophy from the Barbarians. Accordingly in many places, and especially in the *Epinomis*, you may hear him mentioning both Syrians and Egyptians in the following manner:

PLATO   'The cause of this is that he who first observed these phenomena was a Barbarian: for it was a very ancient region which bred those who first took notice of these things because of the

p. 472 beauty of the summer season, which both Egypt and Syria fully enjoy. . . . Whence the knowledge has reached to all countries, including our own, after having been tested by thousands of years and time without end.'

And lower down he next adds:

' Let us take it then that, whatever Greeks may have received from Barbarians, they work out and finish it with greater beauty.'

So says Plato. But Democritus also, still earlier, is said to have appropriated the ethical doctrines of the Babylonians. And somewhere, boasting about himself, he says:

DEMO- b   'But of the men of my time I have wandered over the most
CRITUS   land, investigating the most distant parts, and have seen the most climates and soils, and listened to the greatest number of learned men, nor did any one ever yet surpass me in the construction of lines accompanied by demonstration, nor yet those Egyptians who are called Arpedonaptae, for all which purposes I passed as much as five years in foreign lands.'

For this man also visited Babylon, and Persia, and Egypt, and was a disciple of the Egyptians and their priests.

c   What if I were to count up to you Heracleitus and all the other Greeks, by whom civil life among the Greeks

---

471 d 12 Pseudo-Plato, *Epinomis*, 986 E   472 a 6 ibid. 987 E
b 1 Clement, *l. c.*

is proved to have been left for long ages very poor, and devoid of all learning.

It was embellished indeed with temples of the gods, and images and statues, and prophecies and oracles, and the manifold pomp of the fraudulent daemons, but of true wisdom and of useful science it was utterly destitute.

Nor did their useless oracles contribute aught to the discovery of good counsels: but even their wonderful d Pythian god did not help them at all in philosophy, nor did any other deity assist them in the pursuit of any needful good. But wandering hither and thither, and running about all their life they bedecked themselves, according to the fable, with borrowed plumes; so that now their whole philosophy consisted of what they begged.

For by copying different sciences from different nations, they got geometry from the Egyptians, and astrology from the Chaldeans, and other things again from other countries; but nothing among any other nations like the benefit which some of them found from the Hebrews.

For this was the knowledge of the God of the universe, and the condemnation of their own gods, which our argument as it proceeds a little farther will prove.

But thus much at present it indicates to the readers, p. 473 that the ancient Greeks were destitute not only of true theology, but also of the sciences which are profitable to philosophy; and not of these only, but also of the common habits of civil life.

And I believe that this indication will assist me in the demonstration of the object which I have proposed; inasmuch as my proposal is to uphold the plea, that we have not unreasonably preferred the theology of the Hebrews, and that of the Barbarians, as they would call it, to the philosophy of the Greeks.

If then it should be seen they have themselves gathered b it all long before from Barbarians, and have received from their own gods no help at all in philosophy, but have even found fault justly with their gods ; and if some of them for these reasons have preferred atheism to the worship of the gods, then what right have they any more to find fault with us, instead of welcoming and commending us, because from having loved the better part, or rather from having found and recovered that which alone is true, we have withdrawn from the false-

c hood, without either turning round like the wise men of the Greeks to atheistic reasoning, or on the other hand mixing up the error of polytheism with the knowledge of the Supreme God, in a similar way to their admirable philosophers, nor yet have confused the falsehood with the truth ?

Let us not, however, discuss these points yet, but first let me ask you to consider those proofs by which the Greeks are convicted of having stolen everything from Barbarians, not only their philosophical science, but also the common inventions which are useful in daily life.

CHAPTER V

d FIRST therefore he who introduced to the Greeks the common letters, even the very first elements of grammar, namely Cadmus, was a Phoenician by birth, from which circumstance some of the ancients have surnamed the alphabet Phoenician.

But some say that the Syrians were the first who devised letters. Now these Syrians would be Hebrews who inhabited the neighbouring country to Phoenicia,

p. 474 which was itself called Phoenicia in old times, but afterwards Judaea, and in our time, Palestine. And it is evident that the sound of the Greek letters is very closely connected with these.

For example, each letter among the Hebrews has its name from some significant idea, a circumstance which it is not possible to trace among the Greeks : on which account especially it is admitted that the letters are not originally Greek.

Now the Hebrews have in all twenty-two letters : of which the first is 'Alph,' which translated into the Greek **b** language would mean 'learning': and the second 'Beth,' which is interpreted 'of a house': the third is 'Gimel,' which is 'fullness': the fourth 'Delth,' which signifies 'of tablets': the fifth 'Hê,' which is 'this.' And all these together make up a meaning of this kind, 'Learning of a house, fullness of tablets this.'

Then after these is a sixth letter called among them 'Wau,' which is 'in it': then 'Zaï,' which is 'liveth': after which comes 'Heth,' which is 'the living': that the whole may be 'in it liveth the living.'

After these a ninth letter, 'Teth,' which is 'good': **c** then 'Yoth,' which is interpreted 'beginning'; the two together, 'good beginning.' After these 'Chaph,' which is 'nevertheless': then 'Labd,' which is 'learn': the whole being 'nevertheless learn.'

'After these is a thirteenth letter 'Mem,' which is 'from them': then 'Nun,' which is 'eternal.' Then 'Samch,' which is interpreted 'help': that the meaning may be, 'from them eternal help.'

After these is 'Aïn,' which being translated signifies 'fountain,' or 'eye': then 'Phe,' 'mouth.' Then next 'Sade,' 'righteousness': of which the meaning is 'fountain (or 'eye') and mouth of righteousness.'   **d**

After these is a letter 'Koph,' which is interpreted 'calling': then 'Res,' which is 'head': and after these 'Sen,' which is 'teeth': last of all the twenty-second letter is called with them 'Thau,' which means 'signs.' And the sense would be, 'calling of the head, and signs of the teeth.'

Among the Hebrews such is the paraphrase and interpretation of the letters, making up a meaning in words appropriate to the learning and promise of the letters. But the like you cannot find among the Greeks, whence, as I said, it must be acknowledged that they do not belong originally to the Greeks, but have been imitated directly from the language of the Barbarians.

This is also proved from the very name of each letter.
p. 475 For in what does 'Alpha' differ from 'Alph'? Or 'Beta' from 'Beth'? Or 'Gamma' from 'Gimel'? Or 'Delta' from 'Delth'? Or 'Epsilon' from 'Hê'? Or 'Zeta' from 'Zaï'? Or 'Theta' from 'Teth'? And all the like cases.

So that it is indisputable that these names belong not originally to the Greeks: therefore they belong to the Hebrews, among whom each of them shows some signification. And having originated with them the letters passed on to other nations, and so to the Greeks. About the letters of the alphabet I have said enough: but you must hear also what Clement says in dealing with the
b subject before us.

Chapter VI

CLEMENT   'THE healing art is said to have been invented by Apis the Egyptian . . . and afterwards improved by Aesculapius. Atlas the Libyan was the first who built a ship, and sailed the sea. . . .
c   'Astrology also was first made known among men by the Egyptians and Chaldeans. . . . Some, however, say that prognostication by the stars was devised by the Carians. The Phrygians were the first to observe the flights of birds.

'The inspection of sacrificial victims was accurately practised by the Tuscans who border on Italy. The Isaurians and Arabians perfected augury, and the Telmessians, doubtless, divination by dreams.

'The Tyrrhenians invented the trumpet, and Phrygians the flute; for both Olympus and Marsyas were Phrygians. . . . The Egyptians again first taught men to burn lamps, and divided the
d year into twelve months, and forbade intercourse with women in temples, and enacted that none should enter temples after intercourse without bathing.

---

475 b 3 Clement, *Miscellanies*, i. c. 16

'The same people again were the inventors of geometry. . . . CLEMENT
Kelmis and Damnameneus, the Idaean Dactyls, first discovered
iron in Cyprus. And the tempering of bronze was invented by
Delas, another Idaean, or, as Hesiod says, a Scythian.

'Certainly Thracians were the first who invented the so-called
scimitar, which is a curved sword, and they first used targes on
horseback : in like manner the Illyrians invented the so-called
targe (πέλτη). Further they say that the Tuscans invented the
art of moulding clay : and Itanus, who was a Samnite, fashioned
the long shield.

'Cadmus the Phoenician invented stone-cutting, and discovered **p. 476**
the gold mines near Mount Pangaeus. Moreover another nation,
the Cappadocians, first invented the so-called " nabla," as the
Assyrians the lyre of two strings.

'The Carthaginians were the first to fit out a quadrireme, and
it was built off hand by Bosporus. Medea of Colchis, the daughter
of Aeëtes, first devised the dyeing of the hair.

'The Noropes (a Paeonian tribe, now called Noricum) worked **b**
copper, and were the first to refine iron. Amycus, the king of the
Bebryces, invented boxing-thongs.

'With regard to music, Olympus the Mysian was fond of
practising the Lydian harmony : and the so-called Troglodytes
invented a musical instrument, the sambuca.

'They say also that the slanting pipe was invented by Satyrus
the Phrygian, and in like manner the trichord, and the diatonic
harmony by Hyagnis who also was a Phrygian : notes likewise by
Olympus the Phrygian ; as the Phrygian harmony and the Mixo-
Phrygian, and the Mixo-Lydian by Marsyas, fellow countrymen of **c**
those just named : and the Dorian was invented by Thamyris the
Thracian.

'We have heard too that the Persians were the first who made
a carriage, and couch, and footstool, and that the Sidonians first
built a trireme. The Sicilians who are close to Italy were the
first to invent a lyre, not far inferior to the harp, and devised
castanets.

'Robes of fine linen are said to have been invented in the time
of Semiramis, queen of the Assyrians : and Atossa who reigned **d**
over the Persians is said by Hellanicus to have been the first to
use folded letters.

Clement   ' These things then were related by Scamon of Mitylene, and Theophrastus of Ephesus, and Cydippus of Mantinea, also by Antiphanes, and Aristodemus, and Aristotle, and besides these by Philostephanus, and Straton the Peripatetic in the books *Concerning Inventions*. And I have quoted a few of them in confirmation of the inventive and practical genius of Barbarians, from whom the Greeks have received the benefit of their institutions.'

These things Clement states in these very words in the *Miscellanies*. And to what has now been mentioned I think it well to append also the extracts from the writing of Josephus the Hebrew, which he composed in two books, *Of the Antiquity of the Jews*, on the point that the Greeks are a young nation, and have received help from the Barbarians, and have dissented from each other in their writings. This too will contribute to the

P. 477 accurate and sure confirmation of my statements. Hear therefore what he also writes, word for word.

Chapter VII

Josephus   ' My first thought then is of utter astonishment at those who think it right to attend to none but Greeks concerning the most ancient facts, and to seek to learn the truth from them, but to disbelieve us and the rest of mankind.

' For I see that the very opposite is the case, if at least we are
b not to follow vain opinions, but draw the just conclusion from the facts themselves. For you will find all things among the Greeks to be recent, having come into existence, as one might say, yesterday or the day before; I mean the foundation of their cities, and their invention of the arts, and the registration of their laws : and
c the writing of their histories is almost the latest object of their attention.

' Doubtless, however, they themselves admit that the most ancient and most constant traditional record is that of the events which have occurred among the Egyptians, and Chaldeans, and

---

477 a 3 Josephus, *Against Apion*, i. 2

Phoenicians (for at present I omit to include ourselves with JOSEPHUS these).

' For they all inhabit regions which are least subject to destruction from the surrounding atmosphere, and have taken much care to leave none of the facts of their history unrecorded, but to have all continually enshrined by their wisest men in public registers.

' But the region about Greece has been invaded by thousands of destructive plagues, which blotted out the memory of past events : **d** and as they were always setting up new modes of life, they each of them supposed that their own was the beginning of all.

' Tardily and painfully they learned the nature of letters. Those at least who assign the greatest antiquity to their use of them boast of having learned it from the Phoenicians and Cadmus.

' Nevertheless no one could show any record that is preserved even from that time either in temples or on public monuments : seeing that there has been great doubt and inquiry, whether even those who so many years later went on the expedition to Troy, made use of writing ; and the true opinion is rather that they were ignorant of the use now made of written letters.   **p. 478**

' In short, there is no undisputed writing found among the Greeks older than Homer's poetry : and he was evidently later than the Trojan war. They say too that even he did not leave his poetry in writing, but that it was transmitted by memory and afterwards put together from the songs, and that this is the cause of its many discrepancies.

' Those, however, among them who undertook to write histories —I mean Cadmus of Miletus and Acusilaus of Argos, and any **b** others who are said to have come after him—lived but a short time before the expedition of the Persians against Greece.

' Moreover all with one voice acknowledge, that the first among the Greeks who philosophized about things celestial and divine, as Pherecydes the Syrian, and Pythagoras, and Thales, got their learning from Egyptians and Chaldeans, and wrote but little : and these writings are thought by the Greeks to be the oldest of **c** all, and they do not quite believe that they were written by those authors.

' Is it not then necessarily unreasonable for the Greeks to have been puffed up, as though they alone understood the events of early times, and handed down the truth concerning them cor-

Josephus rectly?   Or who could not easily learn from the same historians, that they had no certain knowledge of anything which they wrote, but gave each their own conjectures about the facts?

'Accordingly in their books they frequently refute one another, and do not hesitate to make the most contrary statements concerning the same events.   But it would be superfluous labour for me to teach those who know better than myself on how many points

d Hellanicus has dissented from Acusilaus in regard to the genealogies, and how often Acusilaus sets Hesiod right; or in what fashion Ephorus exposes Hellanicus as making very many false statements, and Ephorus is exposed by Timaeus, and Timaeus by those who came after him, and Herodotus by them all.

'Nor did Timaeus deign to agree with Antiochus and Philistus or Callias about Sicilian history, nor again have the authors of Athenian histories followed each other's statements about the affairs of Attica, nor the historians of Argos about the affairs of Argolis.

'And why need I speak about the smaller affairs of the several states, seeing that the most celebrated authors have disagreed

P. 479 about the Persian invasion and the events which happened therein?   And on many points even Thucydides is accused by some of falsehood, although he is thought to write the history of his own time with the greatest accuracy.

'Now of dissension such as this many other causes might perhaps be brought to light by those who wish to seek for them; but I myself attach the greatest importance to two causes which shall now be set forth.

'And I will mention first that which seems to me to be the more decisive.   For the fact that from the beginning there was no zealous care among the Greeks to have public records kept of contemporary events—this most of all was the cause of error, and

b gave impunity for falsehood to those who afterwards wished to write about ancient history.

'For not only among the other Greeks was the care of the records neglected, but even among the Athenians themselves, who are said to be aborigines and studious of culture, nothing of this kind is found to have been done: but the oldest of their public records they say are the laws about murder written for them by

c Draco, a man born a little before the tyranny of Peisistratos.

'What need is there to speak of the Arcadians, who boast of JOSEPHUS antiquity? For they even at a later period were scarcely instructed in the use of letters.

'Inasmuch therefore as no record had been published, which would have taught those who wished to learn, and convicted those who were guilty of falsehood, there ensued the great disagreement of the historians among themselves.

'But besides this there is that other second cause to be assigned. For those who set themselves to write made no serious study of the truth—although they have always this profession ready at **d** hand—but tried to display their power of language; and adapted themselves to any style in which they thought to surpass the rest in reputation on this point; and some of them turned to writing mythical tales, and some, to gain favour, took to eulogizing cities or kings; while others had recourse to censuring men's actions or those who had described them, thinking that they should gain reputation herein.

'In short they are constantly doing what is of all things the most contrary to history. For it is a test of true history, whether all spake and wrote the same accounts of the same events; but these men imagined that if they wrote different accounts from others, they should thus appear to be themselves most truthful of all.'

So much says Josephus. And these statements may **p. 480** be confirmed by the testimony of Diodorus, which I shall quote from the first Book of the *Bibliotheca* compiled by him, and which is word for word as follows:

CHAPTER VIII

'AFTER having thoroughly explained these points, I must state DIODORUS how many of those who have been famed among the Greeks for intelligence and culture made a voyage to Egypt in ancient **b** times, in order that they might gain some knowledge of its customs and culture.

'For the priests of the Egyptians report from the records in their sacred books that they were visited by Orpheus, and

---

480 a 5 Diodorus Siculus, i. 96

DIODORUS Musaeus, and Melampus, and Daedalus, and besides these by the
poet Homer, and Lycurgus the Spartan; also by Solon the
c Athenian, and Plato the philosopher; and that there came also
Pythagoras of Samos, and Eudoxus the mathematician, Democritus
of Abdera also, and Oenopides of Chios.

'And as evidences of all these they point to the images of some,
and the names of places or buildings called after others. Also
from the branch of learning studied by each the priests bring
proofs of the fact that they had brought over from Egypt
everything whereby they gained admiration among the Greeks.

d 'Thus Orpheus, they say, brought away from the Egyptians
most of the mystic rites, and the orgiastic celebration of his own
wandering, and the fable concerning those in Hades. For the
rite of Osiris is the same as that of Dionysus : and that of Isis is
very similar to that of Demeter, with only the change of names.
And the punishments of the ungodly in Hades, and the meadows
of the godly, and the making of moulded images (of the shades)
common among the multitude he is said to have introduced in
imitation of the Egyptian customs in regard to burial.

'For Hermes the conductor of souls, according to the ancient
custom among the Egyptians, having brought up the body of Apis
to a certain place gives it over to him who wears the face of
Cerberus. And after Orpheus had made this known among the
Greeks, Homer, it is said, following him wrote in his poem :

p. 481   "Cyllenian Hermes waved his golden wand,
               And summoned forth the souls of heroes slain." '

Then again farther on he adds :

'They say that Melampus brought from Egypt the customary
rites performed in honour of Dionysus among the Greeks, and the
mythological tales concerning Kronos, and those concerning the war
of the Titans, and the entire history of the sufferings of the gods.

'Daedalus, it is said, imitated the winding of the labyrinth
b which remains up to the present time, but was built, as some say,
by Mendes, or, as others say, by king Marus many years before
the reign of Minos : the proportion too of the ancient statues in
Egypt is said to be the same with that of the statues made by
Daedalus in Greece.

---

481 a 1 Homer, *Od.* xxiv. 1   a 4 Diod. Sic. i. 97

'Daedalus was also said to have been the architect of the very DIODORUS
beautiful vestibule of Hephaestus in Memphis, for which he was
admired, and received a wooden statue in the said temple, wrought c
by his own hands. And at last being held in great honour
for his genius, and having made many more discoveries, he
received divine honours. For in one of the islands near
Memphis there is still a temple of Daedalus venerated by the
inhabitants.

'Of Homer's visit to Egypt they bring forward among other
proofs especially the drugging of Telemachus by Helen in the
house of Menelaus, and his oblivion of the evils that had befallen
him. For it is evident that the poet had carefully examined
the soothing drug which he says that Helen had obtained from d
Egypt, from Polydamna the wife of Thôn.

'Even at the present time they still say that the women in
this country use the same medicine, and they assert that a remedy
for anger and sorrow has been discovered from ancient times
among the women of Diospolis only : and that Thebes and
Diospolis are the same city : also that among the inhabitants
Aphrodite is called the " golden " from an ancient tradition, and
that near the city named Momemphis there is a so-called " plain
of golden Aphrodite."

'Also the mythical tales concerning Zeus and Hera and their
intercourse, and their travelling to Ethiopia, Homer is said to
have brought thence. For among the Egyptians, year by year, the
shrine of Zeus is carried across the river into Libya, and after p. 482
some days it returns again, as if the god were come from Ethiopia:
and that the intercourse of these deities takes place when at
their festivals both their shrines are carried up into a mountain
crowned with all kinds of flowers by the priests.

'They say that Lycurgus also, and Plato, and Solon, inserted
many of the customs of Egypt in their codes of law, and that
Pythagoras learned from the Egyptians the doctrines of the *Sacred
Word,* and the theories of geometry, and the science of numbers,
and besides these the migration of the soul into every kind of
animal.   b

'They suppose also that Democritus spent five years among

---

c 6 Homer, *Od.* iv. 220-230

DIODORUS them, and was taught many of the principles of astrology; and that Oenopides in like manner lived with the priests and astrologers and learned, among other things, that the sun's orbit has an oblique path, and that he is carried in the opposite direction to the other heavenly bodies.

'In like manner also it is said that Eudoxus studied astrology c with them, and published much useful information to the Greeks, whereby he acquired a notable reputation.

'And of all the ancient statuaries those whose names are most widely known had sojourned with them, Telecles and Theodorus the sons of Rhoecus, who had made the statue of the Pythian Apollo for the Samians.'

Thus far Diodorus. But here I must let this argument, with such proof as has been given, come to an end. Henceforth then we ought not to be charged with unreasonableness, if in our desire for the true religion we have ourselves resorted to the teachers of the wise Greeks d and even of their philosophers, I mean the Barbarians, if at least the Hebrews are Barbarians.

Now it would be well to examine their chronology, I mean the dates at which Moses and the prophets after him flourished: since this would be one of the most conclusive evidences for the argument before us, that before dealing with the learned men among the people we should first decide about their antiquity; in order that, if the Greeks should be found to hold the same doctrines with the prophets and theologians of the Hebrews, you may no longer be in doubt who were likely to have borrowed from the others; whether the elder from the younger, Hebrews from Greeks, and Barbarians from philosophers, p. 483 whose language even they were not likely to understand; or, what is more likely, that the younger borrowed from the elder, and that those Greeks who had most busily studied the history of the various nations were not unacquainted with the writings of the Hebrews, which had been long before translated into the Greek language.

CHAPTER IX

WITH regard to Moses and the antiquity of the prophets **b** who came after him, very many others have carefully laid down the evidence in their own writings, from which I shall presently make some few quotations.

But I myself shall take a more novel course than the said authors, and shall adopt the following method. As there is an acknowledged agreement between the times of the Roman emperor Augustus and the birth of our Saviour, and as Christ began to teach the gospel in the fifteenth year of Tiberius Caesar, any one who may choose to count up the number of the years from this point proceeding to the earlier times, until Darius king of the **c** Persians, and the restoration in his time of the temple in Jerusalem, which took place after the return of the Jewish nation from Babylon, will find that from Tiberius to the second year of Darius there are five hundred and forty-eight years.

For the second year of Darius coincides with the first year of the sixty-fifth Olympiad : and the fifteenth of the reign of Tiberius at Rome falls in with the fourth year of the two hundred and first Olympiad.

The Olympiads therefore between Darius the Persian **d** and Tiberius the Roman emperor are a hundred and thirty-seven, which make up a period of five hundred and forty-eight years, four years being counted to the Olympiad.

But since the seventieth year of the desolation of the temple in Jerusalem was in the second year of Darius, as the records of Hebrew history show, if we run back from this point again, from the second year of Darius to the first Olympiad there would be made up two hundred and fifty-six years, sixty-four Olympiads : and the same you would find to be the number of years from the last year of the desolation of the said temple going back to the fiftieth year

of Uzziah king of Judah, in whose time prophesied Isaiah
p. 484 and Hosea, and all who were contemporary with them.
So that the first Olympiad of the Greeks falls in with
the time of the prophet Isaiah and his contemporaries.

Again, going back from the first Olympiad to the
previous times as far as the capture of Troy, you will find
a sum of four hundred and eight years, as contained in
the chronological records of the Greeks.

And according to the Hebrews, from the fiftieth year
of Uzziah king of Judah going back to the third year of
b Labdon as judge of Israel, you will make up the same
number of years, four hundred and eight; so that the
capture of Troy was in the times of Labdon the judge,
seven years before Samson ruled over the Hebrews, who
is said to have been irresistible in strength of body, like
the famous Hercules among the Greeks.

If from this point also you go back to the earlier
generations, and count up to yourself four hundred years,
you will find among the Hebrews Moses, and among the
Greeks Cecrops the earthborn.

Now the history of the events so celebrated among the
c Greeks is later than the times of Cecrops. For after
Cecrops comes the deluge in the time of Deucalion, and
the conflagration in the time of Phaethon, and the birth
of Erichthonius, and the rape of Persephone, and the
mysteries of Demeter, the establishment of the Eleusinian
mysteries, the husbandry of Triptolemus, the abduction
of Europa by Zeus, the birth of Apollo, the arrival of
Cadmus at Thebes, and, still later than these, Dionysus,
Minos, Perseus, Asclepius, the Dioscuri, and Hercules.

d   Now Moses is proved to have been older than all these,
as having been in the prime of life at the time of Cecrops.
And going back again from Moses to the first year of the
life of Abraham, you will find five hundred and five
years. And counting up as many for the earlier time
from the aforesaid year of the reign of Cecrops, you will
come to Ninus the Assyrian, who is said to have been

the first ruler of all Asia except India : after him was named the city Ninus, which among the Hebrews is called Nineve ; and in his time Zoroastres the Magian reigned over the Bactrians. And the wife of Ninus and his successor in the kingdom was Semiramis ; so Abraham was contemporary with these.

Now in the Canons of Chronology composed by us these events were proved to demonstration to be as I have said. But on the present occasion in addition to what has been stated I shall adduce as witness of the antiquity of Moses the very bitterest and fiercest enemy both of the **p. 485** Hebrews and of us Christians, I mean that philosopher of our time, who having in his excessive hatred published his compilation against us, subjected not us only, but also the Hebrews and Moses himself and the prophets after him, to the like slanders. For I believe that I shall thus confirm my promise beyond controversy by the confession of our enemies.

Well then in the fourth Book of his compilation against us Porphyry writes what follows, word for word :

'The truest history of the Jews, as being that which most **b** Por-
perfectly accords with their localities and names, is that of   PHYRY
Sanchuniathon of Berytus, who received their records from
Hierombalus the priest of the God Jevo ; he dedicated his history
to Abelbalus king of Berytus, and was approved by him and by
his examiners of truth. Now the times of these men fall before
the date of the Trojan war, and approach closely to that of Moses, **c**
as is shown by the successions of the kings of Phoenicia. And
Sanchuniathon, who with careful regard to truth made a collection
of all ancient history from the records of each city and the registers
of the temples, and wrote it in the language of the Phoenicians,
lived in the time of Semiramis queen of Assyria.'

So says Porphyry. We must then calculate the proposed dates as follows. If Sanchuniathon lived in the time of Semiramis, and she is acknowledged to have

---

485 b 1 Porphyry, *Against the Christians*, bk. iv ; cf. p. 31 a

been long before the Trojan war, Sanchuniathon also must be older than the Trojan war.

But he is said to have received the records from others d older in time than himself: and they being themselves older than he are said to have approached closely to the times of Moses, though not even themselves contemporary with Moses, but approaching closely to his times : so that Sanchuniathon was as much younger than Moses, as he was later than his own predecessors who were acknowledged to approach near to Moses.

It is difficult, however, to say by how many years Moses probably preceded those of whom I speak : for which reason I think it well to pass over this point. But granting that Moses lived in the very time of this Sanchuniathon, and no earlier, I shall follow up the proof in this way.

If Sanchuniathon was becoming well known in the time of Semiramis queen of Assyria, even granted that p. 486 Moses was no earlier, but flourished in his time, then he too would be contemporary with Semiramis.

But whereas our calculation went to show that Abraham was in her time, our philosopher's calculation proves that even Moses was older. Now Semiramis is shown to have been full eight hundred years before the Trojan war. Therefore Moses also will be as many years earlier than the Trojan war according to the philosopher.

Now the first king of Argos is Inachus, the Athenians at that time having as yet no city and no name. But the first ruler of the Argives is contemporary with the b fifth king of Assyria after Semiramis, a hundred and fifty years after her and Moses, in which time nothing remarkable is recorded to have happened among the Greeks. But at this period of time the Judges were ruling among the Hebrews.

Then again more than three hundred years later, when more than four hundred were now completed from the time of Semiramis, the first king of the Athenians is

Cecrops their celebrated Autochthon when Triopas was ruler of Argos, who was seventh from Inachus the first Argive king.

And in the interval between these the flood in the c time of Ogyges is recorded, and Apis was the first to be called a god in Egypt, and Io the daughter of Inachus, who is worshipped by the Egyptians under the altered name of Isis, became known, as also Prometheus and Atlas.

From Cecrops to the capture of Troy are reckoned little short of other four hundred years, in which fall the marvellous tales of Greek mythology, the flood in the time of Deucalion, and the conflagration in the time of Phaethon, there having been, probably, many catastrophes on the earth in various places.

Now Cecrops is said to have been the first to call God Zeus, He not having been previously so named among d men : and next to have been the first to found an altar at Athens, and again the first to set up an image of Athena, as even these things were not existing of old.

After his time come the genealogies of all the gods among the Greeks. But among the Hebrews at this time the descendants of David were reigning, and the prophets who succeeded Moses were flourishing: so that according to the published testimony of the philosopher there are more than eight hundred years reckoned in all from Moses to the capture of Troy.

But far more recent still than the Trojan war are the traditional times of Homer and Hesiod and the rest. And after these, only yesterday as it were, about the p. 487 fiftieth Olympiad, Pythagoras and Democritus and the subsequent philosophers gained a name, somewhere about five hundred years after the Trojan war.

Moses therefore and the Hebrew prophets who succeeded him are proved to be fifteen hundred years earlier than the philosophers of the Greeks, according to the confession of the aforesaid author.

Such then is in brief my statement. But it is time to examine also the arguments upon the same subject of those who have preceded me. There have been then among us men of learning, second to none of the culti-
b vated class, who have also devoted themselves with no little care to sacred literature, and who, after an accurate examination of the present subject, defended the antiquity of the Hebrews by the use of a rich and varied arrangement of proof.

For some of them computed the times from certain well acknowledged histories, and others confirmed their testimony by quotations of an earlier date. And some made use of Greek authors, and others of those who had recorded the history of the Phoenicians and of the
c Chaldeans and Egyptians. But all of them together, having collected the Greek and the Barbarian records and those of the Hebrews themselves, and having set all their histories side by side, and, as it were, shaken them together one against the other, have made a combined examination of the things done about the same periods in all those nations.

Then, after each had made his arrangement of the events to be proved by methods of his own, they brought forward their proof with common consent and agreement. And for this reason especially I thought it right to give place in the present discussion to their own
d words, in order that the authors of the arguments might not be deprived of their due rewards, and at the same time the maintenance of the truth might receive indisputable confirmation not by one witness but by many.

CHAPTER X

AFRI-
CANUS
'UNTIL the beginning of the Olympiads no accurate history has been written by the Greeks, the earlier accounts being all confused and in no point agreeing among themselves: but the

---

487 d 6 Africanus, *Chronography*, bk. iii. Cf. Routh, *Rell. Sacr.* ii. p. 269

Olympiads have been accurately recorded by many, because the
Greeks compared the registers of them at no long interval of
time, but every four years.

'For which reason I shall collect and briefly run over the most
celebrated of the mythical histories down to the first Olympiad:
but of the later any which are remarkable I shall combine
together in chronological order each to each, the Hebrew with
the Greek, carefully examining the Hebrew and touching upon
the Greek, and shall fit them together in the following manner.
By seizing upon one action in Hebrew history contemporary **b**
with an action narrated by Greeks, and adhering to it, while
either deducting or adding, and indicating what Greek or Persian
or any one else synchronized with the Hebrew action, I shall
perhaps succeed in my aim.

'Now a most remarkable event is the migration of the Hebrews,
when carried captive by Nebuchadnezzar king of Babylon, which
continued seventy years, according to the prophecy of Jeremiah.
Now Nebuchadnezzar is mentioned by Berossus the Babylonian.

'After the seventy years of the Captivity Cyrus became king of **c**
Persia, in the year in which the fifty-fifth Olympic festival was
held, as one may learn from the *Bibliotheca* of Diodorus, and the
histories of Thallus and Castor, also from Polybius and Phlegon,
and from others too who were careful about Olympiads : for the
time agreed in all of them.

'So then Cyrus in the first year of his reign, which was the first
year of the fifty-fifth Olympiad, made the first partial dismissal of
the people by the hand of Zerubbabel, contemporary with whom
was Jesus the son of Josedek, after the completion of the seventy
years, as is related in the Book of Ezra among the Hebrews.   **d**

'The narratives therefore of the reign of Cyrus and of the end
of the Captivity synchronize : and the calculations according to
the Olympiads will thus be found to agree down to our time ; for
by following them we shall fit the other histories also one to
another according to the same principle.

'And the Athenian chronology computes the earlier events
in the following way ; from Ogyges, who was believed among
them to be an aboriginal, in whose time that great and first flood

---

488 d 1 Ezra i

occurred in Attica, when Phoroneus was king of Argos, as
Acusilaus relates, down to the first Olympiad from which the
Greeks considered that they calculated their dates correctly, a
p. 489 thousand and twenty years are computed, which agrees with
what has been stated before, and will be shown to agree also
with what comes after.

'For both the historians of Athens, Hellanicus and Philochorus
who wrote *The Attic Histories,* and the writers on Syrian history,
Castor and Thallus, and the writer on universal history, Diodorus
the author of the *Bibliotheca,* and Alexander Polyhistor, and some
of our own historians recorded these events more accurately even
than all the Attic writers. If therefore any remarkable narrative
occurs in the thousand and twenty years, it shall be extracted as
may be expedient.'

And soon after he proceeds:

b   'We assert therefore on the authority of this work that Ogyges,
who has given his name to the first deluge, as having been saved
when many perished, lived at the time of the Exodus from Egypt
of the people with Moses, proving it in the following way.

'From Ogyges to the first Olympiad aforesaid there will be
shown to be a thousand and twenty years: and from the first
Olympiad to the first year of the fifty-fifth, that is the first year of
the reign of Cyrus, which was the end of the Captivity, two hundred
and seventeen years. From Ogyges therefore to Cyrus there were
c one thousand two hundred and thirty-seven years. And if any
one would carry back a calculation of one thousand two hundred
and thirty-seven years from the end of the Captivity, there is
found by analysis the same distance to the first year of the Exodus
of Israel from Egypt by the hand of Moses, as from the fifty-fifth
Olympiad to Ogyges who founded Eleusis. Which is the more notable
point to take as the commencement of the Athenian chronology.'

Again after an interval:

'So much for events prior to Ogyges. Now about his times
Moses came out of Egypt: and that there is no reason to disbelieve that these events occurred at that time, we show in the
following manner.

---

489 b 1 Cf. Routh, *Rell. Sacr.* ii. p. 272   c 10 Cf. ibid. ii. 274

' From the Exodus of Moses to Cyrus, who reigned after the Cap- d AFRI-
tivity, there were one thousand two hundred and thirty-seven years.   CANUS
For the remaining years of Moses' life were forty : of Joshua, who
became the leader after him, twenty-five years : of the elders who
were judges after him, thirty years ; and of those included in the
Book of Judges, four hundred and ninety years. Of the priests
Eli and Samuel, ninety years. Of the kings of the Hebrews, who
came next, four hundred and ninety years : and seventy of the
Captivity, the last year of which was, as we have said before, the
first year of the reign of Cyrus.

' From Moses to the first Olympiad there were one thousand and **P. 490**
twenty years, since there were one thousand two hundred and
thirty-seven years to the first year of the fifty-fifth Olympiad :
and the time in the Greek chronology agreed with this.

' But after Ogyges, on account of the great destruction caused
by the flood, what is now called Attica remained without a king
one hundred and eighty-nine years until the time of Cecrops. For
Philochorus asserts that that Actaeon who comes after Ogyges, and
the fictitious names, never even existed.'

And again :

' From Ogyges therefore to Cyrus there were as many years as
from Moses to the same date, namely one thousand two hundred
and thirty-seven. And some of the Greeks also relate that Moses **b**
lived about those same times ; as Polemon in the first book of his
Hellenic histories says, that " in the time of Apis son of Phoroneus
a part of the Egyptian army was expelled from Egypt, who took
up their abode not far from Arabia in the part of Syria called
Palestine," being evidently those who went with Moses.

' And Apion the son of Poseidonius, the most inquisitive of
grammarians, in his book *Against the Jews*, and in the fourth
Book of his *Histories*, says that in the time of Inachus king of
Argos, when Amosis was reigning in Egypt, the Jews revolted,
with Moses as their leader.

' Herodotus also has made mention of this revolt and of Amosis **c**
in his second Book ; and, in a certain way, of the Jews themselves, enumerating them among those who practise circumcision,

---

490 a 11 Cf. Routh, *l. c.*, ii. p. 275   c 1 Cf. Herod. ii. c. 162
c 3 ibid. c. 104

AFRI-
CANUS

and calling them the Assyrians in Palestine, perhaps on account of Abraham.

'And Ptolemaeus of Mendes, in writing the history of the Egyptians from the beginning, agrees with all these, so that the variation of the dates is not noticeable to any great extent.

'But it is to be observed that whatever especial event is mentioned in the mythology of the Greeks because of its antiquity,
d is found to be later than Moses, their floods, and conflagrations, their Prometheus, Io, Europa, Sparti, Rape of Persephone, Mysteries, Legislations, exploits of Dionysus, Perseus, labours of Hercules, Argonauts, Centaurs, Minotaur, tale of Troy, return of the Heracleidae, migration of Ionians, and Olympic Festivals.

'It seemed good then to me, when about to compare the Hellenic histories with the Hebrew, to explain the aforesaid date of the monarchy in Athens : for it will be open to any one who will, by taking his starting-point from me, to calculate the number of years in the same way as I do.

'So then in the first year of the thousand and twenty years set
P. 491 forth from the time of Moses and Ogyges to the first Olympiad there occurs the Passover, and the Exodus of the Hebrews from Egypt, and in Attica the flood in the reign of Ogyges; and very naturally.

'For when the Egyptians were being scourged by the wrath of God with hailstorms and tempests, it was natural that some parts of the earth should suffer with them; and that the Athenians should experience the same fate with the Egyptians was natural, being supposed to be emigrants from them, as is asserted, among others, by Theopompus in the *Three-headed*.

'The intermediate time, in which no special event has been
b recorded by the Greeks, is passed by. But after ninety-four years, as some say, came Prometheus, who was said in the legend to form men; for being a wise man he tried to reform them out of their extreme uncouthness into an educated condition.'

Thus writes Africanus. And now let us pass on to another.

---

490 c 5 Cf. 497 a 6   491 a 10 Cf. Pausanias, vi. c. 18

CHAPTER XI

'But now I think it behoves me to prove that our philosophy c Tatian
is older than the institutions of the Greeks. And Moses and
Homer shall be set as our limits : for since each of them is very
ancient, and the one the oldest of poets and historians, and the
other the founder of all Barbaric wisdom, let them now be taken
into comparison by us.

'For we shall find that our doctrines are older not only than d
the learning of the Greeks, but even than the invention of letters.
And I shall not adopt our own native witnesses, but rather make
use of Greeks as my allies. For the one course would be injudi-
cious, because it would not be accepted by you; but the other, if
proved, would be admirable, if at any time by opposing you with
your own weapons I should bring against you proofs beyond
suspicion.

'For concerning the poetry of Homer, and his parentage, and
the time at which he flourished, previous investigations have been
made by very ancient writers, as Theagenes of Rhegium who
lived in the time of Cambyses, and Stesimbrotus of Thasos, and
Antimachus of Colophon, Herodotus also of Halicarnassus, and
Dionysius of Olynthus : and after them Ephorus of Cumae, p. 492
and Philochorus of Athens, and Megacleides and Chamaeleon the
Peripatetics : then the grammarians, Zenodotus, Aristophanes,
Callimachus, Crates, Eratosthenes, Aristarchus, Apollodorus.

'Now of these Crates says that he flourished before the return
of the Heracleidae, within eighty years after the Trojan war; but
Eratosthenes says, after the hundredth year from the capture of b
Troy; while Aristarchus says, at the time of the Ionian migration, which is a hundred and forty years after the Trojan war;
and Philochorus says, forty years after the Ionian migration, in
the archonship at Athens of Archippus, a hundred and eighty
years after the Trojan war; and Apollodorus says, a hundred
years after the Ionian migration, which would be two hundred
and forty years after the Trojan war : but some said that he lived
before the Olympiads, that is four hundred years after the capture c
of Ilium; while others brought down the time, and said that

---

c 1 Tatian, *Address to the Greeks*, c. 31

TATIAN Homer had been contemporary with Archilochus; now Archilochus flourished about the twenty-third Olympiad, in the time of Gyges king of Lydia, five hundred years after the Trojan war.

'With regard then to the times of the aforesaid poet, I mean Homer, and the dispute and disagreement among those who gave an account of him, let this our summary statement suffice for d those who are able to examine the matter carefully. For it is in every man's power to show that their opinions also about the historical statements are false; for with those authors whose record of times is inconsistent, the history cannot possibly be true.'

Again shortly after:

'Granted, however, that Homer was not only not later than the Trojan war, but let him be supposed to have lived at that very time of the war, and further even to have shared in the expedition with Agamemnon, and, if any wish to have it so, to have lived even before the invention of letters had taken place: for the aforesaid Moses will be shown to be very many years older than the actual capture of Troy, much more ancient too than the building of Troy was, and than Tros and Dardanus.

'And for proof of this I will employ the testimony of Chaldeans, Phoenicians, and Egyptians. But why need I say much? For one who professes to persuade ought to make his narration of the facts to his hearers very brief.

P. 493 'Berossus, a Babylonian, a priest of their god Belus, who lived in the time of Alexander, composed the history of the Chaldaeans in three Books for Antiochus the third successor of Seleucus; and in setting forth the account of the kings he mentions the name of one of them Nabuchodonosor, who made an expedition against the Phoenicians and Jews; events which we know to have been announced by our prophets, and which took place long after the age of Moses, and seventy years before the Persian supremacy.

b 'Now Berossus is a most competent man, and a proof of this is given by Iobas, who writing *Concerning the Assyrians* says that he has learned their history from Berossus: he is the author of two books *Concerning the Assyrians*.

'Next to the Chaldaeans, the case of the Phoenicians is as

---

492 d 6 Tatian, *l. c.*, c. 36

follows. There have been among them three authors, Theodotus, Tatian
Hypsicrates, Mochus. Their books were rendered into the Greek
language by Laetus, who also wrote an accurate treatise on the
lives of the philosophers.

' In the histories then of the aforesaid authors the rape of **c**
Europa is shown to have taken place in the time of one of the
kings, also the arrival of Menelaus in Phoenicia, and the story of
Hiram, who gave his daughter in marriage to Solomon king of the
Jews, and presented him with timber of all kinds for the building
of the Temple.

' Menander also of Pergamus wrote the record of the same
events. Now the date of Hiram approaches somewhat near to the
Trojan war; and Solomon the contemporary of Hiram is much
later than the age of Moses.

' Then the Egyptians have accurate registers of dates. And **d**
Ptolemy, not the king but a priest of Mendes, the translator of
their writings, in narrating the actions of their kings says that
the journey of the Jews from Egypt to whatever places they
chose, under the leadership of Moses, took place in the time of
Amosis king of Egypt.

' And this is how he speaks : " Now Amosis lived in the time of
king Inachus." After him Apion the grammarian, a man of great
reputation, in the fourth Book of his *Egyptian History* (there are
five of his Books) among many other things says that Amosis
demolished Avaris, and that he lived in the time of Inachus the
Argive, as Ptolemy of Mendes recorded in his *Chronology*.

' Now the time from Inachus to the capture of Troy makes up **p. 494**
twenty generations; and the mode of the proof is as follows :

' The kings of the Argives have been these :—Inachus, Phoroneus,
Apis, Argeius, Criasus, Phorbas, Triopas, Crotopus, Sthenelaus,
Danaus, Lynceus, Abas, Proetus, Acrisius, Perseus, Eurystheus,
Atreus, Thyestes, Agamemnon, in the eighteenth year of whose
reign Troy was taken.

' Also the intelligent reader must understand quite distinctly **b**
that according to the tradition of the Greeks there was no written
record of history among them. For Cadmus, who taught the
aforesaid people the alphabet, landed in Boeotia many generations
afterwards.

' After Inachus Phoroneus with difficulty put an end to their

TATIAN savage and wandering mode of life, and the people were brought into a state of order.   Wherefore if Moses has been shown to have been contemporary with Inachus, he is four hundred years earlier than the Trojan war.

'And this is proved to be so both from the succession of the kings of Athens, and Macedonia, and the Ptolemies, and also
c those of the dynasty of Antiochus; whence it is manifest that if the most illustrious deeds among the Greeks were recorded in writing and begin to be known after the time of Inachus, they were also later than the time of Moses.

'For as contemporary with Phoroneus who followed Inachus the Athenians mention Ogyges, in whose time the first flood occurred : and as contemporary with Phorbas Actaeus, from whom Attica was called Actaea : and as contemporary with Triopas Prometheus, and Epimetheus, and Atlas, and Cecrops of double sex, and Io.

d   'In the time of Crotopus there was Phaethon's conflagration, and Deucalion's flood : in the time of Sthenelaus was the reign of Amphictyon, and the arrival of Danaus in the Peloponnese, and the colonization of Dardania by Dardanus, and the abduction of Europa from Phoenicia to Crete.

'In the time of Lynceus there was the rape of Persephone, and the foundation of the sanctuary at Eleusis, and the husbandry of Triptolemus, and the arrival of Cadmus at Thebes, and the reign of Minos.

'In the reign of Proetus occurred the war of Eumolpus against the Athenians ; and in that of Acrisius the crossing of Pelops from Phrygia, and the arrival of Ion at Athens, and the second Cecrops, and the exploits of Perseus.   And in the reign of Agamemnon Troy was taken.

P. 495   'Therefore from what has been said above Moses is shown to be older than all heroes, cities, or daemons : and he who preceded them in age ought rather to be believed than the Greeks who drew his doctrines from the fountain-head without fully understanding them.

'For there were many sophists among them, who indulged a meddling curiosity, and these attempted to put a false stamp on all that they had learned from Moses and those who agreed with his philosophy, in order first that they might be thought to say something original; and secondly that, disguising what they **b** Tatian did not understand by a kind of rhetorical artifice, they might misrepresent the truth as being a mere fable.

' With regard, however, to our polity, and the history of our laws, and all that the learned among the Greeks have said, and how many and who they are that have mentioned us, proof shall be shown in my " Answer to those who have set forth opinions concerning God."

' But for the present I must endeavour with all accuracy to make it clear that Moses is earlier not only than Homer, but also than the writers before him, Linus, Philammon, Thamyris, **c** Amphion, Orpheus, Musaeus, Demodocus, Phemius, the Sibyl, Epimenides the Cretan, who came to Sparta, Aristaeus of Proconnesus, who wrote the *Arimaspia*, and Asbolus the Centaur, and Basis, and Drymon, and Euclus of Cyprus, and Horus of Samos, and Pronapides of Athens.

' For Linus was the teacher of Hercules, and Hercules has been shown to be one generation earlier than the Trojan war ; and this **d** is manifest from his son Tlepolemus, who joined the expedition against Troy.

' Orpheus was contemporary with Hercules; moreover, the writings afterwards attributed to him are said to have been composed by Onomacritus of Athens, who lived during the government of the Pisistratidae about the fiftieth Olympiad.

' Musaeus was a disciple of Orpheus. And as Amphion was two generations earlier than the Trojan war, this prevents our collecting more about him for the information of the studious. Demodocus too and Phemius lived at the very time of the Trojan war ; for they abode, the one among the suitors, the other with the Phaeacians. Thamyris also and Philammon are not much more ancient than these.

' So then with regard to their work of various kinds and **p. 496** their dates and record, I think I have described them to you with all possible accuracy. But that we may also complete what is as yet deficient, I will further set forth the evidence concerning those who are considered the Sages.

' For Minos, who was considered to be pre-eminent in all wisdom, and sagacity, and legislation, lived in the time of Lynceus who reigned after Danaus, in the eleventh generation

TATIAN after Inachus.   And Lycurgus, born long after the capture of
b Troy, made laws for the Lacedaemonians a hundred years before
the commencement of the Olympiads.

'Draco is found to have lived about the thirty-ninth Olympiad,
and Solon about the forty-sixth, and Pythagoras about the sixty-
second.   Now we showed that the Olympiads began four hundred
and seven years after the Trojan war.

'So then, after these facts have been thus proved, a few more
words will suffice to record the age of the Seven Sages.   For as
Thales the eldest of them lived about the fiftieth Olympiad, the
approximate dates of those who came after him are thus stated
concisely.

'This is what I have composed for you, O men of Greece,
I, Tatian, a follower of the Barbarians in philosophy, born in the
c land of the Assyrians, but instructed first in your doctrines, and
afterwards in such as I now profess to preach.   And knowing
henceforward who God is, and what is the doing of His will,
I present myself to you in readiness for the examination of my
doctrines, while my mode of life according to God's will remains
incapable of denial.'

Thus much says Tatian.   But let us now pass on to
Clement.

CHAPTER XII

d   'THE subject has indeed been carefully discussed by Tatian in
CLEMENT his *Discourse to the Greeks*, and by Cassian in the first book of his
Exegetics.   But nevertheless my commentary demands that I also
should run over what has been said upon the topic.

'Apion then the grammarian, who was surnamed Pleistonices,
in the fourth Book of his *Egyptian Histories*, although being
P. 497 an Egyptian by birth he was so spitefully disposed towards
the Hebrews as to have composed a book *Against the Jews*,
when he mentions Amosis the king of Egypt and the trans-
actions of his time, brings forward Ptolemaeus of Mendes as a
witness.

'And his language is as follows :

'"But Avaris was demolished by Amosis, who lived in the time

---

496 d 1 Clement of Alexandria, *Miscellanies*, i. c. 21

of Inachus the Argive, as Ptolemaeus of Mendes recorded in his CLEMENT
Chronology."

' Now this Ptolemaeus was a priest, who published *The Acts of
the Kings of Egypt* in three whole books, and says that the
departure of the Jews out of Egypt under Moses as their leader
took place in the time of Amosis king of Egypt; from which it is **b**
clearly seen that Moses flourished in the time of Inachus.

' Now Dionysius of Halicarnassus teaches us in his *Chronology*
that the history of Argos, I mean the history from Inachus downwards, is mentioned as older than any Hellenic history.

' Forty generations later than this is the Athenian history,
beginning from Cecrops the so-called aboriginal of double sex,
as Tatian says in so many words : and nine generations later the
history of Arcadia from the time of Pelasgus, who also is called
an aboriginal.

' More recent than this last by other fifty-two generations is the **c**
history of Phthiotis from the time of Deucalion. From Inachus
to the time of the Trojan war twenty or twenty-one generations
are reckoned, four hundred years, we may say, and more.

' And whether the Assyrian history is many years earlier than
the Hellenic, will appear from what Ctesias says. In the four
hundred and second year of the Assyrian empire, and in the
thirty-second year of the reign of Beluchus the eighth, the movement of Moses out of Egypt took place in the time of Amosis
king of Egypt, and of Inachus king of Argos.

' And in Hellas in the time of Phoroneus the successor of **d**
Inachus the flood of Ogyges occurred, and the reign in Sicyon,
of Aegialeus first, then of Europs, and then of Telchis, and in
Crete the reign of Cres.

' For Acusilaus says that Phoroneus was the first man : whence
also the author of the poem "Phoronis" says that he was "the
father of mortal men."

' Hence Plato in the *Timaeus*, following Acusilaus, writes :
" And once when he wished to lead them on to a discussion
about antiquity, he said that he attempted to speak of the most
ancient things in this city, about Phoroneus who was called
' the first ' man, and about Niobe, and the events that followed
the flood."

497 d 9 Plato, *Timaeus*, 22 A

p. 498
CLEMENT 'Contemporary with Phorbas was Actaeus, from whom Attica was called Actaea : and contemporary with Triopas were Prometheus, and Atlas, and Epimetheus, and the biform Cecrops, and Io : in the time of Crotopus there was Phaethon's conflagration, and the flood of Deucalion : and in the time of Sthenelaus was the reign of Amphictyon, and the arrival of Danaus in the Peloponnese, and the colonization of Dardania by Dardanus, whom Homer calls

"The first-born son of cloud-compelling Zeus,"

and the abduction of Europa from Crete to Phoenicia.

'In the time of Lynceus was the rape of Core, and the
b foundation of the sanctuary at Eleusis, and the husbandry of Triptolemus, and the arrival of Cadmus in Thebes, and the reign of Minos. In the time of Proetus there was the war of Eumolpus against the Athenians : and in the time of Acrisius the migration of Pelops from Phrygia, and the arrival of Ion in Athens, and the second Cecrops, and the exploits of Perseus and Dionysus, and also Orpheus and Musaeus.

'And in the eighteenth year of the reign of Agamemnon Troy was taken, in the first year of the reign in Athens of Demophon son of Theseus, on the twelfth day of the month Thargelion, as Dionysius the Argive says.

c 'But Agius and Dercylus in their third Book say, on the eighth day of the last decade of the month Panemus : Hellanicus says, on the twelfth of Thargelion ; and some of the writers of Athenian history say, on the eighth of the last decade, in the last year of the reign of Menestheus, at the full moon. The poet who wrote *The Little Iliad* says :

"At midnight, when the moon was rising bright."

But others say, on the same day of the month Scirophorion.

'Now Theseus, who was a rival of Hercules, is older than the
d Trojan war by one generation : Homer at least mentions Tlepolemus, who was the son of Hercules, as having joined in the expedition against Troy.

'Moses therefore is shown to be six hundred and four years older than the deification of Dionysus, if at least he was deified in the thirty-second year of the reign of Perseus, as Apollodorus says in his *Chronicles*.

---

498 a 8 Hom. *Il.* xx. 215   c 7 *Little Iliad*, Fr. 6

'And from Dionysus to Hercules and the chiefs who sailed in CLEMENT the Argo with Jason, there are sixty-three years comprised. Asclepius too and the Dioscuri sailed with them, as Apollonius Rhodius testifies in the *Argonautica*.

'From the reign of Hercules in Argos to the deification of Hercules himself and of Asclepius there are comprised thirty-eight years, according to Apollodorus the chronicler : and from that point to the deification of Castor and Pollux fifty-three years : **p. 499** and somewhere about this time was the capture of Troy.

'And if we are to believe the poet Hesiod, let us hear what he says :

"Admitted to the sacred couch of Zeus,
Fairest of Atlas' daughters, Maia bare
Renownèd Hermes, herald of the Gods.
And linked with Zeus in sweetest bonds of love
Fair Semele conceived a glorious son,
Great Dionysus, joy of all mankind."

'Cadmus the father of Semele came to Thebes in the reign of **b** Lynceus, and became the inventor of the Greek letters. And Triopas was contemporary with Isis in the seventh generation from Inachus.

'But there are some who say that she was called Io from her going (ἰέναι) through all the earth in her wanderings : and Istrus in his book *Of the migration of the Egyptians* says that she was the daughter of Prometheus : and Prometheus was contemporary with Triopas, in the seventh generation after Moses ; so that Moses would be earlier even than the origin of mankind was according to the Greeks.

'Now Leon, who wrote a treatise *On the gods of Egypt*, says that **c** Isis was called by the Greeks Demeter, who is contemporary with Lynceus in the eleventh generation after Moses.

'Apis also the king of Argos was the founder of Memphis, as Aristippus says in the first Book of the *Arcadica*.

'Moreover Aristeas of Argos says that this Apis was surnamed Sarapis, and that it is he whom the Egyptians worship.

'But Nymphodorus of Amphipolis, in the third Book of *The Customs of Asia*, says that when Apis the bull died and was **d**

---

d 12 Cf. Apollonius Rhodius, *Argonautica*, i. 146   **499** a 5 Hesiod, *Theogony*, 938

CLEMENT embalmed, he was deposited in a coffin (σορός) in the temple of the daemon who was worshipped there, and thence was called Soroapis and afterwards Sarapis. And Apis is the third from Inachus.

'Moreover Latona is contemporary with Tityus:

> "For Leto erst he strove to violate,
> The noble consort of immortal Zeus."

'And Tityus was contemporary with Tantalus. With good reason therefore the Boeotian Pindar writes:

> "For late in time Apollo too was born."

'And no wonder, since he is found in company with Hercules serving Admetus

> "A whole long year."

'Zethus too and Amphion, the inventors of music, lived about the age of Cadmus. And if any one tell us that Phemonoe was **p. 500** the first who uttered an oracle in verse to Acrisius, yet let him know that twenty-seven years after Phemonoe came Orpheus, and Musaeus, and Linus the teacher of Hercules.

'But Homer and Hesiod were much later than the Trojan war, and after them far later were the lawgivers among the Greeks, Lycurgus and Solon, and the Seven Sages, and Pherecydes of Syros, and the great Pythagoras, who lived some time later about the beginning of the Olympiads, as we proved.

'So then we have demonstrated that Moses was more ancient than most of the gods of the Greeks, and not merely than their **b** so-called Sages and poets.'

So far Clement. But since the question before us was carefully studied before our Christian writers by the Hebrews themselves, it would be well to consider also what they have said: and I shall use the language of Flavius Josephus as representative of them all.

CHAPTER XIII

c 'I WILL begin then first with the writings of the Egyptians.
JOSEPHUS It is not possible, however, to quote their own actual words; but Manetho an Egyptian by birth, a man who had a knowledge of

---

499 d 6 Hom. *Od.* xii. 579   d 10 Pind. *Fr.* 11 (114)   d 13 Cf. Hom.
Il. xxi. 443   500 c 1 Josephus, *Against Apion*, i. 14

Hellenic culture, as is evident from his having written the history JOSEPHUS
of his own country in the Greek language, and translated it, as
he says himself, out of the sacred books, who also convicts Herodotus of having from ignorance falsified many things in Egyptian
history—this Manetho then, I say, in the second Book of his
Egyptian History writes concerning us as follows: and I will d
quote his words, just as if I brought himself forward as a
witness.

'"We had a king whose name was Timaeus. In his time God
was angry with us, I know not why, and men from the Eastern
parts, of obscure origin, were strangely emboldened to invade the
country, and easily took possession of it by force without a battle."'

And soon after he adds:

'"The name of their whole nation was Hycsos, that is 'shepherd-
kings.' For 'Hyc' in the sacred language means ' king,' and Sos
is ' shepherd,' and ' shepherds ' in the common dialect: and thus
combined it becomes ' Hycsos.' But some say that they were Arabs."

' But in another copy he says that " kings " are not meant by **p. 501**
the name " Hyc," but on the contrary " captive-shepherds " are
signified. For Hyc in Egyptian, and Hac, aspirated, expressly
means " captives." And this seems to me more probable, and
in agreement with ancient history.

' Now these before-named kings, both those of the so-called
" Shepherds," and their descendants, ruled over Egypt, he says,
five hundred and eleven years.

' But after this, he says, there was a revolt of the kings from b
the Thebaid and the rest of Egypt against the Shepherds, and a
great and long war broke out. But in the time of a king whose
name was Misphragmuthosis, he says that the Shepherds were
defeated, and though driven out of the rest of Egypt, they were
shut up in a place having a circumference of ten thousand
arurae: the name of the place was Avaris.

' The whole of this, Manetho says, the Shepherds surrounded
with a great and strong wall, that so they might have all their c
possessions and their booty in a stronghold.

' But Thmouthosis the son of Misphragmouthosis attempted to
subdue them by a siege, having sat down against their walls

---

501 a I Josephus, *l. c.*

JOSEPHUS with four hundred and eighty thousand men : but after giving
up the siege in despair, he made terms of agreement with them,
that they should leave Egypt, and all go away uninjured whither-
soever they chose. And upon these conditions they with their
whole families and possessions, being not less in number than
two hundred and forty thousand, made their way from Egypt
across the desert into Syria.

d   ‘ But being afraid of the power of the Assyrians (for they were
at that time the rulers of Asia), they built a city in what is now
called Judaea, to suffice for so many thousands of inhabitants,
and called it Jerusalem.’

Next to this he recounts the succession of the kings of
Egypt, together with the duration of their reigns, and
adds :

‘ So says Manetho.   And when the time is calculated according
to the number of years mentioned, it is evident that the so-called
Shepherds, our ancestors, departed from Egypt and colonized this
country three hundred and ninety-three years before Danaus arrived
in Argos : and yet he is considered by the Argives as very ancient.

‘ Two things therefore of the greatest importance Manetho has
p. 502 testified in our favour out of the writings of the Egyptians.   First
their arrival in Egypt from some other country, and afterwards the
departure thence at so ancient a date as to be nearly a thousand
years before the Trojan war.’

The extracts from Egyptian history have been recorded
thus somewhat at large by Josephus. But from Phoenician
history, by employing the testimony of those who have
written on Phoenician affairs, he proves that the Temple
b in Jerusalem had been built by King Solomon a hundred
and forty-three years and eight months earlier than the
foundation of Carthage by the Tyrians : then he passes
on, and quotes from the history of the Chaldaeans their
testimonies concerning the antiquity of the Hebrews.

---

501 d 8 Josephus, *Against Apion*, c. 16

Chapter XIV

But why need I heap up proofs upon proofs, when c
every one who is a lover of truth, and not of spitefulness,
is satisfied with what has been stated, as containing
varied confirmation of the proposed argument? For our
proposal was to prove that Moses and the Prophets were
more ancient than Greek history.

Since therefore Moses has been proved to have lived
long before the Trojan war, let us look also at all those
who came after him. Now that Moses appeared in the d
world later in time than those former true Hebrews,
Heber and Abraham, from whom the derived name has
been applied to the people, and than all the other godly
men of old, is manifest from his own history.

Next to Moses therefore Jesus ruled the nation of the
Jews thirty years, as some say: then, as the Scripture
says, foreigners ruled eight years. Then Gothoniel, fifty
years: after whom Eglom king of Moab eighteen years:
after whom Ehud eighty years. After him strangers
again twenty years: then Debbora and Barak forty p. 503
years. Then the Madianites seven years: then Gedeon
forty years. Abimelech three years. Tola twenty-three
years: Jair twenty-two years: the Ammonites eighteen
years: Jephtha six years: Esbon seven years: Aealon
ten years: Labdon eight years: strangers forty years:
Samson twenty years: then Eli the Priest, as the Hebrew
says, forty years; about whose time the capture of Troy
occurred. And after Eli the Priest Samuel was the ruler
of the people.

After him their first king Saul reigned forty years:
then David forty years: then Solomon forty years; who
also was the first to build the Temple in Jerusalem. After b
Solomon Roboam reigns seventeen years: Abia three
years: Asa forty-one years: Jehoshaphat twenty-five years:

---

502 d 8 Cf. Judges iii. 8, ibid. 9 ' Othniel '   503 a 5 Judges xii. 10–13

Joram eight years: Ahaziah one year: Athaliah seven years: Joash forty years: Amaziah twenty-seven years: Uzziah fifty-two years; in whose reign prophesied Hosea, Amos, Esaias, Jonah: and after Uzziah Jotham reigned sixteen years: after whom Ahaz sixteen years. In his time was held the first Olympic festival, in which Coroebus of Elis won the foot-race.

c   Hezekiah succeeds Ahaz for twenty-nine years; and in his time Romulus built Rome and became king. And after Hezekiah Manasses reigned fifty-five years: then Amon two years: then Josiah thirty-one years; in whose time prophesied Jeremiah, Baruch, Huldah, and other prophets.

Then Jehoahaz three months: after whom Jehoiachim eleven years; and after him last of all Zedekiah twelve years. In his time Jerusalem having been besieged by the Assyrians, and the Temple burned, the whole nation d of the Jews is carried away to Babylon, and there Daniel prophesies, and Ezekiel.

And after the number of seventy years Cyrus becomes king of Persia, and he remitted the captivity of the Jews, and allowed those of them who would to return to their own land, and to raise up the Temple again: at which time Jesus the son of Josedek returned, and Zerubbabel the son of Salathiel, and they laid the foundations, when Haggai, and Zechariah, and Malachi prophesied last of all, after whom there has been no more a prophet among them.

In the time of Cyrus Solon of Athens was flourishing, and the so-called Seven Sages among the Greeks, than whom their records mention no more ancient philosopher.

Of these seven then Thales of Miletus, who was the first natural philosopher among the Greeks, discoursed con-
p. 504 cerning the solar tropics and eclipse, and the phases of the moon, and the equinox. This man became most distinguished among the Greeks.

A pupil of Thales was Anaximander, the son of

Praxiades, himself also a Milesian by birth. He was the first designer of gnomons for distinguishing the solar tropics, and times and seasons, and equinox.

And a pupil of Anaximander was Anaximenes son of Eurystratus of Miletus ; and his pupil was Anaxagoras, son of Hegesibulus, of Clazomenae. He was the first who clearly defined the subject of first principles. For he not **b** only published his opinions concerning the essence of all things, like his predecessors, but also concerning the moving cause thereof. 'For in the beginning,' he says, ' all things were confused together. But mind entered and brought them out of disorder into order.'

Anaxagoras had three pupils, Pericles, Archelaus, and Euripides. Pericles became the first man of Athens, and excelled his contemporaries both in wealth and birth : Euripides turned to poetry, and was called by some ' the **c** philosopher of the stage ' : and Archelaus succeeded to the school of Anaxagoras in Lampsacus, but migrated to Athens and lectured there, and had many Athenians as pupils, and among them especially Socrates.

At the same time with Anaxagoras there flourished the physical philosophers Xenophanes and Pythagoras. Pythagoras was succeeded by his wife Theano, and his sons Telauges and Mnesarchus.

A pupil of Telauges was Empedocles, in whose time Heracleitus ' the obscure ' became famous. Xenophanes is said to have been succeeded by Parmenides, and **d** Parmenides by Melissus, and Melissus by Zeno the Eleatic, who, they say, concocted a plot against the tyrant of that time, and was caught, and when tortured by the tyrant that so he might give a list of those who were his accomplices, paid no regard to the tyrant's punishments, but bit through his tongue, and spat it at him, and died in this obstinate endurance of the tortures.

He had for his pupil Leucippus, and Leucippus Demo-

---

504 b 4 cf. Diogenes, *Laertius*, ii. 6.   **c** 1 Cf. Clement of Alexandria, *Miscellanies*, v. 71

critus, and he Protagoras, in whose time Socrates
flourished. One may also find scattered here and there
other physical philosophers who lived before Socrates:
all, however, beginning with Thales appear to have
flourished later than Cyrus king of Persia: and it
is manifest that Cyrus lived long after the carrying
p. 505 away of the Jewish nation into captivity at Babylon,
when the Hebrew prophets had already ceased, and their
holy city had been besieged. So you must admit that
Greek philosophy was much later than Moses and the
Prophets who came after him ; and especially the philosophy of Plato, who having been at first a hearer of
b Socrates, afterwards associated with the Pythagoreans, and
shot far beyond all his predecessors both in eloquence
and wisdom and in his philosophical doctrines.

Now Plato lived about the end of the Persian monarchy,
a little earlier than Alexander of Macedon, and not much
more than four hundred years before the Emperor
Augustus.

If therefore it should be shown to you that Plato and
his successors have agreed in their philosophy with the
Hebrews, it is time to examine the date at which he
lived, and to compare the antiquity of the Hebrew
theologians and prophets with the age of all the philosophers of Greece.

c   But since this has been already proved, it is now the
proper time to turn back and observe that the wise men
of the Greeks have been zealous imitators of the Hebrew
doctrines, so that our calumniators can no longer
reasonably find fault with us, if we ourselves, admiring
the like doctrines with their philosophers, have determined to hold the Hebrew oracles in honour.

BOOK XI

CONTENTS

PREFACE CONCERNING THE ARGUMENT

d   THE preceding Book, which is the tenth of the *Evangelical Preparation*, was intended to prove by no statements of my own, but by external testimonies, that as the Greeks had contributed no additional wisdom from their own resources, but only their force and elegance of language, and had borrowed all their philosophy from Barbarians, it was not improbable that they were also not unacquainted with the Hebrew Oracles, but had in part seized upon them also ; seeing that they did not keep their hands clean from theft even of the literary efforts of their own countrymen. For, as I said, it was not my statement but their own that proved them to be thieves.

p. 508   Moreover in the same Book we learned by the comparison of dates that they were very young in age as well as in wisdom, and fell very far short of the ancient literature of the Hebrews.

Such were the contents of the preceding Book : but in this present one we hasten on at once to pay as it were a debt, I mean the promise which was given, and

b to exhibit the agreement of the Greek philosophers with the Hebrew Oracles in some if not in all their doctrinal theories. Dismissing therefore those of whom it is superfluous to speak, we call up the leader of the whole band, deeming it right to adopt as umpire of the question Plato alone as equivalent to all : since it is likely that as he surpassed all in reputation he will be sufficient by himself for the settlement of our question.

But if at any point it should be necessary, for the sake of giving clearness to his thought, I shall also make use of the testimony of those who have studied his philosophy, and shall set forth their own words for the settlement of the question before us.

Let me, however, make this reservation, that not every c matter has been successfully stated by the master, although he has expressed most things in accordance with truth. And this very point also we shall prove at the proper season, not in order to disparage him, but in defence of the reason for which we confess that we have welcomed the Barbarian philosophy in preference to the Greek.

CHAPTER I

WHEREAS Plato divided the whole subject of philosophy d into three branches, Physics, Ethics, Logic, and then again divided his Physics into the examination of sensibles, and the contemplation of incorporeals, you will find this tripartite form of teaching among the Hebrews also, seeing that they had dealt with the like matters of philosophy before Plato was born.

It will be right then to hear Plato first, and so afterwards to examine the doctrines of the Hebrews. And **p. 509** I shall quote the opinions of Plato from those who give the highest honour to his system ; of whom Atticus, a man of distinction among the Platonic philosophers, in the work wherein he withstands those who profess to support the doctrines of Plato by those of Aristotle, recounts the opinions of his master in the following manner :

CHAPTER II

' SINCE therefore the entire system of philosophy is divided b into three parts, the so-called Ethical topic, and the Physical, ATTICUS

---

509 b 1 Atticus, *Fragment* preserved by Eusebius. Cf. Mullach, *Fr. Phil. Gr.* iii. 185

ATTICUS and also the Logical; and whereas the aim of the first is to make each one of us honourable and virtuous, and to bring entire households to the highest state of improvement, and finally
c to furnish the whole commonalty with the most excellent civil polity and the most exact laws; while the second pertains to the knowledge of things divine, and the actual first principles and causes, and all the other things that result from them, which part Plato has named *Natural Science*; the third is adopted to help in determining and discovering what concerns both the former. Now that Plato before and beyond all others collected into one body all the parts of philosophy, which had till then been scattered and dispersed, like the limbs of Pentheus, as some one
d said, and exhibited philosophy as an organized body and a living thing complete in all its members, is manifestly asserted by every one.

‘For it is not unknown that Thales, and Anaximenes, and Anaxagoras, and as many as were contemporary with them spent their time solely on the inquiry concerning the nature of existing things. Nor moreover is any one unaware that Pittacus, and Periander, and Solon, and Lycurgus, and those like them, applied their philosophy to statemanship. Zeno too, and all this Eleatic School, are also well known to have studied especially the dia-
p. 510 lectic art. But after these came Plato, a man newly initiated in the mysteries of nature and of surpassing excellence, as one verily sent down from heaven in order that the philosophy taught by him might be seen in its full proportions; for he omitted nothing, and perfected everything, neither falling short in regard to what was necessary, nor carried away to what was useless.

‘Since therefore we asserted that the Platonist partakes of all three, as studying Nature, and discussing Morals, and practising Dialectic, let us now examine each point separately.’

So speaks Atticus. And the Peripatetic Aristocles also adds his testimony to the same effect, in the seventh Book of the treatise which he composed *Of Philosophy*,
b speaking thus word for word:

Chapter III

'If any man ever yet taught a genuine and complete system Aris-
of philosophy, it was Plato. For the followers of Thales were tocles
constantly engaged in the study of Nature: and the school of
Pythagoras wrapped all things in mystery: and Xenophanes c
and his followers, by stirring contentious discussions, caused the
philosophers much dizziness, but yet gave them no help.

'And not least did Socrates, exactly according to the proverb,
add fire to fire, as Plato himself said. For being a man of great
genius, and clever in raising questions upon any and every
matter, he brought moral and political speculations into philosophy, and moreover was the first who attempted to define the
theory of the Ideas: but while still stirring up every kind
of discussion, and inquiring about all subjects, he died too early
a death.

'Others took certain separate parts and spent their time upon d
these, some on Medicine, others on the Mathematical Sciences,
and some on the poets and Music. Most of them, however,
were charmed with the powers of language, and of these some
called themselves rhetoricians and others dialecticians.

'In fact the successors of Socrates were of all different kinds,
and opposed to each other in their opinions. For some sang the
praises of cynical habits, and humility, and insensibility; but
others, on the contrary, of pleasures. And some used to boast of
knowing all things, and others of knowing absolutely nothing.

'Further some used to roll themselves about in public and p. 511
in the sight of all men, associating with the common people,
while others on the contrary could never be approached nor
accosted.

'Plato however, though he perceived that the science of things
divine and human was one and the same, was the first to make
a distinction, asserting that there was one kind of study concerned
with the nature of the universe, and another concerned with
human affairs, and a third with dialectic.

'But he maintained that we could not take a clear view
of human affairs, unless the divine were previously discerned:

---

510 b 2 Aristocles, *De Philosophia*; cf. Mullach, iii. p. 206

ARIS- **b** for just as physicians, when treating any parts of the body, attend
TOCLES   first to the state of the whole, so the man who is to take a clear
view of things here on earth must first know the nature of the
universe ; and man, he said, was a part of the world; and good
was of two kinds, our own good and that of the whole, and the
good of the whole was the more important, because the other was
for its sake.

'Now Aristoxenus the Musician says that this argument comes
from the Indians: for a certain man of that nation fell in with
Socrates at Athens, and presently asked him, what he was doing
in philosophy : and when he said, that he was studying human
c life, the Indian laughed at him, and said that no one could
comprehend things human, if he were ignorant of things divine.

'Whether this, however, is true no one could assert positively :
but Plato at all events distinguished the philosophy of the universe,
and that of civil polity, and also that of dialectic.'

Such being the philosophy of Plato, it is time to
examine also that of the Hebrews, who had studied
philosophy in the like manner long before Plato was
born.   Accordingly you will find among them also this
d corresponding tripartite division of Ethical, and Dialec-
tical, and Physical studies, by setting yourself to observe
in the following manner:

CHAPTER IV

As to Ethics then, if you thoroughly examine what the
Hebrews taught, you will find that this subject before all
others was zealously studied among them in deeds much
earlier than in words.   Since as the end of all good, and
the final term of a happy life, they both admired and
p. 512 pursued religion and that friendship with God which is
secured by the right direction of moral habits; but not
bodily pleasure, like Epicurus; nor again the threefold
kinds of good, according to Aristotle, who esteems the
good of the body, and external good on an equality with
the good of the soul; no, nor yet the utter void of know-

ledge and instruction, which some have announced by
a more respectable name as 'suspension of judgement';
nay, nor even the virtue of the soul; for how much is
there of this in men, and what can it contribute by
itself without God to the life that knows no sorrow?

For the sake of that life they fastened their all on hope **b**
in God, as a cable that could not break, and declared
that the friend of God was the only happy man: because
God the dispenser of all good, the purveyor of life and
fountain of virtue itself, being the provider of all good
things for the body, and of outward fortune, must be
alone sufficient for the happy life to the man who by
thoroughly true religion has secured His friendship.

Hence Moses, the wisest of men and the first of all to
commit to writing the life of the godly Hebrews before
his time, has described in an historical narrative their
mode of life both political and practical.   In beginning **c**
that narrative he drew his teaching from universal principles, assuming God as the cause of the universe, and
describing the creation of the world and of man.

Thus from universal principles he next advanced in his
argument to particulars, and by the memory of the men
of old urged his disciples on to emulation of their virtue
and piety; and moreover being himself declared the
author of the holy laws enacted by him, it must be
manifest that on all points he was careful to promote the **d**
love of God by his attention to moral habits, a point
which in fact our argument anticipated and made clear
in what has gone before.

It would be too long to set down in this place the
prophets who came in succession after Moses, and their
arguments to encourage virtue, and dissuade from all
kinds of vice.   But what if I were to bring before you
the moral precepts of the all-wise Solomon, to which he
devoted a special treatise and called it a book of *Proverbs*,
including in one subject many concise judgements of the
nature of apophthegms?

p. 513 And in this way from old times, before the Greeks had
learned even the first letters, the Hebrews were both
themselves instructed in the ethical branch, and freely
imparted of the same instruction to those who came to
them.

Chapter V

Also the dialectic branch of Hebrew philosophy they
thought it right to pursue not, as the Greeks were wont,
b with clever sophistries, and arguments cunningly framed
to deceive, but by the conception of actual truth, which
with souls illumined by divine light their religious
philosophers discovered, and were by it enlightened.

And to make those who were being instructed in the
learning of their country more keen in pursuit of this
truth, they used even from the age of infancy to deliver
to them recitations of holy words, and tales from sacred
histories, and metrical compositions of psalms and can-
ticles, problems also and riddles, and certain wise and
allegorical theories, combined with beauty of language,
c and eloquent recitation in their own tongue.

Moreover they had certain expositors (δευτερωταί) of
primary instruction (for so it pleases them to name the
interpreters of their scriptures), who by translation and
explanation made clear what was obscurely taught in
riddles, if not to all, at least to those who were fitted
to hear these things.

Thus again Solomon the wisest among them started
d from this principle in the beginning of his book of
Proverbs, teaching us that this was mainly the cause
of his writing, by stating in express terms that
every man ought to know wisdom and instruction, and to
discern the words of understanding, and to perceive the turns
of language, and understand true righteousness, and give right
judgement. 'That I may give,' he says, 'subtilty to the simple,

and to the young man perception and thoughtfulness. For the wise man will hear these things and be wiser, and the man of understanding will obtain guidance : he will understand a proverb and a dark saying, the words of the wise, and riddles.'

Such were the terms of the promise of the said book : and the particular questions proposed and their solutions, **p. 514** and the dialectic treatment carried through all their prophetic scriptures in a manner proper to the wisdom and language of the authors, any one who wishes may learn by taking in hand and studying at leisure the books of their discourse. And if any one were also to study the language itself with critical taste, he would.see that, for Barbarians, the writers are excellent dialecticians, not at all inferior to sophists or orators in his own **b** language.

There would also be found among them poems in metre, like the great Song of Moses and David's 118th Psalm, composed in what the Greeks call heroic metre. At least it is said that these are hexameters, consisting of sixteen syllables : also their other compositions in verse are said to consist of trimeter and tetrameter lines, according to the sound of their own language.

While such is the relation of their diction to its logical sense, the thoughts must not be brought into comparison with those of men. For they comprise the oracles of God **c** and of absolute truth to which they have given utterance, prophecies, and predictions, and religious lessons, and doctrines relating to the knowledge of the universe.

And of the authors' accuracy in reasoning you may find indications from their correctness in the application of names, concerning which it will be evident that Plato also bears witness to the opinion of the Hebrews, and is on this very point in agreement with the philosophy of their authors, as indeed it is easy to discern from what follows.

Chapter VI

d   Long before the name of philosophy was known to the Greeks, Moses had been the first throughout all his writing to treat in numberless instances of the giving of names, and sometimes had arranged the names of all things about him in exact accordance with their nature, and at other times referred to God the decision of the new name given to devout men, and had taught that names are given **p. 515** to things by nature and not conventionally; Plato in following him assents to the same opinions, and does not omit to mention Barbarians, and affirm that this custom is maintained among them, hinting probably at the Hebrews, since it is not easy to observe a theory of this kind among other Barbarians.

He says, at all events, in the *Cratylus*:

PLATO   'The name of anything is not whatever men agree to call it, pronouncing over it some small portion of their own language, but there is a kind of natural correctness in names, the same for all both Greeks and Barbarians.'

And then farther on he says:

b   'So then as long as the legislator, whether here or among the Barbarians, assigns to each thing the form of name that properly belongs to it, whatever syllables he may use, you will not deem him to be a worse legislator, whether in this country or anywhere else.'

Then again after asserting that the man who understands the correctness of names is a dialectician and a legislator, he next speaks thus:

'A carpenter's work then is to make a rudder under the superintendence of a pilot, if the rudder is to be a good one.
'Evidently.
'And a legislator's work, as it seems, is to give a name, having **c** a dialectician to direct him, if the name is to be rightly given.
'That is true.

---

515 a 8 Plato, *Cratylus*, 383 A   b 1 ibid. 390 **A**   b 9 ibid. 390 D
55²

'The giving of names then, Hermogenes, is likely to be no light Plato matter, as you suppose, nor a work for light persons, nor for chance comers : and Cratylus speaks truly, when he says that things have their names by nature, and that not every one is an artist in names, but only that man who looking to the name which by nature belongs to each thing is able to impose its form upon both the letters and the syllables.'

After these statements, and many more, he again d brings up the mention of the Barbarians, and then expressly acknowledges that most of the names have come to the Greeks from the Barbarians, saying in exact words :

'I have an idea that the Greeks, and especially those who live under the Barbarians, have taken many names from them.

'Well, what then ?

'If any one should try to find how these names are fitly given according to the Greek language, and not according to that language from which each name happens to be derived, you know that he would be in difficulty.

'Naturally.'

So says Plato. He is anticipated, however, by Moses ; for hear what he says, as being a wise legislator and withal a dialectician. 'And out of the ground God formed p. 516 all the beasts of the field and all the fowls of the heaven, and brought them to Adam, to see what he would call them. And whatsoever Adam called a living being, that was the name thereof.'

For by saying 'that was the name thereof' does he not show that the appellations were given in accordance with nature ? For the name just now given, he says, was long before contained in the nature, and that in each of the things named there existed from the beginning this name which the said man inspired by a superior power has b given it.

Moreover the very name Adam, being originally a Hebrew noun, would become with Moses an appellation

---

d 6 Plato, *Cratylus,* 409 D   **516 a** 1 Gen. ii. 19

of the earth-born man, because among the Hebrews the earth is called Adam, wherefore also the first man made out of the earth is with true etymology called by Moses Adam.

But the name may also have another meaning, being otherwise taken for 'red,' and representing the natural colour of the body. However, by the appellation 'Adam' c he signified the earthlike, and earthly, and earthborn, or the man of body and of flesh.

But the Hebrews also call man otherwise, giving him the name 'Enos,' which they say is the rational man within us, different in nature from the earthlike 'Adam.' Enos also has a meaning of its own, being in the Greek language interpreted 'forgetful.'

And such the rational part within us is by nature apt to be, on account of its combination with the mortal and irrational part. For the one being altogether pure, and incorporeal, and divine, and rational, comprehends not only the memory of the things that are past, but also the d knowledge of the things that are to come, through the supreme excellence of its vision. While the other close-packed in flesh, pierced through with bones and nerves, and laden with the great and heavy burden of the body, was seen by the Hebrew Scripture to be full of forgetful-ness and ignorance, and called by an apt designation 'Enos,' which means 'the forgetful.'

It is written at least in a certain Prophet 'What is man, that Thou art mindful of him? Or the son of man, that Thou visitest him?' For which the Hebrew, in the first naming of 'man,' contains the word 'Enos': as if he said more plainly, What is this forgetful one, that Thou, O God, rememberest him, forgetful though he is?' And the p. 517 other clause, ' Or the son of man that Thou visitest him? is read among the Hebrews, 'Or the son of Adam': so that the same man is both Adam and Enos; the fleshly nature being represented by Adam, and the rational by Enos.

In this way do the Hebrew oracles distinguish the

etymology of the two words. But Plato asserts that man is called ἄνθρωπος in the Greek language from looking upward, saying:

'But man no sooner sees, that is the meaning of ὄπωπε, than he PLATO both looks up (ἀναθρεῖ), and considers that which he has seen, that he may be one who looks up at what he sees (ἀναθρῶν ἃ ὄπωπε).'   **b**

Again the Hebrews call the man 'Ish' (Eἲs): and the name is derived by them from Ἔs, by which they signify fire, that the man may be so named because of the hot and fiery temper of the masculine nature.

But the woman, since she is said to have been·taken out of man, also shares the name in common with the man : for the woman is called among them ' Issha,' as the man is 'Ish.' But Plato says that the man (ἀνήρ) is so named because of the upward flux (τὴν ἄνω ῥοήν) ; and he adds—

' And γυνή (woman) seems to me to be the same as γονή (birth).'

Again Moses calls the heaven in the Hebrew tongue **c** *the firmament* etymologically, because the first thing after the incorporeal and intellectual essence is the *firm* and sensible body of this world. But Plato says that the name οὐρανός is rightly given to the heaven, because it makes us look upward (ὁρᾶν ἄνω).

Again the Hebrews say that the highest and proper name of God may not be spoken or uttered, nor even conceived in the imagination of the mind : but this actual name by which they speak of God, they call Elohim, from El, as it seems : and this they interpret as 'strength,' and 'power '; so that among them the name **d** of God has been derived by reasoning from His power and strength, by which He is conceived as Allpowerful and Almighty, as having established all things. But Plato says that the names θεός and θεοί (god and gods) were given because the luminaries in heaven are always running (θέειν).

---

517 a 9 Plato, *Cratylus*, 399 C   b 11 ibid. 414 A   c 5 ibid. 396 C
d 5 ibid. 397 D

Of some such kind, to speak generally, are the investigations of the Hebrews and those of Plato on the correctness of names. The names also among men, Plato says, have been given with some meaning, and he tries to render the reason of them: for he says that Hector somehow or other is named from having and ruling (ἔχειν καὶ

p. 518 κρατεῖν) because he was king of the Trojans; and Agamemnon because he was very persistent (ἄγαν μένειν), and persevered vigorously and constantly in his determinations about the Trojans; Orestes because of the mountainous (ὀρεινόν) and fierce and savage quality of his disposition; and Atreus, because of his having been a mischievous (ἀτηρόν) sort of person in character; and Pelops as one who saw nothing at a distance, but only the things that were close and near (πέλας). Tantalus, he says, means a most miserable man (ταλάντατον) because of the misfortunes which beset him.

These examples and countless others such as these you will find stated by Plato, in endeavouring to teach that the first men had their names given to them by nature **b** and not by convention.

But you would not say that the explanations found also in Moses are forced, nor framed according to any sophistical invention of words, when you have learnt that the Hebrew 'Cain' is translated among the Greeks as 'jealousy'; and the person in question was judged deserving of this appellation because he was jealous of his brother Abel.

'Abel' also is interpreted 'sorrow,' because he too became the cause of such suffering to his parents, who **c** by some diviner foresight gave these names to their children at birth.

But what if I should quote Abraham to you? He was a kind of meteorologist, and formerly, while he was acquir-

---

517 d 13 Plato, *Cratylus*, 393 A   518 a 1 395 A   a 4 394 E
a 6 395 B   a 8 395 C   a 9 395 E   b 5 Gen. iv. 1
556

ing the wisdom of the Chaldees, he had become learned
in the contemplation of the stars and in the knowledge
of the heavens, and was called Abram ; and this in the
Greek language means 'high father.'

But God leading him on from things of this world
to things invisible and lying beyond the things that are
seen, employs an appropriate change of name, saying,
'Thy name shall no more be called Abram, but Abraham shall **d**
be thy name ; for a father of many nations have I made thee.'

Now it would be long to tell with what thought this
is connected: but it is sufficient in this matter also to
adopt Plato as a witness to my statement, when he
says that some names have been given by a more divine
power.

He says indeed in express words :

'For here most of all ought care to have been taken in the PLATO
giving of names : and perhaps some of them may even have been
given by a higher power than that of men.'

This very point is also certified by many examples in
the sacred Scriptures of the Hebrews ; and first of all by
Moses, who taught that Abraham, and his son Isaac, and
also Israel, received their names from a diviner power. **p. 519**
'Isaac' is interpreted 'laughter,' bringing with it the
token of the virtuous joy, which God has promised to
give as a special reward to the friends of God.

His son Israel had formerly borne the name of 'Jacob,'
but instead of 'Jacob' God bestows upon him the name
'Israel,' transforming the active and practical man into
the contemplative.

For 'Jacob' is interpreted 'supplanter,' as one who
strives in the contest of virtue : but 'Israel' is interpreted
'seeing God,' a description which would suit the mind
in man that is capable of knowledge and contemplation. **b**

Why need I now refer to the perfect wisdom of Moses,

---

d 1 Gen. xvii. 5   d 9 Plato, *Cratylus*, 397 B   **519 a 6 Gen.**
xxxii. 28   a 9 Gen. xxvii. 36   a 10 Gen. xxxii. 28

or to the sacred oracles of the Hebrews, to explain, by countless other examples, the correctness of their imposition of proper names, when the details of the subject require longer leisure?

To go no farther, the Greeks would be unable to state the etymologies even of the letters of the alphabet, nor could Plato himself tell the meaning or the reason of the vowels or the consonants.

But the Hebrews would tell us the reason of 'Alpha,'
c which with them is called 'Al'ph,' and this signifies 'learning': and of 'Beta,' which it is their custom to call 'Beth,' which name they give to a house; so as to show the meaning, 'learning of a house,' or as it might be more plainly expressed, 'a kind of teaching and learning of household economy.'

'Gamma' also is with them called 'Gimel': and this is their name for 'fullness.' Then since they call tablets 'Delth,' they gave this name to the fourth letter, signifying therewith by the two letters, that 'written learning
d is a filling of the tablets.'

And any one going over the remaining letters of the alphabet, would find that they have been named among the Hebrews each with some cause and reason. For they say also that the combination of the seven vowels contains the enunciation of one forbidden name, which the Hebrews indicate by four letters and apply to the supreme power of God, having received the tradition from father to son that this is something unutterable and forbidden to the multitude.

And one of the wise Greeks having learned this, I know not whence, hinted it obscurely in verse, saying as follows:

p. 520   'Seven vowels tell My Name,—the Mighty God,
                The everlasting Father of mankind:
                The immortal lyre am I, that guides the world,
                And leads the music of the circling spheres.'

You would find also the meanings of the remaining Hebrew letters, by fixing your attention on each ; but this we have already established by our former statements, when we were showing that the Greeks have received help in everything from the Barbarians.   b

And any one diligently studying the Hebrew language would discover great correctness of names current among that people : since the very name which is the appellation of the whole race has been derived from Heber ; and this means the man that 'passes over,' since both a passage and the one who passes over are called in the Hebrew language 'Heber.'

For the term teaches us to cross over and pass from the things in this world to things divine, and by no means c to stay lingering over the sight of the things that are seen, but to pass from these to the unseen and invisible things of divine knowledge concerning the Maker and Artificer of the world. Thus the first people who were devoted to the one All-ruler and Cause of the Universe, and adhered to Him with a pure and true worship, they called Hebrews, naming men of this character as travellers who had in mind passed over from earthly things.

But why should I spend more time in collecting all the instances of the propriety and correctness of the Hebrew names, when the subject requires a special d treatise of its own. However, speaking generally, I think that even by what has been said I have supplied the evidence of the art of reasoning among the Hebrews : if indeed, as Plato said, it is a task for no mean or ordinary men, but for a wise lawgiver and dialectician, to discover the kind of names naturally belonging to things,—a man such as Moses who has made known to us the Hebrew oracles. So then what follows next after the subject of Dialectics, but to examine what was the condition of the Hebrew people in regard to Physics ?

---

520 b 5 Gen. xiv. 13

Chapter VII

p. 521   THIS third branch also of Hebrew philosophy which, we said, is Physics, was divided among them also into the contemplation of things incorporeal and discerned only by the mind, and the Natural Science of things sensible. This too their all-accomplished Prophets knew, and mingled in their own discourses, when the occasion
b required; for they had not learned it by conjectures and by application of human thought, nor did they boast of men as their teachers, but ascribed their knowledge to the inspiration of a Higher Power, and the afflatus of a divine Spirit.

From this source came their countless prophecies concerning future events, and countless physical explanations of the constitution of the world, and descriptions likewise countless of the nature of animals, and very many things concerning plants which each set down in his own prophecies.

And Moses, understanding also the qualities of precious
c stones extremely well, exercises a very careful consideration of them in the case of the High Priest's dress. Again that Solomon, above all others, excelled in knowledge of the nature of such things is testified by the sacred Scripture in the following words:

'And Solomon spake three thousand proverbs, and his songs were five thousand; and he spake of trees, from the cedar that is in Lebanon even unto the hyssop that springeth out of the wall: he spake also of beasts, and of fowl, and of creeping
d things, and of fishes. And there came all peoples to hear the wisdom of Solomon, and from all the kings of the earth, as many as heard his wisdom.'

Starting from this description the author who ascribed to his person the perfection of wisdom, spake also thus: 'For Himself gave me an unerring knowledge of the things that are, to know the constitution of the world, and the operation

---

521 c 6 1 Ki. iv. 32   d 6 Wisdom vii. 17

of the elements; the beginning and end and middle of times, the alternations of the solstices and the changes of seasons, the circuits of the year and the positions of stars; the natures of living creatures and the ragings of wild beasts, the violences of winds and the thoughts of men, the diversities of plants, and the virtues of roots; and all things that are either secret or manifest I learned, for Wisdom the artificer of all things taught me.'   **p. 522**

And again the same Solomon, explaining the nature of the fleeting substance of bodies, says in *Ecclesiastes*: 'Vanity of vanities, all is vanity. What profit hath man in all his labour, wherein he laboureth under the Sun.' And he adds: 'What is that which hath been? The very thing that shall be. And what is that which hath been done? The very thing that shall be done. And there is nothing new under the sun.'

For these and such as these were his physiological conclusions concerning corporeal substance. And you **b** will find, if you go on, that the other wise Hebrews were not without a share of the like science. At all events, as I said before, there are numberless sayings of theirs about plants and animals, whether of the land or of the water, and moreover about the nature of birds.

Nay further, about the constellations in the heaven also: since there is conveyed in the writings of the said authors especial mention of Arctos and Pleias, Orion and Arcturus, which the Greeks are wont to call Arctophylax and Boötes.

Also concerning the constitution of the world, and the revolution and change of the universe, and concerning **c** the essence of the soul, and the creation of the nature, both visible and invisible, of all rational beings, and the universal Providence, and still earlier than these, the opinions concerning the First Cause of the universe, and the doctrine of the divinity of the Second Cause, and the arguments and speculations about the other things that can be perceived only by thought, they have comprehended

----

522 a 4 Eccles. i. 1   a 6 ibid. 9

accurately and well: so that one would not err in saying, that those among the Greeks who have afterwards investigated the nature of these things have been like younger men following the guidance of the old.

d   This then is what we have to say of their Natural Science of the Universe. But as they divided this subject into two parts, the one which concerns things perceived by the senses they did not think it necessary to make known accurately to the multitude, nor to teach the common people the causes of the nature of existing things, except only so far as it was necessary for them to know that the universe has not been self-created, and has not been produced causelessly and by chance from an irrational impetus, but is led on by the Divine Reason as its guide, and governed by a power of ineffable Wisdom.

With regard, however, to things seen only by the mind, that they exist, and what they are, and what their condition is in regard to arrangement, power, and diversity, has been already mentioned and is laid down in the Sacred Books, and has been audibly delivered to all men, p. 5?3 so far as the knowledge was necessary for those who profess religion, with a view to the recovery of a pious and sober life.

But the deep and occult reason of these things they left to be sought out and learned in secret communications by those who were capable of being initiated in matters of this kind. It will be well, however, to describe in a general way a few points in the contemplation of these matters, and to show that herein also Plato entertained the sentiments which were dear to the said people.

Chapter VIII

b   But in fact it is manifest from his own words that the admirable Plato followed the all-wise Moses and the Hebrew Prophets in regard also to the teaching and speculation about things incorporeal and seen only

by the mind; whether it were that he learned from
hearsay which had reached him (since he is proved c
to have made his studies among the Egyptians at the
very time when the Hebrews, having been driven the
second time out of their own country, were in the habit
of visiting Egypt during the Persian supremacy), or
whether of himself he hit upon the true nature of the
things, or, in whatever way, was deemed worthy of this
knowledge by God. 'For God,' says the Apostle, 'manifested it unto them. For the invisible things of Him from the
creation of the world are clearly seen, being perceived by means
of the things that are made, even His eternal power and divinity,
that they may be without excuse.' And you may learn what
I have stated by examining the matter as follows:

CHAPTER IX

MOSES in his declarations of sacred truth uttered a d
response in the person of God: 'I AM THAT I AM. Thus
shalt thou say unto the children of Israel, I AM hath sent me
unto you, and so represented God as the sole absolute
Being, and declared Him to have been properly and fitly
honoured with this name.

And Solomon again spake concerning the origin and **p. 524**
the decay of things corporeal and sensible: 'What is that
which hath been? The very thing that shall be. And what
is that which hath been done? The very thing that shall be
done. And there is nothing new under the sun, whereof a man
shall speak and say, See, this is new. It hath been already, in the
ages which were before us.'

In accordance with them we also divide the All into
two parts, that which can be perceived only by the
mind, and that which can be perceived by the senses:
and the former we define as incorporeal and rational in
its nature, and imperishable and immortal; but the
sensible as being always in flux and decay, and in change

---

523 c 8 Rom. i. 20   d 2 Ex. iii. 14   524 a 2 Eccles. i. 9

and conversion of its substance. And all things being summed up and referred to one beginning, we hold the

b doctrine that the uncreate, and that which has proper and true being, is One, which is the cause of all things incorporeal and corporeal.

Now see in what manner Plato, having imitated not only the thought, but also the very expressions and words of the Hebrew Scripture, appropriates the doctrine, explaining it more at large, as follows:

PLATO 'What is that which always is and has no becoming? And what is that which is always becoming and never is? The former is that which may be comprehended by intelligence combined with reason, being always in the same conditions. The latter is that which may be conjectured by opinion with the help of unreasoning sensation, becoming and perishing but never really being.'

Does it not plainly appear that the admirable philo-

c sopher has altered the oracle which in Moses declared 'I AM THAT I AM' into 'What is that which always is and has no becoming?' And this he has made still clearer when he says that true 'being' is nothing else than that which is not seen by eyes of flesh, but is conceived by the mind. So having asked, What is 'being'? he makes answer to himself, saying: 'That which may be comprehended by intelligence combined with reason.'

And as to Solomon's maxim which said, 'What is that which hath been? The very thing that shall be. And what is

d that which hath been done? The very thing that shall be done,' it must be evident that he translated this almost in the very words, saying, 'But that which may be conjectured by means of irrational sensation is becoming and perishing, but never really "being."' To which he also adds:

PLATO 'For all these are parts of time, the "was" and "shall be"; which we unconsciously but wrongly transfer to the eternal essence. For we say that "It was, and is, and shall be." But

524 b 8 Plato, *Timaeus*, 27 D   c 2 Ex. iii. 14   c 9 Eccles. i. 9
d 6 Plato, *Timaeus*, 37 E

to this essence the " is " alone is truly appropriate ; and the " was " PLATO
and the " will be " are proper to be spoken of the generation
in time, for they are movements. But to that which is always
immovably in the same conditions it belongs not to become
either older or younger through time : nor that it ever became, **p. 525**
nor has now become, nor will be hereafter at all, nor be subject
to any of the conditions which becoming attaches to the things
which pass to and fro in sensation : but these are forms of time,
imitating eternity and moving by number in a circle. And
besides these there are such expressions as the following ; what
has become is become, and what becomes is becoming, and what
will become is about to become.'

And lest any one should suppose that I am misinter-
preting the philosopher's words, I will make use of
commentaries which explain the meaning of these state- b
ments. There are indeed many who have set themselves
to the consideration of these matters ; but at present
it is enough for me to quote the expressions of an
illustrious man, Numenius the Pythagorean, which he
uses in his second Book *Concerning the Good,* as follows :

CHAPTER X

' COME then, let us mount up as nearly as we possibly can c
to true " being," and let us say that " being " neither at any time NUMENIUS
" was," nor ever can " become," but always " is " in a definite
time, the present only.

' If, however, any one wishes to rename this present time
eternity, I too am willing. But the time past we ought to consider
altogether gone, already so gone away and escaped as to exist
no longer : and on the other hand the time to come as yet is not, d
but professes to be able at some future time to come into being.

' It is not therefore reasonable to suppose " being," at least
in one and the same sense, either not to be or to be no longer,
or not yet. Since when this is so stated, there arises in the
statement one great impossibility, that the same thing at the
same time should both be and not be.

---

525 c 1 Numenius, a Fragment preserved by Eusebius only

N<small>UMENIUS</small>   'For if this were so, scarcely would it be possible for anything else to be, if " being " itself in regard to its very " being " be not. For " being " is eternal and constant, ever in the same condition, nor has it been generated and destroyed, nor increased and diminished: nor did it ever yet become more or less: and certainly neither in other senses nor yet locally will it be moved.

'For it is not right for it to be moved, either backward or forward: nor upward ever, nor downward: neither to the right
p. 526 hand nor to the left shall " being " ever pass: nor shall it ever be moved around its own centre; but rather it shall stand fast, and shall be fixed and set firm, ever in the same conditions and same mode.'

And then, after other statements, he adds:

'So much then for my introduction. But for my own part I will no longer make pretences, nor say that I do not know the name of the incorporeal; for now at length it seems likely to be pleasanter to speak than not to speak it. And so then I say that its name is that which we have so long been examining.

b   'But let no one laugh, if I affirm that the name of the incorporeal is "essence" and "being." And the cause of the name " being " is that it has not been generated nor will be destroyed, nor is it subject to any other motion at all, nor any change for better or for worse; but is simple and unchangeable, and in the same idea, and neither willingly departs from its sameness, nor is compelled by any other to depart.

c   'Plato too said in the *Cratylus* that names are exactly adapted to a likeness of the things. Be it granted then and agreed that " being " is the incorporeal.'

Then lower down he adds:

'I said that " being " is incorporeal, and that this is that which can be perceived by the mind only. Their statements then, so far as I can remember, were certainly of this kind: but any one who feels the want of an explanation I am willing to encourage with just this suggestion, that if these statements do not agree with the doctrines of Plato, yet at least he must consider them to be those

---

526 c 1 Plato, *Cratylus*, 430 A, and frequently

of some other great man of the highest ability, such as Pytha- NUMENIUS
goras.

'Plato at all events says—come, let me remember how he says **d**
it—What is that which always is and has no becoming? And
what that which is always becoming, and never is? The first
that which may be comprehended by intelligence combined with
reason, and the other that which may be conjectured by opinion
with the aid of unreasoning sensation, becoming and perishing,
but never really "being."

'For he was inquiring what is "being," and saying that it is
unquestionably without beginning. For he said that for "being"
there is no becoming : for then it would be changed, but that which
is liable to change is not eternal.'

Then below he says :

'If then "being" is altogether and in every way eternal and
unchangeable, and by no means departs in any way from itself,
but abides in the same conditions, and remains fixed in the same
manner, this surely must be that which can be comprehended
by intelligence combined with reason.

'But if body is in flux and is carried off by the change of the
moment, it passes away and no longer exists. Wherefore is it **p. 527**
not utter folly to deny that this is something undefinable, and that
can only be conjectured by opinion, and, as Plato says, becoming
and perishing, but never really "being"?'

Thus then speaks Numenius, explaining clearly both
Plato's doctrines and the much earlier doctrines of Moses.
With reason therefore is that saying currently attributed
to him, in which it is recorded that he said, 'For what
else is Plato than Moses speaking Attic Greek?'

But see, besides this, whether Plutarch in further **b**
unfolding the same thought may not agree both with
the statements of philosophers which have been brought
forward, and the theological doctrines of the Hebrews
set forth again in other places, whereby at one time the
God who makes answer is introduced as saying : 'For I am

---

d 1 Plato, *Timaeus*, 27 D ; see p. **524 b** above   527 b 6 Malachi
iii. 6

the Lord your God, and I am not changed': and at another
time the Prophet directs his speech with a view to Him,
saying that the things which are seen would all some
time be changed and removed, 'but Thou art the same, and

c Thy years shall not fail.' Observe then whether—when He
who spake in Moses, as if proposing a question, said, 'I Am
that I Am,' and, 'I am the Lord your God, and I am not
changed': and again, 'But Thou art (εἶ) the same'—whether,
I say, Plutarch would not seem to be interpreting the
meaning of this in his treatise *Concerning the* Εἶ *at
Delphi*, when he speaks word for word thus:

Chapter XI

d   'Neither number therefore, nor order, nor conjunction, nor any
Plutarch other of the non-significant particles, does the letter seem to
indicate.   But it is an address and appellation of the god complete in itself, which as soon as the word is uttered sets the speaker
thinking of the power of the god.

'For the god, welcoming as it were each of us who approach
him here, addresses to us the words " Know thyself," which is
nothing less than " Hail ": and we answering the god again say
" Thou art " (Εἶ), rendering to him the appellation of " being " as
his true and unerring and solely appropriate name.

p. 528   'For we have in reality no share in " being," but every mortal
nature is set in the midst between becoming and perishing, and
presents a phantom and a faint and uncertain seeming of itself.

'And if any one closely press the thought, from wishing to
grasp it, then just as the violent grasping of water by pressing
and squeezing it together causes what was enclosed to slip through
and be lost, so when Reason seeks too much actuality in any
thing passible and subject to change, it goes astray on this side
to the part that is becoming, and on that to the part that is

b perishing, being unable to lay hold of anything permanent, or
of any true " being."

'For it is not possible, according to Heracleitus, to step twice

---

527 b 10 Ps. ci. 28   d 1 Plutarch, *Moralia*, 391 F   528 b 3
Heracleitus, *Fr.* xli, xlii (Bywater)

into the same river, nor to touch a mortal substance twice in the PLUTARCH
same condition, but by the swiftness and suddenness of its change
it scatters and again collects, or rather we must not say " again "
nor " afterwards," but it is at the same time both combining and
passing away, both coming on and going off.

'Wherefore neither does the part that is becoming attain
to being, because the becoming never ceases nor stands still;
but from a seed by constant change it makes an embryo, then
a babe, then a child, in due order a youth, a young man, a man,
an elder, an old man, destroying the first becomings and ages by c
those which come after.

' We, however, are ridiculously afraid of one death, although
we have already died and are dying so many. For not only,
as Heracleitus used to say, is "the death of fire the birth of air,"
but still more manifestly in our own case the man in his prime
perishes when the old man is coming, and the young man has
passed away into the man in his prime, and the child into
the young man, and the infant into the child, and the man
of yesterday has died into the man of to-day, and the man of
to-day (is dying) into the man of to-morrow; and not one abides
nor is *one*, but we become many, while matter is circulating around d
some one phantom and common mould, and then slipping away.

'Else how is it, if we remain the same, that we delight now in
some things, formerly in others, that we love and hate the
contrary things, and praise and blame, use different language,
have different feelings, retain no more the same appearance, form,
or thought?

'For neither is it natural to have different feelings without a
change, nor can one who changes be the same. But if he is not
the same, he *is* not, but is changing from *this*, and becoming other
from other: and our sense, through ignorance of true "being,"
falsely declares the apparent to "be."   p. 529

'What then is true "being"? The eternal and uncreate, and
imperishable, to which no time brings change. For time is something moveable, and imagined in connexion with the movement
of matter, and ever flowing and not holding water, as it were
a vessel of perishing and becoming. And so when it is said

---

c 5 Heracleitus, *Fr.* xxv.

PLUTARCH of time "after" and "before," and "will be" and "has been," there is at once an acknowledgement of "not-being."

'For to say of that which has not yet come into being, or has already ceased from being, that it "is" is silly and absurd. But at the very moment when, trying to fix our perception of time, we say "it is present," "it is here," and "now," our reason slips

b away again from this and loses it. For it is thrust aside into the future and into the past, just as a visual ray is distorted with those who try to see what is necessarily separated by distance.

'And if the nature which is measured is subject to the same conditions as the time which measures it, this nature itself has no permanence, nor "being," but is becoming and perishing according to its relation to time.

'Hence nothing of this kind may be said of "being," such as "was" or "will be": for these are a kind of inflexions, and transitions, and alternations of that which is not fitted by nature to continue in "being."

c 'But we ought to say of God, HE IS, and is in relation to no time, but in relation to eternity the motionless, and timeless, and changeless, in which is no "before" nor "after," nor future, nor past, nor elder nor younger: but being One He has filled the "Ever" with the one "Now"; and is the sole self-dependent real "Being," having neither past nor future, without beginning and without end.

'Thus then ought we in worship to salute and address Him, or even indeed as some of the ancients did, THOU ART ONE. For the Deity is not many, as each of us is, a promiscuous

d assemblage of all kinds compounded of numberless differences arising in its conditions: but "being" must be *One*, just as One must be "being": for *otherness*, as a differentia of "being," inclines towards a becoming of "not-being."'

CHAPTER XII

WHEREAS Moses and all the Hebrew Prophets teach

p. 530 that the Divine nature is ineffable, and indicate the symbol of the ineffable Name by the notation which may not be pronounced among them, hear how Plato also in agreement with them speaks in his great *Epistle* word for word.

'For it can by no means be defined in words as other branches Ps.-Plato
of learning, but from long converse on the subject itself, and from
living with it, on a sudden a light, as it were kindled from a
spark leaping out of the fire, comes to the soul, and thenceforth
is self-sustained.'

This example also of 'light' another Hebrew Prophet b
had previously set forth, saying, 'The light of Thy countenance, O Lord, was shown upon us.' And again another, 'In
Thy light shall we see light.'

Chapter XIII

As Moses declared concerning the God of all the world, c
'Hear, O Israel, the Lord our God is one Lord,' Plato again
concurring with him teaches that there is one God as also
one heaven, speaking thus in the *Timaeus* :

'Have we then been right in speaking of one heaven, or was Plato
it more correct to say that there are many and infinite? One, if
indeed it is to have been created according to the pattern. For
that which includes the ideals of all living creatures whatsoever
cannot possibly be second to another.'

But that he has a knowledge of one God, even though
in accordance with the custom of the Greeks he commonly speaks of them as many, is evident from the
Epistle to Dionysius, in which, giving marks to distinguish
his letters written in earnest from those thrown off at d
random, he said that he would put the name of 'The gods'
as a sign at the head of those which contained nothing
serious, but the name of 'God' at the head of those
which were thoughtfully composed by him. Accordingly
he thus speaks word for word :

'With regard then to the distinctive mark concerning the Ps.-Plato
letters which I may write seriously, and which not, though I
suppose you remember it, nevertheless bear it in mind and give

---

530 a 6 Ps.-Plato, *Ep.* vii. p. 341 C   b 2 Ps. iv. 7   b 3 Ps. xxxvi. 9
c 2 Deut. vi. 4   c 5 Plato, *Timaeus,* 31 A   d 7 Ps.-Plato, *Ep.* xiii.
p. 363 B

Ps.-PLATO great attention to it.   For there are many who bid me to write,
whom it is not easy for me openly to refuse.   So then the serious
letter begins with " God," and the less serious with "gods." '

And the same author expressly acknowledges that he
has learned the doctrine of the one ' God' from men of
p. 531 old, as he says in the *Laws* :

PLATO   ' God then, as the old tradition says, holding the beginning
and end and middle of all things that exist, passes straight
through while travelling round in nature's course.   Justice is
ever His companion, taking vengeance on those who depart from
the divine law : and the man who is to be happy holds fast to
her and follows on humbly in orderly array.   But if any man
lifted up by arrogance, or elated by riches or honours, or personal
beauty, has his soul inflamed with youthfulness and folly combined
b with insolence, as feeling no need of a ruler or guide, but being
competent even to guide others, he is left forsaken of God : and
when he is thus forsaken, and has also taken to himself others of
like mind, he prances about and throws all things into confusion,
and to many he seems to be somebody, but after no long time pays
to justice no contemptible penalty, and brings utter destruction
upon himself as well as on his family and city.'

Thus Plato writes.   And now beside the description,
' God holding the beginning and end and middle of all things
that exist,' set thou this from Hebrew prophecy, ' I God am
first and I am with the last ' : and beside the sentence,
c ' passes straight through while travelling on in nature's course,'
set this, ' His countenance doth behold uprightness.'

Also with the phrase, ' Justice is ever His companion, taking
vengeance on those who depart from the divine law,' compare
this, ' Righteous is the LORD, and He loveth righteousness ' ; and
this, ' Vengeance is Mine, I will repay, saith the LORD ' ; and this,
' For the Lord is an avenger, and repayeth them that work exceed-
ing proudly ' ; and with this, ' the man who is to be happy
holds fast to her and follows on humbly in orderly array,' there
d agrees, ' Thou shalt walk after the LORD thy God.'   And with

531 a 2 Plato, *Laws*, iv. 715 E   b 10 Is. xli. 4   c 2 Ps. xi. 7
c 5 Ps. xi. 7   c 6 Rom. xii. 20 ; (cp. Deut. xxxii. 35)   c 7 1 Thess.
iv. 6, and Ps. xxxi. 23   d 1 Deut. xiii. 4

this, ' But he that is lifted up by pride is left forsaken of God,' PLATO agrees, ' God resisteth the proud, but giveth grace unto the humble '; and, ' But the joy of the ungodly is a sudden fall.'

These then are a few out of countless passages concerning Him who is God over all.   But observe also the passages concerning the Second Cause.

CHAPTER XIV

IN regard then to the First Cause of all things let this be our admitted form of agreement.   But now consider p. 532 what is said concerning the Second Cause, whom the Hebrew oracles teach to be the Word of God, and God of God, even as we Christians also have ourselves been taught to speak of the Deity.

First then Moses expressly speaks of two divine Lords in the passage where he says, ' Then the LORD rained from the LORD fire and brimstone upon the city of the ungodly ' : where he applied to both the like combination of Hebrew letters in the usual way ; and this combination is the mention of God expressed in the four letters, which is b with them unutterable.

In accordance with him David also, another Prophet as well as king of the Hebrews, says, ' The LORD said unto my Lord, sit Thou on My right hand,' indicating the Most High God by the first LORD, and the second to Him by the second title.   For to what other is it right to suppose that the right hand of the Unbegotten God is conceded, than to Him alone of whom we are speaking?

This is He whom the same prophet in other places more clearly distinguishes as the Word of the Father, supposing c Him whose deity we are considering to be the Creator of the universe, in the passage where he says, ' By the Word of the LORD were the heavens made firm.'

---

d 3 Ja. iv. 6   d 4 Job xx. 5 (Sept.)   532 a 7 Gen. xix. 24
b 4 Ps. cx. 1   c 3 Ps. xxxiii. 6

He introduces the same Person also as a Saviour of those who need His care, saying, 'He sent His Word and healed them.'

And Solomon, David's son and successor, presenting the same thought by a different name, instead of the 'Word' called Him Wisdom, making the following statement as in her person :

'I Wisdom made prudence my dwelling, and called to my aid d knowledge and understanding.' Then afterwards he adds, 'The LORD formed me as the beginning of His ways with a view to His works : from everlasting He established me, in the beginning before He made the earth, . . . before the mountains were settled, and before all hills He begat me. . . . When He was preparing the heaven, I was beside Him.'

And there is this again of the same author, ' God by Wisdom founded the earth, and by understanding He prepared the heavens.' The following also is said to be the same author's : 'And all things that are either secret or manifest I learned : for Wisdom, the artificer of all things, taught me.'

Then he adds, ' But what wisdom is, and how she came into being, I will declare, and will not hide mysteries from you, but will trace her out from the beginning of creation.'

And afterwards he gives such explanations as the following : ' For she is a spirit quick of understanding, holy, alone in kind, manifold, subtil, freely moving, clear in utterance, unpolluted, . . . all-powerful, all-surveying, and penetrating through all spirits, that are quick of understanding, pure, most subtil. P. 533 For wisdom is more mobile than any motion ; yea, she pervadeth and penetrateth all things by reason of her pureness. For she is a breath of the power of God, and a clear effluence of the glory of the Almighty. Therefore can nothing defiled find entrance into her. For she is an effulgence from everlasting light, and an unspotted mirror of the operation of God, and an image of His goodness. . . . And she reacheth from end to end with full strength, and ordereth all things graciously.' Thus the Scripture

---

532 c 6 Ps. cvii. 20   c 12 Prov. viii. 12   d 2 Prov. viii. 22
d 7 Prov. iii. 19   d 10 Wisdom vii. 21   d 12 Wisdom vi. 22
d 16 Wisdom vii. 22   533 a 7 Wisdom viii. 1

speaks : but Philo the Hebrew, explaining the meaning of the doctrine more clearly, represents it in the manner **b** following :

Chapter XV

'For it becomes those who have made companionship with Philo knowledge to desire to behold the true Being, but should they be unable, then at least to behold His image, the most holy Word.'

Also in the same treatise he says this :   c

'But even if one be not as yet worthy to be called the son of God, let him strive earnestly to be adorned after the likeness of His first-begotten Word, who is the eldest of the Angels, and as an Archangel has many names.

'For He is called the Beginning, and the Name of God, and the Word, and the Man after God's image, and He who seeth Israel. For which cause I was induced a short time ago to praise the virtues of those who assert that we are all sons of one Man.

'For even if we have not yet become fit to be deemed children **d** of God, yet surely we may be children of His eternal Image, the most holy Word : for His eldest Word is the Image of God.'

And again he adds :

'I have, however, heard also one of the companions of Moses utter an oracle of this kind : Behold ! the man whose name is the East. A very strange appellation, if you suppose the man who is composed of body and soul to be meant : but if you mean that incorporeal Being who wears the divine form, you will fully acknowledge that the 'East' was happily given to Him as a most appropriate name : for the Universal Father made Him rise as His eldest Son, whom elsewhere He named "First-begotten." And indeed He that was begotten, imitating the ways of His Father, looked to His archetypal patterns in giving form to the **p. 534** various species.'

---

b 3 Philo Iudaeus, *On the Confusion of Tongues*, c. xx   **c** 2 ibid. c. xxviii   **c** 9 Gen. xlii. 11.   **d** 5 Philo Iudaeus, l. c., c. xiv **d** 6 Zech. vi. 12

Let it suffice at this point to have made these quotations from the Hebrew Philo, taken from the treatise inscribed with the title, *On the worse plotting against the better.* But already in an earlier part of *The Preparation for the Gospel*, in setting forth the doctrines of the religion of the ancient Hebrews, I have also sufficiently discussed those which relate to the Second Cause, and to those passages I will now refer the earnest student. Since **b** therefore these have been the theological opinions held among the Hebrews in the way that I have described concerning the Second Cause of the Universe, it is now time to listen to Plato speaking as follows in the *Epinomis*:

Chapter XVI

Ps.-Plato   'And let us not, in assigning offices to them, give to this one **c** a year, and to that a month, and to others appoint no portion, nor any time in which to perform his course, and help to complete the order, which Reason (λόγος), of all things most divine, appointed; Reason, which the happy man at first admires, and then gets a desire to understand, as much as is possible for mortal nature.'

Also in the Epistle to Hermeias, and Erastus, and Coriscus, he has laid down the doctrine with excellent caution, writing as follows word for word:

'This letter you three must all read, together if possible; but **d** if not, by two and two together, as you can, as often as possible: and must make an agreement and valid law, adding an oath as is right, and with earnestness not unworthy of the Muses, and with culture the sister of earnestness, invoking the God who is the Ruler of all things that are and that shall be, and Father and Lord of Him who is the Ruler and the Cause: Whom, if we rightly study philosophy, we all shall know clearly as far as is possible for favoured mortals.'

---

534 a 5 A wrong reference; the quotations are from *The Confusion of Tongues*   b 6 Ps.-Plato, *Epinomis*, 986 C   c 10 Ps.-Plato, *Ep.* vi. 323 C

Does it not seem to you that in speaking thus Plato has followed the doctrines of the Hebrews? Or from what other source did it occur to him to name another God who is mightier than the cause of all things, whom also he calls Father of the All-ruler? And whence came **p. 535** his idea of setting the name of Lord on the Father of the Demiurge, though never before him had any one brought this to the ears of the Greeks, nor even set it down in his own mind.

And if we yet want other witnesses for an indisputable confirmation of the philosopher's meaning, and of the construction of our argument, hear what explanations Plotinus gives in the treatise which he composed *Concerning the three Primary Hypostases*, writing as follows:

Chapter XVII

'If any one admires this world of sense, beholding at once **b** Plo-its greatness and beauty and the order of its eternal course, and   tinus the gods that are therein, some visible, and some invisible, the daemons, and animals and all kinds of plants, let him mount up to its original pattern and to the more real world, and there let him see all intelligible things, and things which are of themselves eternal in their own understanding and life, see also the pure **c** intelligence and the infinite wisdom that presides over them.'

Then afterwards in addition to this he says:

'Who then is He that begat Him? He who is simple, and prior to a plurality of this kind, who is the cause both of His being, and of His plurality. For number came not first: since before the duad is the one; and the duad is second, and produced from the one.'

And again he goes on and adds:

'How then and what must we conceive concerning that abiding substance? A light shining around and proceeding from it, while it remains itself unchanged, as from the sun proceeds

---

535 b 1 Plotinus, *Ennead*, v. bk. i. p. 484 D   c 4 ibid. p. 486 A
c 10 ibid. p. 487 D

PLO- **d** the bright surrounding light that runs around it, ever produced
TINUS   out of it, while it remains unchanged itself.

'And all existing things, so long as they remain, give forth
necessarily from their own essence and from the power present
in them the substance which surrounds them externally and is
dependent upon them, being as it were an image of the archetypes from which it sprang.

'Thus fire gives forth the heat which proceeds from it, and snow
does not merely retain its cold within itself. And especially all
fragrant things bear witness to this fact : for as long as they
exist, a something from them goes forth around them, which is
enjoyed by whatever is near.

'Moreover all things as soon as they are perfect begin to
generate : so that which is always perfect is always generating
p. 536 a something eternal, and what it generates is less than itself.

'What then must we say concerning the Most Perfect ? That
He either generates nothing from Himself, or the things which
are the greatest next to Himself. But after Him mind is the
greatest and the second. For the mind beholds Him and has need
of Him alone, but He has no need of it : and that which is
begotten from a superior mind, must be mind ; and mind is
superior to all things, because all the rest come after it.'

After this he says further :

'Now everything desires and loves that which begat it, and
b especially when that which begat and that which is begotten
exist alone. And when that which begat is also the very best,
the begotten is necessarily so joined with it, as to be separated
only by its otherness. But, since it is necessary to speak more
plainly, I mean that mind is His image.'

And to this again he adds :

'This is the reason also of Plato's trinities : for he says that
around the King of all are all the primaries, and around the
second the secondaries, and around the third the tertiaries. He
says also that the Cause has a Father, meaning that Mind is the
Cause, for with Plato Mind is the Creator.

c 'And Mind, he says, makes the Soul in that cup of his. And

---

536 a 10 Plotinus, ibid. p. 488   b 7 ib.d. p. 489.

the Cause which is Mind has for its Father, he says, the Good, and PLOTINUS that which transcends both Mind and essence. But in many places he speaks of Being and of Mind as the Idea. So that Plato recognizes Mind as proceeding from the Good, and the Soul from Mind : and these are no new doctrines, nor now first stated, but long since, though not publicly divulged : and the doctrines of the present time have been interpretations of the former, which by the testimony of Plato's own writings have confirmed the antiquity of these opinions.'

This is what Plato says. And Numenius highly **d** commending Plato's doctrines in his treatise *Of the Good* gives his own interpretation of the Second Cause, as follows:

CHAPTER XVIII

' THE man who is to understand about the First and Second NUMENIUS God must previously distinguish the several questions by some orderly arrangement : and after this seems to be set right, he must **p. 537** then endeavour also to discuss the matter in a becoming manner, or otherwise not at all. Else he who handles it prematurely, before the first steps have been taken, will find his treasure become dust, as the saying is.

' Let us then not suffer the same ; but after invoking God to be the guide of our discussion concerning Himself, and to show us the treasure of His thoughts, so let us commence. At once we must offer our prayer, and then make our distinction.

' The First God, being in Himself, is simple, because, being united throughout with Himself, He can never be divided. God however the Second and Third is one : but by being associated with matter which is duality, He makes it one, but is Himself **b** divided by it, because it has a tendency to concupiscence, and is always in flux.

' Therefore by not adhering to the intelligible (for so He would have been adhering to Himself), because He regards matter and gives attention to it, He becomes regardless of Himself.

' And He lays hold of the sensible and busies Himself with it,

---

d 5 Numenius, *Of the Good*, a Fragment preserved by Eusebius. Cf. Mullach, iii. 167

NUMENIUS and moreover from setting His desire upon matter He takes it up into His own moral nature.'

And after other statements he says:

'For it is not at all becoming that the First God should be the Creator; also the First God must be regarded as the father of the God who is Creator of the world.

'If then we were inquiring about the creative principle, and asserting that He who was pre-existent would thereby be pre-eminently fit for the work, this would have been a suitable c commencement of our argument.

'But if we are not discussing the creative principle, but inquiring about the First Cause, I renounce what I said, and wish that to be withdrawn, but will pass on in pursuit of my argument, and hunt it out from another source.

'Before capturing our argument, however, let us make an agreement between ourselves such as no one who hears it can doubt, that the First God is free from all kinds of work and reigns as king, but the Creative God governs, and travels through the heaven.

'And by Him comes also our equipment for the chase, mind being sent down in transmission to all who have been appointed to partake of it.

d   'So when God is looking at and turned towards each of us, the result is that our bodies then live and revive, while God cherishes them with His radiations. But when He turns away to the contemplation of Himself, these bodies become extinguished, but the mind is alive and enjoying a life of blessedness.'

This is what Numenius writes. And now do you set beside it the passages from David's prophecy, sung of old among the Hebrews in the following fashion: 'How **p. 538** mighty are Thy works, O Lord: in wisdom hast Thou made them all. The earth is filled with Thy creation. . . . All things wait upon Thee, to give them their meat in due season. When Thou givest it them, they will gather it; and when Thou openest Thine hand, they all will be satisfied with goodness. But when Thou turnest away Thy face, they will be troubled: if Thou takest away their breath, they will die, and turn again to their dust. Thou wilt

---

537 d 8 Ps. (ciii) civ. 24   538 a 2 ibid. 27

send forth Thy Spirit, and they will be created, and Thou wilt
renew the face of the earth.'

For in what would this differ from the thought of the
philosopher, which declares, as we saw, that 'When God
is looking at and turned towards each of us, the b
result is that our bodies then live and revive, while
God cherishes them with His radiations ; but when God
turns to the contemplation of Himself, these become
extinguished.'

And again, whereas with us the Word of Salvation
says, ' I am the vine, . . . My Father is the husbandman, . . . ye
are the branches,' hear what Numenius says concerning
the deity of the Second Cause.

' And as again there is a relation between the husbandman c NUME-
and him that planteth, exactly in the same way is the First God NIUS
related to the Demiurge.   The former being the seed of all soul
sows it in all things that partake of Himself.   But the Lawgiver
plants, and distributes, and transplants into each of us the germs
which have been previously deposited from that higher source.'

And afterwards again he speaks as follows of the mode
in which the Second Cause arose out of the First.

' Now all things which, when given, pass to the receiver, and
have left the giver, such as are attendance, property, silver un- d
stamped or coined,—these things, I say, are mortal and human :
but divine things are such as, when they are distributed and
have come from one to another, have not forsaken the former, and
have brought with them benefit to the latter, without hurting the
other ; nay, have brought him a further benefit by recalling to
memory what he understood before.

' Now this excellent thing is that good knowledge which brings
profit to the receiver and is not lost to the giver.   Just as you
may see a lamp lit from another lamp shining with a light of
which it did not deprive the former, but had its own material
kindled at the other's flame.

' Such a thing is knowledge, which when given and received

---

b 7 John xv. 1, 5   c 1 Numenius, *Fr.* 10.   c 9 Numenius, ibid.

NUMENIUS remains the same with the giver, and is communicated to the receiver.

p. 539   ' And the cause of this, my friend, is not anything human ; but that the state and essence which possesses knowledge is the same both in God who has given, and in you and me who have received it.

' Wherefore also Plato said that wisdom was brought to mankind " with a brilliant flame of fire by Prometheus." '

And again afterwards lower down he says:

' Now the modes of life of the First God and of the Second are these : evidently the First God will be at rest, while the Second b on the contrary is in motion.   So then the First is engaged with intelligibles, and the Second with both intelligibles and sensibles.

' And be not surprised at my saying this, for you are going to hear something far more surprising.   For instead of that motion which belongs to the Second I assert that the rest which belongs to the First is His natural motion, from which both the order of the world, and its eternal continuance, and its safety is diffused throughout the universe.'

After this in the sixth Book also he adds the following:

' Since Plato knew that the Creator alone was known among c men, but that the First Mind, which is called Absolute Being, is altogether unknown among them, therefore he spoke in this way, just as if one were to say: The First Mind, my good sirs, is not that which you imagine, but another mind before it, more ancient and more divine.'

And after other passages he adds:

' A pilot when driven along in mid ocean, sits high above the d helm, and steers the ship by the tillers, but his eyes and mind are strained directly at the sky, looking at things aloft, as his course passes across the heaven above, while he sails upon the sea below. So also the Creator having bound matter together in harmony that it may neither break out nor slip away, is Himself seated above matter, as above a ship on the sea : and in directing the harmony He steers by the ideas, while instead of the sky He looks to the

---

539 a 5 Plato, *Philebus*, 16 C   a 8 Numenius, *Fr.* 10   b 11 Numenius, ibid.

582

High God who attracts His eyes, and takes His judgement from
that contemplation, and His energy from that impulse.'

Also the Word of our Salvation says, 'The Son can do
nothing of Himself, but what He seeth the Father doing.'
Enough, however, has been said by Numenius on this
subject : and there is no need to add anything to his own
words to show that he was explaining not his own **p. 540**
opinions but Plato's. And that Plato is not the first who
has made these attempts, but has been anticipated by the
Hebrew sages, has been proved by the examples already
set forth. Naturally therefore Amelius also, who was
distinguished among recent philosophers, and above all
others an admirer of Plato's philosophy, who moreover
called the Hebrew theologian a Barbarian, even though
he did not deign to mention John the Evangelist by
name, nevertheless bears witness to his statements,
writing exactly what follows word for word :   b

Chapter XIX

' AND this then was the Word, on whom as being eternal AMELIUS
depended the existence of the things that were made, as
Heracleitus also would maintain, and the same forsooth of whom,
as set in the rank and dignity of *the beginning*, the Barbarian c
maintains that He *was with God and was God* : *through whom*
absolutely *all things were made* ; in whom the living creature, and
life, and being had their birth : and that He came down into
bodies, and clothed Himself in flesh, and appeared as man, yet
showing withal even then the majesty of His nature ; aye,
indeed, even after dissolution He was restored to deity, and is
a God, such as He was before He came down to dwell in the body,
and the flesh, and Man.'   d

This, it must be evident, is paraphrased from the Barbarian's theology no longer under any veil, but openly at
last and ' with forehead bold and bare.' And who was

---

d 10 John v. 19   540 b 2 Amelius, a Fragment preserved by
Eusebius   b 4 Heracleitus, *Fr.* ii   d 4 Plato, *Phaedrus,* 243 B (Jowett)

this Barbarian of his but our Saviour's Evangelist John, a Hebrew of the Hebrews? Who in the beginning of his own Scripture states the doctrine of the deity thus, ' In the beginning was the Word, and the Word was with God, and the Word was God. The same was in the beginning with God. All things were made by Him, and without Him was not anything made that hath been made. In Him was life, and the life was the light of men. . . . And the Word became flesh, and dwelt among us, and we beheld His glory, glory as of the Only-begotten from the Father.'

p. 541   Hear also what another Hebrew theologian says concerning the same Person: ' Who is the image of the invisible God, the first-born of all creation : for in Him were all things created, in the heavens and upon the earth, whether visible or invisible, ... and by Him all things consist, and in Him were they all created.'

But since we have found such agreement between the philosophers of the Greeks and the doctrines of the Hebrews concerning the constitution and substantiation of the Second Cause, let us then pass on to other matters.

CHAPTER XX

b   WHEREAS next to the doctrine of Father and Son the Hebrew oracles class the Holy Spirit in the third place, and conceive the Holy and Blessed Trinity in such a c manner as that the third Power surpasses every created nature, and that it is the first of the intellectual essences constituted through the Son, and third from the First Cause, observe how Plato also intimated some such thoughts, speaking thus in his *Epistle to Dionysus*:

PLATO   ' I must explain it to you then in riddles, that if the tablet suffer any harm in the remote parts of sea or land, the reader may learn nothing. For the matter is thus : Around the King of the Universe are all things, and all are for His sake, and that is the cause of all things beautiful : and around the Second are the

secondary things, and around the Third the tertiary. The soul d Plato
of man therefore strains after them to learn what sort of things
they are, looking upon the things akin to its own nature.'

These statements are referred, by those who attempt to
explain Plato, to the First God, and to the Second Cause,
and thirdly to the Soul of the Universe, defining it also
as a third God. But the sacred Scriptures regard the
Holy and Blessed Trinity of Father and Son and Holy
Ghost as the beginning, according to the passages already
set forth.

The next point to this is to examine the nature of the
Good.

Chapter XXI

The Sacred Scripture of the Hebrews explains the p. 542
nature of the Good in various ways, and teaches that the
Good itself is nothing else than God, both in the statement, ' The Lord is good to all them that wait for Him, to the
soul that will seek Him,' and in this, ' O give thanks unto the
Lord; for He is good : for His mercy endureth for ever '; and
also by what the Word of our Salvation declared to the
man who asked Him concerning this, saying, ' Why askest
thou Me concerning that which is good ? None is good save one, b
even God.'

Now then listen to what Plato says in the *Timaeus* :

' Let me then tell you for what cause the Creator formed a
creation, and made this universe. He was good. And in one
who is good no jealousy of anything ever finds place : and being
free from jealousy He desired that all things should be made as
like to Himself as possible.'

In the *Republic* also he speaks thus :

' Is it not true then that the sun though not itself sight, is yet
the cause of sight, and is itself discerned by this very sight ? It
is so, said he. Well then, said I, you may say that this is he whom
I call the offspring of the good, whom the good begat as analogous to c

542 a 4 Lam. iii. 25. Nahum i. 7   a 5 Ps. cvi. 1   a 8 Matt. xix. 7
b 4 Plato, *Timaeus*, 29 E   b 10 ibid. *Republic*, 508 B

PLATO itself, that this should be in the visible world in relation to sight and the things of sight, what the good is in the intellectual world in relation to mind and the things of mind.'

And afterwards he adds:

' Well then, this which imparts truth to the things which are known, and bestows on the knower his faculty of knowledge, this you may call the idea of the good.'

And again he says:

' You would say, I suppose, that the sun imparts to visible things not only their power of being seen, but also their genera- tion, growth, and nourishment, though he is not himself generation. How could it be otherwise ?   You would also say then that things which become known receive from the good not only the property

d of being known, but also their existence and their essence, though the good is not an essence, but far transcends essence in dignity and power.'

Herein Plato says most distinctly that the intellectual essences receive from ' the good,' meaning of course from God, not merely the property of being known, but also their existence and essence ; and that ' the good ' is ' not an essence, but far transcends essence in dignity and power.' So that he does not regard the ideas as co- essential, nor yet suppose that they are unbegotten, because they have received their existence and their essence from Him who is not an essence, but far trans-

p. 543 cends essence in dignity and power, whom alone the Hebrew oracles with good reason proclaim as God, as being the cause of all things.

So then things which have neither their existence nor their essence from themselves, nor yet are of the nature of the good, cannot reasonably be regarded as gods, since the good does not belong to them by nature : for to One only and to no other can this be ascribed, to the Only Good, which Plato admirably proclaimed as ' far transcend-

b ing all essence both in dignity and power.'   Again

---

542 c 6 Plato, *Republic,* 508 E   c 10 ibid. 509 B

Numenius also in his treatise *Of the Good*, in explaining
Plato's meaning, discourses in the following manner:

Chapter XXII

'BODIES, therefore, we may conceive by inferences drawn from NUMENIUS
observing similar bodies, and from the tokens existing in the
bodies before us: but there is no possibility of conceiving the c
good from anything that lies before us, nor yet from anything
similar that can be perceived by the senses.   For example, a man
sitting on a watch-tower, having caught a quick glimpse of
a small fishing-boat, one of those solitary skiffs, left alone by
itself, and caught in the troughs of the waves, sees the vessel at
one glance.   Just so, then, must a man withdraw far from the
things of sense, and commune in solitude with the good alone,
where there is neither man nor any other living thing, nor
body great or small, but a certain immense, indescribable, d
and absolutely divine solitude, where already the occupations, and
splendours of the good exist, and the good itself, in peace and
benevolence, that gentle, gracious, guiding power, sits high above
all being.

'But if any one, obstinately clinging to the things of sense,
fancies that he sees the good hovering over them, and then in luxurious living should suppose that he has found the good, he is
altogether mistaken.   For in fact no easy pursuit is needed for it,
but a godlike effort : and the best plan is to neglect the things
of sense, and with vigorous devotion to mathematical learning to
study the properties of numbers, and so to meditate carefully on
the question, What is being ? '

This is in the first Book.   And in the fifth he speaks **p. 544**
as follows :

'Now if essence and the idea is discerned by the mind, and if
it was agreed that the mind is earlier than this and the cause of
it, then mind itself is alone found to be the good.   For if God the
Creator is the beginning of generation, the good is the beginning
of essence.   And God the Creator is related to the good, of which

---

543 b 4 Numenius, Fragment preserved by Eusebius.   Cf. Mullach, iii.
p. 170   **544 a** 3 Numenius, ibid.

NUMENIUS He is an imitator, as generation is to essence, of which it is a likeness and an imitation.

'For if the Creator who is the author of generation is good,
b the Creator also of essence will doubtless be absolute good, innate in essence. For the second god, being twofold, is the self-maker of the idea of Himself, and makes the world as its Creator: afterwards He is wholly given to contemplation.

'Now as we have by our reasoning gathered names for four things, let them be these four. The first, God, absolute good; His imitator, a good Creator: then essence, one kind of the First God, another of the Second; and the imitation of this essence, the beautiful world, adorned by participation in the beautiful.'

Also in the sixth Book he adds :

c   'But the things which partake of Him participate in nothing else, but only in wisdom : in this way then, but in no other, they may enjoy the communion of the good. And certainly this wisdom has been found to belong to the First alone. If then this belongs exclusively to Him alone, from whom all other things receive their colouring and their goodness, none but a stupid soul could doubt any longer.

'For if the second God is good, not of Himself but from the First, how is it possible that He, by communion with whom this Second is good, should not Himself be good, especially if the Second has partaken of Him as being good ?

'It is in this way that Plato has shown by syllogistic reasoning to any one who is clear-sighted that the good is one.'

d   And again afterwards he says :

'But Plato represented these things as true differently in different places; for in the *Timaeus* peculiarly he wrote the common inscription on the Creator, saying, " He was good." But in the *Republic* he called the good the idea of good : meaning that the idea of the Creator was the good, because to us He is manifested as good by participation in the First and only Good.

'For as men are said to have been fashioned by the idea of man, and oxen by that of an ox, and horses by the idea of a horse; so also naturally if the Creator is good by participation in

---

544 d 4 Plato, *Timaeus*, 29 E

the First Good, the first Mind would be an idea, as being absolute good.'

CHAPTER XXIII

'AND having been created in this way' (evidently the world **p. 545**
is meant) 'it has been framed with a view to that which is ^{PLATO}
apprehended by reason and thought and which is unchangeable.
And if this be so, it necessarily follows that this world is an
image of something. . . . For that contains in itself all intelligible
beings, just as this world contains us.'   b

So Plato speaks in the *Timaeus*. And the meaning of
his statements I will set forth from the collections of
Didymus *Concerning the Opinions of Plato* : and this is
how he writes :

' He says that the Ideas are certain patterns arranged class by DIDYMUS
class of the things which are by nature sensible, and that these
are the sources of the different sciences and definitions. For
besides all individual men there is a certain conception of man :
and besides all horses, of a horse ; and generally, besides the
animals, a conception of an animal uncreated and imperishable. c

' And in the same way as many impressions are made of one
seal, and many images of one man, so from each single idea of
the objects of sense a multitude of individual natures are formed,
from the idea of man all men, and in like manner in the case of
all other things in nature.

' Also the idea is an eternal essence, cause, and principle,
making each thing to be of a character such as its own.

' As, therefore, the particular archetypes, so to say, precede the
bodies which are perceived by sense, so the Idea which includes
in itself all Ideas, being most beautiful and most perfect, exists
originally as the pattern of this present world ; for that has been d
made by its Creator like this Idea, and wrought according to the
providence of God out of the universal essence.'

These are extracts from the aforesaid author. Moses,
however, the all-wise, anticipates even these doctrines,

---

545 a 1 Plato, *Timaeus*, 29 A   a 5 ibid. 30 E   b 6 Areius
Didymus, *De Platonis opinionibus*, a Fragment preserved by Eusebius

teaching us that before the visible sun and stars and before
the heaven that we behold, which he calls the firmament,
and before this our dry land, and before our day and
night, another light besides the light of the sun, and day
and night, and the rest, had been made by God the
universal Ruler and Cause of all.

p. 546   Moreover the Hebrews who came after Moses declare
that there is a certain incorporeal sun not visible to all,
nor subjected to mortal eyes, as says the Prophet speaking in the person of God, ' And to them that fear Me shall
the Sun of righteousness arise.'

Also righteousness itself, not that of a certain kind
among men, but the Idea of that, is known to another
Hebrew Prophet, who said concerning God, ' Who raised
up righteousness from the East ?   He called it before His face,
b and it shall go forth as it were before the nations.'

Also a divine Word, incorporeal and essential, was just
lately shown to us by our ordinary word in the previous
quotations from the Hebrew Scriptures : concerning
which Word there is also the following statement among
the same people : ' Who was made unto us wisdom from God,
and righteousness, and sanctification, and redemption.'

He is called also Life, He is called Wisdom, and Truth.
Also the Scriptures of the Hebrews (since the Apostles
also and disciples of our Saviour are Hebrews) make
c known to us all things which have essential being and
subsistence, nay more, they show us myriads of other
incorporeal powers beyond both heaven and all material
and fleeting essence ; and the images of these powers,
they say, He expressed in things sensible, after which
they have now received the name each of its image.

Man, for instance, they have expressly stated to be
the image of an ideal pattern, and the whole life of
men *passeth on in an image.*   Moses in fact says, ' And
God created man, in the image of God created He him.'   And

---

again another Hebrew writer, following the philosophy d
of his forefathers, says, ' Surely man walketh in an image.'
And now hear how the interpreters of the sacred laws
explain the thought contained in the writings of Moses.
The Hebrew Philo, in fact, speaks thus word for word
in interpreting the doctrines of his forefathers.

Chapter XXIV

' Now if any one should wish to use names in a plainer way, Philo
he would not call the intelligible world anything else than the
Word (or, Reason) of God already engaged in the creation of a
world.   For neither is the intelligible city anything else than the P. 547
reasoning of the architect, when already designing to build the
visible city [by help of the intelligible].

' But this is Moses' doctrine, not mine. For instance, in recording the creation of man he expressly avows, in what follows, that
he was fashioned after the image of God.

' Now if the part (man) is an image of an image, evidently
also the whole species, I mean the whole of this visible world,
which is greater than the human image, is a copy of a divine
image ; and the archetypal seal, as we call the intelligible world,
must itself evidently be the archetypal pattern, the Idea of the
Ideas, the Word (Reason) of God.   b

' He says too that " In the beginning God created the heaven and
the earth "; taking the beginning to be not, as some suppose, the
beginning in time ; for time was not before the world, but either
has begun with it, or after it.

' For since time is the interval of the motion of the universe,
and motion could not begin before that which was to be moved,
but must necessarily be established either after it or with it, so
time also must necessarily either have been of the same age as the
universe or younger than it, and to venture to represent it as c
older is unphilosophical.

' But if in the present passage *the beginning* is not taken to be
the beginning in time, then the beginning according to number

---

d 2 Ps. xxxix. 7   d 7 Philo Judaeus, *On the Creation of the World*, § 5
547 a 5 Gen. i. 27   b 2 Gen. i. 1

PHILO would naturally be signified, so that *in the beginning God created* would be equivalent to " first He created the heaven." '

Then afterwards he says:

' First, therefore, the Maker proceeded to make an immaterial heaven, and an invisible earth, and an ideal form of air and of empty space, the former of which He called *darkness,* because the air is by nature black, and the latter He called *the deep,* for the empty space is very deep and vast.

' Then He made the incorporeal essence of water and of wind, **d** and over all the essence of light, the seventh in order, which again was incorporeal, and then an intelligible model of the sun, and of all stars that were destined to be established as luminaries in the heaven.

' And the wind and the light were honoured with special privilege : for the one he called *the Spirit of God,* because spirit is the most life-giving thing, and God is the author of life; and light, because it excels in beauty. For the intelligible is, I suppose, as much more brilliant and radiant than the sensible, as the sun is than darkness, and day than night, and the mind, which is the guide of the whole soul, than the criteria of sense, and the eyes than the body.

p. 548   ' But that invisible and intelligible light is made an image of the Divine Word, which explained its origin; and it is a super-celestial star the source of the visible stars, which one would not be wrong in calling " universal light," from which sun and moon and the other planets and fixed stars draw their appropriate splendours in proportion to the power of each, while that unmingled and pure light becomes obscured, whenever it begins to turn in direction of the change from intelligible to sensible ; for **b** of the things subject to sense none is pure.'

Also after a few words he adds:

' But when light came, and darkness yielded and retired, and bounds were set in the intervals between them, namely evening and morning, there was at once completed, according to the necessary measure of time, that which the Creator rightly called " day," and not *the first day* but *one day,* which it is called

---

547 c 8 Philo Judaeus, ibid. § 6   **548 b** 3 ibid. § 7

because of the singleness of the intelligible world, which has the Philo
nature of unity.

'So then the incorporeal world was now complete, being
founded in the divine Reason (Word); and after the model c
thereof the sensible world was now to be produced in its perfection: so the Creator proceeded to make first that which was also
the best of all its parts, namely the heaven, which He rightly
named *the firmament,* as being corporeal. For body is by nature
solid, because it is of three dimensions: and what other idea is
there of a solid and a body, except extension in every direction?
Naturally therefore He called this the firmament, as contrasting
the sensible and corporeal world with the intelligible and incorporeal.'

So writes Philo. And Clement also agrees with him,
speaking as follows in the Fifth *Miscellany.*

Chapter XXV

'And again the Barbarian philosophy knows one world of d
thought, and another of sense, the one an archetype, and the Clement
other an image of the fair model. And the former it assigns
to Unity, as being perceptible to thought only; but the sensible
it assigns to the number six: for among the Pythagoreans six
is called marriage, as a number that generates.

'And in the Unity it establishes an invisible heaven, and a p. 549
holy earth, and an intellectual light. For " In the beginning," says
Moses, " God created the heaven and the earth: and the earth was
invisible." Then he adds, " And God said, Let there be light, and there
was light." But in the cosmogony of the sensible world He
creates a solid heaven (and the solid is sensible), and a visible
earth, and a light that is seen.

'Does it not seem to you from this passage that Plato leaves
the ideas of living creatures in the intelligible world, and creates
the sensible species *after their kinds* in the intelligible world?

'With good reason then Moses says that the body was fashioned
out of earth, which Plato calls an " earthly tabernacle," but that b

---

d 1 Clement of Alexandria, *Miscellany,* v. 14   549 a 2 Gen. i. 1
a 4 ibid. i. 3   b 1 Plato, *Phaedrus,* 246 C; *Timaeus,* 64 C

CLEMENT the reasonable soul was breathed by God from on high into man's face.

'For in this part, they say, the ruling faculty is seated, interpreting thus the accessory entrance of the soul through the organs of sense in the case of the first-formed man; for which reason also man, they say, is made *after the image and likeness* of God. For the image of God is the divine and royal Word, the impassible Man; and an image of that image is the human mind.'

But let us now listen to what remains to be said.

CHAPTER XXVI

FURTHER than this Plato follows the doctrines of the
c Hebrews, when he says that there are not only good incorporeal powers but also those of opposite nature, writing as follows in the tenth Book of the *Laws*:

PLATO d   'As then the soul directs and inhabits all things that move in any direction, must we not say that it also directs the heaven? Of course. One soul, or more? More, I will answer for you. Less than two surely we must not suppose, the one that does good, and the other that has power to work evil.'

Then lower down he says:

'For since we have agreed that the heaven is full of many good things and also of many evil things, and these the more numerous, a conflict of this kind, we say, is immortal, and requires marvellous watchfulness. But gods and daemons are our allies, and we are their possessions.'

Whence these ideas came to Plato, I cannot explain:
p. 550 but what I can truly say is that thousands of years before Plato was born this doctrine also had been acknowledged by the Hebrews.

Accordingly their Scripture says, 'And there was, as it were, this day when the angels of God came to stand before God; and the devil came in the midst of them, after going round the

---

549 b 2 Gen. ii. 7   d 1 Plato, *Laws*, x. 896 D   d 7 ibid. x. 906 A
550 a 4 Job i. 13 a, 6 b

earth and walking about in it'; where it calls the adverse power *devil*, and the good powers *angels of God.*

And these good powers it also calls divine spirits, and God's ministers, where it says, 'Who maketh His angels spirits, and His ministers a flame of fire.'   **b**

Moreover the conflict of the adverse powers is thus represented by him who said, 'Our wrestling is not against blood and flesh, but against the principalities, against the powers, against the world-rulers of the darkness of this age, against the spiritual hosts of wickedness in the heavenly places.'

Also the oracle of Moses which said, 'When the Most High was dividing the nations, when He was separating the children of Adam, He set the bounds of the nations according to the number of the angels of God,' seems to be directly paraphrased by Plato in the words whereby he defined **c** the whole human race to be 'the possessions of gods and daemons.'

Chapter XXVII

In the doctrine of the immortality of the soul Plato **d** differs not at all in opinion from Moses. For Moses was the first to define the soul in man as being an immortal essence, when he said that it is originally an image of God, or rather has been made 'after the image of God.' For his words were, 'God said, Let us make man after our image, and after our likeness. . . . And God made man, in the image of God made He him.'

And afterwards dividing the compound man in his description into the visible body and the man of the soul that is discerned only by the mind, he adds, 'And God took dust from the earth and formed man, and breathed into his face the breath of life, and man became a living soul.'

Moreover he says that man was made fit to be ruler **p. 551** and king of all the creatures upon earth. So he says, 'And God said, Let us make man after our image, and after our likeness, and let them have dominion over the fishes of the sea, and over the fowls of the heaven, and over the cattle, and over all the earth. . . . And God created man in His own image, in the image of God created He him.'

Now in what other way could an image and likeness of God be conceived than in reference to the powers that are in God, and to the likeness of virtue ? Hear then how in the *Alcibiades* Plato speaks on this point also as one who had been taught by Moses :

PLATO **b**   ' Can we then mention any part of the soul that is more divine than that with which knowledge and wisdom have to do ?

' We cannot.

' This then is the part of it like God ; and any one who by looking upon this has learned all that is divine, both God and wisdom, will thus get to know himself also most perfectly.

' It is evident.

[' So then, just as there are mirrors clearer than the mirror in the eye, and purer and brighter, so God is something purer and brighter than the best that is in our soul.

' It seems so, Socrates.

' In looking then on God, we should be using that noblest mirror of man's nature also for looking into the virtue of the **c** soul; and in this way should best see and learn to know ourselves. Certainly.']

This is in the *Alcibiades*.   But in the dialogue *On the Soul* observe how he explains these topics more at length.

' May we then, said he, assume two kinds of existing things, one visible and the other invisible ?

' Let us assume it, said he.

' And the invisible constant and immutable, but the visible **d** never constant ?

' This also let us assume.

' Well then, said he, is not the one part of ourselves body, and the other soul ?

' Exactly so, said he.

---

551 b 1 Ps-Plato, *Alcibiades*, i. 133 C   b 8 The passage in brackets is not in the MSS. of Plato   c 6 Plato, *Phaedo*, 79 A

'To which class then should we say that the body is more like PLATO and more akin?

'Oh, that is manifest to every one, said he; to the visible.

'And what of the soul?   Is it visible or invisible?

'Not visible at any rate by men, Socrates.

'But we surely were speaking of the things that are visible or not visible to the nature of man; or was it, think you, to some other nature?

'To man's nature.

'What do we say then about the soul? Is it visible or invisible?

'Invisible.

'Then it is unseen?

'Yes.

'Soul then is more like the unseen than body is, and body like the visible?

'It must certainly be so, Socrates.

'Well then, were we not also saying long ago, that whenever **p. 552** the soul uses the help of the body to examine anything, either by sight, or by hearing, or by any other sense (for this is what is meant by "the help of the body," to examine a thing by the help of sense), that then she is dragged by the body into the midst of these ever-changing objects, and loses her own way, and becomes confused, and giddy as if drunken, from trying to lay hold of things of this same kind?

'Quite so.

'But whenever she is contemplating anything by herself alone, she passes at once into yonder world, to the pure, and eternal, and immortal, and unchangeable, and there and with that world she ever communes as one of kindred nature, whenever she can **b** be alone, and have opportunity; and so she has rest from her wandering, and with that world she is constant and unchangeable, as trying to lay hold of things of this same kind. And this condition of the soul is called thoughtfulness.

'Very nobly and truly spoken, Socrates, said he.

'To which class then does it now seem to you, from both our former and our present arguments, that the soul is more like and more akin?

'Every one, I think, Socrates, said he, even the most stupid, **c**

PLATO would from this method of inquiry agree that soul is in every way much more like to that which is ever constant than to that which is not.

'And what of the body?

'More like the other.

'Look at it then again in this way; that, when soul and body are combined in one, nature orders the body to serve and to obey, and the soul to rule and to govern. Now in these respects again which of the two seems to you to be like the divine, and which like the mortal? Do you not think that the divine is naturally fitted to rule and to lead, and the mortal to be ruled and to serve?

'I think so.

d   'To which of the two then is the soul like?

'Evidently, Socrates, the soul is like the divine, and the body like the mortal.

'Consider then, Cebes, said he, whether from all that has been said we obtain these results: that soul is most like the divine, and immortal, and intelligible, and uniform, and indissoluble, and ever unchangeable and self-consistent; and the body on the other hand most like the human, and mortal, and unintelligible, and multiform, and dissoluble, and never consistent with itself.

'Have we anything else to say against this, my dear Cebes, to show that it is not so?

'We have not.

'Well then? This being so, is it not a property of body to be quickly dissolved, but of soul on the other hand to be altogether indissoluble, or nearly so?

'Certainly.

p. 553   'Do you then observe, that after a man is dead, the body, the part of him which is visible and lies in the visible world, and is called a corpse, the property of which is to be dissolved, and decomposed, and scattered by the winds, does not at once suffer any change of this kind, but remains for a considerable time — if the man die with his body in a vigorous state and at a vigorous time of life, for a very considerable time indeed. For when the body

b has shrunk and been embalmed, like those who were embalmed in Egypt, it remains almost entire an incredible time. And even if the body be decayed, some parts of it, bones and sinews and all such parts, are nevertheless, so to say, immortal, are they not?

598

' Yes.

' But then the soul, the unseen, that has passed to another place like herself, noble, and pure, and unseen, the true Hades, to the presence of the good and wise God, whither, if it be God's will, my own soul is presently to go—is then, I say, this soul of ours, such as she is and so endowed by nature, on being released from the body, immediately scattered to the winds and lost, as **c** most men say ?

' Far from it, my dear Cebes and Simmias ; but the truth is much rather this. If the soul is pure when released, drawing nothing of the body after her, as she never during this life had any communication with it willingly, but shrank from it, and was gathered up into herself, as making this her constant study, and this is nothing else than practising true philosophy, and preparing in reality to die cheerfully,—Or would not this **d** be a preparation for death ?

' Certainly.

' In this condition then the soul departs to that world which is like herself, the unseen, the divine, and deathless, and wise : and on arriving there she finds ready for her a happy existence, released from error, and folly, and fears, and wild desires, and all other human ills, and, as they say of the initiated, she truly passes the rest of her time with the gods. Is it thus, Cebes, that we ought to speak, or otherwise ?

' Thus assuredly, said Cebes.

' But, I suppose, if when she departs from the body she is **p. 554** polluted and impure, from being in constant communion with the body, and cherishing it, and loving it, and having been so bewitched by it, I mean by its desires and pleasures, as to think that nothing else is true except the corporeal, just what a man might touch, and see, and eat, and drink, and use for his lusts— but accustomed to hate and fear and shun what to the eyes is dark and invisible, but intelligible to thought and attainable by philosophy—in this condition then do you suppose that a soul will depart pure in herself and unalloyed ?

' By no means, said he.'   **b**

This is what Plato says. And his meaning is explained by Porphyry in the first Book of his *Answer to Boëthus*

Concerning the Soul, where he writes in the following manner :

CHAPTER XXVIII

POR- c   'FOR example, he said, the argument from similarity was
PHYRY   thought by Plato to be forcible in proof of the immortality
of the soul. For if she is like that which is divine, and
immortal, and invisible, and inseparable, and indissoluble,
and essential, and firmly established in incorruption, how can
she fail to be of the corresponding class to the pattern ?

'For whenever there are two extremes manifestly contrary,
as rational and irrational, and it is a question to which side
some third thing belongs, this is one mode of proof, by showing
to which of the opposites it is like. For thus, although the human
d race in the first stage of life is held down in an irrational
condition, and although many even to old age are full of the
errors of unreason, nevertheless, because it has many similarities
to that which is purely rational, this race was believed to be from
the beginning rational.

'Since therefore there is a divine constitution manifestly
incapable of admixture and of damage, namely that of the gods,
and since there is evidently on the other hand the earthly, and
soluble, subject to corruption, and since with some it is doubted
to which side of the said opposition the soul is attached, Plato's
opinion was that we should trace out the truth from similarity.

p. 555   'And since she is in no way like to the mortal and soluble
and irrational and inanimate, which is therefore also tangible, and
sensible, and becoming, and perishing, but like the divine, and
immortal, and invisible, and intelligent, which partakes of life,
and is akin to truth, and has all the properties which he enume-
rates as belonging to her,—since this is so, he thought it not
right, while granting that she had the other points of likeness
to God, to consent to deny her the similarity of essence, which is
the cause of her having received these very properties.

'For as the things which were in their operations unlike God
b were at once found to differ also in the constitution of their

---

essence, so he thought it followed, that the things which partook Porphyry
in a measure of the same operations had previously possessed the
similarity of essence. For because of the quality of the essence
the operations also were of a certain quality, as flowing from it,
and being offshoots of it.'

Hear then what Boëthus, in detracting from the force
of this argument, has written in the very beginning of his
treatise, as follows:

'To show whether the soul is immortal, and is a nature too Boëthus
strong for any kind of destruction, a man must persistently travel c
round many arguments.

'But one would not need much discussion to believe that
nothing about us is more like God than the soul, and that,
not only because of the continuous and incessant motion which
she generates within us, but also because of the mind belonging
to her.

'In view of which fact the physical philosopher of Crotona
said that the soul as being immortal naturally shrank from
all quiescence, like the bodies that are divine.

'But also to the man who had once discerned the idea of the
soul, and especially how great purposes and what impulses the mind d
that rules within us often sets in motion, there would gradually
appear a great likeness to God.'

And afterwards he adds:

'For if the soul is shown to be of all things most like to the
divine, of what further use is it to require by way of preface
all the other arguments in proof of her immortality, instead
of reckoning this as one among the many, sufficient as it is to
convince the fair-minded, that the soul would not have partici-
pated in the activities which are similar to those of the divine,
if she were not also divine herself.

'For if, although buried in the body which is mortal, and p. 556
soluble, and unintelligent, and by itself dead, and constantly
perishing and wasting away towards its change of final destruction, the soul both forms it and holds it together, and displays her
own divine essence, although she is obstructed and impeded by the

---

555 b 10 Boëthus, a Fragment preserved by Eusebius

Boëthus   all-ruinous mould which lies around her, must she not, if by our
hypothesis she were separated as gold from the clay plastered
round it, at once display her own specific form as being like
b God alone, and moreover preserving through Her participation
in Him the similarities in her operations, and even in her most
mortal condition (as she is when imprisoned in the mortal body)
escaping dissolution for this reason, that she is, as we said, of the
nature which has nothing in common with decay?' *

And lower down he says:

'But naturally she appears to be both divine from her assimilation to the Indivisible, and mortal from her approaches to the
mortal nature: and she descends and ascends, and is both akin
to the mortal, and yet like the immortals.

c 'For even he who stuffs himself full and hastes to be surfeited
like the cattle is a man: and he too is a man, who by knowledge
is able in perils by sea to save the ship, and he who can save life
in diseases, and he who discovers truth, and has devised methods
for the attainment of knowledge, and inventions for kindling
fire, and observations of horoscopes, and manufactures imitations
of the works of the Creator.

'For it was a man who thought of fashioning upon earth the
conjunctions of the seven planets together with their motions,
d imitating by mechanism the phenomena in heaven. And in fact
what did not man devise, showing thereby the mind within him
that is divine and on a par with God?

'And though thereby he displayed the daring efforts of an
Olympian and divine and altogether immortal being, yet
because the multitude through the selfishness of their own
downward inclination were not able to discern his character,
he misled them into supposing from the outward appearances
that he was like themselves of mortal nature: there being but
this one mode of deriving consolation from their baseness, that
because of external appearances they found satisfaction in seeing
others share equally in their wretchedness, and persuaded themselves that as in external things so also in their inner nature all
men are alike.'

p. 557   Of all these doctrines Moses has been seen to be the
teacher, for in describing the first creation of man in

the language already quoted, he by his assimilation to the divine confirmed the arguments concerning the immortality of the soul.

But since the opinions of Moses and Plato were in full harmony and accord concerning the incorporeal and invisible essence, it is time to review the remaining portions of Plato's philosophy, and to show that he was friendly to the Hebrews on all points, except where perchance he was b led astray and induced to speak more after the manner of man, than in accordance with the word of truth.

For instance, all the philosopher's sayings which have been rightly expressed will be found to agree with the doctrines of Moses, but in whatever he assumed that did not agree with Moses and the prophets, his argument will not be well established. And this we shall prove at the proper season. But meanwhile, since his positions in the contemplation of the intelligible world have been discovered to be in perfect agreement and harmony, it is time to go back again to the physical theory of the sensible world, and briefly run over the philosopher's c agreement with the doctrines of the Hebrews.

Chapter XXIX

MOSES declared that this universe had a beginning as having been made by God; he says at all events in the commencement of his own writing, 'In the beginning God d created the heaven and the earth,' and after the particulars he adds, ' This is the book of the generation of heaven and earth, when they were created, in the day that God made the heaven and the earth.' And now listen to Plato, how close he keeps to the thought, when himself writing as follows:

'And again all that comes into existence must of necessity PLATO proceed from some cause; for it is impossible for anything to have been generated without a cause.'

---

557 d 1 Gen. i. 1   d 3 ibid. ii. 4   d 7 Plato, *Timaeus*, 28 A

And he adds:

PLATO   'The whole heaven then or world, or by whatever other name it would most acceptably be called, so let us call it—we have first to ask a question concerning it, which it is assumed that one must ask on every subject at the outset—did it always exist, without any beginning of generation, or has it been generated and had some beginning?

'It has been generated: for it is visible, and tangible, and has **p. 558** a body; and all such things are sensible: and all sensible things were shown to be apprehensible by opinion and generated. But that which is generated must, we say, have been generated by some cause. It is a hard task, however, to discover the maker and artificer of this universe, and after discovering Him it is impossible to speak of Him to all men.'

And again afterwards he says:

'Thus therefore we must say, according to probable reason, that this world was in truth made through the providence of God **b** a living being endowed with soul and mind.'

CHAPTER XXX

AGAIN Moses, by what he said of the heavenly bodies, taught that they also are created: 'And God said, Let there be lights in the firmament of the heaven to give light upon the **c** earth; . . . and let them be for signs, and for seasons, and for days and for years. . . . And God made the two great lights, . . . and the stars; and set them in the firmament of the heaven.'

In like manner Plato speaks:

'Such then being the reason and the thought of God in regard to the generation of time, in order that time might be brought into existence there have been created the sun and moon and five other bodies which are called planets, for distinguishing and preserving the numbers of time. And when He had made their bodies, God set them in their orbits.'

---

557 d 11 Plato, *Timaeus*, 28 B   558 a 8 ibid. 30 B   b 3 Gen. i. 14
c 5 Plato, *Timaeus*, 38 C

Now observe whether Plato's expression, 'Such then being the reason (λόγου) and thought of God,' must not be like that **d** of the Hebrew who says, 'By the word (λόγῳ) of the Lord were the heavens established, and all the powers thereof by the breath of His mouth.' Moreover as Moses said, 'And He set (ἔθετο) them in the firmament,' Plato has used a like word, 'set,' when he says, 'And when He had made their bodies, God set (ἔθηκεν) them in their orbits.'

Chapter XXXI

As the Hebrew Scripture after each of the creations adds the phrase, 'And God saw that it was good,' and after **p. 559** the summing up of all says, 'And God saw them all, . . . and behold they were very good'; now hear how Plato speaks:

'If then indeed this world is fair, and its Creator good, it is evident that He was looking to that pattern which is eternal.'

And again:

'For the world is the fairest of things created, and He the best of causes.'

Chapter XXXII

On this point also the whole Hebrew Scripture speaks **b** throughout, at one time saying, 'And the heaven shall be rolled together as a scroll,' and at another adding, 'And the heaven shall be new, and the earth new, . . . which I make to remain before Me, saith the Lord'; and again at another time saying, 'For the fashion of this world passeth away.' Hear then how Plato also confirms the doctrine, saying in the *Timaeus*:

'And He established a visible and tangible heaven: and for **c** Plato these reasons, and out of these elements such as I have described, being four in number, the body of the world was formed in harmony by due proportion, and gained from them a friendly

---

d 2 Ps. xxxiii. 6   559 a 2 Gen. i. 31   a 4 Plato, *Timaeus*, 29 A
a 7 ibid.   b 2 Isa. xxxiv. 4   b 3 Isa. lxv. 17, lxvi. 22   b 6 1 Cor.
vii. 31   c 1 Plato, *Timaeus*, 32 B

PLATO union, so that having entered into unity with itself it became indissoluble by everything else except Him who bound it together.'

Then afterwards he says:

' So then time has come into existence together with the heaven, that having been produced together they may also be dissolved together, if there should ever be any dissolution of them.'

And again he adds:

' Ye gods and sons of gods, the works whereof I am the Creator .and Father are indissoluble save by my will.'

d   Afterwards he adds:

' Therefore though all that is bound may be dissolved, yet only an evil being would wish to dissolve that which is well combined and in right condition. Wherefore also since ye have been created, though ye are not altogether immortal nor indissoluble, nevertheless ye shall not be dissolved, nor incur the fate of death, since in my will ye have found a still stronger and more valid bond than those by which ye were bound together at the time of your creation.'

Also in the *Politicus* or *Statesman* the same author speaks as follows:

' For there is a time when God Himself goes round with the universe, which He helps to guide and wheel; and there is a time when the revolutions having now completed their proper measure of time, He lets it go, and the universe, being a living creature and having received intelligence from Him who arranged it at first, revolves again of its own accord in the opposite **p. 560** direction. And this retrogression has of necessity been implanted in its nature for the following reason.

' For what reason, pray?

' Because it is a property of none but the most divine things to be always changeless in condition and self-consistent and the same, and bodily nature is not of this class. And though that which we have called the heaven and the world has been endowed by its

---

Creator with many blessings, nevertheless it also partakes of Plato
body; whence it is impossible for it to be always free from
change; as far as possible however, and in a very great degree,
it moves in the same orbit in one and the same relative course, **b**
because the reversal to which it is subject is the least possible
alteration of its proper motion.

'But it is almost impossible for anything to continue for ever
turning itself, except for the Ruler of all things that are moved.
And for Him to move anything now one way, and now again in
the opposite way, would not be right. From all this then we
must neither say that the world always turns itself, nor that it
is all turned by God in two opposite courses, nor again that some
two gods, who are of opposite minds, turn it, but, as was said
just now, and this alone remains possible, that at one time it is **c**
guided in its course by another divine cause, acquiring again
its life, and receiving from its Creator a restored immortality,
and at another time when let go it moves of itself, having been
let go at such a time that it travels backwards during countless
periods, because being of vast size and most perfectly balanced
it moves upon the smallest pivot.

'Certainly all the details which you have described seem to be
very probable.

'Let us then draw our conclusions and consider closely the
effect produced from what I have just mentioned, which effect
we said was the cause of all the wonders : for surely it is this **d**
very thing.

'What thing ?

'The fact that the course of the world at one time is guided
in the direction of its present revolution, and at another time
in the opposite direction.

'How then ?

'This change we must believe to be the greatest and most
complete of all variations in the heavenly motions.

'It seems so indeed.

'We must suppose therefore that very great changes occur at
that time to us who dwell under the heaven.

'This too is probable.

'But do we not know that animal nature ill endures many **p. 561**
great and various changes occurring at the same time ?

P<small>LATO</small> ' Of course.

' Very great destruction therefore of all other animals necessarily occurs at that time, and moreover very little of the human race survives. And with regard to these survivors, among many other marvellous and strange effects which occur the greatest is this, which also follows immediately upon the reversal of the motion of the universe at the time when the revolution opposite to that which is at present established takes place.'

Afterwards lower down he adds to all this the following remarks on the restoration of the dead to life, taking a

b similar course to the opinions of the Hebrews.

C<small>HAPTER</small> XXXIII

' B<small>UT</small> how were animals produced in those days, Stranger, and in what way were they begotten one of another ?

c ' It is evident, Socrates, that the generation of one animal from another did not exist in the order of nature at that time, but the earth-born race which was said to exist formerly—this it was that in this other period sprang up out of the earth again. The tradition was recorded by our earliest ancestors, who in the following period were not far from the end of the former revolution, but were born in the beginning of the present : for they were the heralds to us of these traditions, which are now disbelieved by many without good reason.

' For we ought, I think, to observe what follows therefrom.

d With the fact that old men pass on to the natural condition of the child it is consistent, that from those who have died and been laid in the earth, some being brought together again there and restored to life should follow the changed order, the wheel of generation being at the same time turned back in the opposite direction : and so in this manner necessarily springing up out of the earth they are thus named and accounted earth-born, except any whom God reserved for another destiny.

' This is certainly quite consistent with what was said before.'

Then again, as he goes on further, he discourses in the

------

561 b 2 Plato, *Politicus,* 271 A

following manner concerning the consummation of the
world, in agreement with the doctrines of the Hebrews:

Chapter XXXIV

' For when the period of all these events was completed, and **p. 562**
a change was to take place, and moreover the earth-born race Plato
had now all perished, each soul having fulfilled all its generations, and fallen into the earth for as many sowings as were
appointed for each, then at length the pilot of the universe let go, **b**
as it were, the handle of the rudder, and withdrew into his own
watch-tower, and Fate and an innate desire began to turn the
course of the world back again.

' So all the gods who locally share the government of the chief
divinity, as soon as they learnt what was going on, let go in
turn the portions of the world belonging to their charge. And
the world turning back and clashing together, as having received
an opposite impulse from before and from behind, was mightily
convulsed in itself, and wrought another destruction of animals **c**
of all kinds.

' And after this in long process of time the world ceasing from
tumults and confusion and convulsions welcomed a calm, and
entered in orderly array upon its own accustomed course, having
charge and control over itself and all things in it.'

Again after a little while he says:

' Wherefore God, who had first set the world in order, when
at length He saw that it was in helpless strait, being anxious
that it should not be shattered in the confusion of the storm,
and sink down into the infinite gulf of disorder, again takes His **d**
seat at the helm, and having turned back what had suffered
harm and dissolution into the former circuit appointed by
Himself, He arranges and restores it, and endows it with immortality and perpetual youth. Here then the story of the end of
all things is told.'

Chapter XXXV

' These things, then, said I, are nothing in number nor in
greatness in comparison with those other rewards which await

562 a 1 Plato, *Politicus*, 272 D   c 8 ibid. 273 D   d 7 Plato, *Republic*,
x. 614 A

p. 563 each of them after death.   And you ought to hear them, in order
PLATO that each may receive in full what is due to be told to them by
our argument.

'You may speak, said he, as to one who will not find the
story too long, but listen all the more gladly.

'But indeed, said I, it is not the story of Alcinous that I am
going to tell you, but that of a brave man Er the son of Armenius,
a Pamphylian by birth, who was killed in battle, and when the
dead were gathered up after ten days in a state of putrefaction,
his body was taken up undecayed and carried home to be buried,
and on the twelfth day when laid on the funeral pile, he came
back to life, and after his revival told what he had seen in the
other world.

b   'And he said that when his soul had departed from his body,
it travelled with many others, until they came to a certain
wonderful place, in which were two chasms in the earth close to
each other, and others opposite to them in the heaven above.

'And between them there sat judges, who, after they had
decided each case, commanded the just to proceed by the way
on the right hand leading upward through the heaven, having
hung around them on their breast the records of the judgements
given, and the unjust by the way leading downwards on the
left, these also having on their backs the records of all their
deeds.

'And when he himself came forward, they said that he must
c be the messenger to mankind of what was done there, and they
commanded him to hear and see everything in that place.'

So Plato speaks.   And Plutarch also in the first Book
Concerning the Soul tells a story similar to this:

CHAPTER XXXVI

d   'WE were present ourselves with this Antyllus : but let me
PLUTARCH tell the story to Sositeles and Heracleon.   For he was ill not
long ago, and the physicians thought that he could not live :
but having recovered a little from a slight collapse, though he
neither did nor said anything else showing derangement, he

---

563 d 1 Plutarch, *On the Soul*, Fragment iii, preserved by Eusebius
610

declared that he had died and been set free again, and was not PLUTARCH
going to die at all of that present illness, but that those who
had carried him away were severely reproved by their lord; for
having been sent for Nicandas, they had brought him back
instead of the other. Now Nicandas was a shoemaker, besides
being one of those who frequent the palaestrae, and familiar
and well known to many. Wherefore the young men used to **p. 564**
come and mock him, as having run away from his fate, and as
having bribed the officers sent from the other world. It was
evident, however, that he was himself at first a little disturbed
and disquieted; and at last he was attacked by a fever, and died
suddenly on the third day. But this Antyllus came to life again,
and is alive and well, and one of our most agreeable friends.'

I wish to quote these statements because of the fact
that in the Hebrew Scriptures there are cases mentioned
of restoration to life. But since in their promises it is
also contained that a certain land shall be given to the **b**
friends of God only, according to the oracle which says,
'But the meek shall inherit the land,' and that this is a
heavenly land is made clear by the saying which
declares, 'But Jerusalem which is above is free, which is the
mother of us all'; the prophet also intimates in an allegorical way that this same city consists of costly and precious
stones, saying, 'Behold, I prepare for thee a carbuncle for thy
stone, and will make thy battlements jasper, and thy foundations **c**
sapphire . . . and thy border choice stones': now see how Plato
also confesses in the dialogue *Concerning the Soul* that
he is persuaded of the truth of these very things, or the
like. He assigns the statement to Socrates in the following manner:

CHAPTER XXXVII

'BUT indeed, Simmias, I do not think it requires the skill of **d** PLATO
Glaucus to describe to you what it is: but to decide whether it
be true, appears to me too hard even for Glaucus' skill. And

---

564 b 3 Ps. xxxvii. 11, Matt. v. 5   b 5 Gal. iv. 26   b 8 Isa. liv. 12
d 1 Plato, *Phaedo*, 108 D

PLATO not only should I perhaps find myself unable to do so, but even if I knew how, my life seems hardly long enough, Simmias, for an argument of such length.   Nevertheless there is nothing to prevent my describing to you the figure of the earth, such as I am convinced it is, and its various regions.

'Well, said Simmias, even that is enough.

'My own conviction, then, said he, is first of all that, if the earth is spherical and placed in the centre of the heaven, it has no need either of air to prevent its falling, or of any other

p. 565 similar sustaining force, but that the perfect uniformity of the heaven in all its parts, and the very equilibrium of the earth, are sufficient to sustain it : for a thing in equilibrium placed in the centre of a similar body, will have no reason to incline more or less in any direction, but being evenly balanced will remain undeflected.   This then, said he, is my first conviction.

'And quite correct, said Simmias.

'Further then, said he, I am persuaded that it is of vast size, and that we who live between the Pillars of Hercules and the Phasis occupy a very small part of it, dwelling round the sea,

b just as ants or frogs round a pond, and that there are many others elsewhere living in many like regions.

'For in every direction round the earth there are many hollows of various kinds both in shape and size, into which the waters and the mist and the air have flowed together; but the earth itself is pure and situated in a pure part of the heaven, wherein are the stars, and which most of those who are accustomed to speak of such things call the ether, of which these

c three (water, mist, and air) are a sediment, and are always flowing together into the hollows of the earth.

'We therefore are unconscious that we live in the hollows, and suppose that we are living above on the surface of the earth, just as if any one living in the midst of the bottom of the sea should suppose that he was living on the surface, and seeing the sun and the other luminaries through the water should imagine the sea to be heaven, but through sluggishness and weakness had never come up to the top of the water, nor, by rising and lifting his head up out of it into this region of ours, had ever seen how much purer and fairer it is than their own, nor had ever heard this from any one who had seen it.

'We then are in this very same case: for while living in d PLATO some hollow of the earth we imagine that we are living on the surface, and call the air heaven, as if this were the heaven through which the stars run their courses. But the fact is the same, that from weakness and sluggishness we are not able to pass out to the surface of the air: for if any one were to reach the top of it, or take wings and fly up to it, he would put out his head, and, just as the fishes here who jump up out of the water and see the objects on earth, so would a man survey the world beyond: and, if his nature were strong enough to endure the sight, he would learn that yonder is the true heaven, and the true light, and the true earth.

'For this earth and the stones and the whole region here are p. 566 decayed and corroded, as the things in the sea by the brine: and there is nothing worth mentioning that grows in the sea, nor anything that is, so to say, perfect; but there are caves, and sand, and vast slime and mud-banks wherever there *is* land, all utterly unworthy to be compared with the beautiful things of our world.

'But on the other hand yonder world would be seen far more to surpass everything of ours. For if I must tell you a pretty fable, it is worth your while, Simmias, to hear what is the nature of the objects on that earth which lie close under the heaven.   b

'We certainly, Socrates, said Simmias, should be delighted to hear this fable.

'Well then, my friend, said he, it is said in the first place that the earth itself, if any one were to see it from above, is just such to look upon as the balls which are covered with twelve pieces of leather, variegated and marked by different colours, of which the colours used by our painters here on earth are, as it were, samples. But there the earth is wholly made up of colours such as these, and far more brilliant and pure.

'For part of it is purple and of marvellous beauty, and part c like gold, and the part that is white is whiter than chalk or snow, and in like manner it is made up of all the other colours, and yet more in number and more beautiful than all that we have ever seen.

'For even these mere hollows of it, filled as they are with water and air, present a certain species of colour, as they gleam

PLATO amid the diversity of the other colours, so that its form appears
as one continuous variegated surface.

d 'And in this earth such as I have described it, the plants that
grow are in like proportion, both trees and flowers, with their
fruits; and the mountains again in like manner, and the stones
have their smoothness and transparency greater in the same
proportion, and their colours more beautiful : and of these the
gems here, these that are so prized, are fragments, carnelians,
and jaspers, and emeralds, and all such as these : but there
everything without exception is of this kind, and still more
beautiful than these.

'And the cause of this is that those stones are pure, and not
eaten away or spoiled, like those here, by decay and brine, and
by the sediments collected here, which cause ugliness and diseases
in stones and earth, and in animals and plants as well.   But
p. 567 the real earth is adorned with all these jewels, and with gold
and silver besides, and all other things such as these.   For they
shine out on the surface, being many in number and of great
size and in many places of the earth, so that to see it must be
a sight for the blessed to behold.'

CHAPTER XXXVIII

b THE Hebrew Scripture foretells that there shall be
a tribunal of God and a judgement of souls after their
departure hence, in countless other passages, and where
it says : 'The judgement was set, and the books were opened, . . .
and the Ancient of days did sit. . . . A river of fire flowed before
Him; ten thousand times ten thousands ministered unto Him, and
thousand thousands stood before Him.' Now hear how Plato
mentions the divine judgement, and the river even by
c name, and how he describes the many mansions of the
pious, and the various punishments of the impious, in
agreement with the language of the Hebrews.

For he speaks as follows in the dialogue *Concerning
the Soul* :

'And midway between these a third river issues forth, and

---

567 b 4 **Dan.** vii. 10, 9   c 6 Plato, *Phaedo*, 113 A

near its source falls into a vast region burning with a great fire, PLATO
and forms a lake larger than our sea, boiling with water and mud :
and thence it proceeds in a circular course turbid and muddy,
and as it rolls round the earth, arrives, among other places, at the d
extremity of the Acherusian lake, but does not mingle with its
water; and after making many circuits underground, it pours
into a depth below Tartarus.

'Now this is it which they call Pyriphlegethon, fragments of
which are thrown up by our volcanoes, wherever they occur in the
earth. Opposite again to this the fourth river falls out first, as
the tale goes, into a fearful and savage region, which is wholly
of a colour like lapis lazuli; this is called the Stygian region,
and the lake which the influx of the river forms is called Styx.
Then after falling into the lake, and receiving strange properties in
its water, the river sinks under the earth, and is whirled round in
its course in the opposite direction to Pyriphlegethon, and meets it
from the opposite side in the Acherusian lake; and its water also **p. 568**
mingles with no other, but after flowing round in a circle this
river too falls into Tartarus opposite to Pyriphlegethon : and its
name is, as the poets say, Cocytus.

'Such being the nature of these regions, as soon as the dead
have arrived at the place to which each is conveyed by his genius,
first of all they undergo a trial, both those who have lived good
and holy and just lives, and those who have not. And those who
are found to have led tolerable lives proceed to Acheron, and
embarking on such vessels as there are for them, they arrive **b**
on board these at the lake; and there they dwell, and by undergoing purification and suffering punishment for their evil deeds
they are absolved from any wrongs they have committed, or receive
rewards for their good deeds, each according to his deserts. But
any who are found to be incurable by reason of the greatness
of their sins, having either perpetrated many great acts of
sacrilege, or many nefarious and lawless murders, or any other
crimes of this kind—these are hurled by their appropriate doom
into Tartarus, whence they never come forth.   **c**

'But those who are found to have committed sins which are
great though not incurable, as for instance if in anger they have
done any violence to father or mother, and passed the rest of their
life in penitence, or have committed homicide in any other similar

Plato way, these must also be thrown into Tartarus, but after they
have been thrown in and have continued there a year, they
are cast out by the wave, the homicides by way of Cocytus,
d and the parricides by way of Pyriphlegethon: and when they
arrive all on fire at the Acherusian lake, there with loud
cries they call upon those whom they either slew or outraged;
and having summoned them they intreat and beseech them to let
them come out into the lake, and to receive them kindly: and
if they persuade them, they come out, and cease from their
troubles; but if not, they are carried again into Tartarus, and
thence back into the rivers, and never have rest from these
sufferings, until they have won over those whom they wronged;
for this was the sentence appointed for them by the judges.

'But any who are found to have been pre-eminent in holiness
of life—these are they who are set free and delivered from these
p. 569 regions here on earth, as from prison-houses, and attain to the
pure dwelling place above, and make their abode upon the upper
earth. And of this same class those who have fully purified
themselves by philosophy live entirely free from troubles for
all time to come, and attain to habitations still fairer than these,
which it is neither easy to describe, nor does the time suffice
at present. But for the sake of these things which I have
described we ought, Simmias, to make every effort to gain a share
of virtue and of wisdom in our lifetime: for fair is the prize,
and great the hope.'

b So speaks Plato. And now with that passage, 'And
they attain to fairer habitations, which it is neither easy to
describe, nor does the time suffice at present,' you will compare
that which with us runs as follows:

'For eye hath not seen, nor ear heard,
Neither have entered into the heart of man,
The things which God hath prepared for them that love Him.'

And with the 'habitations' mentioned compare the
statement that 'in the Father's house are many mansions,'
promised to those beloved of Him. And with what is
said about Pyriphlegethon compare the eternal fire
c threatened to the ungodly, according to the Hebrew

---

prophet who says to them, 'Who shall announce to us that the fire is kindled? Who shall announce to us the place of eternity?' And again, 'Their worm shall not die, and their fire shall not be quenched, and they shall be for a spectacle to all flesh.'

Now observe how Plato also, after saying in agreement with this that the impious will go into Tartarus, adds, 'whence they never come out.' And again after saying that the pious shall live in abodes of bliss, he adds the words, 'entirely and for all time to come.' Moreover the expression d used by him 'free from troubles' is like 'pain and sorrow and sighing flee away.'

And when he says that those who go away to Acheron not simply arrive there, but 'embarking first in what vessels there are for them,' what vessels then does he mean to indicate but their bodies, in which the souls of the deceased embark, and share their punishment, according to the established opinions of the Hebrews? But now as this subject has been sufficiently discussed, I will pass on to the twelfth Book of the *Preparation for the Gospel.*

---

c 2 Isa. xxxiii. 14   c 4 ibid. lxvi. 24   d 2 Isa. xxxv. 10

BOOK XII

CONTENTS

Chapter I

p. 573 b OUR twelfth Book of the *Preparation for the Gospel* will now from this point supply what was lacking in the preceding Book in proof of Plato's accordance with the Hebrew Oracles, like the harmony of a well-tuned lyre. We shall begin with a defence of our Faith, that is reviled among the multitude.

PLATO c   'It would be another question therefore whether one is right or wrong in finding fault with the constitutions of Lacedaemon and Crete : perhaps, however, I should be better able than either of you to tell what most people say of them.   For if your laws are even moderately well framed, one of the best of them must be a law allowing none of the young to inquire what is right or wrong in them, but bidding all with one voice and one mouth to agree that everything is well settled by the appointment of the gods ; and if any one says otherwise, they must not endure to listen to him at all.   But if an old man observes any fault in your laws, he may discuss such subjects with a ruler and one d of his own age, no young man being present.'

'What you enjoin, Stranger, is perfectly right.'

With good reason then the Hebrew Scriptures at an earlier time require faith before either the understanding

---

573 c 1 Plato, *Laws*, i. 634 D

or examination of the sacred writings, where it says, 'If ye will not believe, surely ye shall not understand,' and again, 'I believed, and therefore have I spoken.'

For which cause also among us those who are newly admitted and in an immature condition, as if infants in soul, have the reading of the sacred Scriptures imparted to them in a very simple way, with the injunction that they must believe what is brought forward as words of God.   But those who are in a more advanced condition, **P. 574** and as it were grown grey in mind, are permitted to dive into the deeps, and test the meaning of the words: and these the Hebrews were wont to name 'Deuterotists,' as being interpreters and expounders of the meaning of the Scriptures.

CHAPTER II

'IN the next place therefore we should say : It seems, Tyrtaeus, **b** PLATO that you praise most highly those who distinguish themselves in foreign and external war.   He would admit this, I suppose, and agree?

' Of course.

' But we say that, though these are brave, those are far braver who show their valour conspicuously in the greatest of all wars. And we too have a poet as witness on our side, Theognis, a citizen of Megara in Sicily, who says :   **c**

> " Cyrnus, when factions rage, a faithful man
>   Is worth his weight in silver and in gold."

'Such a man then, we say, is very much braver than the other in a harder warfare, almost as much as justice and temperance and wisdom combined with valour are better than valour by itself alone.   For a man would never be found faithful and true in civil wars without possessing all virtue.   But there are very many mercenaries who are willing to die in war, standing firm and fighting, as Tyrtaeus says, the greater part of whom, with very few exceptions, are violent and unjust and insolent and the **d** most senseless of mankind.

---

d 5 Isa. vii. 9   d 7 Ps. cxv. i   574 b 1 Plato, *Laws*, i. 629 E
c 2 Theognis, *Elegiac Gnomes*, v. 77 f.   c 10 Tyrtaeus, i. 16

PLATO   'To what conclusion then does our present argument lead? And what does it wish to make clear by these statements? Evidently this, that before all things both the heaven-sent lawgiver in this country, and every other of the least usefulness, will always enact his laws with a view chiefly to the greatest virtue: and this is, as Theognis says, faithfulness in dangers, which one might call perfect justice.'

p. 575 Among us also the Word of salvation, joining wisdom with faith, commends the man who is adorned with both, saying, in His own words: 'Who then is the faithful and wise steward?' and again, 'Well done, good and faithful servant, thou hast been faithful over a few things, I will set thee over many things.' Certainly in these passages He clearly shows that He approves not unreasoning faith, but that which is combined with the greatest virtues, such certainly being wisdom and goodness.

CHAPTER III

b 'FOR indeed it seems to me that in our former arguments we
c stated opportunely that the souls of the dead have a certain power after death, and take an interest in human affairs. There are tales treating of these matters, which are tedious though true: but on such subjects besides the other reports which we ought to believe, as being so many and so ancient, we must also believe the lawgivers who say that these things are true, unless they are shown to be utter fools.'

In the Book of the Maccabees also it is said that Jeremiah the Prophet after his departure from life was seen praying for the people, as one who took thought
d for men upon earth. And Plato also says that we ought to believe these stories.

CHAPTER IV

'THERE are two kinds of stories, the one true, and the other false?

---

575 a 2 Matt. xxiv. 45   a 3 ibid. xxv. 21   b 1 Plato, *Laws*, xi. 926 E
c 8 2 Macc. xv. 12   d 3 Plato, *Republic*, ii. 376 E

' Yes.

' And we must instruct children in both, and in the false first ?

' I do not understand, said he, what you mean.

' Do you not understand, said I, that what we first tell children is a fable ? And this, I suppose, is, generally speaking, fiction, though there is also some truth in it. And we use fables with children earlier than gymnastics.

' That is true.'   p. 576

So Plato writes. And among the Hebrews also it is the custom to teach the histories of the inspired Scriptures to those of infantine souls in a very simple way just like any fables, but to teach those of a trained mental habit the more profound and doctrinal views of the histories by means of the so-called Deuterosis and explanation of the thoughts that are unknown to the multitude.

Chapter V

' Do you not know then that the beginning is the chief **b** part of every work, especially for any young and tender mind ? For at that age any character that one wishes to impress on each is most easily formed and imparted.   **c**

' Quite so.

' Shall we then just carelessly permit our children to listen to casual fables (composed by casual persons), and to receive into their souls opinions for the most part opposite to those which, when they are grown up, we shall think they ought to hold ?

' We must by no means permit it.

' In the first place then, it seems, we must supervise the writers of fables, and approve any good fable they may compose, and reject any that are not good. And we must persuade nurses and mothers to tell their children those which are approved, and **d** to form their souls by the fables much more carefully than their bodies with their hands. But the greater number of the tales which they tell them now must be rejected.'

---

576 b 1 Plato, *Republic,* ii. 377 B

These precautions also had been taken by the Hebrews before Plato's time. For those who had a divine spirit fit for discerning of spirits approved what was rightly said or written with help from the Holy Spirit, and the contrary they rejected, just as they rejected the words of the false prophets. Moreover it was the custom of parents and nurses to soothe their infant children by singing the most edifying narratives from the divine Scriptures, just like any fables, for the sake of preparing beforehand for the religion which they were to learn when approaching to manhood.

CHAPTER VI

'LISTEN then, as they say, to a very pretty story, which you, I suppose, will regard as a myth, but I as a true story, for what I am going to say I shall tell you as being true.'

And after a little more:

'(There was a law) that he who had lived a just and holy life should depart after death to the Islands of the Blessed, and dwell in perfect happiness beyond the reach of all evils. But the man who had lived an unjust and ungodly life must go away to the prison-house of vengeance and punishment, which they call Tartarus.'

And again a little farther on:

'Next they must be stripped of all these wrappings and so tried, for their judgement must be after death. The judge also must be naked, that is to say, dead, examining by his very soul
c the very soul of each immediately after death, when it is bereft of all its kindred, and has left all that apparel behind on earth, in order that the judgement may be just.'

And afterwards he adds:

'This, Callicles, is what I have heard and believe to be true, and from these stories I gather the following conclusion: death, as it seems to me, is nothing else than the separation from each other of two things, the soul and the body.

---

577 b 1 Plato, *Gorgias*, 523 A   c 5 ibid. 524 A

'And after they are separated, each of them retains its PLATO own condition almost the same as it had when the man was alive, the body having its own nature and the results of its d treatment and sufferings all plainly visible.   For instance, if a man's body was large either by nature or by training or both while he was alive, his corpse also after death will be large; and if it was fat, it will be fat also after death, and so on.

'And again, if it was his custom to wear long hair, his corpse also will have long hair; or if a man was often whipped, and bore traces of the stripes in scars on his body either from scourges or from wounds of other kinds, when alive, his body after death may be seen to have these marks.   Or if a man's limbs were broken or distorted during life, the same will be visible also after death. 'And in a word, whatever was a man's condition of body during life, the same conditions are also plainly visible after death, either all or most of them for a certain time.

This same then seems to me to be the case, Callicles, with refer- p. 578 ence to the soul also.   When it is stript of the body, all things are visible in the soul, both its natural qualities, and the effects due to the habits of every kind which the man had contracted in his soul.

'When therefore they have come before the judge, those from Asia before Rhadamanthus, he stops them, and examines the soul of each, without knowing whose it is; but often when he has laid hands on the Great King or some other king or potentate, he b discerns that his soul has no sound part in it, but is scored with scourges, and full of scars from perjuries and injustice, of which each man's deeds have left the print upon his soul, and all crooked from falsehood and imposture, with nothing straight, because it has been reared with no sense of truth : and from power, and luxury, and insolence, and intemperance of conduct he sees the soul full of deformity and ugliness; at sight of which he sends it off c straight to prison in disgrace, where on its arrival it will have to endure its befitting punishments.

'Now every man who is under punishment, if punished rightly by another, ought either to become better and profit by it, or to be made an example to the rest, that others, seeing the sufferings which he endures, may be brought by terror to amendment.

'Those who receive benefit when they are punished by gods and men are they whose sins are remediable; but nevertheless it is by pain

PLATO **d** and suffering that they receive the benefit both here and in Hades, for in no other way is it possible to be delivered from iniquity.

'But if any have been guilty of the worst crimes, and have become incurable by reason of such iniquities, of these the examples are made; and inasmuch as they are incurable, they can no longer receive any benefit themselves, but others are benefited, who see them enduring for ever the greatest and most painful and terrible sufferings for their sins, hung up there in the prison-house in Hades as signal examples, a spectacle and a warning to the wicked who from time to time arrive there. And if what Polus says is true, I foretell that Archelaus will be one of these, and every other tyrant who is like him.

p. 579 'I suppose that the majority of these examples have been taken from among tyrants and kings and potentates, and those who have managed the affairs of states; for these because of their power commit the greatest and most impious crimes.

'Homer too bears witness to this. For he has represented those who are suffering eternal punishment in Hades as kings and potentates, a Tantalus, and Sisyphus, and Tityus. But Thersites, or any other common villain, no poet has represented as involved in extreme punishments as being incurable: for,
b I suppose, he had not the power, and therefore was happier than those who had it. In fact, however, Callicles, the men who become excessively wicked are of the class who have power. Yet there is nothing to prevent good men from being found even among these; and those who are so found are very worthy of admiration. For it is a difficult thing, Callicles, and very praiseworthy for a man who has great power of doing wrong to live always a just life, and few there be of this kind. Some there have been both here and elsewhere, and I doubt not there will be others, endowed with this virtue of administering
c justly whatever may be entrusted to them; and one there has been very celebrated over all Greece, Aristides son of Lysima-chus: yet for the most part, my good friend, men in power turn out bad.

As I was saying therefore, when Rhadamanthus gets hold of such a man, he knows nothing else about him, neither who he

---

578 d 11 Plato, *Gorgias*, 471 A   **579 a 5** Hom. *Od.* xi. 575 ff.

is, nor of what family, but only that he is a villain : and on PLATO
seeing this, he sends him off to Tartarus, with a badge upon him
to show whether he seems to be curable or incurable; and on
arrival there he undergoes the treatment proper to his case.

'But sometimes after looking upon another soul that has lived
a holy life in company with truth, a private man's or any d
other's (most likely, I venture to say, Callicles, the soul of
a philosopher who minded his own work and did not busy
himself in affairs during his life), he is delighted and sends it
off to the Islands of the Blessed.

'Aeacus also does just the same, and each of these two sits in
judgement with a rod in his hand.   But Minos as superintending
sits alone, and holds a golden sceptre, as Ulysses in Homer says
that he saw him,

"Holding a sceptre of gold, as he utters the doom of the dead."

'For my part therefore, Callicles, I am convinced by these
stories, and consider how I shall present my soul before the judge
in the healthiest condition possible.   So renouncing what most men **p. 580**
deem honours, I shall try by really practising truth both to live the
best life in my power, and so, when death comes, to die.

'All other men also I exhort to the best of my ability.   And
you especially I in my turn invite to enter upon this mode of life
and this conflict, which I declare to be worth all other conflicts
here on earth.

'And I make it a reproach to you that you will not be able to
help yourself, when the trial and the judgement of which I was just
now speaking come upon you.   But on coming before that judge, **b**
the son of Aegina, when he lays hold of you and leads you
forward, you will stand agape and turn dizzy there, just as much
as I should here.   And perhaps some one will smite you even to
your shame upon the cheek, and will insult you in every way.

'Perhaps, however, this appears to you a fable, like an old
wife's tale, and so you despise it.   And there would be nothing
strange in despising it, if by any searching we could find something better and truer.

'But as it is you see that though there are three of you, who
are the wisest of the Greeks of the present time, yourself and **c**

---

d 10 Hom. *Od.* xi. 569

PLATO Polus and Gorgias, you are not able to show that we ought to live any other life than this, which appears to be of advantage in the other world as well. But amid so many arguments, while all the rest were refuted, this alone remains unshaken, that to do wrong is to be more carefully avoided than to suffer wrong, and above all a man must study not to *seem* but to *be* good, both in private and in public life.'

So then Plato supposed that Aeacus and Minos and
d Rhadamanthus would be judges of the dead : but the word of God protests that ' all must appear before the judgement-seat of God; that each one may receive the things done in the body, according to what he hath done, whether it be good or bad.'

And again it says, ' In the day when God shall judge the secrets of men, . . . who will render to every man according to his works : to them who by patient continuance in well-doing seek for glory and honour and immortality, eternal life : but unto them that are contentious, and obey not the truth, but obey unrighteousness, there shall be wrath and indignation, tribulation and anguish, upon every soul of man that worketh evil, of the Jew first, and also of the Greek ; . . . for there is no difference.'

CHAPTER VII

p. 581   ' TAKE care, however, that these things come not to the know-
PLATO ledge of uneducated men : for there are, I think, hardly any tales more ridiculous than these to the multitude, nor on the other hand any more admirable and inspiring to the well disposed. But though often repeated and constantly heard even for many
b years, they, like gold, hardly become thoroughly purified with much careful treatment.'

Among us also the Word of salvation says:

' Give not that which is holy to the dogs, neither cast ye your pearls before swine.' And again, ' For the natural man receiveth not the things of the Spirit of God : for they are foolishness unto him.'

---

580 d 2 2 Cor. v. 10   d 6 Rom. ii. 16, 6   d 13 ibid. iii. 22
581 a 1 Plato, *Epistles*, ii. 313 E   b 4 Matt. vii. 6   b 5 1 Cor. ii. 14

628

CHAPTER VIII

'AND indeed (I call it folly) also in the individual, when good C PLATO reasons that are present in his soul produce no good effect, but what is quite contrary to them. All these I should class as the worst kinds of ignorance both in a state and in each individual citizen, and not the ignorance of the craftsmen, if you understand, d Strangers, what I mean.

'Yes, we understand, friend, and admit what you say.

'Let this then be thus laid down as agreed on and stated, that nothing connected with government must be entrusted to those citizens who are ignorant of these things, and they must be reproached for ignorance, even though they may be very clever in argument and thoroughly trained in all accomplishments, and all that naturally tends to quickness of understanding : while those who are of the opposite character to them must be called wise, even though, according to the proverb, they know neither how to read nor how to swim; and offices of authority must be given to them as sensible men.

'For, my friends, how can there be even the smallest kind p. 582 of wisdom without harmony ? It is not possible. But the finest and greatest of harmonies may most justly be called the greatest wisdom; and of this that man partakes who lives according to reason, whereas he who lacks wisdom is the ruin of his family, and by no means a saviour to the state, but on the contrary he will on every occasion be found ignorant in such affairs.'

Let this suffice for my quotation from the *Laws*. But in the *Statesman* also the same author speaks as follows on the subject of not being at all anxious about names b and phrases :

'Very good, Socrates; and if you continue to guard against being anxious on account of names, you will turn out to be richer in wisdom in your old age.'

CHAPTER IX

THE Hebrew Scripture introduces Moses at first as c deprecating the leadership of the people by what he said

---

c I Plato, *Laws*, iii. 689 B   582 b 3 Plato, *Statesman*, 261 E

to Him who conversed with him, 'I beseech Thee, O Lord,
appoint some other that is able, whom Thou shalt send': and
afterwards it represents Saul as hiding himself to avoid
assuming the kingdom, and the prophet Jeremiah as
humbly deprecating his mission. Now hear how Plato
also confirms the reasonableness of declining office,
speaking as follows:

PLATO d   'This then, O Thrasymachus, is now clear, that no art nor
government provides for its own benefit, but as I said before,
both provides and enjoins what is profitable to the governed,
having regard to his advantage though he is the weaker, and not
to that of the stronger.

'It was for these reasons then, my dear Thrasymachus, that
I said just now that no one is ready to accept office of his own
free will, and take in hand other people's troubles to set right,
but all demand a recompense, because he who intends to do
justice to his art never practises nor enjoins what is best for himself,
if he follows the rules of art, but what is best for the governed.
For which reasons, as it seems, there must be a payment for those
who are expected to be willing to take office, either money, or
honour, or a penalty if he refuse.'

CHAPTER X

p. 583   WHEREAS the oracles of the Hebrews teach that their
prophets and righteous men bravely endured the most
extreme insults and outrages and every kind of danger,
  b you may learn the agreement of Plato's opinion on this
point also from these words of his, which he has set
down in the second Book of the *Republic*:

PLATO   'Such then being our representation of the unjust man, let us
now in our argument set the just man beside him " in his nobleness
and simplicity," a man, as Aeschylus says:

"Whose will is not to seem good, but to be."

'We must take away the seeming. For if he is to seem just,

---

582 c 3 Exod. iv. 13   d 1 Plato, *Republic*, i. 346   583 b 4 ibid. ii.
361 B   b 5 Aeschylus, *Seven against Thebes*, 577

he will have honours and rewards for seeming to be so : and then PLATO
it will be uncertain whether he is just for the sake of justice,
or for the sake of the rewards and honours.

'We must strip him then of everything except justice, and
make his condition the reverse of the former. Though never c
doing wrong, he must have the reputation of the worst wrong-
doing, that his justice may be strictly tested by his being proof
against infamy, and its consequences : and he must be immovably steadfast even unto death, being in reality just but "with
a life-long reputation for injustice." '

And soon after he adds :

'Let me therefore describe it; and so, Socrates, if my speech be
somewhat coarse, imagine the speaker to be not me, but those d
who praise injustice above justice. And they will tell you as
follows, that in these circumstances the just man will be scourged,
racked, fettered, will have both· eyes torn out, and at last after
suffering every kind of torture he will be crucified, and will
learn that a man should wish not to be, but to seem, just.'

Such is Plato's description in words, but the righteous
men and prophets among the Hebrews are recorded long
before to have suffered in deed all that he describes.
For though most just, yet as if the most unjust, 'they were
stoned, they were sawn asunder, they were slain with the sword,
they wandered about in sheep-skins and goat-skins, being destitute, afflicted, tormented, ... wandering in deserts, and mountains,
and caves, and the holes of the earth, of whom the world was not
worthy.'

The Apostles also of our Saviour, though following the p. 584
highest path of justice and piety, were by the multitude
involved in the reputation of injustice, and what they
suffered we may learn from themselves when they say,
'We are made a spectacle unto the world, both to angels and to
men ... And even unto this present hour we both hunger, and
thirst, and are naked, and are buffeted, and have no certain
dwelling-place : ... being reviled, we bless; being persecuted, we

---

d 10 Heb. xi. 37   584 a 5 1 Cor. iv. 9   a 6 ibid. 11

endure; being defamed, we intreat: we are made as the filth of
the world.'

Nay, even unto this present time the noble witnesses
b of our Saviour throughout all man's habitable world,
while exercising themselves 'not to seem but to be' both
just and pious, have endured all the sufferings which
Plato enumerated: for they were both scourged, and
endured bonds and racks, and even had their eyes torn
out, and at last after suffering all terrible tortures they
were crucified. None like them will you find by any
searching among the Greeks, so that one may naturally say
that the philosopher did no less than prophesy in these
c words concerning those who among us were distinguished
in piety and true righteousness.

CHAPTER XI

As Moses in some mystic words says that in the beginning of the constitution of the world there had been
a certain Paradise of God, and that therein man had
been deceived by the serpent through the woman, hear
d now what Plato, all but directly translating the words,
and on his part also speaking allegorically, has set
down in the *Symposium*. Instead of the Paradise of God
he called it the garden of Zeus, and instead of the serpent and the deception wrought by it he supposed Penia
(*Poverty*) to lay the plot, and instead of the first man,
whom the counsel and providence of God had set forth
as it were for His new-born son, he spake of a son of
Metis (*Counsel*) called Poros (*Plenty*), and instead of saying
' when this world was being constituted,' he said ' when Aphrodite was born,' speaking in this allegorical way of the
world, because of the beauty with which it is clothed.
He speaks, however, word for word as follows:

p. 585   ' When Aphrodite was born, the gods were holding a feast, and
PLATO among the rest was Poros the son of Metis. And after dinner,

---

585 a ɪ Plato, *Symposium*, 203

Penia, as there was a feast, came to beg and stood about the doors. So Poros being drunk with nectar, for there was no wine as yet, went into the garden of Zeus, where he was weighed down with sleep. So then Penia, to relieve her destitution, plotted to get a child by Poros, and lay down beside him, and conceived Eros.'

PLATO

Such then were the thoughts which in this passage also Plato obscurely hinted in imitation of Moses.

b

CHAPTER XII

AGAIN Moses had said, 'But for Adam there was not found an help meet for him. And God caused a trance to fall upon Adam, and cast him into a sleep, and He took one of his ribs, and filled up the flesh instead thereof. And the Lord God builded the rib, which He had taken from Adam, into a woman.'

c

Plato, though he did not understand in what sense the story is told, was evidently not ignorant of it. But he assigns it to Aristophanes, as a comedian accustomed to scoff even at holy things, introducing him in the *Symposium* as speaking thus:

' Now you must first become acquainted with human nature and its affections. For our original nature of old was not the same as now, but of a different kind. In the first place the sexes of mankind were three, not two as now, male and female, but there was also a third combining them both, of which the name remains now, but the thing itself has disappeared. For Hermaphrodite was then both a real form and a name combined of both, the male and the female.'

d

Then after his usual sarcasms, he adds:

'After this speech his Zeus proceeded to cut the men in two, like those who cut sorb-apples for pickling, or eggs with hairs. And of each whom he cut he bade Apollo turn round the face and half of the neck towards the cutting, that by contemplating the section of himself the man might be more obedient to order : he also bade him heal the other parts.'

---

b 2 Gen. ii. 20-22   c 8 Plato, *Symposium*, 189 D   d 9 ibid. 190 D

Chapter XIII

p. 586 Moses described the original life of the earth-born as having been spent in the Paradise of God, and God as guiding them in a course of life without money or possessions, and all things as growing up for them without sowing or ploughing, and themselves as bare of the clothing afterwards adopted: and now listen to the **b** philosopher all but translating these very statements into the Greek language. He says then:

Plato 'God Himself was their shepherd and guardian, just as now man being another animal of more divine nature tends other kinds inferior to himself. And while God was their ruler, there were no states, nor any possessions of wives and children ; for they all sprang up out of the earth into a new life with no remembrance of their former state : and there were no things of this present kind, but they had fruits in abundance both from trees **c** and many various plants, not growing from cultivation, but sent up spontaneously by the earth. They dwelt for the most part in the open air, without clothes and without bedding ; for their seasons were so tempered as to cause them no trouble, and they had soft couches, where grass sprang up in abundance out of the earth. The life of which I speak, Socrates, was that of the age of Kronos : but the present life, which is said to be in the reign of Zeus, you know by your own experience.'

Chapter XIV

d Again as Moses has recorded that 'the serpent was more subtle than all the beasts,' and how the serpent talked to the woman and the woman to the serpent, and has set forth the persuasions used by the serpent, now listen to what Plato writes:

'If therefore the children of Kronos, with so much leisure and ability to hold intercourse by words not only with men but with

---

586 b 3 Plato, *Statesman*, 271 E   d 1 Gen. iii. 1   d 6 Plato, *Statesman*, 272 B

beasts also, used all these advantages with a view to philosophy, Plato conversing with the beasts as well as with one another, and inquiring from every nature which by the possession of any special faculty discerned anything different from the rest to add to the store of wisdom, it is easy to decide that the men of that age were ten thousand times better than the present in respect of happiness.

'But if filling themselves to the full with meat and drink they discoursed to one another and to the beasts of fables such as now are told of themselves, this also, just simply to declare my own p. 587 opinion, is very easy to decide. Nevertheless let us leave these questions, until there appear some informer competent to tell us in which way the men of that age were inclined in regard to b knowledge and the use of language.'

Chapter XV

When Moses had laid down a plan of legislating for men, he thought that he must have in his preface an account of ancient times: and he makes mention of the c Flood, and of the subsequent life of mankind, and then he describes the social life of the men of old among the Hebrews who were friends of God, and also of those who were proved otherwise in offences, because he considered that the narration of these things would be a parallel to his legislation.

And in like manner Plato also, when he proceeds to write down laws, affects the same method with Moses. In the preface, for instance, of the *Laws*, he has made use of his account of ancient times, making mention of a flood, and of the mode of life after the flood. Listen at least to what he says at the beginning of the third Book of the *Laws*:

'Do you think then that there is any truth in the ancient d traditions?

'What traditions?

---

587 d 1 Plato, *Laws*, 677 A

PLATO   ' That mankind has often been destroyed by floods and diseases
and many other calamities, in which only some small portion of
the human race was left.

' Certainly every one thinks all this very probable.

' Come then, let us consider one of the many destructions,
namely this which was caused by the flood.

' What point are we to observe in regard to it ?

' That those who escaped the destruction at that time would be
chiefly mountain-shepherds, small sparks of the human race preserved on the hill-tops.

' Evidently.

' Moreover such men must necessarily be unacquainted both with
other arts and especially with the devices of men in towns against
each other with regard to selfish advantage and rivalry, and all
p. 588 other evil deeds which they contrive one against another.

' Certainly it is probable.

' Let us suppose then that the cities settled on the plains and
by the sea were utterly destroyed at that time.

' Suppose so.

' Must we not say then that all implements were lost, and every
excellent invention connected with art, whether of political or any
other kind of wisdom, must all have perished at that time ? '

And further on he says :

' Let us say then that, at the time when the destruction had
b just taken place, the condition of mankind was this, a boundless
and fearful desolation, and a very great expanse of fertile land.'

After these and other such statements, he goes on to
describe the lives of mankind after the flood, and then,
just as Moses appends to the history after the flood the
civil state of the godly Hebrews of old, in like manner
Plato also, next to the lives of those who followed the
flood, tries to describe the ancient times of Greek
history, as Moses does of the Hebrews, mentioning the
Trojan war, and the first constitution of Lacedaemon,
and the Persians, and those who had lived among these
c events whether well or ill : and then after the narration

---

588 a 10 Plato, *Laws*, 677 E

of these things he begins his arrangement of the laws, following Moses in this also.

Chapter XVI

Moses made all his legislation and the constitution of **d** his state dependent on piety towards the God of the universe, and inaugurated his legislation with the Creator of all, and then taught that from the good that is divine proceeds all good for man, and referred the divine to the ruling mind of the world, that is the very God of all. Now see how our philosopher also, treading in the same steps, finds fault with the lawgivers of the Cretans and Lacedaemonians, and teaches throughout the law approved by Moses, speaking as follows: **p. 589**

'May I then explain how I should have liked to hear you Plato define the matter further?

'By all means, Stranger.

'You ought to have spoken thus: It is not without reason that the laws of the Cretans are especially celebrated among all the Greeks: for they are rightly framed in that they render those who use them happy; for they provide all good things for them.

'Now goods are of two kinds: some human, and some divine; and the former are dependent on the divine; and if a city accept **b** the greater, it gains the less also; but otherwise, it is deprived of both. Now there are first the lesser goods, of which the chief is health, and beauty second, and the third strength of body for running and all other movements, and wealth fourth, not blind but keen-sighted wealth, if it accompany wisdom.

'For this indeed is the first and chief of divine goods, wisdom I mean, and next a temperate habit of soul joined with intelli- **c** gence, and from these combined with courage a third good would be justice, and a fourth courage. Now all these are by nature set in higher rank than those bodily goods, and the law-giver too must give them this rank.

---

589 a 2 Plato, *Laws*, 631 A

Plato   ' And next he must direct that all the other ordinances for his citizens are to be regarded by them as looking towards these goods, and among these the human to look to the divine, and all the divine to the ruling mind.

d   ' With regard also to mutual contracts of marriage, and then in the procreation and nurture of children, both male and female, he must take care of his citizens in youth and maturer years even till old age, duly awarding honour or disgrace, and after having observed and watched over their pains and pleasures and desires in all these kinds of intercourse, and their pursuit of love of all kinds, he must rightly distribute praise or blame by means of the laws themselves.'

Also a little afterwards he says:

' After careful observation the legislator will appoint guardians over all these matters, some guiding their course by wisdom, and some by true opinion, so that intelligence may bind all these ordinances together and render them subservient to temperance and justice, not to wealth or ambition.

' It is in this way that I, O Strangers, should have wished, and
p. 590 still do wish you to describe how in the so-called laws of Zeus, and those of the Pythian Apollo, which Minos and Lycurgus enacted, all these provisions are contained, and what orderly arrangement in them is discernible to one who by skill and habits has experience about laws, although to the rest of us this is by no means clear.'

Among us also it is said, ' Seek ye first the kingdom (of God) and (His) righteousness, and all these things shall be added
b unto you.'   But long before this Moses also having commenced with the doctrine concerning God, and having next adapted to it his constitution of the state, and the rules about contracts, and the customs of social life, appoints as rulers and guardians over them all those who are consecrated to God, as the scriptures also teach, just men, haters of arrogance, ' some guiding their course by wisdom and some by true opinion.'

---

589 d 10 Plato, *Laws*, 632 C   **590 a** 7 Matt. vi. 33

Chapter XVII

' I tell you then ; and I affirm that the man who is to excel **c** Plato
in anything must practise that very thing from his earliest youth,
both in sport and in earnest, in every particular pertaining to
the subject. Take for instance, the man who is to be a good
husbandman or a builder of some kind ; the one must play at
building children's houses, and the other at tilling the ground, **d**
and he who brings up either of them must provide small copies of
the real tools for him ; and whatever branches of knowledge
must be learnt beforehand they must begin to learn ; the carpenter
for instance must learn to measure by rule or line, and the
soldier to play at riding or some other such exercise ; and by
their sports the teacher must try to turn the children's pleasures
and desires to the point which they must reach to attain their end
in life.

' The chief point then in education, we say, is the right " training
in the nursery," which will best lead the soul of the child in his
play to the love of that, in which, when he has become a man, he
will need to be perfect in the excellence of his work.'

This also Moses had previously enacted, saying, ' And **p. 591**
these words, which I command thee this day, shall be in thy
heart and in thy soul, and thou shalt enforce them upon thy sons.'
This the Hebrews are accustomed to do, training up all
their young children from a tender age in the precepts
of religion : and this is zealously practised to the present
time in accordance with an ancestral custom in the
Jewish nation.

Chapter XVIII

' Let not therefore that which we call education be indefinite. **b**
For at present when we blame or praise the mode in which each
has been brought up we speak of one of us as educated, and
another as uneducated, although sometimes they are men extremely
well educated for retail trade or a ship-master's life or any other **c**
such calling. For in our present discourse, as it seems, we do

---

c 1 Plato, *Laws*, 643 B   591 a 1 Deut. vi. 6.   b 1 Plato,
Laws, 643 D

PLATO not regard this as education, but that training to virtue from childhood, which makes a man desire and long to become a perfect citizen, knowing how to rule and to obey with justice.

'This is the training which, as it seems to me, our present mode of speaking designates, and which alone it would allow us to call education ; but that which aims at wealth or at strength or even
d at any kind of cleverness apart from intelligence and justice (it deems) mechanic and illiberal and not worthy to be called education at all.

'Let us then have no difference with them about a name, but let the present mode of speaking continue as agreed on between us, namely that those who have been rightly educated generally become good men. And so we must never disparage education, as it is of all noblest things the first that comes to the best of men : and if ever it transgresses, but may possibly be reformed, that is what every man should do to the utmost of his power throughout life.'

Also in the second Book of the *Laws* he adds :

'By education then I mean the virtue that comes first to children, that is, if pleasure and friendship and pain and hatred
p. 592 are rightly engendered in their souls when as yet they are incapable of reason, and, when they have attained to reason, agree with their reason that they have been rightly trained by suitable habits. This harmonious agreement is virtue as a whole, but the part of it due to right training in regard to pleasures and pains, so as to hate what one ought to hate, from the very beginning unto the end, and to love what one ought to love, if you
b cut off just this part by your argument and call it education, according to my judgement you would use the name rightly.'

So speaks Plato. But he is anticipated by David in the Psalms, when in teaching us 'to hate what we ought to hate, and love what we ought to love' he speaks as follows : 'Come, ye children, hearken unto me : I will teach you the fear of the Lord. What man is he that desireth life, and would fain see good days ? Keep thy tongue from evil, and thy lips that they speak no guile. Depart from evil, and do good ;
c seek peace, and pursue it.'

---

591 d 12 Plato, *Laws*, ii. 653 B   592 b 6 Ps. xxxiv. 11, 12

Solomon too says in like manner: 'Hear, ye children, the instruction of a father. For I give you a good gift: forget not my laws.' And again: 'Get wisdom, get understanding; forget it not.' And: 'Say that wisdom is thy sister; and gain understanding for thy familiar friend.' Again: 'Enter not upon the paths of the ungodly, and envy not the ways of transgressors.' And numberless other such passages you will find in the Hebrew Scriptures, fitted for teaching the acquisition of piety and virtue, and suited alike to the young and to those of full age.

Chapter XIX

THE answer of God said to Moses: 'See, thou make all **d** things after the pattern which was shown to thee in the mount.' And the sacred word stated more plainly, 'Who served a copy and shadow of the heavenly things;' and taught that the symbols in the writings of Moses plainly contain an **p. 593** image of the more divine realities in the intelligible world. Now then listen how Plato also gives similar interpretations in the sixth Book of the *Republic*, writing as follows:

'The philosopher then by communing with God and with the PLATO order of the world becomes both orderly and divine, as far as is possible to man: slander however is rife in all things.

'In all indeed.

'If therefore, said I, it ever becomes necessary for him to study how to introduce what he sees in yonder world into the habits of mankind both in private and in public life, and so to mould others as well as himself, do you think that he will be found a bad artificer of temperance and justice and civic virtue in general? **b**

'Certainly not, said he.

'But then if the multitude understand that what we say about him is true, will they be angry with the philosophers? And will they disbelieve us when we say that a State can never be prosperous, unless it be planned by artists who follow the divine pattern?

---

592 c 2 Prov. iv. 1   c 5 ibid. iv. 5   c 6 ibid. vii. 4   c 7 ibid. iv. 14
d 1 Exod. xv. 40   d 3 Heb. viii. 5   593 a 6 Plato, *Republic*, 500 C

641

PLATO 'They will not be angry, said he, if they understand it. But now what kind of plan do you mean?

c 'They would take, said I, a State and the moral nature of man for a tablet, and first of all would make a clean board, which is not at all an easy matter. You know, however, that the philosophers would differ at once from other men on this point, that they would be unwilling to touch either individual or State, or to frame laws, before they had either received a clean board, or themselves had made it so.

'Yes, and rightly, said he.

'Next then do you not think they would sketch out the plan of the constitution?

'Of course.

d 'Then, I suppose, in working it out, they would frequently look to this side and to that, both to what is essentially just and beautiful and temperate and everything of that kind, and then to the other side, to what is found in men, and would put upon their tablet the likeness of a man by making a combination and mixture of the various ways of life, and taking their design from that which, when embodied in man, Homer called the form and likeness of God.

'Rightly, said he.

'And one feature, I suppose, they would wipe out, and paint in another, until they made the human characters as pleasing as possible to God.'

CHAPTER XX

p. 594 'It seems to me that for the third or fourth time our argument
b has been brought round to the same point, namely that education is the drawing and leading of children to that which has been declared by the law to be right reason, and which has been approved by the best and eldest men from experience to be truly right.

'In order therefore that the soul of the child may not be accustomed in its joys and sorrows to go contrary to the law and to the rules laid down by the law, but may comply with it by

---

593 d 7 Hom. *Il.* i. 131, iii. 16 594 a 1 Plato, *Laws*, 659 C

rejoicing and sorrowing at the same things as the old man,— PLATO
for this purpose, let these, which we call songs, be now in reality c
charms for the soul, seriously designed with a view to harmony
such as we speak of; but because the souls of the young are
unable to bear seriousness, let them be called and treated as plays
and songs, just as those who are in charge try to offer to the sick
and enfeebled in body the nutriment that is good for them in
some kinds of pleasant food and drink, but that which is unwholesome in unpleasant things, in order that they may like the
one, and be rightly trained to dislike the other.

' And in the same way the good lawgiver will persuade, and,
failing to persuade, will compel the poet rightly to represent by d
noble and praiseworthy language both the gestures in his rhythms
and the music in his harmonies of the temperate and brave and
thoroughly good men.'

With good reason then among us also the children are
trained to practise the songs made by divine prophets
and hymns addressed to God.

CHAPTER XXI

' YOU compel your poets to say that the good man, as being
temperate and just, is happy and blessed, whether he be tall and
strong, or small and weak, and whether he be rich or poor : but **p. 595**
if he should perchance

"Midas and Cinyras in wealth surpass,"
and be unjust, he would be miserable and live a wretched life.

' Also your poet, if he speaks rightly, says,

"Ne'er would I praise, nor count for aught, a man "
who did not combine justice with the practice and attainment of
all things accounted honourable; and, being a just man,

"Close should he stand and strive to reach the foe:"
but if unjust he should

"Not dare to look on battle's bloody death,
Nor outstrip Thracian Boreas in the race,"

---

d 8 Plato, *Laws*, 660 E   595 a 3 Tyrtaeus, i. 6   a 6 ibid. i. 1
a 9 ibid. i. 12   a 11 ibid. i. 11   a 12 ibid. i. 4

PLATO **b** nor ever have any other of the so-called good things, for the things called good by the many have no right to the name.

'For health is called the best, and beauty the second, and wealth the third; and numberless other things are called good, such as quick sight and hearing, and the sensitive and sound condition of all organs connected with the senses, and again to be a tyrant and do whatever one likes, and then it is said the consumma-**c** tion of all blessedness is to have acquired all these things and then come to be immortal as soon as possible.

'But you and I say this, I suppose, that to just and holy men these are all excellent possessions, but to the unjust great evils all of them, beginning with health. For indeed to have sight and hearing and sensation and to live at all are the greatest of evils for a man who possesses all the so-called goods without justice and virtue in general if he is to be immortal for ever, but a less evil **d** if such a one survive as short a time as possible.

'These then are the things which I suppose you will persuade and compel your poets to say, as I do, and also by making their rhythms and harmonies correspond thereto, so to train your youths. Do you not see? For I say plainly that evil things so-called are to the unjust good, but evil to the just: and good things to the good are really good, but evil to the evil. As I was asking then before, do you and I agree, or how say you?'

These thoughts are not much unlike David's Psalms, which he had previously composed by divine inspiration, teaching by songs and hymns who is the truly blessed man, and who the contrary. This, at least, is the thought **p. 596** with which his Book begins, where he says: 'Blessed is the man that walketh not in the counsel of the ungodly,' and so on. This is what Plato has altered when he declares that the poets ought to say, 'that the good man being temperate and just is happy and blessed, and if a man be rich but unjust, he is miserable.'

And the very same thought David again expressed thus in the Psalms, saying: 'If riches abound, set not your heart upon them.' And again: 'Be not thou afraid when a man

---

596 a 1 Ps. i. 1   a 7 Ps. lxii. 10   a 8 Ps. xlix. 16

is made rich, and when the glory of his house is increased.' And at your leisure you may find each of the philosopher's sayings stated word for word throughout the whole **b** sacred writing of the Psalms.

Chapter XXII

'NAY rather, how surpassingly worthy of a lawgiver and a PLATO statesman. But other things there you would find to be less worthy : this point, however, about music is both true and worthy **c** of consideration, that it was possible, as it seems, on such subjects for a man of firm courage to get songs established by law which naturally produce right conduct. But this will be work for a god or some godlike man.'

With good reason therefore it had been enacted among the Hebrews also that they should admit no other hymns and songs in religious instructions than those which had been made under the influence of the Divine Spirit by men of God and prophets, and the music corresponding **d** to these sung in the manner customary among them.

Chapter XXIII

' So far I myself agree with the multitude, that music must be judged by pleasure, not however by the pleasure of chance persons, but that the best music generally is that which gives delight to the best persons who are well educated, and especially that which **p. 597** delights the one man pre-eminent both in virtue and education.

' And the reason why I say that the judges of this matter must be virtuous is this, that they ought to be endowed with wisdom in general, and especially with courage.

' For the true judge ought not to judge by what he learns from the theatre, when driven out of his senses by the tumult of the multitude and his own ignorance ; nor if, on the other hand, he knows right, ought he through unmanliness and cowardice carelessly to deliver a false judgement out of the same mouth

---

b 3 Plato, *Laws*, 657 A   d 3 ibid. 658 E

PLATO b with which he invoked the gods before proceeding to give judgement. For the judge sits there not as the learner but rather,
according to right, as the teacher of the spectators, and to oppose
those who neither properly nor rightly give pleasure to the
spectators.'

Among the Hebrews also in old times it was not the
part of the multitude to judge the discourses pronounced
from divine inspiration, and the inspired songs, but they
were few and rare persons, themselves partakers of a
divine spirit, fit to judge of what was said, who alone
c were permitted to approve and consecrate the books of
the prophets, and to reject those of men unlike them
in character.

CHAPTER XXIV

d   'Now the original purpose of my argument, to exhibit in
becoming language the aid that should be given to the Chorus
of Dionysus, has been stated to the best of my power. Let us
then consider whether this has been rightly done. I suppose
that an assembly of this kind necessarily ends by becoming ever
more tumultuous as the drinking goes on, just what we supposed
at the outset must necessarily occur in the circumstances now
under discussion.

'Necessarily.

'Yes, and every man is lifted with lighter heart above himself,
and is gladdened, and grows full of loud confidence, and of
unwillingness in such a state to listen to his neighbours, and
claims to be competent to govern both himself and every one
else.

'Certainly.

'Did we not say then that in these circumstances the souls of
p. 598 the drinkers, becoming like iron heated in the fire, grow softer
and younger, so as to be found tractable by one who has both the
knowledge and the power to train and mould them just as when
they were young? And that this modeller is the same as in their
youth, namely the good legislator, who must make laws for the

---

597 d 1 Plato, *Laws*, 671 A

banquet, able to give an entirely opposite turn to the will of PLATO
the man who is growing confident and bold and impudent beyond
bounds, and refuses to submit to order and to his turn of silence,
and speech, and drinking, and singing; laws able also justly to
inspire that noblest fear, which stoutly resists the entrance of **b**
unbecoming boldness, that divine fear to which we have given
the names of reverence and shame?

' That is true.

' We said too that the quiet and sober must be guardians of
these laws and aid their operation.'

With good reason therefore it has been made a traditional custom for us also in our feasts to sing songs and
hymns composed in honour of God, the proper order being
under the charge of those who are guardians among us.

CHAPTER XXV

' IF, as a serious matter, any city means to practise the custom **c**
now mentioned in a lawful and orderly fashion, as taking anxious
care for the sake of temperance, and in like manner and for the
same reason will not hold aloof from other pleasures, but form **d**
plans for the sake of controlling them, in this way they may all
be used: but if it is to be for sport, and with permission for any
one to drink who will, and whenever he will, and with whomsoever
he will, with the accompaniment of whatever other customs he
will, I should never join in the vote, that this city or this man
ought ever to indulge in drinking; but going even farther than
the usage of the Cretans and Lacedaemonians I should vote for the
law of the Carthaginians, that no one when in camp should ever
taste wine, but accustom himself to water-drinking the whole
time; and that in any city neither male nor female slave should
ever taste wine, nor magistrates during the year in which they
may be in office, nor again should pilots or judges while on duty **p. 599**
taste wine at all, nor any one who is coming to deliberate in any
important council, nor any one at all in the daytime, unless on
account of bodily training or sickness; nor again at night,
when any one whether man or woman thinks of getting

---

598 c 1 Plato, *Laws*, 673 E

PLATO children.   One might also mention many other reasons, why those who hold to reason and law should not drink wine, so that on this principle no city whatever would have need of many vine-yards, but the other forms of husbandry and the whole mode of
b life would be duly regulated.'

Moses also anticipates this by enacting that the priests must not taste wine at the time of their religious service, saying: 'And the Lord spake to Aaron, saying, Ye shall drink no wine nor strong drink, thou and thy sons with thee, whenever ye go into the tent of the testimony, or when ye approach to the altar, so shall ye not die: a statute for ever throughout your generations.'   The same author also gives a law to those who make a vow, saying: 'Whosoever, whether man or woman, shall make a special vow of self-dedication to purity
c unto the Lord, he shall separate himself from wine and strong drink, and vinegar of wine and vinegar of strong drink shall he not drink.'   Solomon too forbids the use of wine to rulers and judges, saying: 'Do all things with deliberation; drink wine with deliberation: princes are passionate, let them not drink wine, lest they drink and forget wisdom ... and troubles.'   The apostle also gives permission to Timothy on account of sicknesses, saying: 'Use a little wine for thy stomach's sake and thine often infirmities.'

CHAPTER XXVI

d   'IF therefore there has either been in the boundless ages of the past, or is even now in some barbarous region lying far away out of our sight, or shall hereafter be a necessity for men eminent in philosophy to take charge of a State, I am ready to argue to the death in defence of this assertion, that the constitution which I have described has existed, and still exists, and will exist,
p. 600 whenever the Muse herself becomes mistress of the State: for it is not impossible that she should become mistress, nor are my descriptions impossible.'

---

599 b 4 Lev. x. 8   b 9 Num. vi. 2, 3   c 4 Prov. xxxi. 4
c 8 1 Tim. v. 23   d 1 Plato, *Republic*, 499 C
648

Chapter XXVII

'But how for a man in relation to himself? Must he be **b** Plato disposed as an enemy towards an enemy, or what do we say in this case ?

' O Athenian stranger, Attic I should not like to call you, since you seem to me worthy rather to be called after the name of the goddess, because you have made the argument clearer by rightly bringing it back to its first principle, so that you will more easily recognize that we were quite right just now in saying that all men are enemies to all, both in public and in private, and every one an enemy to himself.   c

' What do you mean, my good sir ?

' In this last case also, my friend, a man's conquest over himself is the first and noblest of all victories, but to be defeated by himself is at once the basest and worst defeat of all. For this is a sign that there is a war against ourselves going on in every one of us.'

And after other passages he adds to this and says :

' Must we not then reckon each of ourselves as one ?

' Yes.

' But as possessing in himself two counsellors, antagonistic and foolish, which we call pleasure and pain ?

' That is true.

' And in addition to both these certain opinions of things **d** future, which in common are called expectation, but severally the expectation of pain is called fear, and the expectation of the contrary is confidence. And further with all these there is a calculation, which of them is better or worse, and when this calculation has become a common decree of a State it is called law.'

And presently he says :

' But this we know, that these affections in us are like cords and strings which pull us inwardly, and being opposite to each other draw us different ways towards opposite actions; and

---

600 b 1 Plato, *Laws*, 626 D   c 9 ibid. 644 C   d 9 ibid. 644 E

PLATO herein lies the distinction between virtue and vice. For reason affirms that there is one of these drawings to which every man ought always to yield, and never let it go, but pull against the other cords ; and that this one is the golden and sacred guidance

p. 601 of reason, called the public law of the State ; and that others are hard and of iron, but this one soft, as being of gold (and of one form), while the others are like all kinds of forms. We ought therefore always to take part with the best guidance, that of the law. For inasmuch as reason is beautiful and gentle and not violent, its guidance needs assistants, in order that in us the golden kind of motive may prevail over the other kinds.

' And so in this way the fable about virtue, speaking of us as being puppets, would be maintained, and the meaning of the expression about a man being " better or worse than himself " would in a certain way be made clearer ; and that in regard to

b a State or an individual, the latter having found in his own case a true principle with regard to this drawing by cords should live in obedience to it, and a State, having learned the principle either from some god or from this very individual thus informed, should establish it as a law for dealing both with herself and with all other states. Thus vice and virtue would be more clearly distinguished for us.'

Among us also the word of God teaches the like

c doctrines, saying : ' I delight in the law of God after the inward man, but I see another law in my members warring against the law of my mind.' And again : ' Their thoughts one with another accusing or else excusing them.' And other passages which are similar to these.

CHAPTER XXVIII

d ' WE remember, however, that in the former part of our discussion we agreed that, if the soul should be found to be older than the body, the properties also of the soul would be older than those of the body.

' Yes, certainly.

'Then tempers, and dispositions, and wishes, and reasonings, PLATO and true opinions, and meditations, and remembrances must have been prior to length and breadth and thickness and strength of bodies, if soul is prior to body.

'Necessarily.

'Must we not then necessarily grant what follows immediately **p. 602** from this, that the soul is the cause of all that is good and evil, and noble and base, and just and unjust, and of all opposites, if we suppose her to be the cause of all things?'

Let these quotations suffice from the tenth Book of the *Laws*. Now with these Moses frequently agrees in his laws, saying: 'And if a soul sin and commit a transgression,' and all other passages expressed by him in like manner to this.

CHAPTER XXIX

THE Hebrew Scripture says of the earnest philosopher: **b** 'It is good for a man to bear the yoke in his youth: he will sit alone, and keep silence, because he hath taken it upon him:' and of the prophets beloved by God, that they passed their lives in deserts, and mountains, and caves, for the **c** sake of attaining the height of philosophy, fixing their thought upon God alone; and now hear Plato, how he too makes this mode of life divine, giving the following description of one who aspires to the height of philosophy:

'We are to speak then, it seems, since this is your pleasure, of the leaders: for why should one talk about those who spend their time to bad purpose in philosophy? But these leaders, I suppose, in the first place from their youth up have never known the way to the Agora, nor where the court of justice is, or the council-chamber, or any other public assembly of the State: and **d** laws and decrees, whether read or written, they neither see nor hear. The strivings of political clubs to gain offices, and meetings and banquets and revellings with flute-girls, are practices which do not occur to them even in dreams.

---

602 a 7 Lev. vi. 2, 4   b 2 Lam. iii. 27, 28   c 1 Heb. xi. 38
c 7 Plato, *Theaetetus*, 173 C

PLATO   'And what has happened well or ill in the city, or what evil
has come to any one from his ancestors male or female, is less
known to him than, as the proverb says, the number of gallons
in the sea.   And as to all these things he knows not even that
he does not know them, for he does not abstain from them for
the sake of gaining reputation; but in fact it is only his body
that has its place and home in the city, but his mind esteeming
all these things as little or nothing, disdains them and is
" flying all abroad," as Pindar says, measuring both the things

p. 603 beneath the earth and on its surface, and studying the stars
above the sky, and scrutinizing in all ways the whole nature of
existing things each as a universal, but not condescending to anything close at hand.

'How do you mean this, Socrates?

'Just as, when Thales was star-gazing, Theodorus, and looking
upward fell into a well, a clever and witty Thracian handmaid is said to have made a jest upon him, that he was eager to
know about things in heaven, but took no notice of what was

b before his face and at his feet.

'And the same jest holds good against all who pass their lives
in philosophy.   For in fact a man of this kind knows nothing of his
nearest neighbour, not merely as to what he is doing, but hardly
even knows whether he is a man or some other kind of animal.
But what man is as man, and what is becoming to such a nature
to do or to suffer different from all others, this he is investigating,
and takes much trouble in searching it out.   You understand,
I suppose, Theodorus, do you not?

c   'Yes, I do, and what you say is true.

'Therefore, my friend, the man of this character both in his
private intercourse with every one, and in public life, as I said
at first, whenever he is compelled either in a law-court or anywhere else to talk about the things at his feet and before his eyes,
becomes a laughing-stock not only to Thracian girls but also to
the rest of the rabble, by falling into wells and every kind of
trouble from want of experience : and his awkwardness is shock-
ing and makes him seem no better than a fool.

'For when scandal is going on he has nothing personal where-

----

602 d 14 Pindar, *Fragment,* 123 (226)

with to reproach anybody, inasmuch as he knows no harm of any PLATO
one from having paid no attention to it : so he appears ridiculous d
in his perplexity.   And amidst the praises and loud boastings of
others it is evident that he is laughing not in pretence but in
reality, and so he is thought to be silly.

'For when either a tyrant or a king is eulogized, he fancies
that it is some kind of herdsman, as a swineherd, or a shepherd,
or cowherd that he hears congratulated for drawing much milk;
but he supposes that they have a more ill-tempered and more
treacherous animal than those to tend and to milk.

'He supposes also that a man in this position must become
from want of leisure no less boorish and uneducated than the
herdsmen, being shut in by his city-wall as by a fold on the
mountain.   And when he hears how some one or other, possessing **p. 604**
ten thousand plethra of land or yet more, possesses a wonderful
amount, he thinks that what he hears of is very little, being
accustomed to look at the earth as a whole.

'And when men sing the praises of family, saying that some
man of birth can show seven wealthy ancestors, he regards the
commendation as that of very dull and short-sighted persons, who
from want of education cannot look always to the whole, nor
calculate that every man has had countless myriads of ancestors
and forefathers, among whom any man whatever has had many
times over thousands and thousands of rich and poor, and kings **b**
and slaves, barbarians and Greeks : but when men pride themselves upon a pedigree of five and twenty ancestors, or trace back
to Hercules son of Amphitryon, their narrow-mindedness seems
to him extraordinary, and he laughs at their being unable to
calculate that the twenty-fifth upwards from Amphitryon, and the
fiftieth from him, was such as fortune made him, and so to shake
off the vanity of an unintelligent soul.

'In all these matters then such a philosopher is derided by the
multitude, on the one hand as seeming to be arrogant, and on the **c**
other as ignorant of what is before his feet, and at a loss on every
occasion.

'You state exactly what takes place, Socrates.

'But when the philosopher himself, O my friend, draws a man
upwards, and the other is willing to escape with him from the
question, "In what do I wrong you, or, you me," into the con-

PLATO templation of abstract justice and injustice, and what is the essence of each of them, and in what they differ from other things or from each other; or from the question, whether a king possessing much wealth is happy, to the contemplation of abstract d monarchy and human happiness and misery in general, of what nature they are, and in what way it is befitting to human nature to acquire the one of them, and avoid the other,—when in turn that narrow-minded, shrewd and pettifogging creature is required to explain all these subjects, he gives the philosopher his revenge. Turning giddy where he hangs on high, and looking down, unaccustomed as he is, from the upper air, dismayed and perplexed and stammering a barbarous jargon, he makes himself a laughing-stock not to Thracian girls, nor to any other uneducated person, for they do not understand it, but to all who have been brought up otherwise than as slaves.

'This then, O Theodorus, is the character of each. The one is
p. 605 the character of the man who has been really brought up in freedom and leisure, whom you call a philosopher, with whom we need not be indignant at his seeming to be a simpleton and a nobody, when he is thrown into any servile offices, as for instance if he does not understand how to tie up a bundle of bed-clothes, nor to sweeten a sauce or a flattering speech. But the other is the character of the man who is able to render all such services as these smartly and quickly, but does not understand how to throw his cloak over his right shoulder like a gentleman, nor in just harmony of language to hymn the praises of the true
b life of gods and of divinely favoured men.

'If, Socrates, you could persuade all men, as you do me, of the truth of what you say, there would be more peace and fewer evils among men.

'But it is not possible, O Theodorus, either that evils should disappear (for there must always be something antagonistic to good), or that they should be settled among the gods, but they necessarily haunt our mortal nature and this our place of abode.

'Wherefore also we should try to escape from this world to the other as speedily as possible. And escape means assimilation to God as far as is possible, and assimilation means to become just
c and holy and wise withal. But in fact, my good friend, it is not at all an easy thing to persuade men that the reasons for which

654

the multitude say that we ought to shun wickedness and pursue PLATO
virtue are not the right reasons for practising the one and avoiding
the other, I mean the wish not to seem to be bad, but to seem to
be good.

' For this, as it seems to me, is the proverbial old wives' gossip :
but the truth we may state as follows : God is never in any
way unrighteous, but most perfectly righteous : and nothing is
more like Him than any one of us who may likewise become
most righteous. On this depends a man's true ability, or his
nothingness and cowardice.

' For to know this is wisdom and genuine virtue, but not to **d**
know it is manifest ignorance and vice : and all other kinds
of seeming cleverness and wisdom, when they display themselves
in political power, are vulgar, and in arts mechanical. With the
man then who does wrong, and says or does unholy things, it is
far best not to admit that villany makes him a clever man.

' For such men glory in their shame, and suppose that they are
spoken of as no fools, nor mere cumberers of the ground, but men
of the right sort to prosper in a State. We ought therefore to tell **p. 606**
them the truth, that they are all the more what they think they
are not, because they think they are not. For they are ignorant
of the penalty of injustice, the last thing of which they ought to
be ignorant. For it is not the penalty which they fancy, stripes
and death, which wrong-doers sometimes escape altogether, but
a penalty which it is not possible to escape.

' What penalty then do you mean ?

' Though there are two examples set forth in the world of
reality, the divinity being the example of the greatest happiness,
and the godless of the greatest misery, they do not see that this
is true, but from silliness and the extreme of folly they are not
conscious of growing like to the one and unlike the other because **b**
of their evil deeds : and they pay the penalty for this by living
the life fitted for the pattern to which they are growing like.

' And if we tell them that unless they get rid of their cleverness,
the place that is free from all evil will not receive them after
death, but that they will always have a life here on earth corresponding to their own character by a continual association with
evil, being evil themselves, they will listen to this, as men of
the utmost cleverness and cunning listening to fools.

PLATO   ' Quite so, Socrates.

c   'I know it indeed, my friend. There is, however, just one
circumstance in their case, whenever they are obliged to give and
to receive an explanation in private about the studies which they
condemn, and are willing to stand their ground manfully for a
long time, and not run away like cowards, then at last, my good
sir, they are strangely dissatisfied with themselves and their arguments, and their fine rhetoric somehow fades away, so that they
seem to be no better than children.'

CHAPTER XXX

d   AMONG us also there is this saying concerning all
sophistry practised among men: 'For the wisdom of this
world is foolishness with God. For it is written, I will destroy
the wisdom of the wise, and will set at nought the prudence of
the prudent. Where is the wise? Where is the scribe? Where
is the disputer of this world?'

Moreover that those who study a divine philosophy ought
to have no narrow-minded thoughts, we are taught in the
saying: 'While we look not at the things which are seen, but
at those which are not seen: for the things which are seen are
temporal; but the things which are not seen are eternal.'

p. 607   And of the fact that wickedness gathers close around
the earth and this mortal life, the word of God says somewhere: 'Redeeming the time, because the days are evil.' And:
' Sufficient unto the day is the evil thereof.' The prophet also
says: ' Cursing, and stealing, and adultery, and murder, are
poured out upon the earth, and they mingle blood with blood.'

And with regard to escaping from this world to God,
Moses says: 'Thou shalt walk after the Lord thy God, and to
b   Him shalt thou cleave.' And the same Moses teaches us to
imitate God, saying: ' Ye shall be holy, for the Lord your God
is holy.'

David also knowing that God is righteous, and urging
us to become imitators of Him ourselves, says: ' Righteous

---

606 d 2 I Cor. iii. 19   d 3 ibid. i. 19, 20   d 9 2 Cor. iv. 18
607 a 3 Eph. v. 16   a 4 Matt. vi. 34   a 5 Hos. iv. 2   a 8
Deut. x. 20   b 2 Lev. xi. 45   b 5 Ps. xi. 7

is the Lord, and loveth righteousness.' The same David taught us to despise wealth, saying: ' If riches increase, set not your heart upon them'; and, 'Be not thou afraid, when a man is made rich, and when the glory of his house is increased : for when he dieth, he shall carry nothing away, nor shall his glory descend with him.'

Also in the following words he taught us not to c admire the ruling powers among mankind: 'Put not your trust in princes, nor in any sons of men, in whom there is no safety. His breath will go forth, and he will return to his earth : in that day shall all his thoughts perish.'

Chapter XXXI

'But even if the case were not such as our argument has d Plato now proved it to be, if a lawgiver, who is to be of ever so little use, could have ventured to tell any falsehood at all to the young for their good, is there any falsehood that he could have told more beneficial than this, and better able to make them all do everything that is just, not by compulsion but willingly ?

' Truth, O Stranger, is a noble and an enduring thing ; it seems, however, not easy to persuade men of it.'

Now you may find in the Hebrew Scriptures also thousands of such passages concerning God as though He were jealous, or sleeping, or angry, or subject to any **p. 608** other human passions, which passages are adopted for the benefit of those who need this mode of instruction.

Chapter XXXII

' Are we then agreed as to our former statements ?   **b** Plato
' About what ?

' That every one, man and boy, free and slave, male and female, and the whole city, should never cease from reciting to themselves these charms which we have just described, changed from time to time in some way or other, and presenting every kind of variation,

---

b 6 Ps. lxii. 10   b 7 Ps. xlix. 16   c 2 Ps. cxlvi. 3
d 1 Plato, *Laws*, 663 D   608 b 1 ibid. 665 B

PLATO so that the singers may have an insatiable desire for the hymns,
c and pleasure in them.

'How could there be any doubt that this practice ought to be
adopted?'

In the fifth Book also of the *Republic* he writes to the
like effect, saying as follows:

'Do you then know any human occupation, in which the male
sex is not superior in all these respects to the female? Or need
we waste time by mentioning the art of weaving, and the making
of pancakes and preserves, in which the female sex is thought
forsooth to be great, and in which their utter inferiority is most
ridiculous?

d   'You say with truth, said he, that the one sex is far surpassed
by the other, I might almost say, in everything. Many women,
no doubt, are better than many men in many points, but the
general truth is as you say.

'No occupation then, my friend, of those who manage the
affairs of the state belongs to a woman as woman nor to a man
as man; but the natural qualities are found here and there in
both sexes alike, and while woman has by nature a share in all
pursuits, and man in all, yet woman is in all weaker than man.

'Yes, certainly.

'Are we then to assign all employments to men, and none to
women?

'How can we?

'In fact, we shall say, I suppose, that among women also one
has a natural gift of healing and another has not, and one is
musical and another unmusical?

'Certainly.

'Also one fit for gymnastics and for war, and another unwar-
like and with no taste for gymnastics?

'So I suppose.

'Again, one woman is a philosopher, another hates philosophy?
p. 609 And one is high-spirited, another spiritless?

'This too is true.

'So there is one woman fit for a guardian, and another unfit.

---

608 c 6 Plato, *Republic*, 455 C

Or was not such the nature which we selected as that of men PLATO
who were fit for guardians?

'Yes, it was such.

' Both woman and man therefore have the same natural fitness
for guardianship of the state, except in so far as one is weaker
and another stronger.

' So it appears.

' We must then select women also who are of this character to
live with men of the same character, and to share in their
guardianship, since they are competent, and akin to them in
nature.'

With good reason then our Word also admits to its b
divine instruction and philosophy every class not only
of men but also of women, and not only of free men and
slaves, but also of Barbarians and Greeks.

CHAPTER XXXIII

' LET us look at it then in this way. Now suppose some one c
were to praise the breeding of goats, and the animal itself as
a fine property; and some one else, having seen goats feeding
without a goatherd in cultivated ground and doing mischief,
should find fault with them, and on seeing any kind of cattle
without a keeper or with bad keepers, should in this case blame
them, do we think that such a man's censure would convey any
just blame whatever?

' How should it ? '

Also after a few sentences :

' And what would you say of one who praises or blames any
kind of community, which ought naturally to have a ruler, and
which with his aid is useful, whereas the critic had never d
seen it in its rightful association with a ruler, but always
without rule, or with bad rulers ?   Do we suppose that observers
such as these could pronounce any useful censure or praise on
communities of this kind ?

' How could they ? '

---

609 c 1 Plato, *Laws*, 639 A

If then among us also it should appear that some without any president and ruler, or with evil rulers, were doing evil, one ought not to find fault with our whole school, but rather to admire our religious constitution from the conduct of those who follow it rightly.

CHAPTER XXXIV

p. 610 IN the *Proverbs* of Solomon it is briefly stated : ' The memory of the just is associated with praises, but the name of the ungodly is extinguished '; and again it is said : ' Call no man blessed before his death ' : so now hear how Plato **b** interprets the thought in the seventh Book of the *Laws*, saying :

PLATO ' Whosoever of the citizens should reach the end of their life after having wrought good and laborious works either in body or soul, and been obedient to the laws, it would be fitting that they should receive eulogies.

' By all means.

' It is not safe, however, to honour those who are still alive with eulogies and hymns, before a man has finished his whole course of life, and crowned it with a noble end. And let us have all these honours common to men and to women who have **c** been conspicuously good.'

CHAPTER XXXV

As Solomon had said in *Proverbs* : ' Give me neither poverty nor riches,' so Plato says in the fourth Book of the *Republic* :

' But we have found, it seems, some other things for the guardians, against which they must watch in every way, that **d** they may not creep in unobserved into the state.

' What kind of things ?

' Riches, said I, and poverty ; as the one engenders luxury, and idleness, and revolution, and the other meanness and mischievousness, as well as revolution.'

By mischievousness is meant every disgraceful action.

---

610 a 1 Prov. x. 7   **a** 3 Ecclus. xi. 28   **b** 3 Plato, *Laws*, 801 E
c 2 Prov. xxx. 8   **c** 5 Plato, *Rep.* 421 E

Chapter XXXVI

Again Moses says in his laws: 'Let every man fear his father and his mother,' and 'Honour thy father and thy mother, that it may be well with thee'; and Plato, like Moses, bids us both honour and fear them, speaking thus in the *Laws*:

'Every man of sense fears and honours the prayers of his parents, knowing that many times and for many persons they have been accomplished.' **p. 611** Plato

And again in another place he says:

'We would have every one reverence his elder both in word and deed. And any one who is twenty years older than himself, whether male or female, let him regard as father or mother, and treat with reverence.'

Chapter XXXVII

Moses in his laws forbade Hebrews to have Hebrews **b** as slaves, and said: 'If thou buy an Hebrew servant, six years shall he serve thee: and in the seventh year thou shalt send him away free.' And in like manner Plato says in the *Republic*:

'They should therefore themselves own no Greek as a slave, and advise the other Greeks to the same effect.

'Certainly, said he.

'Thus then they would be more ready to turn their arms against Barbarians, and abstain from war against each other.'

Chapter XXXVIII

'Let no man move landmarks, either of his own fellow **c** citizen who is a neighbour, or of one whose property marches with his on the borders, if he be neighbour to a foreigner, considering that this is really to move what should be immoveable.'

And presently he says:

'Whosoever ploughs over his neighbour's lands, encroaching **d**

---

d 7 Lev. xix. 3   d 8 Exod. xx. 12   611 a 1 Plato, *Laws*, 931 E   a 5 ibid. 879 C   b 2 Exod. xxi. 2 ; Deut. xv. 12   b 6 Plato, *Republic*, 469 C   c 1 Plato, *Laws*, 842 E   d 1 ibid. 843 C

PLATO upon the boundaries, let him repay the damage, and as a cure for both his impudence and his meanness let him pay besides double of the damage to the person injured.'

CHAPTER XXXIX

'AND in a word, let not the disgrace and punishment of a father follow upon any of the children, except when any one's **p. 612** father and grandfather and great-grandfather in succession have paid the penalty of death.'

CHAPTER XL

A LAW of Moses says : 'If a man steal a calf, or a sheep, and slay it, or sell it, he shall repay five calves for the calf, and four sheep for the sheep. . . . But if he be caught, and the theft be found in his hand alive, from a calf or an ass to a sheep, he shall **b** repay double.'   Now hear how Plato follows this, saying :

' But whether a thief steal much or little, let there be one law and one punishment imposed for all alike. For in the first place he must pay double the amount stolen, if he be convicted in a suit of this kind, and if the rest of his substance suffice to pay it, beyond his lot of land ; and if not, he must be kept in prison until he has paid it, or persuaded the man who gained sentence against him to release him.'

CHAPTER XLI

c   AGAIN when Moses says : 'But if the thief be found breaking in, and be smitten that he die, it is not murder,' Plato agrees in this also, saying :

' If a man catch a thief coming into his house by night to steal his goods, and slay him, let him be guiltless : also if he kill a footpad in self-defence, let him be guiltless.'

---

611 d 5 Plato, *Laws*, 856 C   612 a 3 Exod. xxii. 1, 4   b 2
Plato, *Laws*, 857 A   c 1 Exod. xxii. 2   c 4 Plato, *Laws*, 874 B

Chapter XLII

'And so if a beast of burden or any other animal kill a man, d Plato except any animals which, when struggling in any contest of the public games, do such a thing, let the relatives prosecute the slayer for murder, and let the suit be decided by the country guardians, such and so many as the relative shall appoint, and let the beast which is condemned by them be slain and cast outside the borders of the country.'

So says Plato. And Moses in anticipation says : 'But if a bull gore a man or a woman and they die, the bull shall be **p. 613** surely stoned, and his flesh shall not be eaten, but the owner of the bull shall be quit.'

Chapter XLIII

The prophetic scripture says : 'Son of man, behold, the house of Israel are all of them become unto Me a mixture of copper, and tin, and iron, and lead, in the midst of the furnace b are they made a mixture of silver. Therefore say, Thus saith the Lord ; because ye are all become one mixture, therefore, behold, I will gather you into the midst of Jerusalem, even as silver is gathered, and copper, and iron, and lead, and tin, into the midst of the furnace, to blow fire upon them, that they may be melted ' : and now hear what Plato says in like manner :

' Listen then to the rest of the fable. For we in the city are of course all brothers, as we shall say to them in telling the fable, but the god, in forming as many of you as are fit to rule, mixed gold c in their composition ; wherefore they are the most to be honoured ; and for all the auxiliaries, silver ; but iron and copper for the husbandmen and other operatives.

' Inasmuch then as you are all of one family, you will generally beget children like yourselves, but sometimes from a golden parent a silver child will be born, and a golden child from a silver parent, and all the rest in this way, one from another.

' And this is the first and chief command that God lays upon the rulers, that they be above all good guardians of their children

---

d 1 Plato, *Laws*, 873 D   d 8 Exod. xxi. 28   **613 a** 4 Ezek. xxii. 18
b 8 Plato, *Republic*, 415 A

PLATO **d** and watch over them with strictest care, to see what metal is mingled in their souls; and if one of their own children be found to be partly of copper or iron, they must by no means have pity on him, but assign to him the rank befitting his nature, and thrust him down either among the operatives or the husbandmen; and if, on the other hand, from these classes there be born a child with a mixture of gold or silver, they will value them and promote them, some to the rank of guardian, others to that of auxiliary: for there is an oracle that the state will be destroyed, whenever the man of iron or of copper has become its **p. 614** guardian.   Do you know any device then by which they might be brought to believe this fable?'

CHAPTER XLIV

THE Hebrew prophecy says to the princes of the people: 'O ye shepherds of Israel, do shepherds feed themselves?   Do not **b** the shepherds feed the sheep?   Behold, ye devour the milk, and the fat ye slay, and clothe you with the wool, and ye feed not My sheep.... And ye sought not the lost, and the broken ye bound not up, and brought not back that which was going astray.'   Moreover the Word of our salvation says: 'The good shepherd giveth his life for the sheep: but he that is an hireling and not the shepherd, whose own the sheep are not, forsaketh them.' Now listen also to Plato, in the first Book of the **c** *Republic*, how he translates these sayings:

'But as it is, Thrasymachus (for we must still look back upon our former statements), you see that though at first you defined the true physician, you did not afterwards think it necessary to keep strict watch over the definition of the true shepherd; but you suppose that, in so far as he is a shepherd, he fattens the sheep not with a view to what is best for the sheep, but with a view to the good cheer, just as a banqueter who is going to have a feast, or on the other hand with a view to selling them, as a money-maker and not a shepherd.   But surely the **d** art of the shepherd is concerned with nothing else than how to provide what is best for the flock over which he is set: for

---

614 a 4 Ezek. xxxiv. 2   b 5 John x. 11   c 2 Plato, *Republic*, 345 C

surely it has sufficiently provided all that is required for its Plato
own perfection, as long as it lacks nothing of the shepherd's art.
Thus then I was supposing just now, that we must necessarily
admit that every government, in so far as it is a government,
looks solely to what is best for that which is governed and tended
by it, in the case both of public and private government.   But
is it your opinion that the rulers in states, I mean the true rulers,
hold office willingly ? '

Chapter XLV

The Hebrew prophecy says : 'From fear of thee, O Lord, we **p. 615**
have been with child, and we have been in pain, and have
brought forth wind [of deliverance] ': and Plato in the
Theaetetus represents Socrates as speaking thus :

' Those who associate with me are in fact affected in the
same way as women in childbirth : for they travail in pain
and are full of perplexity night and day far more than the
women.   And this pain my art is able both to arouse and to
allay.'   b

Chapter XLVI

The prophet Ezekiel said : 'And the hand of the Lord came
upon me, and I saw, and, behold, an uplifting wind came from
the north.'   And presently he said : 'And in the midst was
the likeness as of four living creatures.   And the appearance of
them was as the likeness of a man upon them, and each one had
four faces.   And the likeness of their faces was as the face of
a man : and they four had the face of a lion on the right side ; and c
they four had the face of a calf on the left side ; they four had
also the face of an eagle.'   Hear now what Plato also says in
like manner :

' Now then, said I, let us discuss it with him, since we have
come to an agreement as to the effect of a course of injustice and
a course of justice respectively.

' How discuss it ? said he

---

615 a 1 Isa. xxvi. 18   a 5 Plato, *Theaetetus*, 151 A   b 2 Ezek. i. 3, 5
c 5 Plato, *Republic*, 588 B

PLATO　'By forming in words an image of the soul, that the author of those remarks may know how he described it.

'What sort of image? said he.

'One of such a kind, said I, as the creatures which, according to the legend, were naturally produced in old times, the Chimaera and Scylla and Cerberus, and many others in which several forms are said to have grown together into one.

'So they say, said he.

d　'Mould then, first, a single form of a motley many-headed beast, having a ring of heads of tame and wild beasts, and able to change all these and to produce them out of itself.

'The task, said he, needs a cunning artist: but nevertheless, since language is more easily moulded than wax and substances of that kind, suppose the model made.

'Now then model a second form of a lion, and a third of a man: but let the first be far the greatest, and the second next to it.

p. 616　'These, said he, are easier, and are already done.

'Well, then, join the three in one, so that they may in a manner be grown together.

'They are so joined, said he.

'Now mould around them on the outside a likeness of one of them, that of the man, so that to one who cannot see the inside, but only the outer cover, there may appear to be one single animal, a man.

'The cover is moulded, said he.

'To the man, then, who says that it is profitable for this human creature to do wrong and not for his interest to do right, let us reply, that his assertion can only mean, that it is profitable for

b him by feeding the multiform beast well to strengthen both the lion and the lion's members, but to starve and weaken the man, so that he may be dragged whichever way either of the others draws him, and not to familiarize them at all or make them friendly one to another, but leave them to bite and struggle among themselves and devour one another.

'Certainly, said he, this is what the eulogist of injustice must say.

'On the other hand, then, would not he who says that justice is profitable assert that the creature ought so to act and speak, that

his inner man shall have the chief control over the whole man, Plato
and take charge of the many-headed beast like a husbandman, c
nourishing and taming the gentle parts and hindering the growth
of the wild, having taken the lion's nature for his ally, and by
his common care for all make them friendly to each other and
to himself, and so train them?

'Yes, this again is quite what the advocate of justice has to
say.'

Chapter XLVII

The whole nation of the Hebrews having been divided d
into twelve tribes, Plato also in like manner enjoins by
law the necessity of maintaining the propriety of this
in the case of his own citizens, speaking as follows:

'Let our whole country be divided into twelve parts as equal
as possible, and for each part let one tribe assigned by lot
furnish annually five men as guardians of the public lands and
commanders of cavalry.'

And again he says:

'Let the generals elected propose for themselves twelve commanders of infantry, one for each tribe.'

Chapter XLVIII

As the royal metropolis established long before among **p. 617**
the Hebrews was far from the sea, and situated among b
the mountains, and possessed of very fruitful land; so
Plato says that the metropolis to be founded by him in
his *Laws* ought to be something of this kind.   His words
are as follows:

'But what I am more desirous of asking concerning it is this,
whether it will be a city on the sea-coast or inland.

'The city of which we spake just now, Stranger, is about
eighty stadia distant from the sea.

'How then?   Are there harbours on this side of it, or is it
altogether without harbours?

---

616 d 5 Plato, *Laws*, 760 B   d 10 ibid. 755 D   617 b 6 ibid. 704 B

PLATO   'Nay, on this side, O Stranger, it is as well provided with harbours as possible.

'Wonderful! You don't say so! Further, then, does the country about it produce everything, or does it need anything besides?

'It hardly needs anything more.

'And will it have any neighbouring city close to it?

c   'None at all, and that is why it is to be founded there: for some emigration that occurred in the place in old times has left this region uninhabited for an immense time.

'Well, again? As to hills, and plains, and forest, what proportion has it of each?

'It is like the general character of the rest of Crete.

'Should you call it rocky rather than level?

'Yes, certainly.

d   'It cannot then be hopelessly bad for the attainment of virtue. For if it was to have been on the coast, and with good harbours, and in need of many things more than it could produce, it would have needed some mighty saviour and lawgivers more than mortal, if, under such natural conditions, its moral tendencies were not to be very promiscuous and evil; but as it is there is some consolation in the eighty stadia. It lies indeed nearer to the sea than it should, considering how very well you say it is provided with harbours; nevertheless we may be content even with this. For when the sea is close to a country, its daily neighbourhood is pleasant, but in reality
p. 618 it is very brackish and bitter: for by filling the city with commerce and retail trade, it engenders shifty and faithless habits in men's souls, and makes the city unfaithful and unfriendly both to herself, and likewise to all other nations. Against this, however, it possesses a consolation in producing all things; yet being rocky it evidently cannot be at the same time productive in abundance and in variety. For if it had both, it would provide large exports, and in return be filled with gold and silver coin; than which, I may say, there could be no greater evil,
b taken singly, for a city in regard to the attainment of just and noble sentiments.'

But now after so many proofs as we have hitherto given, let us observe how, after approving the mode of

education among the Hebrews in the passages which we
have mentioned, he deprecates the Greek method,
writing as follows in the tenth Book of the *Republic*:

Chapter XLIX

' LET me say to you in confidence (for you will not tell of me **c** PLATO
to the tragic poets and all the rest of the imitative tribe), all
such poetry seems to be hurtful to the understanding of those
hearers who do not possess an antidote in the knowledge of its **d**
real nature.

' Pray what is the purport of your remarks ? said he.

'I must speak, said I, although a certain fondness and reverence which I have felt from boyhood for Homer restrains my
speech. For of all those charming tragic poets he seems to
have been the first teacher and leader : nevertheless we must not
respect a person in preference to the truth, but, as I said,
I must speak out.

' Quite so, said he.'

Then afterwards he adds:

'As to other matters, then, let us demand no explanation from
Homer, or any other of the poets, by asking why, if any of them
was skilful in healing, and not a mere imitator of medical
language, none of the poets ancient or modern is said to have
made cures, as Asclepius did, or to have left any school of medical
art behind him, as Asclepius left his descendants : and let us **p. 619**
not ask him about other arts, but let them pass.

' With regard, however, to those grandest and noblest subjects
of which Homer undertakes to speak, such as war, and strategy,
and administration of states, and the education of mankind, it is
fair, I suppose, to ask him this question : "My dear Homer, if
in the representation of virtue you were not a mere image-maker
twice removed from the truth, as we defined an imitator to be, but
only once removed, and capable of knowing what pursuits make
men better or worse both in private and in public, tell us which **b**
of our states owed a better government to you, as Lacedaemon

618 c 1 Plato, *Republic*, x. 595 B   d 12 ibid. 599 B

PLATO to Lycurgus, and many both small and great states to many other legislators? What state alleges that you have been a good lawgiver to them and have conferred a benefit upon them? For Italy and Sicily so speak of Charondas, and we of Solon : but who says this of you ? " Will he be able to mention any ?

'I think not, said Glaucon. At least no one says so, not even the Homeridae themselves.

'Well, but what war in the time of Homer is recorded to C have been waged successfully under his command or advice?

'Not one.

'But are there said to have been many ingenious inventions applicable to arts or any other pursuits, as in the case of a man who is wise in practical work, such as Thales the Milesian, and Anacharsis the Scythian?

'Nothing of the kind whatever.

'Well, then, if not publicly, yet in private, is Homer said during his lifetime to have guided the education of any persons, who loved him for his society, and handed down a certain Homeric way of living to those who came after; just as Pythagoras was wonderfully beloved himself for this kind of association, and his successors, who to this day call their mode of life Pythagorean, seem to be in a manner distinguished among other d men?

'Nothing of this kind either is reported of him. For surely, Socrates, the education of Creophylus, the companion of Homer, would appear even more ridiculous than his name, if the stories told about Homer are true : for it is said that in his lifetime he was much neglected by this very man.

'Yes, so indeed it is said, I replied.

'But do you suppose, O Glaucon, that if Homer had been really able to educate men and make them better, as being himself capable not merely of imitating but of knowing such subjects, he would have failed to gain many companions, by p. 620 whom he would have been honoured and beloved? So then Protagoras of Abdera, and Prodicus of Ceos, and very many others are able in private intercourse to persuade the men of their day, that they will not be able to manage either their own house or their state, unless *they* preside over their

670

education, and are so much beloved for this their wisdom as to PLATO
be almost carried about on the heads of their companions. Can
we then suppose that, if Homer or Hesiod was really capable **b**
of improving men in virtue, their contemporaries would have
allowed them to wander about as rhapsodists, and would not
rather have hugged them closer than gold, and constrained them
to stay with them at home, or, if they could not persuade them,
would themselves have escorted them wherever they went, until
they had received sufficient education?

'It seems to me, Socrates, said he, that what you say is entirely
true.

'Then must we not assume that all the poets, from Homer
downwards, only copy images of virtue and of the other subjects
of their poetry, and do not touch the truth? But, as we were
saying just now, the painter, though he knows nothing himself
about shoemaking, will make what seems to be a shoemaker to
those who likewise know nothing about it, but judge by the **c**
colours and forms?

'Yes, certainly.

'In the same way, then, I suppose, we may say that the poet
also by his names and phrases lays on certain colours proper to
the several arts, of which he knows nothing himself except how to
imitate them, so that to others like him, judging only from the
words, whether he speaks about shoemaking, or generalship, or
any other subject whatever, in metre and rhythm and harmony,
it seems to be extremely well spoken.

'So powerful a charm these musical forms have naturally in
themselves: but when stripped of their musical colouring, you **d**
know, I imagine, how poor the poets' works appear when read
in bare simplicity as prose. Have you observed it, or not?

'I have, said he.'

Now these things being so, it seems good to me to go
through some short passages of Plato, wherein he maintains the dóctrine of God and of providence in a more
logical manner, adhering in this also to the Hebrew
dogmas. And first let us observe how he sets forth the
opinions of the atheists.

Chapter L

p. 621 'There are some who say that all things come, and have come,
Plato and will come into existence some by nature, some by art, and
some by chance.

'Do they not say well then?

'Yes, it is probable, I suppose, that wise men are right in
b what they say. Nevertheless let us follow them up, and inquire
what they on that side mean.

'By all means.

'It seems, they say, that the greatest and fairest things are
wrought by nature and chance, and the less important by art,
which receiving from nature the great original works of creation
moulds and frames all the smaller, which we all call artificial.

'What do you mean?

'I will state it still more plainly thus. Fire and water and
c earth and air, they say, all exist by nature and chance, and none
of them by art. And the bodies which come next to these, the earth,
and sun, and moon, and stars, have been created by help of
these elements, which are absolutely inanimate. And being
severally carried by the chance with which they meet from their
several forces, they combine in some intimate way, hot with cold,
or dry with moist, and soft with hard, and all other principles
which by chance were yet necessarily combined with a mixture
of their opposites, and in this way and according to these conditions they have thus created both the whole heaven and all
things in the heaven, and all animals too and plants, all seasons
being produced, they say, from these elements, not by virtue of
intelligence, nor any god, nor art, but, as we say, by nature and
chance.

'And afterwards from these mortal elements art sprang up
later, mortal like them, and has since produced certain play-
d things, not partaking much of truth, but certain images akin
one to another, such as are produced by painting and music
and all their assistant arts. And the arts which do produce
anything good, are those which combine their own power with
that of nature, as for example medicine, and husbandry, and

---

621 a 1 Plato, *Laws*, 888 E

gymnastics. Moreover it is said that political science also co- PLATO operates in some small measure with nature, but for the most **p. 622** part with art: and thus that all legislation allies itself not with nature but with art, the assumptions of which are not true.

'How do you mean?

'In the first place, my excellent friend, these people say that gods exist not by nature but by art and by certain laws, and that these laws differ in various ways, according as the several states agreed among themselves in establishing their legislation: and moreover that what is honourable by nature is one thing, but by law another; and that principles of justice have no existence at all by nature, but that men go on disputing with one another, and are always changing them; and whatever alterations they make are severally valid at the time when they make them, being made **b** by art and laws, and not by any natural principle.

' All these, my friends, are doctrines of men whom the young think wise, both poets and prose writers, who say that conquest by force is the best right. And from this cause young men are assailed by impious thoughts, as that there are no gods such as the law commands them to believe in, and therefore dissensions arise, from their drawing men towards what they call the right life of nature, which is in reality to live in mastery over all others, and not as serving others according to law.

' What a description you have given, O Stranger, and what injury by young men both publicly to states and to private families!'

                                                                    c

Also after other passages he says:

'But now, Cleinias, answer me again, since you too must take part in the discussion. For the man who talks thus probably believes fire, and water, and earth, and air to be the first elements of all things, and these are what he calls nature, and believes the soul to be made out of them afterwards: and this not only seems to be probable, but he really tries to prove it to us by his argument.

' Yes, certainly.

' Is it possible then that we have discovered a source, as it were, of the senseless opinion of all men who ever meddled **d**

---

622 c 3 Plato, *Laws*, 891 C

PLATO with physical inquiries? Consider and examine every argument: for indeed it is a matter of no small importance, if those who take up impious arguments, and lead others, should be found to be using their arguments not at all rightly, but in a mistaken manner. This seems indeed to me to be the case.

'You say well; but try now to explain how it is.

'It is likely then that we shall have to deal with rather unusual arguments.'

Also soon after he adds this:

'Nearly all of them, my friend, seem to have been ignorant both of the nature and of the power of the soul, and especially p. 623 of its origin, that it is the first of all things, created before all bodies, and the chief ruling principle of all their change and rearrangement. Now if this is so, must not the things which are akin to the soul have of necessity been created before those which belong to the body, if the soul itself is older than the body?

'Necessarily.

'Then thought, and attention, and mind, and art, and law must be prior to hard and soft, and heavy and light: and moreover the great primal works and actions must be works of art, as being first of all; and natural products and nature, which they are wrong in calling by this name, must come afterwards and take their beginning from art and mind.

'How wrong?

'By "nature" they mean the generation of the first principles. But if the soul shall be found to be first, not fire nor air, then the soul having been the very first generated would most rightly be said to exist pre-eminently by nature. This is true, if one b has proved soul to be older than body, but not otherwise.

'What you say is most true.'

CHAPTER LI

c 'COME then, if we ought ever to invoke divine aid, let us do so now: let the gods be invoked with all earnestness to come to the demonstration of their own existence; and let us hold fast to this as a sure cable in embarking upon our present argument.

622 d 11 Plato, *Laws*, 892 A

When I am questioned upon matters of this kind, it seems to be PLATO the safest course to answer such questions in the following **d** manner.

' When any one says to me, Stranger, are all things at rest, and nothing in motion, or the very contrary ?   Or are some of them in motion, and some at rest ?   Some I suppose are in motion, I shall say, and some at rest.   Is there not then some place in which the fixed are at rest, and the moving move ?

' Of course.

' And some, I suppose, would move in one single place, and others in more than one.

' Do you mean, I shall say, that the things which are in the condition of rest at the centre move in one single place, just as the circumference of circles revolves, though the circles are said to be at rest ?

' Yes.'

And afterwards he adds: p. 624

' Let us further state it in the following way, and answer ourselves again.   If all things were somehow combined in one mass at rest, as most of such philosophers are bold enough to say, which of the above-mentioned kinds of motion must first arise among them ?

' Of course the self-moving : for unless there were previously some change in themselves, they could never begin to change from any external cause.

' As the beginning then of all motions, and the first which arises in things at rest and continues in things in motion, the self-moving, we must say, is necessarily the eldest and mightiest of all **b** changes ; and that which is changed by another, and itself moves others, is the second.

' Most true.

' Since therefore we have reached this stage of the argument, let us make the following answer.

' What answer ?

' If we see this self-motion take place anywhere in the element of earth, or water, or fire, whether separate or combined, what condition shall we say exists in such element ?

---

624 a 2 Plato, *Laws*, 895 A

PLATO   'Do you ask me whether we shall say that it is alive, when it moves itself?

'Yes.

'It is alive, of course.

c   'And again, when we see soul in any thing, must we admit that this has a different or the same life as the former?

'The same, and no other.

'Stay then, in heaven's name. Should you not wish to understand three points about every thing?

'What do you mean?

'One, the essence; and one, the definition of the essence; and one, the name: and further, that there are two questions concerning everything that exists

'How two?

'Sometimes one puts forward the name alone and asks for the definition, and at another time one puts forward the definition

d   alone and asks the name. Are we then willing now again to make a statement of the following kind?

'Of what kind?

'There is, I suppose, something divisible into two equal parts in other things as well as in number. And the name of this that is divisible in number is "even," and its definition is "number divisible into two equal parts."

'Yes.

'It is something of this kind that I am trying to explain. 'Is it not the same thing of which we speak in either way, whether on being asked for the definition we give the name, or being asked for the name we give the definition, since it is the same thing that we speak of by name as "even," and by definition as "number divisible into two equal parts"?

'Yes, certainly.

'What then is the definition of that which has the name "soul"?

p. 625   Have we any other except that which was stated just now, "the motion which has the power of moving itself"?

'Do you mean to say that the definition "self-moving" implies the same essence as the name, which we all call "soul"?

'That is what I say. And if this is so, do we any longer feel the want of a sufficient proof that soul is the same as the first creative and moving principle of all things that are, and have been, and shall be, and again of all their contraries, since it PLATO has been shown to be the cause of all change and motion ?

'We want no more : but it has been most satisfactorily proved that soul is the oldest of all things, as having been the beginning **b** of motion.

'Is not then the motion which is produced in one thing because of another, but never presents any self-motion, being in reality a change of a soul-less body, of secondary rank or of a rank as far removed as any number by which one may choose to reckon it?

'Rightly so.

'Should we then have said rightly and properly and with the most perfect truth that soul has existed before body, or not, and that body is secondary and comes after soul, as according to nature the governed comes after the governing principle?

'Yes, with the most perfect truth.

'Do we however remember that we admitted in the former part, **c** that, if soul should be found to be older than body, the things of the soul would also be older than those of the body?

'Yes, certainly.

'Then characters, and moral habits, and wishes, and reasonings, and true opinions, and acts of attention and memory must have existed earlier than length, and breadth, and depth, and strength of bodies, if soul was prior to body.

'Necessarily.

'Must we then necessarily admit what follows immediately on this, that soul is the cause of good and evil, and honourable and base, and just and unjust, and of all opposites, if at least we are to assume it to be the cause of all things?   **d**

'Of course.

'Must we not say then that, as soul governs and inhabits all things that move in any way, it governs the heaven also?

'Certainly.

'One soul, or more?   More than one, I will answer for you both.   Not less than two at least we must suppose, the beneficent, and that which has power to work evil.

You have spoken very rightly.

'Well, to proceed. Soul then conducts all things in heaven, and earth, and sea by her own movements, the names of which are

p. 626 will, consideration, attention, deliberation, opinion right or
PLATO wrong, joy, sorrow, confidence, fear, hatred, affection, and all
movements either akin to these or primary, which again taking
with them the secondary movements of bodies lead all things to
growth and decay, and separation and combination, and their
attendant conditions of heat and cold, heaviness and lightness,
hard and soft, white and black, bitter and sweet, and all
b things by use of which the soul, which is divine, taking ever
with her the divine ·mind, conducts all things rightly and
happily, but, if she allies herself with folly, works all the
contrary effects to these. Are we to assume that these things
are so, or have we still a doubt whether they may not be
otherwise?

'By no means.

'Which kind then of soul, are we to say, rules over heaven and
earth and their whole circuit? That which is full of .wisdom
and virtue, or that which possesses neither? Are you willing
that we should answer this as follows?
c 'How?

'If on the one hand, my excellent friend, we are to say, the
whole path of heaven and the course of all things therein has
a nature similar to the movement and revolution and reasonings
of mind, and proceeds in a manner akin thereto, we must
evidently say, that the best kind of soul takes care of the whole
world; and guides it on that best path.

'True.

'But if it proceeds in an insane and disorderly manner, we
must say that the evil soul is guiding it.

'This too is most true.

'What then is the nature of the movement of mind? Now
d in answering this question, my friends, it is difficult to speak
wisely. And for this reason it is fair that I too should help
you now in the answer.

'You say well.

'Let us then not frame our answer as if looking straight at the
sun and bringing on ourselves darkness at noonday, by supposing
that we shall ever see mind with mortal eyes, and know it
thoroughly. It is safer to observe the subject of our inquiry by
looking upon an image of it.

'How do you mean ?

'Of those ten kinds of motion let us take as its image that
which mind resembles; and when I have helped you to remember
this, I will frame our common answer.

'You could not speak better.

'Well then of our former discourse we remember thus much at
least, that of all things we supposed some to be in motion, and
some at rest.

'Yes.

'And again of those that were in motion we supposed some to **p. 627**
move in one place only, and others in more than one, as they were
carried along.

'That is so.

'Of these two motions then that whose course is always in one
place must necessarily move round some centre, like the wheels
on a lathe, and must be in every way as much as possible akin
and similar to the revolving motion of the mind.

'How do you mean ?

'Surely if we say that mind and the motion which goes on in
one place both move according to the same conditions, and in the
same manner, and in the same course, and round the same centres,
and towards the same direction, and according to one law and
one order, like the motions of a top, we should never be shown to **b**
be bad word-painters of beautiful images.

'What you say is very right.

'Well then this other motion which never proceeds in the same
manner, nor according to the same conditions, nor in the same
course, nor round the same centres, nor towards the same direction, nor in one place, nor in proportion, nor order, nor any law,
must be akin to every kind of folly.

'Most truly it must.

'Now then there is no longer any difficulty in saying expressly,
that since soul is that which carries all things round for us, we
must of necessity affirm that the revolution of the heaven is **c**
carried on by the care and arrangement either of the best soul
or of the worse.

'But according to what has now been said, O Stranger, it
would be impious to say otherwise than that soul or souls
endowed with every virtue carry them round.

PLATO   'You have paid admirable attention to my arguments, Cleinias. But listen further to the following.

'What?

'If soul carries all things round, sun and moon and the stars too, does she not also carry round each one of them?

'Of course.

'Then concerning one of them let us argue in a manner which d we shall find applicable to all the heavenly bodies.

'Which one?

'Every man sees the sun's body, but no one sees his soul, nor yet the soul of any animal's body, either in life or after death.   There is, however, much reason to suppose that this nature of soul invests all our bodily senses though utterly imperceptible thereby to us, but is apprehended by mind alone. By mind therefore and by thought let us grasp the following notion of it.

'What kind of notion?

'If soul carries the sun round, we shall not be far wrong in saying that it does one of three things.

'What three?

p. 628   'That either dwelling within this circular body that we see the soul carries it such as it is safely through in every direction, as our soul carries us about every way; or having from some external source provided herself with a body of fire or a kind of air, as some say, she forcibly drives body by body; or thirdly, being herself without a body, but endowed with certain other exceedingly wonderful powers, she so guides his course.

'Yes.

'This so far must be true, that soul directs all things by one or other of these operations.'

b   These then are the statements of our philosopher in the tenth Book of the *Laws*.   But hear how he arranges the same thought in the *Philebus* also:

'All the wise men say with one voice, in reality magnifying themselves, that mind is our king of heaven and earth.   And perhaps they are right.   But, if you please, let us conduct our examination of the general nature of mind more at length.

---

628 b 4 Plato, *Philebus*, 28 C

'Speak in whatever way you please, Socrates, thinking nothing Plato of length on our account, as you will not be wearisome to us.

'You say well. Let us then begin our further inquiries in the following manner.

'How?

'Whether ought we to assert, Protarchus, that all things and this so-called universe are under the guardianship of the irrational **c** and purposeless force, and mere hap-hazard; or that, on the contrary, as those before us used to say, mind and wisdom of some marvellous kind arrange and govern them?

'They are utterly different assertions, O noble Socrates. For the opinion which you mention seems to me to be impious. But the assertion that mind arranges them all is worthy of the aspect of the world, and of sun and moon and stars and the whole circuit of heaven, and for my part I would never speak nor even think **d** of them otherwise.

'Are you willing then that we also should assent to what was agreed on by those before us, that these things are so?   And not merely think that we must state the opinions of others without risk to ourselves, but also share the danger and bear part of the blame, when some clever man asserts that these things are not as we say but all in disorder?

'Of course I should be willing.

'Come then, scan carefully the argument on this subject which now encounters us.

'Only state it.

'Do we discern in the constitution of the world the elements belonging to the nature of the bodies of all living things, fire and water and air and " land," as the storm-tossed sailors say?

'Certainly. For we are verily tossed by storms of perplexity in our present discussions.

'Well then, concerning each of the elements existing in us, **p. 629** take a statement of this kind.

'What?

'That each of these as existing in us is small, and weak, and in no respect at all pure, and without a power worthy of its nature: and having admitted this in one, conceive the same of all. As for instance there is fire, I suppose, in us, and fire in the universe.

PLATO   ' Of course.

' Is not then the part that is in us small and weak, and mean, but that which is in the universe wonderful both in quantity and beauty, and in every kind of power that belongs to fire ?

' What you say is very true.

' Again, is the fire of the universe generated and fed and ruled
b by this fire that is in us, or on the contrary is it from that fire that mine and yours and that of all other animals receives all these services ?

' This question does not even require an answer.

' Quite right. You will say the same then, I suppose, concerning the earth that is here in the animals and that which is in the universe ; and so of all the other elements about which I asked just now you will give this same answer.

' Yes, for who would ever be thought to be in his right mind, if he answered otherwise ?

' No one probably. But now follow the next point. For when we saw all these elements now mentioned combined in one, did we not call it a body ?

' Of course.

c   ' Assume the same then in regard also to this which we call the world : for because of the same process it must be a body, being composed out of the same elements.

' What you say is very right.

' Is then our body nourished wholly from this body, or does this receive from ours its nourishment and all the further services which we just now mentioned in reference to them ?

' This is another question, Socrates, not worth asking.

' But what of the following ? Is it worth asking ? Or what will you say ?

' Say what it is.

' Shall we not say that this body of ours has a soul ?

' Of course we shall say so.

d   ' Whence, my dear Protarchus, did it get a soul, unless indeed the body of the universe had a soul, inasmuch as it has all things the same as our body, and in every way more beautiful ?

' Evidently from no other source, Socrates.

' For surely we do not think, O Protarchus, that those four classes, the finite, the infinite, their compound, and cause which exists as a fourth class in all things,—that this, which Plato in our bodies supplies a soul, and endows it with the art of exercising the body and healing it when it has fallen ill, and makes various arrangements and remedies in various parts, is to be called entire and complete wisdom; but that, though these **p. 630** same elements exist in the heaven as a whole, and in its great divisions, in more beauty and purity, it has not contrived to create in these the nature of all that is most beautiful and noble.

'Nay, this would be in every way unreasonable.

'If then this is denied, would it not be better for us, with that other argument as our guide, to say, that, as we have often said, there is in the world a vast infinity and an efficient limit, and over them a cause of no little power, ordering and arranging years, and seasons, and months, which cause is most justly called wisdom and mind?   **b**

'Most justly indeed.

'Wisdom however and mind could never exist without soul.

'No indeed.

'Will you not say then that through the power of the cause there is implanted in the nature of Zeus a kingly soul and a kingly mind: and in other gods other noble qualities, according to the names by which they like each to be called?'

Chapter LII

'To the man who believes that there are gods, but that **c** they take no heed of human affairs, we must speak words of encouragement. O best of men, let us say, your believing in gods is perhaps due to some divine affinity that draws you towards your kindred, to honour and believe in them. But the fortunes of evil and unjust men both in private and in public life, though not really happy, yet being in the opinions of men vehemently **d** but unduly commended as happy, and wrongfully celebrated both in poetry and in literature of every kind, tend to draw you towards impiety.

'Or perhaps from seeing unrighteous men at last reach old age,

---

630 c 1 Plato, *Laws*, 899 D

PLATO and leave behind them children's children in the greatest
dignities, you are now disturbed, when, after seeing them in all
these conditions or after hearing or having been yourself an
actual eye-witness of some of them, when many terrible impieties
were committed, you see them in consequence of these very deeds
attain from small beginnings to despotic powers and highest
dignities: then it is evident that because of all such things,
though you would not like to blame the gods as the causes of them,
because they are your kindred, yet being at the same time led
astray by false reasoning and unable to be angry with the gods,
p. 631 you have come to this your present condition of thinking that,
though they exist, they despise and disregard the affairs of men.

' In order therefore that your present doctrine may not grow
into a stronger tendency towards impiety, but that, if it be at all
possible, we may be enabled to avert its progress by arguments,
let us add the sequel to the argument by which at the outset we
reached our conclusion against the man who did not believe in
gods at all, and try now to make further use of it. And do you,
O Cleinias, and you, Megillus, take turns in answering for the
b young man, as before. And if any difficult point arise in the
arguments, I will take it from you, and carry you across the river,
as I did just now.

' You speak well: and if you do this, we to the best of our
ability will do as you say.

' But probably it will not be difficult to prove at least this,
that the gods are not less careful over small matters than over
those of great importance. For he was present, I suppose, and
heard what we were saying just now, that being endowed with
every virtue they hold the care of all things as their own
peculiar right.

' Yes, and he listened attentively.

' Let us then examine the next point together, namely what
c virtue we ascribe to them, when we agree that they are good.
Do we say, pray, that prudence and the possession of mind is
proper to virtue, and the contrary to vice ?

' We do say so.

' Again ? That manliness is part of virtue, and cowardice of
vice ?

' Yes, certainly.

'Shall we also say that of these qualities one class is dis- PLATO graceful, and the other honourable?

'We must.

'And of these shall we say that all the bad belong, if so be, to us, but the gods have no part either great or small in such qualities?

'This also every one must admit.

'Again? Shall we class carelessness, and idleness, and luxury as a virtue of the soul? How say you?   d

'How could we?

'Well then on the opposite side?

'Yes.

'The contraries to these therefore we must set on the other side?

'Yes, on the other side.

'What then? Luxurious, and careless, and idle, every one of this character would be in our opinion a man whom the poet declared to be most like to stingless drones?

'Most truly the poet spake.

'We must not say then that god is of a character such as this, which he himself hates : nor if any one attempts to utter anything of this kind must it be allowed.

'Surely not. How could it be allowed?

'If then it is a man's especial duty to manage and attend to some work, but he attends to the great and neglects the small parts of this kind of work, on what principle can we praise such a man without going altogether wrong? Let us, however, look at it thus. Does not he who acts in this way, whether god or man, **p. 632** act on one of two principles?

'What two principles?

'Either as thinking that it is of no consequence to the whole, if the small matters are neglected, or from slothfulness and luxury, if it is of consequence and he neglects them. Is there any other way in which negligence occurs? For of course, when it is impossible to attend to all, there will then be no negligence on the part of one who fails to attend to any matters either small or great, to which a god or any inferior person deficient in power may be unable to attend.

---

631 d 8 Hesiod, *Works and Days*, 303

PLATO   ' Of course not.

b   ' Now then to answer us three there are two, who both admit
that gods exist, though one says that they may be appeased
by prayer, and the other that they are careless of small matters.
In the first place you both say that gods know and see and hear
all things, and that of all the objects of sensation or knowledge
nothing can possibly escape their notice.   Do you say this is so,
or how?

' It is so.

' Well, again?   Can they do all things which are possible for
mortals and immortals?

' How can they refuse to admit that this also is true?

' Moreover we have agreed, all five of us, that they are not only
good but as good as possible.

' Yes, certainly.

c   ' Is it not impossible then to admit that they do anything whatever from indolence and luxury, if they are such as we say?   For
in us idleness is the offspring of cowardice, and carelessness of
idleness and luxury.

' You speak most truly.

' No god then is ever negligent from idleness and carelessness,
for of course there is no cowardice in him.

' Most true.

' If then they neglect the small and trifling concerns of the
universe, the alternative is that they must do this, either from
knowing that there is no need to attend to any such things at all;
d or—what is the remaining alternative except that they know the
contrary?

' There is none.

' Are we then to suppose, O excellent and best of men, that you
mean to say that they are ignorant and, though they ought to
attend, are negligent from ignorance, or that they know they
ought, just as the worst of men are said to do, when they know
that it would be better to do differently from what they really
do, and do it not, because of some yielding to pleasures or pain?

' How is it possible?

' Do not then human affairs partake of the nature endowed with
soul, and is not man himself of all animals the most religious?

' It seems so indeed.

'We say, however, that all mortal animals are the "possessions PLATO of the gods," to whom also the whole heaven belongs.

'Of course.   p. 633

'Now therefore any one may say that these things are either small or great to the gods; for in neither case can it become our owners to neglect us, being, as they are, most careful and benevolent. Besides this let us consider the following point also.

'What point?

'About sensation and power. Are they not naturally opposed to each other in regard to ease and difficulty?

'How do you mean?

'It is surely more difficult to see and to hear the small than the great; but on the other hand it is easier for any one to carry, and hold, and take care of the small and light, than the opposites.   b

'Very much more.

'If then a physician who is willing and able to cure a whole body committed to his charge, attend to the great but neglect the small parts, will the whole do well with him?

'By no means.

'No, nor yet with pilots, nor generals, nor stewards, nor statesmen, nor any such officials, would the many or the great things do well apart from the few or small. For as the stone-masons say, the large stones do not lie well without the small.

'How could they?

'Let us therefore never think that God is inferior to mortal workmen, who, the better they are themselves, finish their proper c works the more exactly and perfectly, both small and great with the same skill; but that God, most wise as He is, and both willing and able to care for all, takes no care at all for those which it is easier to care for, as being small, but only of the great, just like some idle or cowardly workman giving up work because of the labour.

'By no means, O Stranger, let us admit such a thought as this concerning gods: for our thought in that case would be by no means either pious or true.

'It seems to me that we have now at last had quite sufficient discussion with the censorious young man about the negligence of gods.   d

'Yes.

PLATO   'In forcing him at least by our arguments to confess that he was wrong in what he said. I think, however, that he is still in need of some consoling words.

'Of what nature, my good friend?

'Let us persuade the young man by our arguments, that all things have been arranged by the guardian of the universe with a view to the safety and excellence of the whole, and that each part thereof does and suffers its proper share according to its power. And for each of these parts there are rulers appointed over the very smallest portion of action and suffering, by whom perfection is wrought out even to the minutest subdivision.

p. 634   'And as one of these thy own portion, O bold man, small indeed though it is, ever looks and tends towards the whole. But of this very fact thou art ignorant, that all creation takes place for the sake of that whole, in order that the life of the universe may have a constant supply of happy being, created not for thy sake, but thou for the sake of that whole. For every physician and every skilful workman makes every thing for the sake of all, aiming at that which is most for the common good: each part he makes for the sake of a whole, and not a whole for the sake of a part.

'But thou art discontented, because thou knowest not in what way that which is best for thee is expedient both for the whole b and for thyself, as far as the law of your common origin admits. But since a soul combined now with one body, and now with another, is always undergoing changes of all kinds, either of itself or through some other soul, nothing is left for the player to do but to shift the pieces, moving the disposition that is growing better into a more favourable place, and that which is growing worse into the worse place, in order that each may obtain the lot appropriate to its destiny.

'How do you mean?

'I think I am explaining it in the way in which it would naturally be easy for the gods to take care of all. For if one were c to form and to refashion all things without constantly looking to the whole, as for instance to make living water out of fire, instead of so forming many things out of one, or one out of many, that they partook of a first, or second, or third birth, the contents of the ever-changing arrangement would be infinite in multitude. But now there is wonderful facility for the guardian of the universe.

' How do you mean again ?

' In this way. Our King saw that all actions were full of life, and that there was much virtue in them and much vice, and that soul and body had become indestructible, but not eternal, like those who are gods according to law; for if either of **d** these two, soul and body, had perished, there would never have been any generation of living beings; he also discerned that it was the constant nature of one part, the good in the soul, to be beneficial, and of the evil part to do harm; and when He considered all this, He contrived the place of each part so that it would render virtue victorious in the whole being, and vice overpowered, in the fullest and easiest and best manner.

' With a view then to all this, He has arranged what quality each must be constantly acquiring, and what seat and what regions it must inhabit in its transmutations: but the causes of the production of a certain quality He left to the will of each of us. For every one of us becomes for the most part such at each time as is the tendency of his desires and the quality of his soul. **p. 635**

' Naturally so.

' All things therefore which are endowed with a soul are liable to change, as possessing the cause of change in themselves; and in changing they follow the order and law of destiny. If they make only slight changes of moral character, their changes of place are less and on the level surface of their country; but those which make more and worse changes of character are cast down into the abyss, and the so-called infernal regions, all which under the name of Hades and other similar names men greatly dread and **b** dream about, both in life and after they are separated from their bodies. Whenever therefore a soul undergoes great changes of vice or virtue, through her own will and the strong influence of association, if in the one case from communion with divine virtue she becomes eminently virtuous, she passes into an excellent and all-holy place, being carried away to some other and better region than this; but in the contrary case, she transfers her life to places of the opposite kind.

' " Such the just doom the Olympian gods decree," for you, O boy, or youth, who think the gods care nothing for you; namely, that if you are growing worse you must pass on to the worse souls, and if better to the better, and both in life and in **c**

Plato every successive death must do and suffer what it is fitting for like to do to like.

'Neither shall you nor any other ever boast of having got the better of the gods by escaping this doom, which is the most strictly ordained of all dooms by those who ordained it, and of which you must most carefully beware: for it will never lose sight of you. Neither will you be so little as to sink into the depth of the earth, nor so high as to fly up into heaven; but you shall pay the fitting penalty, d whether while abiding here, or after you have passed into Hades, or been carried away into some yet more savage place than these.

'You must also take the same account of those others, those, I mean, whom you saw grown from small to great by unholy deeds or any such practices, and supposed that they had passed from misery to happiness, and thought that in their deeds, as in a mirror, you had seen the universal carelessness of the gods, not knowing in what way their share contributes to the whole. But think you, O boldest of men, that it is of no importance p. 636 to know this, without knowing which a man can never have an idea of life nor be able to join in a discussion thereon, in regard to a happy or unhappy lot.

'If you can be persuaded of this by Cleinias here, and by all this our company of reverend seniors, that you know not what you say about the gods, God Himself will give you good help: but if you should be in need of any further argument, listen to what we say to the third opponent, if you have any sense at all.'

The meaning of this, if not the actual words, has been previously set down very briefly in the oracles of the Hebrews, the thought being comprised in few words. For b the sentence, 'You will neither be so little as to sink into the depth of the earth, nor so high as to fly up into heaven,' must be similar to the passage in David, which runs thus: 'Whither shall I go from Thy spirit, and whither shall I flee from Thy presence? If I go up into heaven, Thou art there. If I go down into Hades, Thou art there.

---

636 b 4 Ps. cxxxix. 7

' If I should take wings, and abide in the utmost parts of the
sea; there also shall Thy hand lead me.' Also this : 'The
heavens declare the glory of God, and the firmament sheweth His c
handy-work.' And again, this in Isaiah : ' Lift up your eyes
on high, and behold who shewed all these things.' Also
this : ' From the greatness and beauty of created things in
like proportion is their first maker beheld.' And this : ' For
the invisible things of Him from the creation of the world are
clearly seen, being understood by the things that are made, even
His eternal power and godhead.' Also this, 'I was envious at
the wicked, when I saw the prosperity of sinners,' seems to me
to have been paraphrased by Plato in the passage, ' You PLATO
must also take the same account of those others, those, I mean,
whom you saw grown from small to great by unholy deeds, or d
any such practices, and supposed that they had passed from
misery to happiness.'

Also all the other passages expressed like these in the
words of the Hebrews anticipated the interpretation
put forth at length by Plato. And so you will find,
by carefully examining each of them point by point,
that it agrees with the Hebrew writings. And by
doctrines of the Hebrews I mean not only the oracles of
Moses, but also those of all the other godly men after
Moses, whether prophets or apostles of our Saviour, whose
consent in doctrines must fairly render them worthy of
one and the same title.

---

b 8 Ps. xix. 1   c 2 Is. xl. 26   c 4 Wisdom xiii. 5
c 5 Rom. i. 20   c 8 Ps. lxxiii. 3

BOOK XIII

CONTENTS

Preface

p. 639

SINCE it has been seen in the preceding Books that the philosophy of Plato in very many points contains a translation, as it were, of Moses and the sacred writings of the Hebrews into the Greek language, I now proceed to add what is still wanting to the argument, and to go b through the opinions expressed upon the several topics by those who were before me, and at the same time to free myself from a plausible charge of reproach, in case any one should accuse me. Why then, he might say, if Moses and Plato have agreed so well in their philosophy, are we to follow the doctrines not of Plato but of Moses, when we ought to do the reverse, because, in addition to the equivalence of the doctrines, the Greek author would be more congenial to us as Greeks than the Barbarian ?

Being loth to make a retort to this charge from respect to the philosopher, I defer this question to a later period, and will first examine those points which I mentioned first. Take then and read what sort of opinion Plato c used to put forward concerning the Greek poets and writers on religion, and how he used to reject all the traditional notions concerning the gods, and thoroughly expose their absurdity.

CHAPTER I

PLATO **d**   'To tell of the other divinities, and to learn their origin, is beyond our power; but we must give credence to those who have spoken in former times, who being, as they said, the offspring of gods, had certain knowledge, I suppose, of their own ancestors. It is impossible therefore to disbelieve children of the gods, even though they speak without certain or probable proofs: but as they declare that they are reporting family histories, we must in obedience to the law believe them.

'On their authority then let the origin of these gods be admitted and stated thus. The children of Gé and Uranus (Earth and

p. 640 Heaven) were Oceanus and Tethys, and their children Phorcys and Kronos and Rhea and the rest of them; and of Kronos and Rhea sprang Zeus and Hera, and all whom we know as their reputed brethren, and still others who were their offspring.'

In exhorting us hereby to believe the fables concerning gods, and the authors also of the fables as being forsooth the children of gods, in the first place by saying that 'the poets are the offspring of the gods,' it seems to me that he scoffingly implies that the gods also had been men,

b and of the same nature as their children.

And next he brings a direct charge against the theologians, whom he had declared to be the offspring of gods, in the assertion which he adds, 'even though they speak without probable or certain proofs,' and by the addition of the words 'as they said.' He seems too to be jesting when he says, they 'had certain knowledge, I suppose, of their own ancestors': and again, 'It is impossible to disbelieve children of the gods.' Also he expressly shows that he speaks thus against his own judgement on account of the laws, by confessing that it was necessary 'to believe them in obedience to the law.'

---

639 d 1 Plato, *Timaeus*, p. 40 D, quoted also p. 75 d 5, and p. 692 c 1

And in proof that this was his meaning, hear how in c
open and undisguised language he reproaches all the
would-be theologians, smiting them in the *Epinomis*
with the following words:

CHAPTER II

'WITH regard therefore to the origin of gods and of living PLATO
beings, as it has been misrepresented by those of former times,
it seems necessary for me in the first place to give a better
representation in the subsequent discourse, taking up again the
argument which I have undertaken against the impious.'   d

That he has good reason for repudiating the theology
of the earliest writers, he shows in the second Book of
the *Republic*, where it is worth while to fix the attention
upon the number and nature of the statements which he
makes concerning the same poets and theologians, from
the traditions handed down from old times concerning the
Hellenic gods, speaking in the very words that follow:

CHAPTER III

'IN the greater fables, said I, we shall discern the lesser also: **p. 641**
for the general character and the effect of both the greater and
the less must be the same.   Do you not think so?   Yes, I do, said
he: but I do not even understand which you call the greater.
Those, said I, which Hesiod and Homer and the other poets used b
to tell us.   For they, I suppose, used to compose and tell, and
do still tell, false stories to mankind.

'What kind of stories do you mean, said he, and what fault do
you find with them?

'The fault, said I, which before and above all we ought to
reprove, especially if the falsehood is unseemly.

'What is this fault?

'When a man in his discourse concerning gods and heroes
misrepresents their nature, as when an artist paints what is not
at all like the things which he may wish to imitate.

---

640 c 5 Ps.-Plato, *Epinomis*, 980 C   641 a 1 Plato, *Republic*, 377 C,
quoted again p. 692 d 9

PLATO   ' Yes indeed, said he, it is right to condemn such things : but
how, and what kind of faults do we mean ?

c   ' In the first place then, said I, it was an unseemly lie that
was told by the author of that greatest fiction about the greatest
gods, how Uranus wrought what Hesiod says he did, and how
Kronos took revenge upon him.   Again, the doings of Kronos
and his treatment by his son, even if they were true, ought not,
I should have thought, to have been thus lightly mentioned
before young and silly persons, but, best of all, to have been
buried in silence; or, if there were any necessity to tell them,
then as few as possible should have heard them in secret, after
sacrificing no mere pig, but some great and scarce victim, so that
very few might have had a chance of hearing them.

' Yes indeed, said he, these stories are mischievous.   Aye, said I,
and they must not be told in our city, Adeimantus; nor must a young
d hearer be told, that he would be doing nothing extraordinary in
committing the worst crimes, nor on the other hand in inflicting
every kind of punishment upon his father if he did wrong, but
would be doing what the first and greatest of the gods did.

' Certainly not, nor in my own opinion are such stories fit to be
told.

' Nor yet, said I, about gods going to war with gods, and
plotting against each other and fighting (untrue as such things
p. 642 are), ought anything to be said, if the future guardians of our
city are to think it most disgraceful to be quarrelling lightly one
with another.   Far less ought we to tell them in fables and on
tapestry about wars of the giants and many other quarrels of all
kinds between gods and heroes and their own kinsmen and
relations : but if we could in any way persuade them, that no
citizen was ever at enmity with a fellow citizen, and that such
a thing was unholy, these are the kind of tales that ought rather
to be told to children from the first by old men and old women
b and by those who are growing elderly, and the poets should be
compelled to make their tales like these.

' The chaining too of Hera by her son, and the hurling of
Hephaestus out of heaven by his father, when he was going to
defend his mother from a beating, and all the battles of the gods
that Homer has invented, must not be admitted into the city,
whether they are composed with or without allegorical meanings.

'For the youth is not able to judge what is allegory and what PLATO is not: but whatever opinions he accepts at such an age are wont to become indelible and unalterable: and on this account perhaps we ought to regard it of the highest importance, that the tales which they first hear "should be adapted in the most perfect manner to c the promotion of virtue."

'Yes, that is reasonable, said he: but if any one were to ask us again which these fictions are, and what fables we mean, which should we mention? Then said I: My dear Adeimantus, you and I are not speaking at present as poets, but as founders of a state: and founders of a state ought to know the moulds in which poets should cast their fictions, and from which they must not be permitted to deviate, nor must they invent the fables themselves.

'Quite right, said he: but that is the very point, what would be the proper models in the case of theology?   d

'Some such as the following, said I; God must of course always be represented as He really is, whether a poet describes Him in epic verse, or in lyrics, or in tragedy.

'Yes, that must be so.

'Is not God then really good, and to be so described?

'Of course.

'But surely nothing good is hurtful? Is it?

'I think not.

'Does then that which is not hurtful do hurt?

'Of course not.

'And does that which hurts not, do any evil?

'No, again.

'Neither can that which does no evil be the cause of any evil?

'How could it?

'Well then, is the good beneficial?

'Yes.

'It is the cause then of well-being?

'Yes.

'The good then is not the cause of all things, but only of **p. 643** what is right, and not the cause of evils.

'Quite so, said he.

'Neither then, said I, can God, since He is good, be the cause

---

642 c 1 From the translation of Davies and Vaughan.

PLATO of all things, as the many say, but of few things that happen to
men He is the cause, and of many things He is not the cause : for
our good things are far fewer than the evil.   And of the good
we must assign no other cause than God, but of the evil we must
seek the causes in other things, but not in God.

'I think, said he, you speak most truly.

'We must not then, said I, allow either Homer or any other
b poet foolishly to commit such an offence as this against the gods,
and to say that

> "Two coffers lie beside the door of Zeus,
>   With gifts for man ; one good, the other ill."

'And to whom Zeus give a mixture of the two,

> "Him sometimes evil, sometimes good befalls";

'And to whom he gives no mixture, but the ill alone,
c
> "Him ravenous hunger o'er God's earth pursues."

'Nor must we admit that Zeus is to us

> "The sole dispenser both of weal and woe."

'And if any one say that the violation of oaths and treaties
wrought by Pandarus was brought about by Athene and Zeus,
we shall not approve : nor that the strife and contest of the gods
was caused by Themis and Zeus : nor again must we permit our
young men to hear how Aeschylus says that

> "God plants in mortal breasts the cause of sin,
>   When He would utterly destroy a house."

'But if any one writes a poem, in which these iambics are
d found, about the sorrows of Niobe, or the calamities of "Pelops'
line," or the "tale of Troy," or any other such events, either we
must forbid him to call them the work of a god, or, if of a god,
then he must invent some such explanation for them as we are
now seeking, and must say that God did what was just and good,
and the others were the better for being chastised.   But we must
not permit the poet to say that those who suffered punishment
were miserable, and that this was God's doing.

'If, however, they would say that the wicked were miserable
p. 644 because they needed punishment, but were benefited by being
punished by God, that we must approve.

---

643 b 3 Hom. *Il.* xxiv. 527 (Lord Derby)   b 6 ibid. 530   c 1 ibid.
532   c 3 Cf. Hom. *Il.* iv. 84 ; xix. 224   c 4 ibid. iii. 275   c 6
ibid. xx. 4   c 9 Aeschylus, *Niobe*, Fr. 160

'But as to saying that God, who is good, becomes the author of PLATO evil to any, we must by all possible means contend that no one shall make such statements in his own city, if it is to be governed by good laws, nor any one either young or old listen to his tales whether in verse or prose, as such statements if uttered would be impious, and neither profitable to us, nor consistent with themselves.

'I vote with you, said he, for this law, and am pleased with it.

'This then, said I, will be one of the laws and moulds in b which our speakers must speak concerning God, and our poets write, That God is not the cause of all things, but only of the good.

'That is quite satisfactory, said he.

'And what then of this second?   Do you suppose God to be a sorcerer, and of a nature to show Himself craftily now in one form and now in another, at one time actually becoming what He seems, and changing His own proper form into various shapes, and at another deceiving us, and making us imagine such transformations in Him; or do you think that He is a simple essence, and most unlikely to go out of His own proper form?   c

'I am not able, said he, to answer now off-hand.

'Well, what do you say to this?   If anything were to change from its own proper form, must it not be changed either by itself or by some other?

'It must.

'Are not then the things which are in the best condition least liable to be altered or moved by another?   As for example when a body is affected by meats and drinks and labours, and every plant by sunshine and winds and other such influences, is it not the healthiest and the most perfect that is altered least?

'Of course it is.

'And would not the bravest and wisest soul be least disturbed and altered by any influence from without?   d

'Yes.

'Moreover I suppose that, on the same principle, among all manufactured things, furniture, buildings, and clothes, those that are well made and in good condition suffer the least alteration from time and other influences?

Plato   'It is so.

'Everything then which is well constituted either by nature or art, or both, admits the least alteration by any other?

'So it seems.

'But surely God, and the things of God, are in every way most excellent?

'Of course.

'In this way then God is most unlikely to take many shapes.

'Most unlikely indeed.

p. 645   'But would He change and alter Himself?

'Evidently, said he, if He is changed at all.

'Does He then change Himself into what is better and more beautiful, or into what is worse and less beautiful than Himself?

'It must be into what is worse than Himself, if He is changed at all: for surely we shall not say that God is imperfect in beauty or goodness.

'You are quite right, said I.   And this being so, do you think, Adeimantus, that any one, whether god or man, would willingly make himself worse in any way?

'Impossible, said he.

'It is also impossible then, said I, that a god should be willing to change himself, but each one of them, as it seems, being as perfect
b as possible in beauty and goodness, remains ever absolutely in his own form.

'It seems to me quite certain, said he.

'Then, my good friend, said I, let none of the poets tell us that

> " Gods, in the guise of strangers from afar,
>   Wander in various forms from state to state."

'Nor let any one slander Proteus and Thetis, nor introduce Hera in tragedies nor in any other poems transformed as a
c priestess begging alms

> " For Inachus the Argive river-god's
>   Life-giving daughters."

'These and many other such falsehoods let them cease to invent.   Neither let our mothers be persuaded by these poets to terrify their children by the tales which they wickedly tell them,

---

645 b 6 Homer, *Odyssey*, xvii. 485   c 2 Aeschylus, *Xantriae*, a
Fragment known only from Plato's quotation
700

that certain gods forsooth wander about by night in the likeness Plato
of many animals of different kinds, lest they be both guilty of
blasphemy against the gods, and at the same time make their
children more cowardly.

' Let them beware, said he.

' But then, said I, do the gods, though they are not capable of **d**
actual change, make us imagine, by their deception and magic,
that they appear in various forms ?

' Perhaps, said he.

' Well then, said I, would a god be willing to lie either by word
or by deed, in putting phantoms before us ?

' I do not know, said he.

' Do you not know, said I, that the true lie, if one may so speak,
is hated by all both gods and men ?

' How do you mean ? said he.

' You know, of course, said I, that no one willingly consents to
lie to the highest and chiefest part of himself, and concerning
matters of the highest importance, but every one fears above all to
harbour a lie there.

' No, I do not even now understand you, said he.

' Because, said I, you think I have some grand meaning :
but I only mean that to lie to the soul about realities, and to be **p. 646**
deceived and ignorant, and to have and to hold the falsehood
there, is what all men would most dislike, and what in that part
of them they utterly detest.

' Yes, utterly, said he.

' But surely, as I was saying just now, this is what might most
rightly be called " a true lie," this ignorance in the soul of the
deceived : since the lie in words is a sort of imitation of the
affection in the soul, and an image produced afterwards, not at
all a pure unmixed lie. Is it not so ?

' Yes, certainly.

' The real lie then is hated not only by gods, but also by men ? **b**
' I think so.

' Well then ? When and in what case is the lie in words
useful, and so not deserving to be hated ? Is it not in dealing
with enemies, and when any of those who are called our friends
from madness or any kind of folly attempt to do some mischief,
it then becomes useful as a remedy to turn them from their purpose ?

PLATO   'Also in those mythical tales of which we were speaking just now, because we know not how the truth stands about ancient c events, do we not make the falsehood as much like truth as possible, and so make it useful?

'It certainly is so, said he.

'For which of these reasons then is falsehood useful to God? Would He lie from ignorance of ancient events by trying to make them like the truth?

'Nay, that would be ridiculous.

'There is nothing of the lying poet then in God?

'I think not.

'But would He lie through fear of His enemies?

'Far from it.

'Or because His friends are foolish or mad?

'Nay, said he, no fool or madman is a friend of God.

'There is no motive then for a god to lie?

'There is none.

'The nature then of gods and demi-gods is quite incapable of d falsehood?

'Yes, utterly so.

'God then is perfectly simple and true both in deed and word, and neither changes in Himself, nor deceives others, either in apparitions, or by words, or by sending signs, either in dream or waking vision.

'I too think it is just as you say.

'You agree then, said I, that this is a second mould in which speech or poetry about the gods must be cast, that they neither are wizards who transform themselves nor mislead us by falsehoods either in word or in deed?

'I do agree.

'While therefore we commend many other things in Homer, we shall not commend this, the sending of the dream by Zeus to Agamemnon; nor the passage of Aeschylus, in which Thetis says p. 647 that Apollo, singing at her marriage,

> "Dwelt on my happy motherhood,
> The life from sickness free and lengthened years;
> Then all-inclusively he blest my lot,
> Favoured of heaven, in strains that cheered my soul.

---

646 d 14 Homer, *Il.* ii. 5 ff.   647 a 2 Aeschylus, *Fragment*, 266 (281)

And I too fondly deemed those lips divine   PLATO
Sacred to truth, fraught with prophetic skill;
But he himself who sang, the marriage-guest
Himself, who spake all this, 'twas even he
That slew my son."

'When a poet says such things as these about gods, we shall
be angry, and refuse him a chorus; neither shall we allow our **b**
teachers to use them for the education of the young, if our
guardians are to grow up devout and godlike, as far as it is
possible for man to be.

'I entirely assent, said he, to these principles, and would adopt
them as laws.'

Thus speaks Plato: and you would find that the
Hebrew Scripture does not contain disgraceful tales about
the God of the universe, nor yet about the heavenly
angels around Him, nor even about the men who are
beloved of God, in any like manner to the Greek theo-
logies; but it contains the model put forth by Plato,
that God is good, and all things done by Him are of the **c**
same character.

Therefore after each of the works of creation that
admirable man Moses adds, And God saw that it was good:
and at the end of all he sums up his account of the
whole and says, And God saw all things that He had made, and,
behold, they were very good. It is also a doctrine of the
Hebrews that God is not the author of evils, inasmuch as
God made not death, neither hath He pleasure in the destruction
of the living: for He created all things that they might have
being, and the generative powers of the world are healthful;
but by the envy of the devil death entered into the world.   **d**

Wherefore by the prophet also God is introduced as
saying to the man who from his own choice had become
evil, Yet I had planted thee a fruitful vine: how wast thou
turned back into the strange vine? And if it should anywhere be said that evils happen to the wicked from God,
it must be understood as an accidental coincidence of

---

c 4 Gen. i. 10   c 6 ibid i. 31   c 9 Wisd. i. 13   d 1 Wisdom ii. 24
d 4 Jer. ii. 21

name, this name being given to the chastisements which
God in His goodness is said to send not for the hurt of
those who are chastised, but for their benefit and profit :
p. 648 just as a physician to save the sick might be thought to
apply bad things in his painful and bitter remedies.

Wherefore in the sacred Scripture also, where it is said
that evils are brought upon men by God, we must apply
the saying of Plato, 'that God did what was just and
good,' even when He was inflicting stern treatment and
what men think evils upon those who so deserved, and
that ' they were the better for being chastised,' not only
according to the philosopher but also according to the
Hebrew Scripture which says, For whom the Lord loveth
b He chasteneth, and scourgeth every son whom He receiveth.

' But we must not permit the poet to say that they
who were punished were miserable, and that this was
God's doing; if, however, they would say that the wicked
were miserable because they needed chastisement, but
were benefited by being punished by God, that we must
approve. But as to saying that God, who is good, becomes
the author of evil to any, we must by all possible means
contend against it.'

Moreover on the point that God is not subject to
change, the Hebrew prophecy teaches as follows, speaking
in the person of God : For I am the Lord your God, and I
c change not. David also, in his description of God, cries
aloud saying : They all shall wax old as doth a garment, and as
a vesture shalt Thou roll them up, and they shall be changed : but
Thou art the same, and Thy years shall not fail.

Wherever the Hebrew writings introduce the Word of
God as appearing in form and fashion of man, we must
remark that they do not represent Him as appearing to
men in the same manner as Proteus and Thetis and Hera,
according to the Greek legends, nor as the gods who
wander about at night in the likeness of animals of many various

---

648 a 10 Heb. xii. 6; Prov. iii. 12   b 2 Cf. 643 d 6   b 12 Mal. iii. 6
c 2 Ps. cii. 26, 27

kinds; but He came, as Plato himself says is sometimes **d** necessary, for the benefit of friends : 'when through madness or some kind of folly they attempt to do mischief, then as a remedy to turn them from their purpose' the advent of God among men is useful.

Now no species of living creatures on earth is dearer to God than man, a species which is of the kindred and family of the Word of God, by whom also man was made rational in the nature of his soul; with good reason therefore they say that the heavenly Word, in His care for a living creature whom He loved, came for the healing of the whole race, which had become subject to disease and a strange kind of madness, so that they knew neither God their Father, nor the proper essence of their **p. 649** own spiritual nature, nor yet God's providence which preserves the universe, but had almost come into the degenerate state of an irrational animal.

And on this account, they say, the Saviour and Physician at His advent departed not from His own proper nature, nor yet deceived those who saw Him, but preserved the truth of both natures, the invisible and the visible.   For in one way He was seen as true man, and in another way He was the true Word of God, not by witchcraft nor by deluding the spectators; for even Plato thought that the divine nature was rightly free from falsehood.

'Therefore God the Word, being perfectly simple and true both **b** in deed and in word, neither changed Himself, nor deceived others, either by apparitions or by words, or by sending signs, either in dream or waking vision.' For all such actions He performed, as became a Physician of reasonable souls, for the salvation of the whole human race, in reality and not in mere seeming, by means of the human nature which He assumed; and thus He bestowed on all of us reconciliation and friendship with His Father through that knowledge **c** of God and true religion which was announced by Him.

---

d 2 Cf. 646 b 5   649 b 1 Cf. 646 d 2

Such then are our doctrines: and with those who say otherwise ' we shall be angry, and refuse them a chorus, neither shall we allow our teachers to use their sayings for the education of the young, if our guardians are to grow up devout and god-like,' as our philosopher also thought to be best.

CHAPTER IV

PLATO d 'FOR though these men themselves consider Zeus the best and most righteous of the gods, yet they acknowledge that even he bound his own father Kronos, because he used wickedly to devour his sons, and that Kronos too had mutilated his own father for similar reasons; but they are angry with me because I proceed against my father for doing wrong, and so they contradict themselves in regard both to the gods and to me.

p. 650 'Is this then the reason, Euthyphron, why I am prosecuted, because when any one says such things about the gods, I am vexed at hearing them? And for this, it seems, some one will say that I commit a great sin. Now therefore if you, who know so well about such matters, agree with them, it seems that I too must of necessity agree. For what else can I say, since I myself admit
b that I know nothing about them? But tell me, for friendship's sake, do you really believe that these things are so?

'Yes, Socrates, and more wonderful things than these, of which the multitude know nothing.

'Do you then also believe that there has really been war among the gods, and dire quarrels and battles, and many other such things, as are told by the poets, and seen in the decorations of our temples by good painters? Especially at the Great Panathenaea the robe that is carried up to the Acropolis is full of such em-
c broideries. Are we to say that these tales are true, Euthyphron?

'Not these alone, O Socrates, but, as I said just now, I will, if you like, relate to you many other tales concerning the gods, which, I am sure, you will be astonished to hear.'

Thus writes Plato in the *Euthyphron*. And Numenius explains his meaning in his book concerning *The Secrets in Plato*, speaking in the way following:

---

649 c 3 Cf. 647 a 12   d 1 Plato, *Euthyphron*, 5 E

Chapter V

'If Plato, after proposing to write about the theology of the **d** Nume-
Athenians, had then been displeased with it, and accused it   nius
of containing tales of the quarrels of the gods among themselves,
and of singing how some had intercourse with their children, and
others devoured them, and how for these things children took
vengeance upon their fathers, and brothers upon brothers, and
other things of this kind,—if, I say, Plato had taken these stories
and openly censured them, I think he would have afforded to the
Athenians an occasion for showing their wickedness again by
killing him, just as they killed Socrates.

'But since he would not have preferred life to truthfulness, and **p. 651**
saw that he should be able to preserve both life and truth, he
gave the part of the Athenians to Euthyphron, a boastful and
stupid person, and especially bad in theology, but represented
Socrates in his own person, and in his peculiar style, in which he
was accustomed to converse with and confute every one.'

Chapter VI

'My dear Crito, your zeal would be most valuable, if it were **b** Plato
consistent at all with right; but if not, the greater the zeal, the
more dangerous.   We must consider therefore whether we ought **c**
to do this or not; for I not only am now but always have been so
disposed as to yield to no other persuasion from my friends except
the reason which on consideration may appear to me the best.

'The arguments then which I used to urge aforetime, I cannot
reject now, because this mischance has come upon me; but they
appear to me of no less force, and I prefer and honour the same
reasons as I did before: and unless we have any better to urge in
my present position, be assured that I shall never agree with you,
not even if the power of the multitude should try to scare us like
children with more bugbears than at present, threatening bonds,
and all kinds of death, and confiscations of goods.   **d**

'What then will be the fairest way of examining the question?
Should we in the first place take up again this argument which
you urge, I mean that concerning men's opinions, whether it was

---

650 d 1 Numenius, a Fragment preserved by Eusebius   651 b 1
Plato, *Crito*, 46 B

PLATO in every case a right statement or not, that we ought to pay attention to some opinions, and not to others? Or whether the statement was right before I was condemned to die, but now has been manifestly proved to have been urged just for the sake of arguing, while it was in reality mere jesting and trifling?

'My own desire then is to consider with your help, Crito, whether the argument will appear to me to be in any way altered, now that I am in this position, or still the same; and whether **p. 652** we shall renounce it or act according to it. Now I think that by those who thought they were talking seriously, it was generally stated in the same manner as I stated it just now, that of the opinions which men entertain we ought to prize some highly, and not others.

'Pray tell me, Crito, do you not think this a right statement? For you, in all human probability, are in no danger of dying to-morrow, and your judgement will not be perverted by the present mischance. Consider then: do you not think it a satisfactory **b** statement, that we ought not to respect all the opinions that men hold, but to respect some and not others? Nor yet the opinions of all men, but those of some, and not of others? What say you? Is not this a right statement?

'Quite right.

'Must we not then respect the good opinions, and not the bad?

'Yes.

'And are not the opinions of the wise good, and those of the foolish bad?

'Of course.

'Come then, what again was said about such matters as these? Does a man who is learning gymnastics with serious attention give heed to the praise and blame and opinion of every man, or **c** only of that one who may happen to be a physician or a trainer?

'Only of that one.

'He ought then to fear the censures and welcome the praises of that one, and not those of the many?

'That is evident.

'He must act then, and practise, and eat and drink in such way as may seem good to the one who is his master and understands the matter, rather than to all the others together.

'It is so.

' Well; and if he disobey that one, and disregard his opinion PLATO
and praises, and respect those of the many who understand
nothing about it, will he suffer no harm?

' Of course he will.

' But what is this harm? And whither does it tend, and to **d**
what part of the disobedient person?

' Evidently to the body, for it does harm to this.

' You are right. And, Crito, is not the case the same with the
rest, not to go through them all? Moreover, in regard to what
things are just and unjust, and disgraceful and honourable, and
good and evil, which are the subjects of our present consultation,
must we follow the opinion of the many and fear it, or that of
the one, if there is a man of understanding, whom we ought
to reverence and fear more than all the rest together? And if we
fail to follow him we shall corrupt and ruin that part of us
which, as we said, is improved by justice and degraded by
injustice. Or is that part of no importance?

' I think it is important, Socrates.

' Well then, if we ruin that part of us, which is improved by **p. 653**
what is healthful and damaged by what is unwholesome, by
not yielding to the opinion of those who have understanding,
is our life worth living when that is ruined? Now this part,
I suppose, is the body, is it not?

' Yes.

' Is our life then worth living with a wretched and diseased body?

' By no means.

' But is then life tolerable for us with that part of us diseased
which is damaged by injustice and improved by justice? Or do
we believe that part of us, whatever it is, which is concerned **b**
with injustice and justice to be more worthless than the body?

' By no means.

' More precious then?

' By far.

' Then, my good friend, we must not care thus at all what the
many will say of us, but what the man who understands about
justice and injustice will say, the one man, and the very truth. So
in the first place this proposal of yours is not right, when you advise
that we ought to care for the opinion of the many in reference to
what is just and honourable and good, and the contrary.'

The word of salvation also says : ‘ Ye seek the glory which cometh from men, and the glory which cometh from the Only One c ye seek not.’ Wherefore we also in our conflicts for religion do rightly in not considering what the many will say of us, but what is the will of One, even the Word of God, whom having in our judgement chosen once for all, it behoves us still to honour even as we did before, and not to change, no, ‘ not even if the power of the multitude should scare us like children with bugbears.’ Now such were the men who bore illustrious testimony of old among the Hebrews.

Chapter VII

PLATO d   ‘ Do we say that we must not intentionally do wrong in any way, or that we ought to do wrong in one way, and not in another ? Or is it neither honourable nor good to do wrong in any way, as we have often agreed in former times, and as I was p. 654 saying just now ? Or have all those our former admissions been scattered to the winds in these last few days, and have we at our age, dear Crito, while holding earnest discourse with one another, been unaware so long that we are no better than children ? Or is it most surely true, as we used then to say, that whether the many affirm or deny it, and whether we are to receive still harder treatment or more gentle than now, nevertheless to do wrong is in every way both evil and disgraceful to the wrong-doer ? Is this b what we assert or not ?

‘ It is.

‘ We must not then do wrong in any way.

‘ Surely not.

‘ Not even return wrong for wrong then, as is the opinion of the many, since we must never do wrong in any way ?

‘ Evidently not.

‘ Well, again ? Ought we, Crito, to do evil or not ?

‘ Of course we ought not, Socrates.

‘ Well then ? To render evil for evil, as the many say, is that just or not just ?

‘ Not just.

‘ For, I suppose, there is no difference between doing evil to men, and doing them wrong.

---

653 b 12 Joh. v. 44   c 6 Cf. 651 c 11   d 1 Plato, *Crito*, 49 A

'You say well.

'Then we must neither do wrong in return, nor do evil to any man, whatever we may suffer from him.   But take care, dear c Crito, lest you may be making this admission against your real opinion.   For I know that this is what very few people think or ever will think.   Between those then who have adopted this opinion and those who have not there is no common purpose, but they must necessarily despise each other when they look each at the others' intentions.   Therefore do you also consider very carefully whether you share and agree with my opinion, and let us begin our deliberations from this point, that it is never right either to do wrong, or to return wrong, or when evil-entreated to retaliate by rendering evil.   Or do you draw back, and not agree d with my first principle?   For I have long been of this opinion, and am so still.   But if you have formed any other opinion, speak and explain.   If, however, you abide by what you held before, listen to the next step.

'I do abide by it, and agree with you.   But say on.

'I go on then to state the next point, or rather I ask whether a man ought to do whatever he has admitted to any one to be just, or falsely to abandon it?

'He ought to do it.'

Compare with this the saying: 'Render to no man evil for evil'; and this: 'Bless them that curse you: pray for them that despitefully use and persecute you, that ye may be the children of your Father which is in heaven, who maketh His sun to rise **p. 655** upon the evil and upon the good, and sendeth rain upon the just and on the unjust.'   Also this: 'Being reviled, we bless; being persecuted, we endure; being defamed, we intreat': a passage b which occurs in our sacred Scriptures.   The Hebrew prophet also says: 'If I rendered evil to them that rendered evil to me.'   And again: 'With them that hate peace I am for peace.'

Chapter VIII

'But you used to boast then that you were not grieved if you c must die, but preferred death, as you said, to banishment; now,

654 d 11 Rom. xii. 17   d 12 Matt. v. 44, 45   655 a 3 1 Cor. iv. 12
b 3 Ps. vii. 4   b 4 Ps. cxx. 7   c 1 Plato, *Crito*, p. 52 C

PLATO however, you are neither ashamed of those fine sayings, nor pay any respect to us, the laws, but are attempting to destroy us; and you are doing just what the vilest slave would do, in trying to run away contrary to the conditions and agreements on which you consented to be our citizen.

'In the first place, therefore, answer us this very question, whether we state the truth in asserting that you have agreed to be governed according to us in deed, and not only in word; or is it untrue? What are we to say in answer to this, Crito? Must we not admit it?

d   'Yes, Socrates, we must.

'Are you not then, they would say, transgressing the covenants and agreements which you made with us, and to which you agreed under no compulsion, nor deception? Nor were you forced to decide too hastily, but for a period of seventy years you were at liberty to go away, if you were not satisfied with us, and if our agreements appeared to you unjust?

'You did not, however, prefer either Lacedaemon or Crete, which you are always saying are well governed, nor any other state, Hellenic nor Barbarian, but you travelled away from **p. 658**(sic) Athens less than the lame and the blind and the cripples. So much more than other Athenians were you in love with the state, and of course with us the laws; for who would like a state without laws? And will you not now abide by your agreements? You will, if you take our advice, Socrates.'

CHAPTER IX

b   'FOR whoever is a corrupter of laws, would be surely thought a corrupter of young and foolish persons. Will you then flee from the well-governed states, and the best-behaved of men? And if you do this, will your life be worth living? Or will you associate with them, and feel no shame in discoursing with them,—and what arguments will you use, dear Socrates? The same as here, that virtue and justice and institutions and laws are the most **c** precious things for mankind? And do you not think that this conduct of Socrates would be unseemly? You certainly ought to think so.

---

658 b 1 *Crito*, 53 C. The Laws still speak

'But you will depart from these regions, and go to Crito's PLATO
friends in Thessaly : for there forsooth is the greatest disorder
and licence.   And perhaps it will please them to hear from you,
in what a ridiculous fashion you made your escape from the
prison, having wrapped yourself in some disguise, or taken a goat-
skin, or something else such as runaways usually dress themselves
up in, and so transformed your appearance.

'But will there be no one to remark that, being an old man,
with probably but a short time left to live, you dared to show so **d**
greedy a love of life in defiance of the highest laws?   Perhaps
not, if you do not annoy any one : but otherwise, you will have
to listen to many things unworthy, dear Socrates, of you.   So you
will live by cringing to all men, and serving them ; and what will
you be doing but feasting in Thessaly, as if you had gone abroad
to Thessaly for a dinner ?   And those fine discourses about justice
and the other virtues, where will they be ?

'But forsooth you wish to live for the sake of your children,
that you may bring them up and educate them ?

'What then ?   Will you take them to Thessaly and bring them
up and educate them there, making aliens of them, that they may
receive this further benefit from you ?   Or if instead of that they
are brought up here, will they be better brought up and educated **p. 659**
because you are alive though not with them ?   For your friends
will take care of them ?   They will take care of them then if you
are gone away to Thessaly ; but if you are gone to the other
world, will they not take care of them, if indeed there is any
good in those who say that they are your friends ?   You must
surely suppose they will.

'Nay, dear Socrates, listen to us who have reared you, and value
neither children, nor life, nor any thing else as of more account
than justice, that when you come to the unseen world you may **b**
have all these pleas to offer in your defence to the rulers there.
For it is evident that to act in this manner is neither in this life
better or more just or more holy for you or any of yours, nor will
it be better for you when you have arrived in the other world.

'But now, if you go hence, you will go as one who has suffered
injustice not from us, the laws, but from men.   But if you go
abroad in this disgraceful manner, returning injury for injury
and evil for evil, transgressing your own agreements and covenants

PLATO **c** which you made with us, and wronging those whom you ought least to wrong, yourself and your friends and country and us, we shall be angry with you while you live, and in the other world our brethren, the laws in Hades, will give you no friendly reception, knowing that you have tried your best to destroy us.'

CHAPTER X

d   'PERHAPS therefore some one will say, Are you not ashamed then, Socrates, of having pursued such a course of life, that you are now in danger of being put to death for it? But I should return a just answer to him, You are wrong in what you say, Sir, if you suppose that any man who is of the least good ought to take into account the risk of life or death, instead of looking at this point alone in his actions, whether he is doing what is just or unjust, the works of a good or a bad man.

   ' For according to your argument the demi-gods who died at **p. 660** Troy would be good for nothing, especially the son of Thetis, who so despised danger in comparison with incurring disgrace, that though his mother, being a goddess, had spoken to him, I suppose, in this way, when he was so eager to kill Hector, O my Son, if you avenge the murder of your friend Patroclus and kill Hector, you will be killed yourself, for, said she,

> "On Hector's fate thine own will follow close."

And after hearing this he cared little for death and danger, but fearing much more to live as a coward and not avenge his friends, he exclaims :

b   "Would I might die this hour"

after inflicting vengeance on the injurious foe, that I remain not here a laughing-stock,

> " Cumbering the ground, beside the sharp-beaked ships."

   ' Think you that he cared for death and danger? Thus, O men of Athens, the case stands in very truth : wherever a man has chosen his own post because he thought it best, or has been placed by a commander, there, in my judgement, he is bound to await the danger, taking no account either of death or of anything else than disgrace.

'If therefore, O men of Athens, when the leaders whom you chose c PLATO
to be my commanders set me in my post at Potidaea, and Amphipolis, and at Delium, or anywhere else, I remained just like any
other where they placed me and ran the risk of being killed,—how
strangely should I have acted, when the god, as I thought and
supposed, ordered me to live the life of a philosopher, examining
myself and others, if in this case, through fear either of death or
anything else whatever, I should desert my post.

'Strange it would be indeed, and then in truth any one
might justly bring me before the court, on the ground that I do d
not believe in the existence of gods, since I disobey the oracle,
and am afraid of death, and think myself wise when I am not.
For to be afraid to die, Sirs, is nothing else than to think oneself
to be wise, when one is not : for it is to think that one knows,
what one does not know. For no one knows about death even
whether it may not be the greatest of all blessings to man ;
but they fear it as if they certainly knew that it is the greatest
of evils. And what is this but that same disgraceful ignorance,
for a man to think that he knows what he does not know ?

'But I, Sirs, perhaps on this subject also differ from most men
in this ; and were I to say that I am wiser than another in any
respect, it would be in this, that, as I do not know enough about the p. 661
state of things in Hades, so I also think that I do not know. But
I do know that to do wrong and to disobey one's superior, whether
god or man, is evil and disgraceful. Those evils therefore which
I know to be evil I shall always fear and shun, rather than
things which, for aught I know, may really be good.

'Therefore not even if you acquit me now, and refuse to believe
Anytus, who said that either I ought not to have come into this
court at all, or that, since I had come, it was impossible to avoid
putting me to death, and told you that, if I should be acquitted, b
at once your sons would all be utterly corrupted by practising
what Socrates teaches—if in answer to this you should say to me,
Socrates, we are not going to be persuaded by Anytus this time,
but we acquit you, on this condition however, that you cease to
spend your time in this speculation, and in philosophy ; and
if you be convicted of doing so any more, you will be put to
death ;—if then, as I said, you were to acquit me on these
conditions, I should say to you, O men of Athens, I honour and

PLATO I love you, but I shall obey the god rather than you, and as long
c as I have breath and power, I shall never cease from studying
philosophy, and exhorting and instructing any of you whom I may
meet from time to time, in my usual style of discourse.'

And a little further on he adds:

' Let us then consider it also in this way, that there is much
reason to hope that death is a good. For the state of the dead is
one of two things: either it is like non-existence and absence of
all sensation in the dead, or, as is commonly said, it is a sort of
transference and migration of the soul from this region to another.
And if there is no sensation, but as it were a sleep in which the
d sleeper sees nothing even in a dream, death must be a wonderful
gain.

' For I suppose, that if a man were obliged to select the night
in which he slept so soundly as to see nothing even in a dream,
and to compare all the other nights and days of his life with this
night,—if, I say, he were obliged to consider and tell us how
many days and nights in the course of his life he had passed more
happily and more pleasantly than this night, I think that not
merely any ordinary person but even the great King himself would
find these better nights very few in comparison with all the rest
p. 662 of his days and nights. If therefore death is something of this
kind, I call it a gain: for thus all time appears nothing more
than a single night.

' But if on the other hand death is like a departure hence to
another place, and if what is said is true, that all the dead exist
there, what greater good could there be than this, O my judges?
For if on arriving in Hades, after having been delivered from
the self-styled judges here, a man shall find the true judges, who
are said to give judgement there, Minos, and Rhadamanthus, and
b Aeacus, and Triptolemus, and all the other demi-gods who were
just in their own lives, will the change of abode be worth nothing?

Or on the contrary, what would any of you pay to associate with
Orpheus, and Musaeus, and Hesiod, and Homer? For my part
I am willing to die many a death, if indeed these things are true,
since I too should find it a delightful occupation there, when-

---

661 c 5 Plato, *Apology of Socrates*, 40 C

ever I met with Palamedes, and Ajax the son of Telamon, and Plato any other of the ancients who has died through an unjust judge- c ment, to compare my own sufferings with theirs,—no unpleasant thing, methinks it would he. And moreover the chief delight would be to spend my life in examining and scrutinizing the dwellers in that world, as I do those here, to learn which of them is wise, and which, though he thinks so, is not.'

We also have the saying: 'We ought to obey God rather than men.' And : 'Be not afraid of them which kill the body, but are not able to kill the soul.' And we know, 'that if the earthly house of our bodily frame be dissolved, we have a building from God, a house not made with hands, eternal in the heavens': . . . and that 'whilst we are absent from the body we are at home with d the Lord,' who also hath promised to all who have hoped in Him, that they shall rest in the bosoms of Abraham and Isaac and Jacob, and, in company with all the other Hebrew prophets and righteous men beloved of God, shall pass the long eternity in a blessed life.

CHAPTER XI

'Of those then who have been killed in war, shall we not say **p. 663** in the first place that any one who died an honourable death was of the golden race?

'Most certainly.

'But when any of such a race as this have died, shall we not believe Hesiod, that :

> "These still on earth as holy daemons dwell,
>   Brave guardians of mankind from every ill" ?

'Yes, we shall believe him.

'Shall we then inquire of the god how we ought to class daemons and deities, and with what difference, and place them b thus in whatever way he may direct?

'Of course we shall.

'And for all time to come, believing them to have become daemons, we shall so serve and worship their tombs ; and these

---

PLATO same customs we shall observe, when from old age or any other cause any one dies of those who have been judged pre-eminently good in life?'

These customs also may fitly be adopted on the death of those beloved of God, whom you would not do wrong in calling soldiers of the true religion. Hence comes also our custom of visiting their tombs, and offering our c prayers beside them, and honouring their blessed souls, believing that we do this with good reason.

But in truth though I have made these selections out of the writings of Plato, any other student might find still more points of agreement with our doctrines in the same author, and perhaps in others also. Since, however, others before us have touched upon the same subject, I think it would be right for me to look at the results of their work also. And I will quote first the words of the d Hebrew philosopher Aristobulus, which are as follows:

CHAPTER XII

ARISTO-   'IT is evident that Plato closely followed our legislation, and
BULUS   has carefully studied the several precepts contained in it. For
p. 664   others before Demetrius Phalereus, and prior to the supremacy of Alexander and the Persians, have translated both the narrative of the exodus of the Hebrews our fellow countrymen from Egypt, and the fame of all that had happened to them, and the conquest of the land, and the exposition of the whole Law; so that it is manifest that many things have been borrowed by the aforesaid b philosopher, for he is very learned: as also Pythagoras transferred many of our precepts and inserted them in his own system of doctrines.

'But the entire translation of all the contents of our law was made in the time of the king surnamed Philadelphus, thy ancestor, who brought greater zeal to the work, which was managed by Demetrius Phalereus.'

Then, after interposing some remarks, he further says:

---

663 d 2 Aristobulus, cf. p. 411 A

'For we must understand the voice of God not as words spoken, Aristo-
but as construction of works, just as Moses in the Law has spoken BULUS
of the whole creation of the world as words of God. For he
constantly says of each work, "And God said, and it was so."

'Now it seems to me that he has been very carefully followed c
in all by Pythagoras, and Socrates, and Plato, who said that they
heard the voice of God, when they were contemplating the arrangement of the universe so accurately made and indissolubly combined by God. Moreover, Orpheus, in verses taken from his
writings in the *Sacred Legend*, thus sets forth the doctrine that
all things are governed by divine power, and that they have had
a beginning, and that God is over all. And this is what he says :

> " I speak to those who lawfully may hear :   d
> Depart, and close the doors, all ye profane,
> Who hate the ordinances of the just,
> The law divine announced to all mankind.
> But thou, Musaeus, child of the bright Moon,
> Lend me thine ear ; for I have truths to tell.
> Let not the former fancies of thy mind
> Amerce thee of the dear and blessed life.
> Look to the word divine, keep close to that,
> And guide thereby the deep thoughts of thine heart.
> Walk wisely in the way, and look to none,
> Save to the immortal Framer of the world :
> For thus of Him an ancient story speaks :   p. 665
> One, perfect in Himself, all else by Him
> Made perfect : ever present in His works,
> By mortal eyes unseen, by mind alone
> Discerned. It is not He that out of good
> Makes evil to spring up for mortal men.
> Both love and hatred wait upon His steps,
> And war and pestilence, and sorrow and tears :
> For there is none but He. All other things
> 'T were easy to behold, could'st thou but first   b
> Behold Himself here present upon earth.
> The footsteps and the mighty hand of God
> Whene'er I see, I'll show them thee, my son :
> But Him I cannot see, so dense a cloud
> In tenfold darkness wraps our feeble sight.   c
> Him in His power no mortal could behold,
> Save one, a scion of Chaldaean race :
> For he was skilled to mark the sun's bright path,
> And how in even circle round the earth

---

664 d 1 *Orphic Fragment*, ii (Hermann)

ARISTO-
BULUS d

The starry sphere on its own axis turns,
And winds their chariot guide o'er sea and sky;
And showed where fire's bright flame its strength displayed.
But God Himself, high above heaven unmoved,
Sits on His golden throne, and plants His feet
On the broad earth; His right hand He extends
O'er Ocean's farthest bound; the eternal hills
Tremble in their deep heart, nor can endure
His mighty power. And still above the heavens

p. 666

Alone He sits, and governs all on earth,
Himself first cause, and means, and end of all.
So men of old, so tells the Nile-born sage,
Taught by the twofold tablet of God's law;
Nor otherwise dare I of Him to speak:
In heart and limbs I tremble at the thought,
How He from heaven all things in order rules.

b

Draw near in thought, my son; but guard thy tongue
With care, and store this doctrine in thine heart."

Aratus also speaks of the same subject thus:

" From Zeus begin the song, nor ever leave
His name unsung, whose godhead fills all streets,
All thronging marts of men, the boundless sea
And all its ports: whose aid all mortals need;

c

For we his offspring are; and kindly he
Reveals to man good omens of success,
Stirs him to labour by the hope of food,
Tells when the land best suits the grazing ox,
Or when the plough; when favouring seasons bid
Plant the young tree, and sow the various seed."

d   'It is clearly shown, I think, that all things are pervaded by
the power of God: and this I have properly represented by taking
away the name of Zeus which runs through the poems; for it is
to God that their thought is sent up, and for that reason I have
so expressed it. These quotations, therefore, which I have brought
forward are not inappropriate to the questions before us.

'For all the philosophers agree, that we ought to hold pious
opinions concerning God, and to this especially our system gives
excellent exhortation; and the whole constitution of our law is

p. 667 arranged with reference to piety, and justice, and temperance,
and 'all things else that are truly good.'

To this, after an interval, he adds what follows:

'With this it is closely connected, that God the Creator of the

---

whole world, has also given us the seventh day as a rest, because ARISTO-
for all men life is full of troubles : which day indeed might BULUS
naturally be called the first birth of light, whereby all things are
beheld.

'The same thought might also be metaphorically applied in
the case of wisdom, for from it all light proceeds. And it has
been said by some who were of the Peripatetic School that wisdom **b**
is in place of a beacon-light, for by following it constantly men
will be rendered free from trouble through their whole life.

'But more clearly and more beautifully one of our forefathers,
Solomon, said that it has existed before heaven and earth ; which
indeed agrees with what has been said above. But what is
clearly stated by the Law, that God rested on the seventh day,
means not, as some suppose, that God henceforth ceases to do
anything, but it refers to the fact that, after He has brought the
arrangement of His works to completion, He has arranged them **c**
thus for all time.

'For it points out that in six days He made the heaven and
the earth and all things that are therein, to distinguish the times,
and predict the order in which one thing comes before another :
for after arranging their order, He keeps them so, and makes no
change. He has also plainly declared that the seventh day is
ordained for us by the Law, to be a sign of that which is our
seventh faculty, namely reason, whereby we have knowledge of
things human and divine.

'Also the whole world of living creatures, and of all plants **d**
that grow, revolves in sevens. And its name "Sabbath" is
interpreted as meaning "rest."

'Homer also and Hesiod declare, what they have borrowed
from our books, that it is a holy day ; Hesiod in the following
words :

"The first, the fourth, the seventh a holy day."

'And again he says :

"And on the seventh again the sun shines bright."

'Homer too speaks as follows :

"And soon the seventh returned, a holy day."

---

b 5 Prov. viii. 22, 27   d 7 Hesiod, *Works and Days*, 770. The
verses that follow are all spurious

'And again :

> " It was the seventh day, and all was done."

'Again :

> " And on the seventh dawn the baleful stream
> Of Acheron we left."

'By which he means, that after the soul's forgetfulness and vice have been left, the things it chose before are abandoned on the true seventh which is reason, and we receive the knowledge of truth, as we have said before.

'Linus too speaks thus :

b
> " All things are finished on the seventh dawn."

'And again :

> " Good is the seventh day, and seventh birth."

'And :

> "Among the prime, and perfect is the seventh."

'And :

> " Seven orbs created in the starlit sky
> Shine in their courses through revolving years." '

c Such then are the statements of Aristobulus. And what Clement has said on the same subject, you may learn from the following :

CHAPTER XIII

'BUT we must add the further evidence, and show now more clearly the plagiarism of the Greeks from the Barbarian philosophy. For the Stoics say that God, as also the soul of course, is in essence body and spirit. All this you will find directly stated in their writings. For I do not wish you now to consider whether their allegorical interpretations, as the Gnostic verity delivers them, show one thing and mean another, like clever wrestlers. But what they say is that God extends through all being, while we call Him simply the Creator, and Creator by a word.

p. 669 'Now they were misled by what is said in Wisdom : "Yea, she pervadeth and penetrateth all things by virtue of her purity" : since

---

668 d 1 Clement of Alexandria, *Miscellany*, v. 14, p. 699 Potter
669 a 1 Wisdom vii. 24

they did not understand that this is said of that wisdom which CLEMENT was the first-created of God. Yes, say they; but the philosophers, Stoics as well as Plato and Pythagoras and even Aristotle the Peripatetic, suppose matter to be one of the first principles, and do not assume one only principle.

'Let them know, then, that the so-called matter, which is said by them to be without quality or shape, has been previously described more boldly by Plato as "Not-being"; and is it per- **b** chance from knowing that the real and true first cause is one, that he speaks so mysteriously in the *Timaeus* in these very words?

'Now therefore let my position be stated as follows : "Of the first principle or principles of all things, or in whatever way it is thought right to describe them, I must not speak at present, for no other reason than this, that it is difficult to explain my opinions according to our present form of discourse."

'And, besides, that prophetic expression, "The earth was invisible and without order," has given them suggestions of a material **c** essence. In fact, the interposition of "chance" occurred to Epicurus from having misunderstood the language of the following passage : "Vanity of vanities, all is vanity." To Aristotle it occurred to bring Providence down only so far as to the moon, from this Psalm : "Thy mercy, O LORD, is in the heaven, and Thy truth reacheth unto the clouds." For before the coming of the Lord the meaning of the prophetic mysteries was not as yet revealed.

'Again the chastisements after death and the punishment by fire were stolen from our Barbarian philosophy both by every Muse of **d** poetry and even by the Greek philosophy. Plato, for instance, in the last Book of the *Republic* says in express terms : "Hereupon certain fierce men of fiery aspect, who were standing by and understood the sound, seized and led away some of them separately; but Aridaeus and the rest they bound hand and foot and head together, and threw them down, and flayed them, and dragged them along the road outside, carding them like wool on thorns." For his "fiery men" are meant to indicate angels, who seize the unrighteous and punish them. "Who maketh," says the Scripture, "His angels spirits, and His ministers a flaming fire."   **p. 670**

'Now it follows upon this that the soul is immortal. For that

b 4 Plato, *Timaeus*, 48 C   b 9 Gen. i. 2   c 4 Eccles. i. 2   c 6 Ps. (xxxv) xxxvi. 5   d 3 Plato, *Republic*, 615 E   d 9 Ps. (ciii) civ. 4

CLEMENT which is undergoing punishment or correction, being in a state of sensation, must be living, though it be said to suffer. Again, does not Plato know also rivers of fire, and the deep of the earth, called by the Barbarians Gehenna, which he calls poetically Tartarus, and introduces Cocytus, and Acheron, and Phlegethon, and names of this kind, as places of punishment for correctional training? And representing, according to the Scripture, the angels of the least of the little ones which behold the face of God, and

b also His supervision extended to us through the angels set over us, he does not hesitate to write:

'"After all the souls have chosen their lives, according to their lot, they went forward in order to Lachesis, and she sent with each the genius of his choice, to be the guardian of his life, and the fulfiller of his chosen destiny."

'Perhaps also something of this kind was intimated to Socrates by his daemon.

'Nay more, the philosophers borrowed from Moses their doctrine that the world was created, and Plato has said expressly:

'"Was it that the world had no beginning of creation, or has it been created at first from some beginning? For it is visible, and tangible, and

c has a body."

'And again, when he says: "To find therefore the Maker and Father of this universe is a hard task," he not only shows that the world has been generated, but also indicates that it was generated from Him, as from one alone, and sprang up out of non-existence. The Stoics also suppose that the world has been created.

'The devil too, so often mentioned by the Barbarian philosophy, the prince of the daemons, is described by Plato, in the tenth Book of the *Laws*, as being a malignant soul, in the following words:

d "As then a soul directs and inhabits all things that move in every direction, must we not say that it also directs the heaven?

'"Of course.

'"One soul or more? More, I will answer for both of you. Less than two surely we must not suppose, one that does good, and the other that has power to work evil."

'In like manner also he writes in the *Phaedrus* thus: "There

---

670 a 9 Matt. xviii. 10   b 3 Plato, *Republic*, 620 D   b 11 Plato, *Timaeus*, 28 B   c 2 ibid. 28 C   d 1 Plato, *Laws*, 896 D   d 7 Plato, *Phaedrus*, 240 A

are indeed other evils, but with most of them some daemon has mingled CLEMENT
an immediate pleasure." And further in the tenth Book of the *Laws*
he directly expresses that thought of the Apostle : "Our wrestling
is not against blood and flesh, . . . but against the spiritual powers of the
hosts in heaven," when he writes thus :

' "For since we agreed among ourselves that the heaven is full of many **p. 671**
goods, and full also of evils, and of more evils than goods, such a conflict
as this, we say, is immortal, and requires wonderful caution."

'Again, the Barbarian philosophy knows one intelligible
world, and another sensible, the one an archetype, and the
other an image of that fair model; and the former it ascribes
to unity, as being perceptible to thought only, but the sensible
to the number six : for among the Pythagoreans six is called
marriage, as being a generative number. And in the unity it sets **b**
an invisible heaven, and a holy earth, and intelligible light.
For "In the beginning," says the Scripture, "God created the heaven
and the earth : and the earth was invisible." Then it adds, "And
God said, Let there be light, and there was light." But in the
creation of the sensible world He framed a solid heaven (and
what is solid is sensible), and a visible earth, and a light that
is seen. Do you not think that from this passage Plato was led
to leave the "ideas" of living things in the intelligible world,
and to create the sensible forms according to the various kinds of
that intelligible world?

'With good reason, therefore, Moses says that the body was **c**
formed of earth, what Plato calls " an earthly tabernacle," but
that the reasonable soul was breathed by God from on high into
man's face : for they say that the ruling faculty is seated in this
part, and interpret thus the accessory entrance of the soul
through the organs of sense in the first-formed man; for which
reason also man, they say, is made " after the image and likeness
of God."

'For the image of God is the divine and royal Word, the
impassible man; and an image of that image is the human mind.
But if you will admit another name for the growing likeness, **d**
you will find it called in Moses a following of God : for he says,
"Walk after the LORD your God, . . . and keep His commandments."
And all the virtuous are, I suppose, followers and servants of God.

---

d 10 Eph. vi. 12   671 a 1 Plato, *Laws*, 906 A   b 3 Gen. i. 1
b 4 ibid. 3   c 7 Cf. Gen. i. 26   d 3 Deut. xiii. 4

CLEMENT   ' Hence the Stoics have said that the end of philosophy is to live
according to the guidance of nature, while Plato says it is to
become like God, as we showed in the second *Miscellany*; and
Zeno the Stoic having received it from Plato, and he from the
Barbarian philosophy, says that all good men are friends one of
p. 672 another.   For in the *Phaedrus* Socrates says that "Fate has not
ordained that the wicked should be a friend to the wicked; nor the good
fail to be a friend to the good."

'This he also fully showed in the *Lysis*, that friendship can
never be preserved amid injustice and wickedness.   The Athenian
Stranger too says in like manner, "That it is conduct pleasing to
God and like Him, and has one ancient saying in its favour, when 'like
loves like' if it be in measure, but things beyond measure agree neither
with things beyond nor with things within measure.   And God must be
to us the measure of all things."

'Then lower down Plato adds again :

b   ' " For indeed every good man is like every other good man, and conse-
quently being also like God, he is beloved both by every good man and
by God."   Arrived at this point, I am reminded of the following
passage, for at the end of the *Timaeus* he says that " one should
assimilate that which perceives to that which is perceived, according to
its original nature, and by thus assimilating them attain the end of that
life which is proposed by the gods to men as the best both for the
present time and for that which is to follow."

And after a few sentences he adds :

'That we are brethren as belonging to one God and one
teacher, Plato evidently declares in the following terms :

" For ye in the city are all brothers, as we shall say to them in telling
c the fable; but God, in forming as many of you as are fit to rule, mixed
gold in their composition, wherefore they are the most to be honoured :
and for all the auxiliaries silver, but iron and copper for the husbandmen
and other operatives."

'Whence, he says, it has necessarily come to pass that some
embrace and love those things which are objects of knowledge,
and others those which are matters of opinion.   For perhaps
he is prophesying of that elect nature which desires knowledge ;
d unless in assuming three natures he, as some supposed, is

672 a 1 Plato, *Phaedrus*, 255 B   **a** 4 Plato, *Lysis*, 214 C   **a** 6
Laws, 716 C   **b** 4 Plato, *Timaeus*, 90 D   **b** 10 Clement of Alexandria, *Miscellany*, v. 14, p. 706 Potter   **b** 12 Plato, *Republic*, 415 A

describing three forms of polity, that of the Jews silver, that of CLEMENT
the Greeks the third, and that of the Christians in whom there
has been infused the royal gold, the Holy Spirit.

'Also he exhibits the Christian life when writing word for
word in the *Theaetetus* :

"Let us speak then of the leaders ; for why should one talk about those
who spend their time to no good purpose in philosophy ? But these
leaders, I suppose, neither know the way to the Agora, nor where the
court of justice is, or the council-chamber, or any other public assembly
of the State; and laws, and decrees whether read or written, they
neither see nor hear. The strivings of political clubs, and meetings, to **p. 673**
obtain offices, and revellings with flute-girls are practices which do not
occur to them even in dreams. And what has happened well or ill in
the city, or what evil has come to any one from his ancestors, is less
known to them than, as the proverb says, the number of gallons in the
sea. As to all these things he knows not even that he does not know
them : for in fact it is his body only that has its place and home in
the city, but the man himself 'is flying,' as Pindar says, 'underneath the
earth' and above the heaven, studying the stars, and scrutinizing every
nature on all sides."   **b**

'Again, with the Lord's saying, "Let your yea be yea, and your
nay, nay," we must compare this : "But it is by no means right
for me to admit a falsehood, and to suppress a truth." Also
with the prohibition of swearing agrees this saying in the tenth
Book of the *Laws* : "Let there be no praising nor swearing about
anything."   And to speak generally, Pythagoras and Socrates
and Plato, when they say that they hear God's voice, while
carefully contemplating the constitution of the universe as made
by God and held together without interruption, must have heard **c**
Moses say, in describing the word of God as a deed, "He spake,
and it was done."

'Also taking their stand upon the formation of the man out
of dust, the philosophers on every occasion proclaim that the
body is of earth, and Homer does not shrink from putting it in
the light of a curse :

"But may all ye to earth and water turn."

Just as Esaias says : "And tread them down as clay."

'Callimachus too writes expressly :   **d**

---

d 7 *Theaetetus*, 173 C   673 a 8 Pindar, *Fr.* (226), 123   b 2 Matt. v. 37
b 3 *Theaetetus*, 151 D   b 6 *Laws*, 917 C   c 2 Ps. (xxxii) xxxiii. 9   c 8
Hom. *Il.* vii. 99   c 9 Isa. x. 6

CLEMENT

> " It was that year in which the wingèd tribe
> And they that swim the sea or tread the earth
> Spake like the clay Prometheus called to life."

' And again the same poet said :

> " If thou wast fashioned by Prometheus' hand,
> And not of other clay."

' Hesiod also says of Pandora :

> " Renowned Hephaestus bade he with all speed
> Mix earth with water, and therein infuse
> The voice and mind of man."

p. 674   ' Now as the Stoics define nature as an artistic fire which proceeds systematically to generation; so by the Scripture God and His Word are represented figuratively by fire and light. Again, is not Homer also alluding to the separation of the water from the land, and the clear discovery of the dry land, when he says of Tethys and Oceanus :

> " For now have they long time
> From love and from the marriage-bed abstained "?

' Again, the most learned among the Greeks ascribe to God power in all things : thus Epicharmus, who was a Pythagorean, says :

b   " Nothing e'er from God escapeth; this behoves thee well to know;
> He o'erlooks us closely; nothing is to God impossible."

' The lyric poet too :

> " From thickest darkness of the night
> God can call forth the purest light,
> Or with dark clouds at will o'erlay
> The brightness of the orient day."

' He who alone can turn the present day into night, the poet says, is God.

' Aratus also, in the book entitled *Phaenomena*, after saying :

c   " From Zeus begin the song, nor ever leave
> His name unsung, whose godhead fills all streets,
> All thronging marts of men, the boundless sea,
> And all its ports ; whose aid all mortals need,"

' adds :

> " For we his offspring are,"

---

673 d 2 Callimachus, *Fr.* 87   d 6 ibid. 133   d 9 Hesiod, *Works and Days*, 60   **674 a** 1 Diog. Laertius, vii. 156   a 7 Hom. *Il.* xiv. 206   b 1 Epicharmus, *Fr.* 297 (Mullach, i. p. 146)   b 4 Pindar, *Fr.* 106 (3)   c 1 Aratus, *Phaenomena*, 1

as it were by creation,

> ... "and kindly he
> Reveals to man good omens of success.
> In heaven he set those guiding lights, and marked
> Their several course ; and for the year he wove
> The circlet of the stars, to show to man
> What best the seasons suit, that all things set
> In order due may grow. Him ever first,
> Him last our prayers invoke. Hail, Father, hail!
> Wonder and joy and blessing of mankind."

d

'Also before him Homer, in the account of the shield made by Hephaestus, describes the creation of the world in accordance with Moses, saying:

> "Thereon were figured earth, and sky, and sea,
> And all the signs that crown the vault of heaven."

p. 675

'For the Zeus who is celebrated in all poems and prose compositions, carries up our thought to God.

'Then, further, Democritus writes that some few of mankind are in the light, so to say, "who lift up their hands to that place which we Greeks now call the air, and mythically speak of all as Zeus ; and he knows all things, and gives and takes away, and he is king of all." With deeper mystery the Boeotian Pindar, as being a Pythagorean, teaches :

b

> "One race of men and one of gods,
> Both from one mother draw our breath,"

that is, from matter : he teaches also that the Creator of this world is one, whom he calls,

> "Father, of all artificers the best,"

who has also provided the means of advancement to divinity according to merit.

'For I say nothing as to Plato, how he plainly appears in the Epistle to Erastus and Coriscus to set forth Father and Son somehow from the Hebrew Scriptures, when he exhorts them in these words "to invoke both with a graceful earnestness, and with the culture which is akin to such earnestness, the God who is the cause of all, and also to invoke the Father and Lord of Him who is ruler and cause, whom (says he) ye shall know, if ye study philosophy aright."

c

---

675 a 1 Hom. *Il.* xviii. 483 (Lord Derby's translation)   a 6 Cf. Clem.
Al. *Protrept.* c. vi. p. 59 Potter   b 2 Pindar, *Nem.* vi. 1   b 6 *Paean.*
Fr. vi   b 12 Pseudo-Plato, *Epistle*, vi. 323 C

729

CLEMENT   ' Also Zeus in his harangue in the *Timaeus* calls the Creator Father, in these words :

"Ye gods and sons of gods, whose Father I am, and Creator of the works." So that also when he says, "Around the King of all are all things, and for His sake they all are, and that is the cause of all things beautiful ; and around a Second are the secondary things, and around a Third the tertiary," I understand it in no other way than that

d the Holy Trinity is signified. For I think that the Holy Spirit is the third, and the Son the second, "by whom all things were made" according to the will of the Father.

' The same author, in the tenth Book of the *Republic*, mentions Er, the son of Armenius, a Pamphylian by birth, who is Zoroaster. At least Zoroaster himself writes, " Zoroaster the son of Armenius, a Pamphylian by birth, having been slain in war, writes down here all things which when in Hades I learned from the gods." Now Plato says that this Zoroaster when laid upon the funeral pile

p. 676 on the twelfth day after death came to life again. Perhaps he alludes not to the resurrection, but to the circumstance that the way for souls to their reception above is through the twelve signs of the Zodiac, and Plato himself says that their way of return to birth is the same. In this way we must understand also that the labours of Hercules were said to be twelve, after which the soul obtains its release from this world entirely. Empedocles also I do not pass over, who mentions the restitution of all things in merely physical language, saying that there will at some time be a change into the essence of fire.

b   ' And most plainly is Heracleitus of Ephesus of this opinion, who maintained that there is one world eternal, and another that perishes, namely, the world in its orderly arrangement, which he knew to be no other than a certain condition of the former. But that he knew the world, which consisting of all being is eternally of a certain quality, to be eternal, he makes evident in speaking thus :

"The world which is the same for all was made neither by any god nor man, but always was, and is, and shall be, an everliving fire, kindled in measure, and in measure extinguished."

c   ' His doctrine was that the world was created and perishable,

---

675 c 5 *Timaeus*, 41 A   c 6 Pseudo-Plato, *Epistle*, ii. 312 E   d 4
Plato, *Republic*, 614 B   676 b 8 Heracleitus, *Fr.* 27 (Mullach)

as is shown by what he adds : "The transmutations of fire are first CLEMENT
sea, and of sea one half becomes earth and the other half lightning."
For virtually he says, that by God the Word, who administers
the universe, fire is changed through air into moisture, the seed
as it were of the cosmical arrangement; and this moisture he
calls sea.   And out of this again heaven and earth arise, and all
things therein contained.

'How the world is again taken back into the primitive essence,
and destroyed by fire, he clearly shows in these words : "The sea
is spread abroad, and is measured to the same proportion as it was before
it became earth."   In like manner concerning the other elements d
the same is to be understood.

'Doctrines similar to this are taught also by the most celebrated
of the Stoics in their discussions concerning a conflagration and
re-arrangement of the world's order, and concerning both the
world and man in their proper quality, and the continuance of
our souls.   Again, Plato in the seventh Book of the *Republic*
has called our day here a "darkness visible," because, I suppose,
of the world-rulers of this darkness; and the soul's entrance into
the body he has called "sleep" and "death," in the same manner
as Heracleitus.   And is this, perhaps, what the Holy Spirit,
speaking by David, foretold concerning our Saviour: "I laid me
down and slept : I awaked, for the LORD will sustain me."   For he **p. 677**
figuratively calls not only the Resurrection of Christ an
awaking from sleep, but also the Lord's coming down into flesh
a sleep.

'For instance, the same Saviour gives the exhortation "Watch,"
as much as to say, study to live, and try to keep the soul independent of the body.   Also in the tenth Book of the *Republic*,
Plato speaks prophetically of the Lord's day in these words :

"But when those in the meadow had each been there seven days, they
were obliged on the eighth to arise thence and proceed on their journey, **b**
and arrive on the fourth day."

'By the meadow, therefore, we must understand the fixed
sphere, as a quiet and pleasant place, and an abode of the saints;

---

c 2 Heracleitus, *Fr.* 28 (Mullach)   c 7 ibid. *Fr.* 29   d 8 Plato,
Republic, 521 C ; Eph. vi. 12   d 10 Plato, *Phaedo*, 95 D   d 12
Ps. iii. 5   **677 a** 8 Plato, *Republic*, 616 B

CLEMENT and by the seven days, each motion of the seven planets, and the whole effective device which speeds them to their final rest. The journey after passing the planets leads to heaven, that is to the eighth motion and eighth day; and when he says that the souls are four days on the journey, he indicates their passage through the four elements.

c   ' Moreover, the Greeks as well as the Hebrews recognize the holiness of the seventh day, by which the cycle of the whole world of animals and plants is regulated. Hesiod, for instance, speaks of it thus :

> " The first, the fourth, the seventh a holy day."

' And again :

> " And on the seventh again the sun shines bright."

' Homer too :

> " And soon the seventh returned, a holy day."

' And again :

d   " The seventh day was holy."

' And again :

> " It was the seventh day, and all was done."

' And again :

> " And on the seventh day the baleful stream
> Of Acheron we left."

' Moreover, the poet Callimachus writes :

> " All things were finished on the seventh dawn."

' And again :

> " Good is the seventh day, and seventh birth."

p. 678   ' And :

> " Among the prime, and perfect is the seventh."

' Also :

> " Seven orbs created in the starlit sky
> Shine in their courses through revolving years."

' The *Elegies* of Solon also make the seventh day very divine.

b   ' And again : Is it not like the Scripture, which says, " Let us

---

677 d See p. 667 d   678 a 6 Solon *Fr.* **xiv.** (Hermann, *Poet. Min. Gr.* iii. 139)   b 1 Wisdom ii. 12

732

take away from us the righteous man, because he is of disservice to us," CLEMENT when Plato, all but foretelling the dispensation of salvation, speaks thus in the second Book of the *Republic*: "In these circumstances the just man will be scourged, fettered, both eyes torn out; and at last, after suffering every kind of torture, he will be crucified"? Antisthenes too, the Socratic, paraphrases that prophetic Scripture, "To whom did ye liken Me? saith the LORD," when he says that "God is like to none, wherefore no man can come to know Him from an image." The like thoughts Xenophon the Athenian **c** expresses in these words: "That He who moves all things, and is Himself at rest, is a great and mighty Being, is manifest: but what He is in form, is unknown. Neither, indeed, does the sun, which appears to shine on all, seem to allow himself to be seen: but if any one gazes impudently upon him, he is deprived of sight." The Sibyl had said before:

> "What flesh can e'er behold with mortal eyes
> The immortal God, who dwells above the skies?
> Or who of mortal birth can stand and gaze   **d**
> With eyes unshrinking on the sun's fierce rays?"

'Rightly, therefore, does also Xenophanes of Colophon, when teaching that God is one and incorporeal, add this:

> "One God there is, supreme o'er gods and men,
> Not like in form to mortals, nor in mind."

'And again:

> "But mortals fondly deem that gods are born,
> Have voice, and form, and raiment like their own."   **p. 679**

'And again:

> "If then the ox and lion had but hands
> To paint and model works of art, like man,
> The ox would give his god an oxlike shape,
> The horse a figure like his own would frame,
> And each would deify his kindred form."   **b**

'Again, then, let us listen to Bacchylides, the lyric poet, when he says concerning the divine nature:

> "No taint of foul disease can them assail,
> No bane annoy, unlike in all to man."

---

b 4 Plato, *Republic*, 361 E; see notes on p. **583 d**   b 8 Isa. xl. 25
c 2 Xenophon, *Memorabilia*, iv. iii. 13, 14   c 8 Sibylline Oracles,
Fr. i. 10–13   d 5 Xenophanes, *Fr.* i. 1 (Mullach)   d 8 ibid. *Fr.* v
679 a 3 ibid. *Fr.* vi   b 4 Bacchylides, *Fr.* 60 (Kenyon)

CLEMENT   'Hear also Cleanthes, the Stoic, who has written as follows in a certain poem concerning the Deity:

> " Askest thou what good is? List then to me.
c
> Good is well ordered, holy, just, devout,
> Self-mastering, useful, honourable, right,
> Grave, self-dependent, ever full of help,
> Unmoved by fear, by sorrow, and by pain,
> Beneficent, well pleasing, friendly, safe,
> Of good report, acknowledged, and esteemed,
> Free from vainglory, careful, gentle, strong,
> Deliberate, blameless, during to the end."

d   'The same author, tacitly accusing the idolatry of the multitude, adds this:

> " Poor slave is he who to opinion looks,
> In hope, forsooth, some honour thence to gain."

'We must not, therefore, any longer think of the divine nature according to the opinion of the multitude: for, as Amphion says in the *Antiope*:

> " Never can I believe that secretly,
> Disguised in fashion of some wicked knave,
> Zeus visited thy bed in human form."

p. 680   'But Sophocles writes in straightforward language:

> " For this man's mother was by Zeus espoused,
> Not in a shower of gold, nor in disguise
> Of feathered swan, as when he pregnant made
> Fair Leda, but complete in manly form."

'Then farther down he added:

> "Swiftly then the adulterer
> Upon the bridal chamber's threshold stood."

'After which he still more openly describes the incontinence of Zeus as represented in the fable, in the following manner:

b
> "Then he nor feast, nor lustral water touched,
> But hastened to the couch, with heart deep stung
> By lust, and wantoned there that whole night through."

'Let these things, however, be left to the follies of the theatres. Heracleitus expressly says: "Men are found incapable of understand-

---

679 b 8 Cleanthes, *Fr.* l. 45 (Mullach, i. p. 152)   **d** 3 ibid. l. 54
d 8 Euripides, *Antiope, Fr.* 6   **680 a** 2 Sophocles, *Fr.* 708   **b** 1 ibid.
b 5 Heracleitus, *Fr.* ii; Aristotle, *Rhetoric*, iii. 5, 6

ing the reason of what is right on each occasion, both before they have CLEMENT
heard it, and on hearing it for the first time."

'And Melanippides, the lyric poet, sings thus:

> "Hear me, O Father, man's delight,
> Thou ruler of the undying soul."

'Parmenides too, "the Great," as Plato calls him in the c
Sophist, writes in the following manner concerning the Deity:

> " Many the proofs that show
> The Deity knows neither birth nor death,
> Sole of His kind, complete, immovable."

'Moreover, Hesiod says that He is

> "Sole king and lord of all the immortal gods,
> With whom no other may in power contend."

'Nay, further, Tragedy also draws us away from the idols, and d
teaches us to look up to heaven. For as Hecataeus, who composed the *Histories,* says in the passage concerning Abraham and
the Egyptians, Sophocles openly cries out upon the stage:

> "There is in truth One God, and One alone,
> Who made the lofty heavens, and wide-spread earth,
> The sea's blue wave, and might of warring winds.
> But we poor mortals with deceivèd heart,
> Seeking some solace for our many woes,
> Raised images of gods in stone or bronze,
> Or figures wrought of gold or ivory;
> And when we crowned their sacrifice, and held
> High festival, we thought this piety."

p. 681

'Euripides, too, says in his tragedy upon the same stage:

> "Seest thou this boundless ether spread on high,
> With watery arms embracing all the earth?
> Call this thy Zeus, deem this thine only god."

'In the drama of *Pirithous* also the same tragic poet speaks
as follows:

> "Thee we sing, the Self-begotten,   b
> Who all nature dost embrace,
> And mid yon bright ether guidest
> In her everlasting race.
> Day and dusky night returning
> Deck for Thee heaven's wide expanse:

b 9 Melanippides, *Fr.* 8 (Bergk), Farnell's *Greek Lyric Poetry,* p. 275
c 1 Plato, *Sophist,* 237 A   c 3 Parmenides, *Fr.* i. 59 (Mullach)   c 7
Hesiod, *Fr.* 53 (Gaisf.), 152 (Göttling)   d 5 Pseudo-Sophocles, *Fr.* 18.
in Müller, *Fr. Hist. Gr.,* tom. ii   681 a 3 Euripides, Fragment quoted
by Lucian, *Jupiter Trag.,* c. 41   a 8 Euripides, *Pirithous,* Fr. ii.

Myriad stars for ever burning
                    Weave round Thee their mystic dance."

'For here he speaks of the Creative mind as "the Self-begotten," and all things that follow are ranked with the cosmos, in which also are the alternations of light and darkness.

Aeschylus also, the son of Euphorion, speaks very solemnly of God:

"Zeus is the bright pure ether, Zeus the earth,
c   The heaven, the universe, and all above."

'I know that Plato adds his testimony to Heracleitus when he writes: "One, the only wise, wills not to be described, and wills to be named Zeus." And again, "Law is obedience to the will of one." Also if you should wish to trace back the meaning of the saying, "He that hath ears to hear, let him hear," you would find it explained by the Ephesian thus: "Those who hear without understanding are like deaf persons: the proverb witnesses of them that though present they are absent."

'But you wish perhaps to hear from the Greeks an express
d statement of one first cause? Timaeus the Locrian, in his treatise on *Nature*, will testify for me word for word: "There is one beginning of all things, which is unoriginate: for if it had an origin, it would be no longer a beginning, but that from which it originated would be the beginning." For this opinion, which is true, flowed from the passage, "Hear, O Israel, the LORD thy God is One, and Him only shalt thou serve."

"Lo! He is clear to all, from error free,"
as says the Sibyl.

'Also Xenocrates, the Chalcedonian, by naming "the High and Nether" Zeus, admits an indication of Father and Son.
p. 682 And the strangest thing of all is, that the Deity seems to be known to Homer, who represents the gods as subject to human passions, yet even so does not gain the respect of Epicurus. Homer says at least:

"Achilles, why with active feet pursue,
    Thou mortal, me Immortal? Knowest thou not
    My Godhead?"

681 b 9 Aeschylus, *Fr. Incert.* 295   c 3 Heracleitus, *Fr.* 12 (Mullach)
c 4 ibid. *Fr.* 56 (Mullach)   c 6 Luke viii. 8   c 7 Heracleitus, *Fr.* 4
(Mullach)   d 2 Cf. Plato, *Phaedrus*, 245 D   d 6 Deut. vi. 4, 13
d 8 Sibylline Oracles, *Fr.* i (Rzach, p. 234)   d 10 Xenocrates, *Fr.* 2
(Mullach, iii. p. 114) Cf. *Comus*, l. 20.   **682 a** 5 Hom. *Il.* xxii. 8
(Lord Derby's translation)

'For he has made it clear that the deity cannot be apprehended CLEMENT by a mortal, nor perceived by feet, or hands, or eyes, or by the body at all. "To whom have ye likened the Lord ? Or to what likeness b have ye compared Him ? " says the Scripture. " Is He an image that a workman made, or did a goldsmith melt gold and spread it over Him ? " and the rest.

'The Comic poet Epicharmus also, in his *Republic,* speaks evidently of the Word (Reason) in this manner :

"Greatest need hath man of Reason and of number in life's ways ;
    For in them is our salvation, and by them we mortals live."   c

Then he adds expressly :

" Reason is man's guide, to govern and preserve him in the way."

Then :

"Mortal men have use of Reason ; Reason also is divine :
    Reason is the gift of nature for man's life and sustenance.
    Reason man's divine attendant guideth him in all his arts :
    Reason is his sole instructor, teaching what is best to do.
    Art is not of man's invention, but a gift that comes from God,   d
    Man's own reason is the offspring of that Reason all-divine."

'Moreover, the Spirit had cried by the mouth of Esaias, "What is the multitude of your sacrifices unto me? saith the LORD : I am full of the burnt-offerings [of rams], and in the fat of lambs and blood of bulls [and of he-goats] I have no delight"; and added soon after, "Wash you, make you clean, put away your iniquities from your souls." So Menander, the Comic poet, writes what answers to this in these very words :

"For whosoever brings a sacrifice
    Of countless bulls or kids, O Pamphilus,
    Or aught like these, who works of art designs,   p. 683
    Vestments of gold or purple, life-like forms
    Graven in emerald or ivory,
    And hopes thereby God's favour may be won
    He strangely errs, and hath a dullard's mind.
    Man's duty is to help his brother man,
    Nor simple maid nor wedded wife betray,
    Nor steal nor murder for foul lucre's sake.
    Then covet not, dear friend, a needle's thread,   b
    For God is ever near to watch thy deeds."

'"I am a God at hand, and not a God far off. Shall man do aught in

b 1 Is. xl. 18   b 7 Epicharmus, *Republic*   c 3 Cf. Plato,
Republic, vii. 522 : the following fragments of Epicharmus seem to be
otherwise unknown   d 4 Is. i. 11   d 7 ibid. 16   d 10 Pseudo-
Menander (Meineke, p. 306)   683 b 3 Jer. xxiii. 23, 24

CLEMENT secret places, and I not see him?" So God speaks by Jeremiah. And again Menander, paraphrasing that Scripture, "Offer the sacrifice of righteousness, and put your trust in the LORD," writes in this way:

> "Then, dearest friend,
> Ne'er covet even a pin that is not thine;
c
> For God in works of righteousness delights,
> And thine own life permits thee to enrich,
> Ploughing the land and toiling night and day.
> Then be thou ever just, and worship God
> With heart as pure as is thy festal robe.
> And if the thunder roll, flee not, my lord,
> For conscious of no guilt thou need'st not fear:
> Since God is watching o'er thee nigh at hand."

d "Whilst thou art yet speaking, I will say, Behold, here I am," saith the Scripture.

' Diphilus again, the Comic poet, discourses of the Judgement somewhat as follows:

> "Thinkest thou then, Niceratus, the dead,
> Who in this life all luxury enjoyed,
> Escaped from God lie hidden from His sight?
> There is an eye of Justice that sees all,
> And even in Hades we believe there are
> Two paths of destiny, one for the just,
> The other for the ungodly. If men say
p. 684
> The earth shall hide them both alike for ever,
> Go rob, and steal, all right and wrong confound:
> Be not deceived; in Hades judgement waits,
> Which God will execute, the Lord of all,
> Whose Name so terrible I dare not speak.
> He to the sinners length of days accords;
> But if a mortal thinks, that day by day
> He can do evil, and escape the gods,
b
> In this his wicked thought, though Justice lag
> With tardy foot, he shall be caught at last.
> All ye who think there is no God, beware!
> There is, there is: let then the wicked man
> Cease to do ill, and so redeem the time:
> Else his just doom he shall at last receive."

' With this the tragedy also agrees in these words:

> "There comes in after days, there comes a time,
> When yon bright golden ether shall pour forth

683 b 5 Ps. iv. 5   b 8 Pseudo-Menander (Meineke, p. 308)   d 1
Is. lviii. 9   d 5 Pseudo-Philemon (Meineke, p. 865)   684 a 7
Euripides, *Phrixus*, Fr. viii; cf. Valckenär, *Aristobulus*, c. i.   b 3 Cf.
Valckenär, ibid.   b 8 Pseudo-Justin, *De Monarchia*, c. iii.

738

Her store of fire, until the well-fed flame
All things in heaven and earth shall fiercely burn."

And again soon after it adds :

> "And then when all creation is dissolved,
> The sea's last wave shall die upon the shore,
> The bald earth stript of trees, the burning air
> No wingèd thing shall bear upon its breast;
> When all is lost then all shall be restored."

The like thoughts we shall find also expressed in the Orphic d
poems, as follows :

> "He hides them all, then from his heart again
> With anxious care brings all to gladsome light."

And if we live a just and holy life throughout, happy are we
here, and happier after our departure hence, enjoying blessedness
not merely for a time, but enabled to find rest in eternity.

> "Sharing with all the gods one hearth, one feast,
> And free from human sorrows, toil, and death."

So says the philosophic poetry of Empedocles. There is none **p. 685**
so great, even in the opinion of the Greeks, as to be above the
judgement, nor so small as to be hidden from it.

' The same Orpheus says also this :

> "Look to the word divine, keep close to that,
> And guide thereby the deep thoughts of thine heart.
> Walk wisely in the way ; and look to none
> Save to the immortal Framer of the world."   b

And again concerning God, calling Him invisible, he says that
He was made known only to one certain person, a Chaldaean by
birth, whether he so speaks of Abraham, or of his son, in the
following words :

> "Save one, a scion of Chaldaean race:
> For he was skilled to mark the sun's bright path,
> And how in even circle round the earth   c
> The starry sphere on its own axis turns,
> And winds their chariot guide o'er sea and sky."

' Then, as it were paraphrasing the Scripture, " Heaven is my
throne, and earth the footstool of my feet," he adds :

> "But God Himself high above heav'n, unmoved,
> Sits on His golden throne ; and plants His feet   d

d 3 Orph. *Fr.* 123 (Abel), vi (Hermann); Stob. *Ecl.* I. ii. 23   685 a 5
Orph. *Fr.* ii. 6 ; cf. 664 d 6   b 6 ibid. 23   c 4 Is. lxvi. 1   c 6
Orph. *Fr.* ii. 29

CLEMENT   On the broad earth ; His right hand He extends
           O'er Ocean's farthest bound ; the eternal hills
           Tremble in their deep heart, nor can endure
           His mighty power. And still above the heavens
           Alone He sits, and governs all on earth.
           Himself first cause, and means, and end of all.
p. 686   Not otherwise dare I to speak of Him :
           In heart and limbs I tremble at the thought,
           How He from heav'n all things in order rules,"

and the lines that follow these. For herein he has plainly set
forth all those prophetic sayings : "Whosoever shall rend the heaven,
trembling shall seize him : and from Thee the mountains shall melt
away, as wax melteth from the presence of fire." Also what is said by
b the mouth of Esaias : "Who measured the heaven with a span, and
all the earth with his fist?"

'Again, when he says :

           "Lord of the heavens, of Hades, land, and sea,
           Whose thunders shake Olympus' strong-built dome,
           Whom daemons shuddering flee, and all the gods
           Do fear, and Fates implacable obey.
           Eternal Mother and eternal Sire,
           Whose anger shakes the universal frame,
c   Awakes the stormy wind, veils all with clouds,
           And rends with sudden flash the expanse of heav'n.
           At Thy command the stars their changeless course
           In order run. Before Thy fiery throne
           Angels unwearied stand ; whose only care
           Is to perform Thy gracious will for man.
d   Thine is the Spring new-decked with purple buds,
           The winter Thine, with chilling clouds o'ercast,
           And autumn with its merry vintage Thine."

'Then, expressly calling God the Almighty, he adds :

           "Come, then, thou deathless and Immortal Power,
           Whose name none but Immortals can express.
           Mightiest of Gods, whose will is strong as Fate,
           Dreadful art Thou, resistless in Thy might,
           Deathless, and with etherial glory crowned."

p. 687 So then by the word μητροπάτωρ he not only indicated the
creation out of nothing, but gave occasion perhaps to those who
introduce the doctrine of emissions to imagine also a consort of God.
And he paraphrases the prophetic Scriptures, both that which

---

686 a 5 Is. lxiv. 1   b 1 ibid. xl. 12   b 4 *Orphic Fr.* iii. 1
d 5 ibid. iii. 14

was spoken by Hosea (Amos): "Lo! I am he that formeth the CLEMENT
thunder and createth the wind, whose hands founded the host of
heaven": and that which was spoken by Moses: "See, see, that it
is I, and there is no other god but me. I will kill, and I will make
to live: I will wound, and I will heal: and there is none that shall
deliver out of my hand."

> " 'Tis He that out of good for mortals brings   **b**
> Evil and cruel war,"

according to Orpheus.

'Such also is the saying of Archilochus of Paros:

> "Zeus, Father Zeus, the realm of heav'n is thine,
> But knavish and unholy deeds of men
> Scape not thine eye."

'Let Thracian Orpheus again sing for us thus:

> "His right hand He extends
> O'er Ocean's farthest bound; and plants His feet
> On the broad earth."   **c**

These thoughts are manifestly taken from that passage, "The
Lord shall shake inhabited cities, and take the whole world in His
hand, as a nest"; "The LORD who made the earth by His power," as
Jeremiah says, " and established the world by His wisdom."

'Moreover in addition to this Phocylides, calling the angels
daemons, shows in the following words that some of them are
good and some bad, as we also have been taught that some are **d**
apostate:

> " But daemons different in kind o'er men
> At various times preside; some to protect
> Mankind from coming evils."

'Well therefore does Philemon also, the Comic poet, exterminate
idolatry by these words:

> "Fortune is no divinity for us,
> No goddess; only that which of itself
> Happens by chance to each is fortune called."

'Sophocles too, the Tragedian, says:

> "Not even the gods have all things at their will,   **p. 688**
> Save Zeus, the final and first cause of all."

687 a 5 Amos iv. 13   a 7 Deut. xxxii. 39   Cf. Hos. xiii. 4   b 1
Orphic Fr. i. 11   b 5 Archilochus, *Fr.* xvii   b 9 *Orphic Fr.* i 19
c 2 Is. x. 14   c 4 Jer. x. 12   d 3 Phocylides, *Fr.* i. 19 (cf. ii. 31)
d 8 Philemon, *Fr.* xlviii   688 a 1 Fragment otherwise unknown

CLEMENT   'Orpheus also says :

> "One power, one god, one vast and flaming heav'n,
> One universal frame, wherein revolve
> All things which here we see, fire, water, earth,"

and the lines that follow.

b   'Pindar too, the Lyric poet, breaks out as it were in transport, saying expressly :

> "What then is God ? The All."

'And again :

> "God, who for mortals all things makes,
> (Gives also grace to song)."

'Also when he says :

> "Why hope in wisdom to excel
> Thy brother man ?
> It is not well
> For mortals here on earth
> With minds of human birth
> The counsels of the gods to scan."

He has drawn his thought from the passage : "Who hath known the mind of the LORD ? Or who hath been His counsellor ? "

c   'Moreover Hesiod agrees with what has been said above in writing thus :

> "Of men on earth no prophet so inspired
> Can know the mind of aegis-bearing Zeus."

With good reason, therefore, does the Athenian Solon himself follow Hesiod, when he writes :

> "The Immortals' mind is all unknown to men."

d   'Again, as Moses had foretold that the woman because of the transgression should bring forth children to pain and sorrow, a certain poet of no little distinction writes :

> "Never by day from labour and distress
> By night from groaning shall they cease ; so hard
> The cares and troubles which the gods shall give."

'Moreover Homer shows that God is just, when he says :

> "The Eternal Father hung
> His golden scales aloft."

---

688 a 4 *Orph. Fr.* vi. 16 (Hermann)   b 3 Pindar, *Fr.* 104 (Boeckh)
b 5 ibid. *Fr.* 105   b 8 ibid. *Fr.* 33   b 14 Is. xl. 13   c 3 Hesiod,
Fr. iii (Gaisford)   c 7 Solon, *Fr.* x   d 4 Hesiod, *Works and Days,* 174-176
d 8 Homer, *Il.* viii. 689

And Menander, the Comic poet, interprets God's goodness, when   CLEMENT
he says:

"By every man from moment of his birth   **p. 689**
A friendly genius stands, life's mystic guide.
No evil daemon he (forbid the thought!),
With power malign to mar thy happy lot."

And then he adds:

"῎Απαντα δ᾽ ἀγαθὸν εἶναι τὸν Θεόν,"

meaning either " that every god is good," or, what is the truer
meaning, " that in all things God is good."

' Again, Aeschylus, the Tragic poet, in setting forth the power
of God does not hesitate to call Him the Most High in the
following passage:

"Set God apart from mortals in thy thought,   b
Nor deem that, like thyself, He too is flesh.
Thou know'st Him not: as fire He now appears
A mighty force, now water, now dark storm.
Again in likeness of the beasts He comes,
Of wind, or lightning, thunder, cloud, or rain.
The seas, and sea-girt rocks, the springing wells,
The gathering floods, obey His sovereign will.
The pillars of the earth, the vast abyss   c
Of Ocean, and the mountain-tops do shake,
If the dread Master's eye but look on them:
So glorious is the power of God Most High."

Does it not seem to you that he is paraphrasing that passage:
" At the presence of the LORD the earth trembles."

' Besides this, the chief prophet Apollo is compelled, in
testimony to the glory of God, to say of Athena, when the Medes
were marching against Greece, that she entreated and supplicated
Zeus for Attica.   And the oracle is as follows:

"Pallas with many words and counsel wise
May pray, but ne'er appease Olympian Zeus.
For he to the consuming fire will give   d
The shrines of many gods, who now perchance
Stand bathed in chilling sweat, and shake with fear,"

and so forth.   **p. 690**

---

689 a 1 Menander, *Fr.* 18   b 1 Ps.-Aeschylus, *Fr.* in Ps.-Justin,
De Monarchia, c. ii   c 6 Ps. cxiv. 7   c 11 Herodotus, vii. 141 ;
cf. **216 d** 5

CLEMENT 'Thearidas, in his book *On Nature*, writes, "The first cause of things that exist, the real and true cause, is one. For that is in the beginning one and alone."

"There is none other save the mighty King,"

as Orpheus says. And with him the Comic poet Diphilus agrees in a very sententious manner, when he says :

"Him never cease to honour and adore,
Father of all, sole source of every good."

b 'With good reason, therefore, Plato trains " the noblest natures to attain that learning which in the former part of our discussion we declared to be the highest, both to discern the good and to make the great ascent." "This then, as it seems, would be no mere turning of an oyster-shell, but the conversion of a soul passing from a kind 'of darkness visible' to the true upward path of being, which we shall call true philosophy "; and those who have partaken thereof he judges to belong to the golden race, when he says, "Ye are doubtless all brethren "; but those who are of the golden race can judge most accurately, and in every way. . . .

c 'Instinctively, therefore, and without teaching, all things derive from all a conception of the Father and Maker of all, things inanimate by suffering with the animal creation, and of living beings those which are already immortal by working in the light of day, and of those still mortal some (perceive Him) in fear while carried by their mother in the womb, but others by independent reasoning. And of mankind both Greeks and Barbarians all have this conception; and nowhere is there any race either of husbandmen or of shepherds, nay not even of the dwellers in cities,

d who can live without being prepossessed by the belief in that higher power. Wherefore every nation of the east, and every one that touches the western shores, the northern also, and all upon the south, have one and the same presentiment of Him who established the government of the world, inasmuch as the most universal of His operations have pervaded all things alike.

'Much more did the inquisitive philosophers among the Greeks, by an impulse from the Barbarian philosophy, ascribe the pre-eminence to the One invisible most mighty and most skilful

---

690 a 2 Thearidas, *On Nature*, a work otherwise unknown a 5 *Orph. Fr.* i. 13 a 8 Diphilus, *Fr.* 52 b 1 Plato, *Republic*, 519 C b 4 ibid. 521 C b 8 ibid. 415 A b 10 The Greek text is defective here

chief cause of all things most beautiful, without understanding CLEMENT the consequences of this, unless they were instructed by us, nay, not even understanding how God Himself is naturally to be conceived, but only, as we have said many times already, in a true but indirect way.'

p. 691

So far Clement. But since the Philosophy of Plato was shown by us at some length to be in very many things in agreement with the doctrines of the Hebrews (for which we admire the man's wisdom and his candour also in regard to the truth), it is time to consider what the points are in which, as we say, we are no longer so favourably disposed towards him, but prefer that which is accounted the Barbarian philosophy to his. b

Chapter XIV

THE oracles of the Hebrews containing prophecies and c responses of a divine power beyond that of man, and claiming God as their author, and confirming their promise by the prediction of things to come, and by the results corresponding to the prophecies, are said to be free from all erroneous thought. For instance, 'the words of God are declared to be pure words, and silver tried in the fire, tested by earth, purified seven times.'

But not such are the words of Plato, nor yet of any d other of the wise among men, who with the eyes of mortal thought and with feeble guesses and comparisons, as in a dream, and not awake, attained to a notion of the nature of all things, but superadded to the truth of nature a large admixture of falsehood, so that one can find in them no learning free from error.

Now, for example, if you would suppress a little of this self-admiration, and contemplate the true light itself by the faculty of reason, you would perceive that even that wonderful philosopher, who alone of all the Greeks touched the threshold of truth, dishonours the name of

---

691 c 6 Ps. xii. 6

the gods by applying it to perishable matter and carved
p. 692 images fashioned by mechanic hands into a human shape;
and after the lofty height of his magniloquence, wherein
he contended that he knew the Father and Maker of
this universe, is thrust down from his place on high
among the supramundane circles, and sinks with the
common people of Athens into the lowest depth of their
God-detested idolatry; so that he does not shrink from
saying that Socrates had gone down to the Peiraeus to
pray to the goddess, and to see his fellow citizens then
for the first time celebrating their barbarous festival;
b acknowledging also that he had enjoined the offering of
a cock to Aesculapius, and regarded as a god the ancestral prophet of the Greeks, the daemon who sits enshrined
at Delphi.

Wherefore also the blame of the superstitious delusion
of the unphilosophical multitude might with good reason
be ascribed to him. Take up again for instance his discourse a little farther back, and after his incorporeal and
imperishable ‘ideas,’ and after a first god and a second
cause, and after intelligent and immortal essences,
observe what kind of laws the all-wise philosopher
would enact concerning the belief of the common people,
speaking thus:

PLATO **c**   ‘To tell of the other divinities and to learn their origin is
beyond us; but we must give credence to those who have spoken
in former times, who being, as they said, the offspring of gods,
had, I suppose, a clear knowledge of their own ancestors. It is
impossible therefore to disbelieve children of the gods, even
though they speak without certain or probable proofs: but as
they assert that they are reporting family histories, we must in
obedience to the law believe them.

‘On their authority then let the origin of these gods be as
follows and so stated. The children of Earth and Heaven were
d Oceanus and Tethys; and their children Phorcys and Kronos

---

692 c I Plato, *Timaeus*, 40 Ð; cf. 75 d, 639 d

and Rhea, and all the others with them : and of Kronos and PLATO
Rhea came Zeus and Hera, and all whom we know as their
reputed brethren, and still others who were their offspring.'

For these reasons then we must give up the great
philosopher, as having misrepresented the fabulous theo-
gonies of the poets, not like a philosopher, nor in a self-
consistent manner. For you had the opportunity of
hearing himself speak in the *Republic* as follows:

'In the greater fables, said I, we shall also discern the less :
for there must be the same type, and the same tendency in both
the greater and the less : do you not think so?

'Yes, I do, said he : but I do not even understand which you **p. 693**
call the greater.

'Those, said I, which Hesiod and Homer and the other poets
told us : for they, I suppose, were the composers of fictitious tales,
which they told and still tell to mankind';

meaning the stories which we have quoted a little above.

Again there was that passage of his in which he said,

'We shall begin then, said I, with the following verse, and
strike out it and all that are like it :

" Fain would I serve some master in the field,"

and the rest ; also the passage wherein he adds :   b

'Once more then we shall entreat Homer and the other poets
not to represent Achilles, the son of a goddess,

" Now turning on his side, and now again
Upon his back,"

and the rest that follows. To this he adds:

'Or to say that Zeus, while all the other gods and men were
asleep, and he alone awake, lightly forgot all the plans he had
devised, through the eagerness of desire, and was so smitten at **c**
sight of Hera that he would not even wait to go into his chamber,
but wished to lie with her there on the ground like a lark, and
said that he was possessed by a stronger passion than even when

---

d 10 Plato, *Republic*, 377 C   **693** a 8 ibid. 386 C   a 10 Hom. *Od.*
xi. 488   b 2 Plato, *Republic*, 388 A   b 4 Hom. *Il.* xxiv. 10   b 7
Plato, ibid. 390 B

PLATO they first used to meet " without the knowledge of their dear parents."
Nor shall we admit the tale of Ares and Aphrodite being bound
by Hephaestus for acts of the same kind ! '

And then after having told these tales in such a
manner, what does he mean in the saying which comes
after, by calling the poets 'children of the gods,' and
asserting that 'to disbelieve them is impossible,' although he
d protested that they had invented the fictitious stories
about the gods ' without necessary or probable proofs'?

And what is the meaning of this unreasonable belief,
put forward in fear of punishment from the laws ?
And how can Uranus and Gé be first of the gods,
then their offspring Oceanus and Tethys, and after all
these Kronos, and Rhea, and Zeus, and Hera, and all
their sons and brothers and descendants mentioned in
fables by Homer and Hesiod, when he was refuting these
very stories by speaking thus :

' The fault, said I, which we ought to reprove before all and
above all, especially if a man lies in unseemly fashion.

' What fault is that ?

' When a man in his discourse concerning gods and heroes
misrepresents their nature, just as when an artist paints what
p. 694 is not at all like the things which he may wish to imitate.'

And again :

' In the first place, said I, it was no seemly lie that was told
by the author of that greatest lie about the greatest gods, how
Uranus wrought what Hesiod says he did, and how Kronos took
revenge upon him,' and what follows this.

But how could the same poets who are here called
false and untruthful be spoken of on the other hand as
offspring of the gods? However, for these reasons we
must abandon this philosopher, as having through fear
of death played false with the Athenian democracy ; but
b must honour Moses, and the Hebrew oracles, as every-

---

693 c 5 Hom. *Il.* xiv. 291   c 10 Plato, *Timaeus,* 40 D   d 11 ibid.
Republic, 377 D   694 a 3 ibid. 377 E   a 5 Hesiod, *Theogony,* 154, 178

where shining out from the one true religion that is
free from error. Look then at another point.

Chapter XV

THE Hebrews say that the intermediate nature of c
rational beings is generated and not without beginning.
And in their account they distinguish this nature into
intelligent beings whom they call spirits, and powers,
and God's ministering angels and archangels: and from
their fall and transgression they derive the race of
daemons, and the whole species of the adverse and
wicked agency.

For which reason they forbid us to regard as gods
those who are not possessed of virtue and goodness as d
inseparable from their nature, but have .received their
very existence not from themselves but from the Cause
of all, and also acquire their well-being, and their virtue,
and their immortality itself not in the same manner as
either He who is God over all, or He by whom all things
were made.

But Plato although, like the Hebrews, he supposes
the rational natures to be incorporeal and intelligible
essences, yet falls away from consistency, by first asserting that .they, as well as every soul, are unoriginated,
and then saying that they were formed out of an effluence
of the First Cause. For he does not mean to admit that
they have arisen out of nothing.

Wherefore also he supposes that there is a numerous
race of gods, assuming in his argument certain effluences
and emissions of the First and Second Causes : and that
they are in nature good and in no way capable of de- **p. 695**
parting from their proper virtue, whence also he supposes
them to be gods.

But the tribe of daemons he believes to be different
from these, as being capable of baseness and wickedness,
and change for the worse : and some of these are called,

and are, good and some evil. But while he thus makes these suppositions contrary to the Hebrew doctrines, he does not explain from what source it may reasonably be said that the daemons arose.

For that they arose from the matter of the corporeal elements no one in his senses would assert: for this matter is irrational, but rational things can never be born of an irrational, and the daemons are rational. If, **b** however, these come from an effluence of the greater gods, how then are they not themselves gods as much as those who have begotten them? And how if the source is good are the things which flow from it not like it? And whence in these latter did a shoot of wickedness grow up, if the root comes originally from good and passes through good? Or how can bitter come from the sweet?

If then the race of the wicked daemons is worse than any darkness and any bitterness, how can it be said to come from an effluence of the nature of the better powers? If it was from this, it would not have turned aside from its proper lot: and if it has been changed, then it was not at first impassible in its nature: and if it was not such, how then could they be gods who are **c** capable of participating in an evil destiny?

If, however, they were neither from the effluence of the better powers, nor yet from the matter of the corporeal elements, we must now either say that they were unoriginated, and must set over against God in addition to the unoriginated matter of the corporeal elements a third group of unoriginated rational beings, thus no longer representing God as being the Maker of all, and Framer of the Universe, or, if we admit this, we must also admit that He made the non-existent, according to the statements of the Hebrews.

For what do these teach on this subject? They say that the intermediate nature of rational beings arose **d** neither from the matter of the corporeal elements, nor from an effluence of the essence which is unbegotten and ever remains in the same mode and relations; but that having no previous existence it has come into being by the effective power of the Cause of all.

And thus they are no gods, nor have been properly dignified with the title, because they are not equalized in nature with their Maker, nor have goodness inseparably attached to them, like God, but sometimes would even admit the contrary to that which is good through **p. 696** disregard of that study of the higher power, which every one has wrought out for himself, who is by nature master of his own movement and purpose. So much then for this subject; and now let us pass to another.

Chapter XVI

Plato, although he agreed with the Hebrews in sup- **b** posing the soul immortal, and saying that it was like unto God, no longer follows them when he sometimes says that its essence is composite, as if involving a certain part of the indivisible and immutable Cause, and a part of the divisible nature belonging to bodies.

He speaks, for instance, in the *Timaeus* in these very words :

'But to the soul, as a mistress to rule over a subject, He Plato gave priority and precedence over the body both in origin and excellence, and made her out of the following constituents and in the following manner. Of the indivisible and ever immutable essence, and of the other divisible essence belonging to bodies, He compounded a third intermediate species of essence out of both the nature of ' the same ' and the nature of ' the other,' and in this way set it midway between the indivisible part and the divisible part which belongs to bodies. And he took the three, as they now were, and mingled them all together into **c** one " idea," and as the nature of " the other " was hard to combine, he fitted it by force into " the same." '

696 b 9 Plato, *Timaeus*, 34 C

Hence also he has naturally connected the passible part with the rational part of the essence. But though d at one time he has given this decision concerning the essence of soul, at another he involves it in a different and worse absurdity, by declaring that the divine and heavenly essence, which is incorporeal and rational and like unto God, and which by virtue of its great excellence soars above the celestial circles, comes down from above out of the supramundane regions upon asses, and wolves, and ants, and bees, and calls upon us to believe this account without any proof.

He speaks accordingly in the discourse *Concerning the Soul* as follows:

p. 697   'So they continue to wander until, by the craving of that PLATO corporeal nature which still accompanies them, they are again imprisoned in a body: and probably they are imprisoned in animals of such moral nature as the habits which they may themselves happen to have followed in life.

'What kind of natures do you mean, Socrates?

'For example, those who have practised gluttony, and wantonness, and drunkenness, and have taken no good heed, probably sink into the class of asses and other beasts of that kind: do you not think so?

'Yes, what you say is quite probable.

'And those who have preferred a course of injustice and tyranny and plunder go into the classes of wolves, and hawks, b and kites: or whither else should we say that such souls go?

'Certainly into such as these, said Cebes.

'Well then, said he, as to the other cases it is evident what way each soul will go, according to the affinities of their habits.

'Quite evident, said he, for how could it be otherwise?

'Well then, said he, are not the happiest among them and those who pass into the best place the men who have practised the civil and political virtue which is called temperance and justice, produced by habit and attention, without the aid of philosophy and intellect?

---

697 a 1 Plato, *Phaedo*, 81 D

'How now are these the happiest?   c PLATO

'Because it is probable that these pass again into some social and gentle race, of bees perhaps or wasps or ants, or even back again into the human race itself.'

In the *Phaedrus* also hear how he discourses :

'For to the same state from which each soul has come she does not attain within ten thousand years; for before this time none grows wings except the soul of the guileless philosopher, or of the philosophic lover. These in the third period of a thousand years, if they have chosen this life thrice successively, so get their wings and fly away in the three-thousandth year. But the others receive judgement when they have finished their first life : and after judgement some go to the houses of correction beneath d the earth and suffer punishment, and others, lifted by the judgement to some place in heaven, live in a manner worthy of the life which they lived in human form. But in the thousandth year both good and evil souls come to an allotment and choice of their second life, and choose whichever each may wish. And there both a human soul may pass into the life of a beast, and from a beast he who was once a man may pass back into a man again.'

This is what he says in the *Phaedrus*; but now listen to him writing in the *Republic* in the following style :

'For he said that he saw the soul which was once that of **p. 698** Orpheus choosing the life of a swan, out of hatred of the female sex, because he had been killed by them, and would not be conceived and born of woman. Then he saw the soul of Thamyras choose the life of a nightingale : he saw also a swan changing and making choice of a man's life, and other musical animals in like manner, as was natural. And the soul that gained the twentieth lot chose a lion's life; and it was the soul of Ajax, son of Telamon, which shrank from becoming a man because he remembered the judgement concerning the arms.

'And the soul of Agamemnon which came next, and also **b** hated the human race because of his sufferings, changed for the

---

c 6 Plato, *Phaedrus*, 248 E   **698 a** 1 ibid. *Republic*, 620 A

PLATO life of an eagle. The soul of Atalanta, whose lot was about the middle, having observed the great honours of an athlete, could not pass by without choosing that life. Next after her he saw the soul of Epeius, the son of Panopeus, passing into the nature of a female artist. Far off among the hindmost he saw the soul of Thersites, the buffoon, entering into an ape.

c   'The soul of Odysseus, having by chance obtained the last lot of all, came forward to choose; and having been cured of ambition by remembrance of his former troubles, went about for a long time seeking for the life of a private person free from business, and with difficulty found one lying somewhere neglected by all the rest, and when he saw it he said that he would have done the same even if he had gained the first lot, and so chose it gladly. Of the other animals also some in like manner passed into men and into one another, the unjust changing into the savage, and the just into the gentle, and formed all kinds of

d mixtures.'

In these discourses concerning the soul it is evident that Plato is following the Egyptian doctrines: for his statement is not that of the Hebrews, since it is not in accordance with truth. There is, however, no occasion to refute this, because he did not himself attempt the problem in the way of demonstration. But thus much one may reasonably remark, that it was not consistent for the same person to say that at the moment of decease the souls of the ungodly departing hence suffer in Hades the just penalties of their deeds, and there undergo eternal punishment, and then to assert that they choose again their modes of life here according to their own will.

For he says that they become imprisoned in a body through desire of what is bodily; and that some of them who have been reared in wantonness and gluttony become asses, and enter into the bodies of other beasts, choosing

p. 699 them at will and not according to just desert; and the unjust and rapacious become wolves, and kites, having entered into this nature of their own accord. Then he says that the soul of Orpheus wished to be a swan; and the soul of Thamyras chose the life of a nightingale, and Thersites that of an ape.

But where then would be that judgement after their departure hence, which he describes in the dialogue *On the Soul,* saying:

'When the deceased have arrived at the place to which each PLATO is brought by his daemon, ... then those who may be thought to have lived an ordinary life proceed to Acheron, and having embarked in such vessels as there are for them, they arrive **b** in these at the lake; and there they dwell, and are purged and punished for their crimes, and so absolved from any offence which each has committed: and for their good deeds they receive rewards each according to his desert. But any who may be thought to be incurable because of the greatness of their sins, having perpetrated either many great acts of sacrilege or many wicked and lawless murders, or any other crimes of this kind, these, I say, are cast by their suitable destiny into Tartarus, whence they never come out.   **c**

Thus he described the fate of the ungodly; and now hear how he speaks of the pious:

'And of this class those who have thoroughly purified themselves by philosophy live for the time to come altogether free from troubles, and attain to abodes still more beautiful than the former, to describe which is neither easy, nor is the time at present sufficient.'

In the *Gorgias* also observe what he says:

'The man who has lived a just and holy life departs after death to the Islands of the Blessed, and there dwells in perfect happiness beyond the reach of ills. But he who has lived **d** an unjust and godless life goes to the prison-house of vengeance and punishment, which they call Tartarus, ... and whoever may have committed the worst misdeeds, and because of such crimes have become incurable, of these the examples are made. And, being incurable, they receive no more benefit themselves; but others receive benefit, who see them for their

---

699 a 10 Plato, *Phaedo,* 113 D   c 4 ibid. 114 C   c 10 ibid.
Gorgias, 523 A   d 3 ibid. 525 C

PLATO great sins enduring the most painful and terrible sufferings for all time, hung up simply as examples there in the prison-house in Hades, a spectacle and warning to the wicked who are continually arriving.'

p. 700   How can this agree with the statements concerning an exchange of bodies, which the soul, they say, seeks after and chooses? For how can the same soul after its departure hence endure tortures, and prisons, and all this punishment for ever, and on the other hand as one released and free from bonds choose whatever modes of life it will? And if it were likely to choose again the life of pleasure, where then is the prison-house of vengeance and punishment? At leisure one might attack the argument at a thousand other points, on the thought of which there is no time to enlarge.

b   So the first error in Plato's opinion on this subject has been thus detected; but the second slip in the exposition of his doctrine, wherein he laid down that one part of the soul is divine and rational and another part of it irrational and passible, has been condemned even by his own friends, as one may learn from statements of the following kind:

CHAPTER XVII

c   'WITH regard to the soul as described by Plato, which he SEVERUS says was composed by God of an impassible and a passible essence, as some intermediate colour from white and black, this is what we have to say, that when in time a separation of them takes place the soul must necessarily disappear, like the **d** composition of the intermediate colour, when each of its constituents is naturally separated in time into its proper colour. But if this is so we shall show the soul to be perishable and not immortal.

'For if this is admitted, that nothing in nature is without its opposite, and that all things in the world have been arranged by God out of the nature of these opposites, He having impressed upon them a friendship and communion, as of dry with moist,

---

700 c 1 Severus, *On the Soul*, a Fragment preserved by Eusebius

and hot with cold, heavy with light, white with black, sweet Severus with bitter, hard with soft, and on all qualities of this kind **p. 701** one other combination including them all, and then upon the impassible essence a combination with the passible, and if the combined and mingled elements naturally in time undergo a separation from each other, and if it is to be assumed that the soul has been produced out of an impassible and a passible essence, then, in the same way as the intermediate colour, so also this must naturally disappear in time, when the opposite elements in its composition press towards their proper nature.

'For do we not see that what is naturally heavy, even though it be lifted up by us, or by any natural lightness being added **b** to it from without, presses down as before in its own natural direction? How in like manner also that which is by nature light, if borne downward by similar external causes, presses upward itself as before? For things which have been combined into one out of two mutual opposites cannot possibly remain always in the same state, unless there is always in them some third kind of natural substance.

'But soul in fact is not any third thing compounded of two mutual opposites, but simple and in its sameness of nature **c** impassible and incorporeal: whence Plato and his School said that it was immortal.

'Since, however, it is a doctrine common to all that man is made of soul and body, and the motions which take place within us apart from the body, whether voluntary or involuntary, are said to be affections of the soul, most of the philosophers, guessing hereby that its substance is passible, say that it is mortal and of a corporeal nature, not incorporeal. But Plato was driven to **d** interweave the passible element with its naturally impassible essence. That neither, however, is the case we shall endeavour to demonstrate by arguing from what Plato and the others have severally said, and explaining the powers which operate within us.'

Let this suffice for my quotation from Severus the Platonist *On the Soul*.

But in addition to what has been already said consider also the following point in regard to the origin of heaven and the luminaries therein.

CHAPTER XVIII

b PLATO agrees with the Hebrews in the account which he gives of the heaven and its phenomena, according to which it was settled that they have had a beginning, as having been made by the Author of the universe, and that they partake of the corporeal and perishable substance; but he no longer agrees with the Hebrews when he enacts a law that men should worship them and believe them to be gods, speaking thus in the *Epinomis*:

Ps.-PLATO 'Whom then, O Megillus and Cleinias, do I ever with reverence speak of as god? Heaven, I suppose, which it is most right for c us, like all others, daemons as well as gods, to honour, and to pray especially to it: and that it has also been the author of all other blessings to us all men would agree.'

Then lower down in the same work he adds this:

'But of the visible gods, who are the greatest and most honourable, and have the keenest sight in all directions, the first we must declare to be the nature of the stars, and all things that we perceive to have been created with them; and next to these and under them the daemons in order, and, as occupying a third and intermediate abode, an aërial race acting as our interpreters, whom we ought to honour much with prayers for the d sake of their favourable intervention.'

Having hereby declared that the aforesaid beings are gods, he gives in the *Timaeus* a physical explanation of their original constitution, in the following description:

PLATO '(Having arranged that) as fire is to air, so is air to water, and as air to water, so is water to earth, of these He combined and constituted a visible and tangible heaven. And for these reasons and out of these elements, such as I have described, being four in number, the body of the world was formed in harmony by due proportion, and from them gained a friendliness such that after having coalesced in itself it became indissoluble by any other except the author of its combination.'

---

702 b 9 Ps.-Plato, *Epinomis*, 977 A   c 5 ibid. 984 D   d 5 Plato, *Timaeus*, 32 B

Then he adds :   **p. 703**

'And in the centre of it He set a soul, which He not only PLATO
spread throughout, but also wrapped it round the body on the
outside, and so formed one single and solitary heaven as a circle
revolving in a circle.'

And again lower down he says in addition :

'In accordance then with reason and this purpose of God for
the birth of time, that time might begin, sun, and moon, and five
other luminaries, which are surnamed planets, have been created
in order to define and preserve the reckonings of time : and,
after having made their several bodies, God set them in the orbits
traversed by the revolution of "the other." '   **b**

Also he adds :

'And the bodies bound together by animated bonds became
living beings, and learned the law appointed for them.'

In the tenth Book also of the *Laws* he gives a general
explanation concerning every kind of soul, speaking as
follows :

'All things, however, that partake of soul are subject to change,
as possessing in themselves the cause of change.   And when they
have changed they move on in the order and law of their destiny :
if they have made only small change in their moral characters,
they make small changes of place on the surface of the ground;
but if they have fallen away more frequently and culpably, they
pass into the abyss.'

So then if 'all things which partake of soul are liable **c**
to change, as possessing the cause of change in themselves,' and if heaven, and sun, and moon are, according
to Plato himself, partakers of soul, then these also must
change, 'as possessing the cause of change in themselves,'
according to his statement.   How then does he say on **d**
the other hand that they are eternal and therefore gods,
although existing in a mortal body, and liable to be
dissolved ?   At least he says again in the *Timaeus* :

---

703 a 2 Plato, *Timaeus*, 34 B   a 7 ibid. 38 C   b 3 ibid. 38 E
b 8 ibid. *Laws*, 904 C

PLATO   ' When therefore all gods, both those which are visible in their
revolutions and those which appear only as far as they choose,
had been created, the author of this universe spake to them as
follows :

' Ye gods and sons of gods, the works whereof I am the creator
and father, are indissoluble save by My will. Therefore though
all that is bound may be dissolved, yet only an evil being would
wish to dissolve that which is well composed and in right condition. Wherefore also since ye have come into existence, though
ye are not altogether immortal nor indissoluble, nevertheless ye
p. 704 shall not be dissolved nor incur the fate of death, since in My
will ye have found a still stronger and more valid bond than
those by which ye were bound together at the time of your
creation.'

So speaks Plato. With good reason therefore do Moses
and the Hebrew oracles forbid to worship these and to
regard them as gods ; but leading us upward to the God
who is King of all, the very creator of sun and moon
and stars and the whole heaven and world, who by a
divine word combined and fitted all things together, he
b bids us by his law to believe in Him alone as God, and
to ascribe the honour of worship to Him only, saying,
' Lest, when thou see the sun and moon and all the stars and
all the host of heaven, thou be deceived and worship them.'

This command is interpreted and explained at large
by Philo, the man so learned in the affairs of the
Hebrews, speaking thus word for word :

PHILO   ' Some supposed that sun and moon and the other luminaries
are gods of absolute power, to whom they attributed the causes
c of all things that are made. But Moses thought that the world
was both created, and was the greatest of all States, having
rulers and subjects, the rulers being all in heaven, such as
are planets and fixed stars, and the subjects being the natures
beneath the moon, in the air, and near the earth.

' But the so-called rulers, he thought, were not independent,

---

703 d 5 Plato, *Timaeus*, 41 A   704 b 3 Deut. iv. 19   b 8 Philo
Iud. *De Monarchia*, i. c. i. p. 213

but deputies of one universal Father, by imitating whose P<small>HILO</small> superintendence they succeed in ruling every thing in creation in accordance with justice and law. But they who did not discern Him who sits as charioteer ascribed the causes of all **d** things which are done in the world to those who are yoked under Him, as if they worked independently. But the most sacred Law-giver changes their ignorance into knowledge, when He speaks thus : " Lest, when thou beholdest the sun and the moon and the stars and all the host of heaven, thou be deceived and worship them."

' With well-directed aim and nobly did he call the acceptance of the above-mentioned as gods a deception. For they saw that the seasons of the year, in which the generations of animals and plants and fruits are brought to completion in definite periods of time are settled by the advance and retreat of the Sun ; they saw also that the Moon as handmaid and successor of the Sun had taken up by night the care and superintendence of the same as the Sun by day, and that the other luminaries in **p. 705** accordance with their sympathy towards things terrestrial were working and doing countless services for the permanence of the whole ; and so they fell into an endless delusion in supposing that these were the only gods.

' Whereas if they had been attentive to walk by the unerring path they would have learned at once that in the same way as sense is the servant of mind, so also were all who can be perceived by sense made ministers of Him whom mind alone can perceive.'

Also he further says :

' So having transcended by reason all visible being, let us go **b** on to the dignity of Him who is without bodily form and invisible, and can be apprehended by thought alone, who is not only the God of the worlds both of thought and sense, but also the Creator of all things. But if any one assign the worship of the Eternal Maker to another younger and begotten being, let him be written down as a madman and guilty of the greatest impiety.'

These are the truly genuine and divine teachings of the Hebrew religion which we have preferred to their

---

d 5 Deut. iv. 19   705 b 1 Philo Iud. *De Monarchia,* i. c. i. p. 214

c vain philosophy. Why need I enlarge further, and bring
to light the other errors of Plato, when it is easy from
what has been already said to guess also what points
I have now passed over in silence? It was not, however,
for the sake of accusing him that I was led to speak of
these things, since for my part I very greatly admire
the man, and esteem him as a friend above all the Greeks,
and honour him as one whose sentiments are dear and
congenial to myself, although not the same throughout;
but I wished to show in what his intelligence falls short
in comparison with Moses and the Hebrew prophets.

And yet to one prepared to find fault it were easy to
pass censure on countless points, such as his solemn and
d sapient regulations with regard to women in the *Republic*,
or such as his fine phrases about unnatural love in the
Phaedrus. If, however, you desire to listen to these
subjects also, take and read his utterances which follow:

Chapter XIX

p. 706   ' Perhaps now, said I, many points connected with our present
Plato subject will appear more than usually ridiculous, if they are to
be carried out as described.

' Certainly, said he.

' What then, said I, is the most ridiculous thing that you see
in them? Is it not, of course, that the women are to practise
gymnastics naked in the palaestra with the men, and not only
the young women but even the elder also; just as the old men
in the gymnasia, when though wrinkled and not pleasing in
appearance, they nevertheless love to practise gymnastics.'

And next he adds:

b   ' But the man who laughs at the women taking exercise naked
for the best of purposes, as though forsooth he were " reaping fruit
of wisdom " in his laughter, seems not even to know at what he is
laughing.'

He says also in the seventh Book of the *Laws*:

'It will therefore evidently be necessary for the boys and girls PLATO
to learn dancing and gymnastics; and there will be dancing-
masters for the boys and mistresses for the girls, that they may
go through the exercise with the greater advantage.'

He also writes therein as follows:

'Again, I suppose, our virgin Queen, who delighted in the
practice of the dance, did not think fit to play with empty hands,
but to be arrayed in full armour and so perform the dance: an c
example which most surely it would become both youths and
maidens alike to imitate.'

He also enacts a law that women should even go to
war, in the following words:

'And in all these schools teachers of the several subjects, being
resident foreigners, should be induced by payments to give all
instructions relating to war to those who come as pupils, and
all relating to music, not merely to one who may come at his
father's wish, while another, without such wish, neglects his
education; but, as the saying is, every man and boy, as far
as possible, must receive compulsory education, as belonging
more to the State than to their parents. All the same rules my
law would enjoin for women as much as for men, that the d
females also should practise the same exercises. And neither
as to horsemanship nor gymnastics should I have any fear in
making this statement, that, though becoming to men, it would
not be becoming to women.'

And again a little lower down he says:

'Let us consider as gymnastics all bodily exercises relating to
war, in archery, and in throwing all kinds of missiles, and the
use of the target, and all fighting in heavy armour, and tactical
evolutions, and all kinds of marching, camps and encamping,
and all instructions pertaining to horsemanship. For there must **p. 707**
be public teachers of all these arts, earning pay from the State,
and their pupils, all the boys and men in the city and girls and
women, must be skilled in all these matters; having while still

---

b 6 Plato, *Laws*, 813 B   b 11 ibid. 796 B   c 6 ibid. 804 C
d 7 ibid. 813 D

PLATO girls practised every kind of dancing and fighting in heavy
armour, and as women having applied themselves to evolutions,
and tactics, and grounding and taking up arms.'

b   But neither to these rules would the Hebrew doctrine
assent, but would assert the very opposite, ascribing
success in war not even to the strength of men, much
less to that of women, but attributing all to God and to
His aid in battle.   And so it says : ' Except the Lord build
the house, their labour is but lost that build it.   Except the Lord
keep the city, the watchman waketh but in vain.'

But observe how the wonderful philosopher also brings
the women into the gymnastic contests, speaking thus :

' But as to women, let girls who are still young contend naked
in the foot-race, and double course, and horse-race, and long
race on the race-course itself : but those of thirteen years are to
c go on until their union in marriage, but not beyond twenty
years nor less than eighteen ; and they must come down to
contend in these races clothed in befitting dress.

' So let these be our rules of racing for both men and women.
But as to trials of strength, instead of wrestling and all such
contests which now are severe, let there be fighting in armour,
both single combats, and two against two.'

And next, after saying,

' So also we must call to our aid those who excel in fighting
in armour, and bid them help us to frame the like laws,'

he adds these words:

d   ' Let also the same laws be in force in regard to the females
until the time of marriage.'

Then after having appended immediately to these
laws those concerning the training of peltasts, and
the pancratium, and archery, and throwing stones from
the hand and with a sling, and concerning the horse-
race, here again he adds these words concerning the
females :

---

707 b 5 Ps. cxxvii. 1   b 10 Plato, *Laws*, 833 C   c 9 ibid. 833 E
d 1 ibid. 834 A

'But it is not right to force females by laws and ordinances PLATO to participate in these contests; if, however, just from their former training passing into a habit their natural constitution without inconvenience allows children or maidens to take part, we must permit it and not blame them.'

So far the laws of Plato concerning women.   But the **p. 708** following extraordinary law is also his:

'If any have left female children, let the judge go back through brothers and brothers' sons, first on the male side, and afterwards on the female, in one and the same family: and let him judge by examination the fitness or unfitness of the time for marriage, inspecting the males naked, and the females naked as far as the navel.'

Moreover at the festivals he says that they must dance naked, speaking in the sixth Book of the *Laws* as follows:

'For this so serious purpose therefore they ought to perform their sports and dance together youths and maidens, both seeing **b** and being seen within bounds of reason and of a certain age implying suitable causes, both sexes being naked so far as sober modesty in each permits.'

In addition to all this hear also the following passages in the *Republic* on the law that the women should be in common:

'This law, said I, and the others which went before have, I suppose, the following law as their consequence.

'What is that?

'These women must all be common to all these men, and none live with any man as his own: and the children too must be common, and neither any parent know his own offspring, nor any **c** child his father.'

Next he adds:

'It is probable, said he.   You therefore, said I, as their law-giver will select the women as well as the men, and, as far as

---

d 9 Plato, *Laws*, 834 D   708 a 3 ibid. 924 E   a 12 ibid. 771 E
b 8 Plato, *Republic*, 457 C   c 4 ibid. 458 C

PLATO possible assign those who are of like nature: and they, as having houses and meals in common, and none possessing anything of this kind privately, will of course be together, and being mixed up together both in the gymnasia and in their general mode of life will be led, I suppose, by the necessity of nature to intercourse with each other. Or do you think that what I say will not necessarily occur?

d   ' Not by any mathematical necessity, said he, but by constraints of love, which are likely to be keener than the other kind in persuading and drawing the mass of mankind.'

But some one perhaps will explain the meaning of these passages in a different way, and will say that they do not suggest what is commonly supposed; since he does not say that all the women without distinction are to be in common, so that wantonness may be allowed to every chance-comer, but that the assignment of them among the men is to lie in the power of the magistrates. For they are to be common in the same way as one may say that the public money is common, being distributed to the proper persons by those who are entrusted with it. Suppose then that this is so.

But what would you say on learning that he also bids them not to bring forth into light what they conceive, speaking as follows?

p. 709

' For a woman, said I, let the law be that beginning from the twentieth year she should bear children for the State until the fortieth year: and for a man, after he has passed the most vigorous prime of his course, henceforward to beget children for the State until his fifty-fifth year.'

After which he says:

' But when both the women and the men, I suppose, have passed the age for begetting children, we shall let them go free perhaps to have intercourse with whomsoever they please.'

And he adds:

b   ' Having strictly charged them, if possible, to bring forth no embryo to light, if such there should be; but should any force its way, to deal with it on the understanding that there is no PLATO maintenance for such a child.'

Such are his directions concerning the conduct of women: and concerning unnatural love [*for which he makes a long apology*—ED.], how unlike are his senti- 710 d ments to those of Moses, who in laws expressly contrary pronounces with loud voice the fit sentence against sodomites.

Why need we still urge the charge that this most wise **p. 711** philosopher after acquitting such sinners, against whom he did not think it fit to prescribe sentence of death, directs in his *Laws* that the slave who failed to give information of a treasure discovered by another should be punished with death. But that you may not suspect me of bearing false witness, listen also to what follows:

CHAPTER XXI

'WHATEVER answer the god may give in regard to the **b** property and the man who removed it, that let the city execute in obedience to the oracles of the god. And if the informer be a free man, let him have the reputation of goodness; but if he fail to inform, of baseness. But if he be a slave, the informer **c** may rightly be made free by the city, on payment of his value to his master; but if he fail to give information, let him be punished by death.'

Here again the punishment of death is enacted not against the man who has purloined some forbidden property, but against him who failed to inform against another who had done wrong: and in another case too he declares a master free from guilt if he kill his own slave in anger. He says in fact:

'If he have killed a slave of his own, let him undergo purification; but if he have killed another man's slave in anger, let him pay the owner twofold for the loss.'   **d**

---

711 b 1 Plato, *Laws*, 914 A   c 11 ibid. 868 A

Listen also to this passage of the laws which he enacted in regard to murderers:

PLATO   'If therefore any one with his own hand slay a free man, and the deed have been done in a passion without premeditation, let him suffer all other penalties that were deemed right for one who slew another without anger to suffer, but let him undergo compulsory exile for two years to correct his passion.'

And then he appends to this another law of the following kind:

'But let the man who has slain another in anger, yet with premeditation, suffer all other the same penalties as the former offender; but just as the other was banished for two years, let him be banished for three, being punished for a longer term because of the violence of his passion.'

Then next he enacts such laws as the following in regard to one who has committed homicide a second time:

p. 712   'But if ever after returning from exile either of them be overcome by anger and commit this same offence again, let him be banished and never return.'

And again afterwards he says:

'But if, as occurs sometimes, though not often, a father or mother from anger kill a son or a daughter by blows or any manner of violence, let them undergo the same purifications as the others, and spend three years in exile. But when the homicides have returned from exile, let the wife be separated from her husband and the husband from the wife, and not beget children together any more.'

To this also he adds:

'But if any man in anger slay his wedded wife, or a wife do
b the same in like manner to her own husband, let them undergo the same purifications, but continue three years in banishment. And when the author of such a deed has returned, let him have no communion in sacred rites with his children, nor ever sit at the same table with them.

---

711 d 4 Plato, *Laws*, 867 C   d 11 ibid. 867 D   712 a 1 ibid. 868 A
a 5 ibid. 868 C   a 13 ibid. 868 D

'And if a brother or sister slay brother or sister in anger, be it PLATO enacted that the same purifications and banishments as have been appointed for parents and children be undergone by them; and let them never have the same home with those whom they have deprived of brothers, or of children, nor share in their sacred rites.

'But if brother slay brother in a faction fight, or in other like c manner, while defending himself against an assault, let him be guiltless, as if he had slain an enemy in war. And in like manner if a citizen slay a fellow citizen, or a foreigner a foreigner. But if a foreigner slay a citizen, or a citizen a foreigner in self-defence, let him be in the same position as to being guiltless: and in like manner if a slave kill a slave. But if on the other hand a slave kill a free man in self-defence, let him be subject to the same laws as the slayer of a father.

'Whosoever designedly and wrongfully slays with his own d hand any one of his kinsmen, in the first place let him be excluded from legal rights, polluting neither agora, nor temples, nor harbours, nor any other public assembly, whether any one interdict the doer of these deeds or not: for the law interdicts him. . . . And let the man who fails to prosecute him, when he ought, or fails to proclaim him be excluded from kinship: . . . and in the second place let him be liable to prosecution by any one who wishes to exact retribution for the deceased. And if a woman has wounded her husband, or a man his wife, with design to kill, let either suffer perpetual banishment.'

Such are the laws of the philosopher: and if we are to **p. 713** bring those of Moses into comparison with them, hear what sort of ordinances he makes concerning cases of homicide.   'If one smite a man and he die, let him surely be put to death. And if he did it not purposely, but God delivered him into his hands, I will give thee a place whither the slayer shall flee. But if a man set upon his neighbour to slay him with guile, and flee for refuge, thou shalt take him from Mine altar to put him to death. He that smiteth his father, or his mother, shall surely be put to death. . . . And if two men revile one another, and one b

---

b 6 Plato, *Laws*, 869 B   d 1 ibid. 871 A   d 10 ibid. 877 C
713 a 4 Ex. xxi. 12

smite his neighbour with a stone or with his fist, and he die not, but be laid upon his bed, if the man rise again, and walk abroad upon his staff, then shall he that smote him be quit : only he shall pay for his loss of time, and the fees of his physician.   And if a man smite his servant, or his maid, with a staff, and he die under his hands, he shall surely be punished.   But if he live a day or two he shall not be punished ; for he is his money. . . . And if a man smite the eye of his servant, or the eye of his handmaiden, and blind him utterly, he shall send them forth
c free for their eyes' sake.'

Such then are the laws of Moses.   Now hear again in what way, and for what kind of offences, Plato orders that the slave shall be punished with scourging without hope of pardon :

PLATO   'When a man wishes to gather the vintage of what are now called fine grapes, or the so-called fine figs, if he be taking them from his own property, let him gather the fruit however and whenever he will: but if from the property of others without having gained permission, let that man always be punished, in accordance with the principle of *not taking up what one laid not down*.   But if a slave touch any of such things without having gained permission of the owner of the farms, for every berry of
d the grapes and every fig of the fig-tree let him be scourged with an equal number of stripes.'

Such are the enactments against these offences, unworthy of the magnanimity of Plato.   But how noble and humane those of Moses are you may learn by listening to him while he speaks as follows : 'When thou art come into thy neighbour's vineyard, thou shalt eat grapes until thy soul be satisfied, but shalt not put any into thy vessel.'   And again : 'If thou come into thy neighbour's standing corn, and pluck the ears with thy hands, then thou shalt not put a sickle to thy neighbour's standing corn.'   And again : 'If thou reapest thy harvest in thy field, and hast forgotten a sheaf in thy field, thou shalt not turn back again to take it : it shall be for the

---

713 b 9 Ex. xxi. 26   c 6 Plato, *Laws*, 844 E   d 6 Deut. xxiii. 24, 25
d 11 Deut. xxiv. 19

poor, for the stranger, for the fatherless, and for the widow, that
the LORD thy God may bless thee in every work of thine hands.
And if thou gather thine olives, thou shalt not turn back to p. 714
glean what is left behind thee : it shall be for the stranger, and
the fatherless, and the widow. And if thou gather the grapes of
thy vineyard, thou shalt not glean over again what is left behind
thee : this shall be for the stranger, for the fatherless and for the
widow.'

These then are the enactments found in Moses. And
Plato's are well known, in which you may find thousands
irreproachable, whereof we most gladly welcome all that
is noble and excellent in him, and bid a long leave
to what is not of such a character. But since we have
travelled so far through these matters, and have shown
cause why we have not chosen to follow Plato in philosophy, it is time to bring the rest of our promise to
completion, and to review the other sects of Greek
philosophy.

BOOK XIV

CONTENTS

Chapter I

Preface concerning the Subject of the Book.   p. 717

HAVING described in the preceding Book all that there
was to say and to hear about the philosophy of Plato and
his agreement with the Hebrew oracles, for which we are
struck with admiration of him, and on the other hand
concerning his dissent from them, for which no man of b
good sense could approve him, I will now pass on to the
remaining sects of those who have been famed for philosophy among the Greeks.

And in their case again I shall set their lapse from the
truth before the eyes of my readers, not in my own
person nor of my own authority, but as before by the
testimony of the very words of Greek authors : not indeed
from dislike to any of them personally, since I confess
that I have a great admiration for them, when I compare
the persons with the rest of mankind as men.

But when I compare them with the sacred writers and
prophets of the Hebrews, and with God who through c
them has both uttered predictions of things to come
and exhibited marvellous works, nay more, has laid the
foundations of instruction in religious learning and true

doctrines, I no longer think that any one ought with reason to blame us, if we prefer God before men, and truth itself before human reasonings and conjectures.

All this I have striven to prove in the argument of this present *Preparation*, as at once an answer and a defence against those who shall inquire, what beauty or majesty we have seen in the writings of the Barbarians, d that we have decided to prefer them to our ancestral and noble philosophy, that, I mean, of the Greeks. However, it is time now to let our proof proceed by way of facts.

CHAPTER II

Now, I think, we ought before all things to begin from p. 718 the first foundation of philosophy among the Greeks, and to learn concerning the so-called physical philosophers before the time of Plato, who they were, and what sort of men their philosophy found as champions of its system ; then we must pass on to the successors of Plato, and learn who they also were, and survey their mutual disputations, and review also the dissensions of the other sects, and the oppositions of their opinions, wherein I shall exhibit the noble combatants like boxers eagerly exchanging blows as on a stage before the spectators.

b Let us, for instance, at once observe how, on the one hand, Plato used to scoff at the earliest philosophers who preceded him, and how others scoffed at Plato's friends and successors : and again in turn how Plato's disciples used to criticize the wise doctrines of Aristotle's fertile thought : and how those who boasted of Aristotle and the Peripatetic School used to prove that the views of those who preferred the opposite sect were nonsense.

You will also see the clever and precise doctrines of the subtlety of the Stoics ridiculed in turn by others, and all the philosophers on all sides struggling against their c neighbours, and most bravely joining in battle and wrestling, so that even with hands and tongue, or rather with

774

pen and ink, they raise strongholds of war against each
other, striking, as it were, and being struck by the spears
and various weapons of their wordy war.

And in this strife of athletes our arena will include,
in addition to those already mentioned, men stripped of
all truth, who have taken up arms in opposition to all
the dogmatic philosophers alike; I mean the Pyrrhonists,
who declared that in man's world there is nothing comprehensible; and those who said with Aristippus that the
feelings were the sole objects of perception; and then **d**
again those who with Metrodorus and Protagoras said
that we ought to believe only the sensations of the
body.

Over against these we shall at the same time strip
for the combat the schools of Xenophanes and Parmenides, who arrayed themselves on the opposite side and
annihilated the senses.

Neither shall we omit the champions of pleasure, but
shall enroll their leader Epicurus also with those already
mentioned.   But against all alike we shall use their own
weapons to set forth their confutation.

Also of all the so-called physicists alike I shall drag **p. 719**
out to light both the discrepancies of their doctrines and
the futility of their eager studies; not at all as a hater
of the Greeks or of reason, far from it, but to remove all
cause of slanderous accusation, that we have preferred
the Hebrew oracles from having forsooth been very little
acquainted with Hellenic culture.

Chapter III

THE Hebrews on their part from long time of old and, **b**
so to say, from the very first origin of man, having found
the true and religious philosophy have carefully preserved
this undefiled to succeeding generations, son from sire
having received and guarded a treasure of true doctrines,

so that no one dared to take away from or add to what had been once for all determined.

So neither has Moses the all-wise, who has been shown
c by our former discourse to have been older than all the Greeks, but last in time of all the ancient Hebrews, ever thought of disturbing and changing any of the doctrines held by his forefathers concerning dogmatic theology, except so far as to found for the people under his charge a certain conduct of life towards each other, and a code of laws for a kind of moderate republic.

Nor have the prophets after him, who flourished for countless periods of years, ever ventured to utter a word of discord either against each other, or against the opinions held by Moses and the elders beloved of God.
d   Nay not even has our Christian School, which derives its origin from them, and by a divinely inspired power has filled alike all Greece and Barbarian lands, introduced anything at variance with the earlier doctrines ; or perhaps one should rather say that not only in the doctrines of theology but also in the mode of life Christianity prescribes the same course as the godly Hebrews before Moses.

Our doctrines then thus described, and testified to by all authors, first middle and last, with one mind and one voice, confirm with unanimous vote the certainty of that which is both the true religion and philosophy, and are
p. 720 filling the whole world, and growing afresh and flourishing every day, as if they had but just established their first prime : and neither legal ordinances, nor hostile plots, nor the oft-sharpened weapons of enemies have exhibited a power superior to the excellence of the reasons which we followed.

But now let us observe what strength has ever been exhibited by the doctrines of the philosophy of the Greeks, tossed as they were in shallow waters ; and first
b of them all let us send down into the battle those who are called physicists. As then these are said to have

flourished before Plato, we may learn from Plato himself how they were at variance one with another ; for he
exposes the feud of Protagoras, Heracleitus, and Empedocles against Parmenides and his school.

For Protagoras, who had been a disciple of Democritus,
incurred the reputation of atheism : he is said, at least,
to have used an introduction of the following kind in his
book *Concerning the gods* : 'As to gods I neither know that
they exist, nor that they do not exist, nor of what nature they
are.' And Democritus said that 'the first elements of the c
universe were vacuum and plenum,' and the plenum he
called 'being' and 'solid,' but the vacuum 'not-being.'
Wherefore he also says that 'being' no more exists than
'not-being' ; and that 'the things which partake of " being "
have from eternity a continuous and swift motion in the vacuum.'

But Heracleitus said that fire was the first principle of
all things, out of which they all come, and into which
they are resolved. For all things are change, and there
is a time determined for the resolution of them all into
fire, and for their production out of it.

These philosophers then said that all things are in d
motion ; but Parmenides, who was by birth an Eleatic,
held the doctrine that 'the all is one,' and that it subsists
without beginning and without motion, and is spherical
in shape. And Melissus, who was a disciple of Parmenides, held the same opinions with Parmenides. So
now listen to what Plato relates with regard to these
men in the *Theaetetus* :

Chapter IV

'And so from drift and motion and mixture of one with Plato
another, all things are " becoming," though we forsooth speak of
them as " being," not using a right term. For nothing ever p. 723

---

720 b 10 Diogenes Laertius, ix. c. 8, § 51   c 1 Aristotle, *Metaphysics*,
A 4   c 7 Bywater, *Heracl. Rell.* Fr. xxii   d 9 Plato, *Theaetetus*, p. 152 D
723 a Viger's edition, from which this notation is taken, passes at once
from 720 to 723

PLATO " is," but is always " becoming." And on this point grant that, except Parmenides, all the wise men in succession were agreed, Protagoras, and Heracleitus, and Empedocles, and the chief poets in either kind of poetry, Epicharmus in Comedy, and Homer in Tragedy, who, when he calls

" Oceanus sire and Tethys mother of gods,"

b says that all things are the offspring of flux and motion. Do you not think that this is what he means?

' I think so.

' Who then could any longer escape derision, if he disputed against so great an army with Homer for their leader? '

Then afterwards proceeding in his argument he further says :

' One must come then to closer quarters, as the argument in defence of Protagoras enjoined, and by sounding this floating essence observe whether it gives a true or a false note. At all events there has been no small conflict about it with no few disputants.

Far indeed from being small, it is making great advance in c Ionia. For the disciples of Heracleitus take a very vigorous lead in this argument.

' So much the more then, my dear Theodorus, are we bound to examine it, and that from its first principle, as they themselves suggest.

' Yes, by all means : for in fact, Socrates, about these Heracleitean doctrines, or, as you call them, Homeric and still older, it is no more possible to argue with the men themselves at Ephesus who pretend to be experts than with men in a frenzy. For in absolute accordance with his writings they are always adrift, and as to dwelling upon an argument and a question, d and quietly answering and asking in turn, they have less than no power at all; or rather the expression " not even nothing " is preferable in view of the absence of even the least quietness in the men. But if you ask any of them a question, they pull out as from a quiver dark little phrases which they shoot off at you, and if you try to get an explanation of what this means, you will presently be struck with another new-fangled phrase, and will

never come to any conclusion at all with any of them, no, nor yet PLATO
they themselves with one another; but they watch most carefully
not to allow anything to be settled either in argument, or in
their own souls, thinking, I suppose, that it would be something
stationary; and with that they are altogether at war, and drive
it out everywhere to the utmost of their power.   p. 724

'Perhaps, Theodorus, you have seen the men fighting, but have
never been in their company when at peace; for they are no
friends of yours. But, I suppose, they explain doctrines of this
peaceful kind at leisure to their disciples, whomsoever they wish
to make like themselves.

'Disciples, my good Sir! Such people do not become disciples one of another, but they grow up of themselves, inspired
each of them from any chance source, and the one thinking that
the other knows nothing. From these men therefore, as I was
going to say, you can never get a reason, either willingly or
unwillingly; but we must take the matter over ourselves and
examine it like a mathematical proposition.   b

'Yes, you speak with discretion. As to the proposition then,
have we not received it from the ancients, who concealed it from
the multitude in poetry, that Oceanus and Tethys, the origin of
all things, are flowing streams, and that nothing is at rest; and
now from their successors, who in their superior wisdom openly
declare it, in order that even their cobblers may hear and learn
their wisdom, and may cease from foolishly supposing that some
things are at rest and others in motion, and when they have c
learned that all are in motion, may honour them?

'But I nearly forgot, Theodorus, that others set forth the
opposite doctrine to this, namely,

"That only is unmoved, whose name is All,"

and all other assertions which men like Melissus and Parmenides,
in opposition to all these doctrines, stoutly maintain, that all is one
and stands self-contained, having no place in which to move.

'How then, my friend, are we to deal with all these? For
going on little by little we have unconsciously fallen between d
both armies, and unless we can in some way defend ourselves

---

724 c 5 Parmenides, *Fr.* i. l. 98 (Mullach, i. p. 124)

PLATO and retreat, we shall pay the penalty, just like those who play across a line in the palaestra, when they are caught hold of by both sides and dragged in opposite directions.'

This is what Plato says in the *Theaetetus*. Passing next to the *Sophist*, he speaks again concerning the physical philosophers his predecessors as follows:

' It seems to me that Parmenides, and every one who has ever yet adventured upon a trial of determining the number and nature of things existent, have discoursed to us in an easy strain. How ? Each seems to me to be relating a sort of fable to us, **p. 725** as if we were children. One says that existences are three, and some of them are sometimes warring in a manner with one another, and then becoming friends again they exhibit marriages, and births, and rearing of offspring: another says that they are two, moist and dry, or hot and cold, and he makes them dwell together and marries them. But all the Eleatic tribe in our part, beginning with Xenophanes and still earlier, assume that all things so-called are one, and so proceed with their fables. But certain Ionian and Sicilian Muses afterwards conceived that it is safer to combine both principles, and say that "being" is both **b** many and one, and is held together by enmity and friendship. For it is ever separating and being united, as the more strong-minded Muses assert; but the weaker relax the perpetual continuance of these conditions, and say that in turn the universe is now one and friendly under the influence of Aphrodite, and then many and at war with itself through some discordance. But whether in all this any of them has spoken truly or not, it would be hard and offensive to find fault in such important matters with famous men of antiquity.'

Then after a few sentences he adds :

' Well then, though we have not discussed all those who give **c** precise definitions about "being" and "not-being," nevertheless let it suffice : and on the other hand let us look at those who speak otherwise, in order that we may see from them all that it is by no means easier to say what " being " is than what " not-being " is.

' We must proceed then to consider these also.

---

724 d 9 Plato, *Sophist*, 242 C   b 11 ibid. 245 E

'Moreover it seems that among them there is, as it were, a kind PLATO
of war of the Giants, through their disputing with one another
about the nature of " being."

'How ?

'One side are for dragging all things down from heaven and
from the invisible to earth, actually grasping rocks and oaks in
their hands. For they lay hold of everything of this kind, and
stoutly maintain, that " being " belongs only to that which admits
some kind of contact and handling, defining body and " being " d
as the same, and should any one else say that a thing without
body has " being," they utterly despise him, and will not listen
to anything else.

'Truly they are terrible men that you speak of : for I too ere
now have met with many of them.

'For this reason those who dispute against them defend themselves very cautiously from some high place in an unseen world,
contending that certain intelligible and incorporeal " forms " are
the true " being." But the corporeal atoms of the other side, and
that which they call the truth, these shatter in pieces by their
arguments, and call them a floating kind of " becoming," instead
of " being." And between the two armies, O Theaetetus, there is **p. 726**
always a mighty battle joined on these subjects.

'True.'

So far, then, has Plato censured the physical philosophers who preceded him. And the kind of opinion
which he himself was for introducing on the matters in
question we have declared in the preceding Books, when
we were showing his agreement with the Hebrew doctrines and with the teaching of Moses in regard to
' Being.'

But come, let us examine in our argument Plato's own
successors also. It is said that Plato, having established his School in the Academy, was the first called an
Academic, and was the founder of the so-called Academic **b**
philosophy. And after Plato Speusippus, the son of
Plato's sister Potone, succeeded to the School, then
Xenocrates, and afterwards Polemon.

And these, it is said, began from his own hearth at

once to undo the teaching of Plato, distorting what had
been clear to the master by introducing foreign doctrines,
so that you might expect the power of those marvellous
c dialogues to be extinguished at no distant time, and the
transmission of the doctrines to come to an end at once
on the founder's death: for a conflict and schism having
hereupon begun from them, and never ceasing up to the
present time, there are none who delight to emulate the
doctrines which the Master loved, except perchance one
or two in all our lifetime, or some others very few in
number, and themselves not altogether free from false
sophistry; since even the earlier successors of Plato have
been blamed for such tendencies.

Polemon's successor, it is said, was Arcesilaus, and
d report says that he forsook the doctrines of Plato, and
established a sort of alien and, as it is called, second
Academy. For he declared that we ought to suspend
judgement about all things, for all are incomprehensible,
and the arguments on either side equal each other in
force, also that the senses and reason in general are un-
trustworthy. He used, for instance, to praise this saying
of Hesiod,

'The gods have spread a veil o'er human thought.'

He used also to try to make some paradoxical novelties.
After Arcesilaus, Carneades and Cleitomachus are said
to have abandoned the opinion of their predecessors, and
become the authors of a third Academy. ' And some add
also a fourth, that of the followers of Philo and Charmides : while
p. 727 some reckon even a fifth, that of the disciples of Antiochus.'

Such were the successors of Plato himself: and as to
their character take and read the statements of Numenius
the Pythagorean, which he has set down in the first Book
of his work entitled *Of the revolt of the Academics
against Plato*, to the following effect.

---

726 d 9 Hesiod, *Works and Days*, l. 42   d 11 Sextus Empiricus,
Pyrrh. Hyp. i. 220

Chapter V

' For the time then of Speusippus, sister's son to Plato, and **b** Nume-
Xenocrates the successor of Speusippus, and Polemon who suc-   nius
ceeded Xenocrates in the School, the character of the doctrine
always continued nearly the same, so far as concerned this much
belauded suspension of judgement which was not yet introduced,
and some other things perchance of this kind. For in other
respects they did not abide by the original tradition, but partly
weakened it in many ways, and partly distorted it : and
beginning from his time, sooner or later they diverged purposely **c**
or unconsciously, and partly from some other cause perhaps other
than rivalry.

' And though for the sake of Xenocrates I do not wish to say
anything disparaging, nevertheless I am more anxious to defend
Plato. For in fact it grieves me that they did not do and suffer
everything to maintain in every way an entire agreement with
Plato on all points. Yet Plato deserved this at their hands, for
though not superior to Pythagoras the Great, yet neither perhaps
was he inferior to him; and it was by closely following and
reverencing him that the friends of Pythagoras became the chief **d**
causes of his great reputation.

' And the Epicureans, having observed this, though they were
wrong, were never seen on any point to have opposed the
doctrines of Epicurus in any way; but by acknowledging that
they held the same opinions with a learned sage they naturally
for this reason gained the title themselves : and with the
later Epicureans it was for the most part a fixed rule never to
express any opposition either to one another or to Epicurus on
any point worth mentioning : but innovation is with them
a transgression or rather an impiety, and is condemned. And for
this reason no one even dares to differ, but from their constant **p. 728**
agreement among themselves their doctrines are quietly held in
perfect peace. Thus the School of Epicurus is like some true
republic, perfectly free from sedition, with one mind in common

727 b 1 Numenius, *The revolt of the Academics against Plato*, a Fragment
preserved by Eusebius

Numenius and one consent; from which cause they were, and are, and seemingly will be zealous disciples.

'But the Stoic sect is torn by factions, which began with their founders, and have not ceased even yet. They delight in refuting one another with angry arguments, one party among them having still remained steadfast, and others having changed.

b So their founders are like extreme oligarchs, who by quarrelling among themselves have caused those who came after to censure freely both their predecessors and each other, as still being more Stoical one party than the other, and especially those who showed themselves more captious in technicalities; for these were the very men who, surpassing the others in meddlesomeness and petty quibbles, were the more quick to find fault.

'Long before these, however, there was the same feeling in those who drew their doctrines from Socrates in different directions, Aristippus in his own way, and Antisthenes in his, and c elsewhere the Megarians and Eretrians in ways of their own, and others with them.

'And the cause was, that as Socrates assumed three gods, and philosophized before them in the strains appropriate to each, his hearers did not understand this, but thought that he spoke all at random, and according to the breath of fortune which at any moment prevailed, sometimes one, sometimes another, as it chanced to blow.

'But Plato had been a Pythagorean, and knew that Socrates for the same reason took such sayings from no other source than that, and had known what he was saying; and so he too wrapped up his subjects in a manner that was neither usual nor plain to d understand; and after conducting them each in the way that he thought fit, and disguising them so as to be half seen and half unseen, he wrote in safety, but himself gave occasion to the subsequent dissension, and distraction of his doctrines, not indeed from jealousy nor yet from ill will—but I am unwilling to speak unfavourable words of men of earlier times.

'But now that we have learned this, we ought rather to apply our judgement to a different point, and as we proposed at the commencement to distinguish Plato from Aristotle and Zeno, so now again separating him from the Academy, if God help us, we p. 729 will allow him to be in and of himself a Pythagorean. Since

now being torn in pieces more furiously than any Pentheus Numenius
deserved, he suffers limb by limb, but is by no means transformed from his whole self and retransformed.

' As a man therefore who stood midway between Pythagoras
and Socrates he reduced the sternness of the former to benevolence, and the wit and playfulness of the latter he raised from
irony to dignity and gravity, and by making just this mixture of
Socrates and Pythagoras he showed himself more affable than
the one and more grave than the other.   b

' This, however, is not at all what I was going to discuss, my
present inquiry having no concern herewith : but I will pass on
to what I had intended, lest I should be thrown out of the way
that leads thither, or else I seem likely to run away altogether.

' Arcesilaus and Zeno became disciples of Polemon, for I am
going to mention them again at last. Of Zeno I remember to have
said that he attended Xenocrates and then Polemon, and afterwards became a Cynic in the School of Crates : but now let him be
accounted to have also derived something from Stilpo and those c
Heracleitean discourses.

' For since as fellow disciples of Polemon Arcesilaus and Zeno
were emulous of each other, the one of them took as his allies
in their mutual contest Heracleitus, and Stilpo, and also Crates,
among whom he was made by Stilpo a disputant, by Heracleitus
austere, and by Crates cynical : but the other, Arcesilaus, has
Theophrastus, and Crantor the Platonist, and Diodorus, and then
Pyrrho, and of these Crantor made him persuasive, Diodorus
sophistical, and Pyrrho versatile, and reckless, and nothing at all. d

' And this was the meaning of a certain hexameter verse often
applied to him in an insulting parody:

" Plato before, and Pyrrho behind, in the midst Diodorus."

But Timon says that he was also taught and equipped by Mene-
demus in the art of disputation, if at least it is of him that he
says :
　　　　　" With Menedemus' lead beneath his breast
　　　　　He runs apace to Pyrrho's mass of flesh,
　　　　　Or Diodorus' dialectic craft."

---

729 d 4 Cf. Hom. *Il.* vi. 181   d 8 Timon, *Fr.* l. 72 (Mullach, i. p. 90)
Diogenes Laertius, iv. c. 6

p. 730 'So by interweaving the reasonings and scepticism of Pyrrho
NUMENIUS with the subtleties of Diodorus, who was skilled in dialectics, he
arrayed a kind of mouthy chatter in Plato's forcible language,
and would say and unsay, and roll over from this side and
from that, and from either side, whichever it might chance,
retracting his own words, obscure, and contradictory withal,
and venturesome, and knowing nothing, as he said himself, so
candid as he was : and then somehow he would turn out like
b those who did know, after having exhibited himself in all kinds
of characters by the sketchiness of his discourses.'

CHAPTER VI

'THERE was no less uncertainty about Arcesilaus than about
Tydides in Homer, when you could not know on which side he
was, whether associated with Trojans or with Achaeans. For to
c keep to one argument and ever say the same thing, was not
possible for him, nor indeed did he ever think such a course by
any means worthy of a clever man. So he went by the name of a

"Keen sophist, slayer of men unskilled in fence."

'For by preparation and study in the delusive show of his
arguments he used to stupefy and juggle like the Empusae,
and could neither know anything himself nor let others know:
he spread terror and confusion, and in carrying off the prize
for sophistries and deceitful arguments, he rejoiced over his
disgrace, and prided himself wonderfully on not knowing either
what is base or noble, or what is good or bad, but after saying
d whichever came into his thoughts, he would change again and
upset his argument in many more ways than he had constructed it.

'So he would cut himself and be cut in pieces like a hydra,
neither side being distinguished from the other, and without
regard to decency ; nevertheless he pleased his hearers, who
while they listened saw also that he was good-looking : he was
most pleasing therefore both to hear and to see, after they
grew accustomed to accept from him arguments proceeding from

---

730 b 3 Cf. Hom. *Il.* v. 85

a beautiful face and mouth, besides the kindliness which shone in NUMENIUS
his eyes.

'Now this description must not be taken loosely, but from the **p. 731**
beginning such was his character.   For having associated in boyhood with Theophrastus, a man of gentle and amorous disposition,
Arcesilaus being beautiful and still in the bloom of youth gained
the love of Crantor the Academic, and attached himself to him;
and being not without natural ability, he let it run its swift and
easy course, and fired by love of disputation he gained help from
Diodorus in those elegant and artfully studied plausibilities, and
also attended the School of Pyrrho (now Pyrrho had begun somewhere or other from the School of Democritus),—so Arcesilaus, b
equipped from this source, adhered, except in name, to Pyrrho, as
one who overthrew all things.

'Mnaseas at least, and Philomelus, and Timon, the Sceptics,
call him a Sceptic, as they were themselves, because he also overthrew truth and falsehood and probability.

'Therefore, although on account of his Pyrrhonistic doctrines
he might have been called a Pyrrhonist, yet from respect for his
lover he submitted to be still called an Academic.   He was therefore a Pyrrhonist, except in name: but an Academic he was not,
except in being so called.   For I do not believe what Diocles of
Cnidos asserts in his Diatribae so-entitled, that through fear of
the followers of Theodorus, and of the Sophist Bion, who used to c
assail the philosophers, and shrank from no means of refuting
them, Arcesilaus took precautions, in order to avoid trouble, by
never appearing to suggest any dogma, but used to put forward
the "suspense of judgement" as a protection, like the black juice
which the cuttle-fishes throw out.   This then I do not believe.

'Those, however, who started from this School, Arcesilaus and
Zeno, with such auxiliary forces of arguments helping both sides
in the war, forgot the origin from which they had started in
the School of Polemon:

> "And parting, formed in order of attack."   d

> "Together rushed
> Bucklers and lances, and the furious might

---

731 d 1 Hom. *Il.* xii. 86 (Lord Derby)   d 2 ibid. iv. 447–449

Of mail-clad warriors ; bossy shield on shield
Clattered in conflict ; loud the clamour rose."

" Buckler to buckler pressed, and helm to helm,
And man to man."

" Man struggling hand to hand with man."

p. 732   "Then rose too mingled shouts and groans of man,
Slaying and slain " ;

the Stoics being the slain ; for they could not strike the
Academics, because they could not discover in what part they
were most liable to be beaten. But beaten they would be, and
their foundation shaken, if they were to have neither principle
nor starting-point for the battle. Now the principle was to
prove that they did not express the thoughts of Plato ; and their
starting-point was lost, if they altered the definition concerning
the conceptual presentation by the removal of a single word.

b   'It is not now the proper time for me to show this, but I will
mention it again, when I arrive exactly at this point. When,
however, they had come to open variance, it was not that
the two struck at each other, but only Arcesilaus at Zeno. For
Zeno in his fighting had a certain solemnity and heaviness, not
more effective than the oratory of Cephisodorus : for he, Cephisodorus, when he saw his own teacher Isocrates attacked by Aristotle,
though he was ignorant and unacquainted with Aristotle, yet
from perceiving that the works of Plato were highly esteemed,
supposed that Aristotle's philosophy agreed with Plato's, and in
c trying to make war upon Aristotle struck at Plato, and having
drawn his first accusation from the " Ideas," ended by attacking
his other doctrines, of which he knew nothing himself, but guessed
the received opinions concerning them by the way in which they
are usually described.

'However, this Cephisodorus instead of fighting the man with
whom he was at war, fought with the one against whom he
wished not to make war. But if Zeno himself after getting rid
of Arcesilaus, had abstained also from making war upon Plato,
he would have shown himself, in my judgement, an excellent
philosopher, in so keeping the peace. But if he acted with
a knowledge perhaps of the doctrines of Arcesilaus, though in

---

731 d 6 Hom. *Il.* xiii. 131   d 8 ibid. iv. 471   732 a 1 ibid. iv. 450

ignorance of Plato, to judge from what he wrote against him, NUMENIUS
he is convicted of taking an inconsistent course, in not striking **d**
the one whom he knew, and insulting most foully and disgrace-
fully the man whom he had no right to assail, and treating him
far worse than he should have treated a dog.

'However, he certainly showed a high spirit in his disregard
of Arcesilaus: for either through ignorance of his doctrines,
or through fear of the Stoics, he turned aside "the mighty jaws
of bitter war" against Plato. But of Zeno's vile and utterly
shameless revolts against Plato I shall speak again, if I can spare **p. 733**
time from philosophy. I hope, however, never to have so much
time to spare, at least for this purpose, unless it be in sport.

'So, when Arcesilaus saw that Zeno was a professional rival,
and worth conquering, he shrank from nothing in trying to
overthrow the arguments set forth by him.

'Now of the other points on which he was at war with him,
I perhaps am not able to speak, or even if I were able, there
would be no need to mention them now: but as Zeno was the
first inventor of the following doctrine, and as he, Arcesilaus,
saw that both itself and its name were famous at Athens, I mean
the *conceptual presentation*, he employed every device against **b**
it. But the other being in the weaker position could suffer no
injury by keeping quiet, and so disregarded Arcesilaus, against
whom he would have had much to say, but was unwilling, or
rather perhaps there was some other cause; but Plato being no
longer among the living he proceeded to fight with his shadow, and
tried to cry him down by uttering all kinds of vulgar buffoonery,
thinking that neither could Plato defend himself, nor would
any one else care to avenge him: or if Arcesilaus should care to
do so, he thought that at all events he should be a gainer **c**
by diverting the attack of Arcesilaus from himself. He knew
also that Agathocles of Syracuse had practised this artifice upon
the Carthaginians.

'The Stoics listened in amazement. For their Muse was
not even then learned nor productive of such graces as those
by which Arcesilaus talked them down, knocking off this
argument, cutting away that, and tripping up others, and so

---

d 7 Hom. *Il.* x. 8

Numenius succeeded in persuading them. When therefore those against whom he argued were worsted, and those in whose midst he was
d speaking were astounded, the men of that day were somehow convinced that neither speech was anything, nor feeling, nor any single work however small, nor on the contrary would anything ever have seemed useless, except what so seemed in the opinion of Arcesilaus of Pitane. But he, as we said, held no opinion, nor made any more definite statement than that all these were little phrases and bugbears.'

Chapter VII

p. 734   'Now there is a pleasant story about Lacydes which I wish to tell you. Lacydes was rather stingy, and in a manner the proverbial Economist; for this man, who was in such general good repute, used to open his storeroom himself and shut it himself.
b And he would take out what things he wanted, and do all other such work with his own hands, not at all as approving self-dependence, nor as being in any poverty, nor in want of servants, for he certainly had servants such as they were: but the reason you are at liberty to guess.

'However, I will go on to tell the pretty story which I promised. For while acting as his own steward he thought that he ought not to carry the key about on his own person, but he used after locking up to hide the key in a certain hollow writing-case: and
c after sealing this with a ring, he used to roll the ring down through the keyhole and leave it inside the house, so that afterwards when he came back, and opened with the key, he would be able to pick up the ring, and lock up again, and then to seal, and then to throw the ring back again inside through the keyhole.

So the servants having discovered this clever trick, whenever Lacydes went out for a walk or anywhere else, they too would open the storeroom, and then, after eating this and drinking up that according to their desire, and carrying other things away, they went through this same round, they shut up, and sealed,
d and the ring they let down through the keyhole into the house, laughing heartily at their master.

'So Lacydes, when he had left his vessels full and found them empty, was puzzled by what occurred; and when he heard that the doctrine of incomprehensibility was taught in the philosophy N<small>UMENIUS</small> of Arcesilaus, he thought that this was the very thing that was occurring in regard to his storeroom. And from this beginning he took to studying with Arcesilaus the philosophy that we can neither see nor hear anything clear or sound; and having once drawn one of his companions into the house, he began to argue with him on "the suspense of judgement" with extraordinary vehemence, as it seemed, and said, This indeed I can state to you as an indisputable fact, having learned it from my own case, not from questioning any other.

'And then he began and described the whole misfortune which **p. 735** had happened to him about the storeroom. What then, said he, could Zeno now say against "incomprehensibility" thus in all points proved manifest to me in such circumstances as these? For as I locked it up with my own hands, sealed it myself, and myself threw the ring inside, and when I came again and opened it, saw the ring inside but not my other property, how can I fail to be justly incredulous of all things? For I shall not dare for my part to say that any one came and stole the things, as there was the ring inside.   **b**

'Then his hearer, who was an insolent fellow, having heard out the whole story as well as he could listen, being scarce able hitherto to contain himself, burst out into a very broad laugh, and still laughing and chuckling tried between whiles to refute his silly notion. So beginning from that time Lacydes no longer used to throw the ring inside, and ceased to use in argument the "incomprehensibility" of his storeroom, but began to comprehend his losses, and found that he had been philosophizing over them in vain.

'Nevertheless his servants were impudent knaves, and not to **c** be caught with one hand, but just such as the slaves you see in comedy, a Geta or a Dacus, loud-tongued in Dacian chatter; and after they had listened to the Stoics' sophisms, or had learned them in some other way, went straight at the venture, and used to take off his seal, and sometimes they would substitute another instead of it, but sometimes they did not even this, because they thought it would be all incomprehensible to him, whether this way or any other.

'So when he came in, he used to examine, and when he saw the writing-case unsealed, or, though sealed, yet with a different d seal, he was very angry: but when they said that it was sealed, for they could themselves see his own seal, he would begin a subtle argument and demonstration. And when they were beaten by his demonstration, and said that, if the seal was not there, perhaps he had himself forgotten and not sealed it up, Yes, certainly, he said, he remembered that he had himself sealed it up, and began to prove it, and argue all round, and thinking that they were making sport of him, he would make violent complaints against them with many oaths.

'But they suspected his attacks, and began to think that he was making sport of them; since Lacydes, who was a philosopher, had decided that he could have no opinion, and therefore no memory, for memory is a kind of opinion; a short time ago p. 736 at least they had heard him, they said, speak thus to his friends.

'But when he overthrew their attempts and used language not at all Academic, they would go themselves to the school of some Stoic, and learn anew what they ought to say, and with that preparation would meet sophistry with sophistry, and show themselves rivals of the Academic school in the art of thievery. Then he would find fault with the Stoics; but his servants would put aside his accusations by alleging " incomprehensibility " with no little jeering.

'So discussions went on there on all points, and arguments and counter-arguments; and in the meanwhile there was not a single b thing left, no vessel, nor anything that was put in the vessel, nor any other things that make up the furnishing of a house.

'And Lacydes for a while was at a loss, seeing that the support of his own doctrines was of no help to him; and thinking that, if he could not convict them, everything he had would be upset, he fell into perplexity, and began to cry out upon his neighbours and upon the gods, *Oh! Oh!* and *Alas! Alas!* and *By all the gods*, and *By the goddesses*, and all the other artless affirmations of men who in cases of distrust take to strong language—all these were uttered with loud shouting and asseveration.

c 'But at last, since he had a battle of contradiction in the house, the master, doubtless, took to playing the Stoic with his servants, and when the servants insisted on the Academic doctrines, in order that they might have no more trouble, he became a constant stay-at-home, sitting before his storeroom. And when he could

do no good, he began to suspect what his philosophy was coming Numenius
to, and opened his mind. Of these things, my boys, said he, we
talk in our discussions one way, but we live in another.'

This is what he tells about Lacydes. But the man d
found many hearers, one of whom, Aristippus of Cyrene,
was distinguished. But of all his disciples his successor
in the School was Evander, and those who came after him.

After these Carneades took up the teaching and established a third Academy. In argument he employed the
same method as Arcesilaus, for, like him, he too practised
the mode of attacking both sides, and used to upset all
the arguments used by the others : but in the principle
of 'suspension of judgement' alone he differed from him,
saying that it was impossible for a mortal man to suspend judgement upon all matters, and there was a
difference between 'uncertain' and 'incomprehensible,'
and though all things were incomprehensible, not all
were uncertain. But this Carneades was also acquainted p. 737
with the Stoic doctrines, and by his contentious opposition to them grew more famous, by aiming not at the
truth but at what seemed plausible to the multitude :
whence he also gave the Stoics much displeasure. So
Numenius writes about him as follows :

Chapter VIII

' Carneades having succeeded to the leadership disregarded b
the teacher whose doctrines he ought to have defended, both those
which were unassailable and those which had been assailed, and
referring everything back to Arcesilaus, whether good or bad,
renewed the battle after a long interval.'

And afterwards he adds :

' So this man also would bring forward and take back, and
gather to the battle contradictions and subtle twists in various
ways, and be full both of denials and affirmations, and contra- c
dictions on both sides : and if ever there was need of marvellous
statements, he would rise up as violent as a river in flood, over-

Numenius flowing with rapid stream everything on this side and on that, and would fall upon his hearers and drag them along with him in a tumult.

'While therefore he swept off all others he himself remained infallible, an advantage not enjoyed by Arcesilaus : for while he used with his quackery to come round his frenzied companions, he was unconscious of having first deluded himself in this, that d he had not been guided by sensation, but convinced of the truth of his reasoning in the overthrow of all things at once.

'But Carneades after Arcesilaus must have been evil upon evil, as he made not even the smallest concession, unless his opponents were likely to be disconcerted by it, in accordance with what he called his positive and negative presentations from probability, that this individual thing was an animal or was not an animal.

'So after such a concession, just as wild beasts who recoil throw themselves all the more violently upon the spear-points, he too after giving in would make a more powerful assault. And when he had stood his ground and was successful, then at once he would voluntarily disregard his previous opinion, and make no mention of it.

p. 738   'For while granting that there are both truth and falsehood in all things, as if he were co-operating in the method of inquiry, he would give a hold like a clever wrestler and thereby get the advantage. For after granting each side according to the turn of the scale in probability, he said that neither was comprehended with certainty.

'He was in fact a more clever freebooter and conjurer than Arcesilaus. For together with something true he would take a falsehood like it, and with a conceptual presentation a concept similar to it, and after weighing them till the scales were even, he would admit the existence neither of the truth nor of the falsehood, or no more of the one than of the other, or more only from probability.

b   'So dreams followed dreams, because the false presentations were like the true, as in passing from an egg of wax to the real egg.

'The evil results therefore were the more numerous. And nevertheless Carneades fascinated and enslaved men's souls ; as an undetected cozener, and an open freebooter, he could conquer whether by craft or by force even those who were very thoroughly equipped.

' In fact every opinion of Carneades was victorious, and never NUMENIUS
any other, since those with whom he was at war were less powerful
as speakers.

' Antipater, for instance, who was his contemporary, was in- c
tending to write something in rivalry; in face, however, of the
arguments which Carneades kept pouring forth day by day, he
never made it public, neither in the Schools, nor in the public
walks, nor even spoke nor uttered a sound, nor, it is said, did any
one ever hear from him a single syllable : but he kept threatening
written replies, and hiding in a corner wrote books which he
bequeathed to posterity, that are powerless now, and were more
powerless then against a man like Carneades, who showed himself
eminently great, and was so considered by the men of that time.   d

' But nevertheless, although from his jealousy of the Stoics he
stirred up confusion in public, he would himself in secret with
his own friends agree, and speak candidly, and affirm, as much
as any other ordinary person.'

Then next he adds :

' Mentor was a disciple of Carneades at first, yet not his successor : for while still living Carneades found him familiar with
his mistress, and not merely from a probable presentation, nor
as failing to comprehend, but most fully believing his own eyes,
and with a clear comprehension, rejected him from his School.
So he departed and became his opponent in sophistry, and his
rival in art, refuting the " incomprehensibility " which he taught in
his discourses.'

Again he adds :   p. 739

' But Carneades, as teaching a self-contradictory philosophy,
used to pride himself upon his falsehoods, and hide the truths
beneath them.   So he used his falsehoods as curtains, and hiding
within spoke the truth in a somewhat knavish way.   Thus he
suffered from the same fault as beans, of which the empty ones
float on the water and rise highest, while the good ones lie below
and are unseen.'

This is what is said about Carneades.   In the School
Cleitomachus is appointed his successor, and after him
Philon, of whom Numenius makes mention as follows :

CHAPTER IX

NUMENIUS   'So then this Philon on first succeeding to the School was beside himself with joy, and by way of making a grateful return used to worship and extol the doctrines of Cleitomachus, and

c   "arm himself in gleaming brass"

against the Stoics.

'But as time went on, and their doctrine of "suspense" was going out of fashion from familiarity, he was not at all consistent in thought with himself, but began to be converted by the clear evidence and acknowledgement of his misfortunes. Having therefore already much clearness of perception, he was very desirous, you may be sure, to find some who would refute him, that he might not appear to be turning his back and running away of his own accord.

'A disciple of Philon was Antiochus, who founded a different Academy: at least he attended the School of Mnesarchus the Stoic, and adopted the contrary opinions to his teacher Philon, d and fastened countless strange doctrines upon the Academy.'

These anecdotes and thousands like these are recorded of the successors of Plato. It is time, however, to take up our subject anew, and examine the opinions, alike false and contradictory, of the physical philosophers, men who wandered over the wide earth, and had set the highest value on the discovery of truth, and been familiar with the opinions of all the ancients, and carefully studied the exact nature of the theology p. 740 which existed among all, Phoenicians and Egyptians and the Greeks themselves, in much earlier times. It is worth while then to hear from themselves what was the fruit they found from their labours, that so we may learn whether any worthy notion of God had come down to them from the men of an older time.

For the superstition of polytheism was formerly prevalent from ancient times among the nations, and shrines, and temples, and mysteries of the gods were everywhere customarily maintained, both in city and country

---

739 c 1 Hom. *Il.* vii. 206

districts. So then there was no need even of human NUMENIUS
philosophy, if indeed the knowledge of things divine
had preoccupied the ground : nor was there any necessity
for the wise to invent novelties, if forsooth the doctrines **b**
of their forefathers were right, nor any cause for factions
and dissensions among the noble philosophers, if the
ancestral opinion about their gods had been tested and
proved to be harmonious and true.

Or what need was there to war and fight with one
another, or run about and wander up and down the long
course, and filch the learning of the Barbarians, when
they ought to have been staying at home, and learning
all from the gods, if forsooth there were any gods, or to
learn from the writers on religion the true and infallible
statements of the matters investigated in philosophy, **c**
about which they spent infinite toil and contention, yet
fell far short of discovering the truth?

Why too need they have ventured to make novel
inquiries about gods or to quarrel and pummel one
another, if forsooth a safe and sure discovery of gods and
a true knowledge of religion was contained in sacred
rites and mysteries and the rest of the theology of the
most ancient races, when they might have cultivated that
very religion undisturbed and in harmonious agreement?

But then if it should be found that these men had
learned no truth about God from their predecessors, but
had set themselves to the examination of nature by their **d**
own devices, and used conjectures rather than clear conception, why should they any longer refuse to acknowledge that the ancient theology of the nations offered
nothing beyond the account which has been rendered in
the books preceding this?

Now that the philosophy of the Greeks was a product
of human conjectures and much disputation and error,
but not of any exact conception, you may learn from
Porphyry's *Epistle to Anebo the Egyptian*, when you hear
him acknowledge this very fact in these words:

CHAPTER X

p. 741
PORPHYRY

'I WILL begin my friendship with you by an inquiry con-
b cerning the gods and good demons and the philosophical
doctrines relating to them, subjects upon which very much has
been said by Greek philosophers also, the greater part, however,
of their statements having only conjecture for the foundation of
their credibility.'

And lower down he adds again:

' For among us there is much verbal controversy, as we derive
c the notion of "the good" by conjecture from human reasonings:
and those who have formed plans of communication with the
higher nature, have exercised their wisdom in vain, if this
branch of the subject has been disregarded in the investigation.'

Moreover in what he wrote *Against Boëthus, On the
Soul*, the same author makes the following confession in
writing, word for word:—

'The evidence of our thoughts and that of history unquestionably establish the immortality of the soul: but the arguments
brought forward by philosophers in demonstration of it seem easy
to be overthrown through the ingenious arguments of the Eristics
on every subject.   For what argument in philosophy could not be
d disputed by men of a different opinion, when some of them thought
fit to suspend judgement even about matters that seemed to be
manifest?'

Also in the work which he entitled *Of the Philosophy
derived from Oracles* he expressly acknowledges that the
Greeks have been in error, and calls his own god as
a witness, saying that even Apollo had proclaimed this
by oracles, and had testified to the discovery of the
truth by the Barbarians rather than by the Greeks, and
moreover had even mentioned the Hebrews in the testimony which he bore.

In fact, after quoting the oracle he has immediately
made use of these concluding words:

---

741 a 1 Porphyry, *Epistle to Anebo*, § 1   b 7 ibid. § 47   c 8
Porphyry, *Against Boethus, On the Soul*

' Have you heard how much pains have been taken that a man PORPHYRY
may offer the sacrifices of purification for the body, to say nothing
of finding the salvation of the soul?   For the road to the gods **p. 742**
is bound with brass, and steep, and rough, and in it Barbarians
found many paths, but Greeks went astray, while those who
already held it even ruined it; but the discovery was ascribed
by the testimony of the god to Egyptians, Phoenicians, and
Chaldeans (for these are Assyrians), to Lydians, and to Hebrews.'

This is the statement of the philosopher, or rather of
his god.   Is it right then after this to blame us, because
forsooth we forsook the Greeks who had gone astray and
chose the doctrines of the Hebrews, who had received
such testimony for comprehension of the truth?

And what are we to expect to learn from philosophers? **b**
Or what hope is there of assistance from them, if indeed
their statements for the most part derive the first principles of their proof from conjectures and probabilities?
And what is the benefit of disputation, if forsooth all the
arguments of the philosophers are easily overthrown,
because of the sophistical use of language on all subjects?
For these are the statements heard just now not from us,
but from themselves.

Wherefore it seems to me that not unreasonably but
rightly and with well-proved judgement, we have despised teaching of such a character, and have welcomed the
doctrines of the Hebrews, not because they have received **c**
testimony from the demon, but because they are shown to
partake of the excellence and power of divine inspiration.

In order, however, that you may learn by actual facts
the disputations of the wonderful philosophers, and their
dissensions about first principles, and about gods, and the
constitution of the universe, I will set out their own
words before you a little later.

But first we must notice another point; for they go
about boasting everywhere of their mathematical sciences
and saying that it is altogether necessary for those who

---

d 14 Porphyry, *Of the Philosophy derived from Oracles*

are going to attempt the comprehension of truth to
d pursue the study of astronomy, arithmetic, geometry,
music,—the very things which were proved to have come
to them from Barbarians,—for that without these a man
cannot be accomplished in learning and philosophy, nay,
cannot even touch the truth of things, unless the knowledge of these sciences has been previously impressed
upon his soul. And then, priding themselves upon their
learning in the subjects which I have mentioned, they
think that they are lifted up on high and almost walking
upon the very ether, as though forsooth they carried God
Himself about with them in their arithmetic ; and
because we do not pursue the like studies, they think
us no better than cattle, and say that we cannot in this
p. 743 way know God, nor anything grand. Come then, let us
first set straight what is wrong in this, by holding out
true reason as a light before them.

And that will show thousands of Greeks and thousands
of Barbarian races also, of whom the former with the
help of the aforesaid sciences recognized neither God,
nor virtuous life, nor anything at all that is excellent
and profitable, while the latter without all these sciences
have been eminent in religion and philosophy. For
instance, you may learn what sort of opinions were held
on these subjects by one so celebrated among them all as
b Socrates, if you give credit to what Xenophon narrates
in the *Memorabilia* as follows :

Chapter XI

XENOPHON ' HE also used to teach how far it was necessary for a well-
educated man to be acquainted with each subject. For example,
c he said that he ought to learn geometry so far as to be able, if
ever it should be necessary, rightly to measure land either in
taking or giving possession, or in allotting it, or marking out
work. And this, he said, was so easy to learn that one who
gave his mind to the measuring could know at once how much

---

743 b 3 Xenophon, *Memorabilia of Socrates*, iv. c. 7

land there was, and go away acquainted with the mode of XENOPHON
measuring it.

'But of learning geometry so far as to reach those unintelligible diagrams he disapproved, for he said he did not see of
what use these were, although he was not unacquainted with them.
But they were enough, he said, to exhaust a man's lifetime, and
hindered him from many other useful branches of learning.   d

'He bade them also become acquainted with astronomy, but
this also only so far as to be able to know the time of night, or of
the month, or of the year, for the sake of travelling, or voyaging, or
keeping watch, and to be able to make use of the indications
relating to all other things that are to be done either in the night,
or in the month, or year, by knowing the different seasons for the
works before mentioned. These also, he said, were easy to learn
from nocturnal hunters, and pilots, and many others, whose **p. 744**
business it is to know these things.

'But he strongly dissuaded from learning astronomy to such an
extent as to know the bodies which are not in the same orbit,
and the planets and comets, and to waste time in investigating their distances from the earth, and their periods, and the
causes of them. For he said that in these matters he did not see
any benefit, and yet even in these he was not uninstructed. But
he said of these also that they were enough to wear out a man's
lifetime, and to hinder him from many useful pursuits.

'And he wholly dissuaded one from anxiously inquiring in
what way the heavenly bodies are each contrived by God; for he **b**
neither thought that these things could be discovered by mankind, nor did he believe that the gods would be pleased with the
man who sought to know what they had not been willing to
make clear. But he said that the man who troubled himself
about these things would be in danger even of going as mad as
Anaxagoras was, who prided himself very highly upon explaining
the contrivances of the gods.

'For when he used to say that fire and the sun were the same,
he ignored the fact that though men easily discern the fire, yet **c**
they cannot look upon the sun; and by being exposed to the sunshine they have their complexions darkened, but not so by fire.
Also he was ignorant that of plants which spring out of the earth
none can make good growth without the light of the sun, while

XENOPHON all perish when heated by fire.   And in saying that the sun was a fiery stone he was ignorant also of this fact, that while a stone set in the fire neither shines nor lasts long, the sun continues all the time to be the brightest of all things.

    ' He also used to bid us learn to count; but here also as in d everything else he bade us guard against useless trouble: yet as far as it was useful he would himself help his companions in examining and discussing all things.'

    So writes Xenophon in the *Memorabilia*.   And in the *Epistle to Aeschines* the same author writes as follows concerning Plato, and those who boast of their physiology of the universe :

CHAPTER XII

p. 745 ' THAT the things of the gods are beyond us is manifest to every one; but it is sufficient to worship them to the best of our power.   What their nature is it is neither easy to discover nor b lawful to inquire.   For it pertains not to slaves to know the nature or conduct of their masters, beyond what their service requires.   And what is of most importance, in proportion as we ought to admire one who spends labour upon the interests of mankind, so to those who strive to get fame from many inopportune and vain attempts it brings the more trouble.   For when, O Aeschines, has any one ever heard Socrates talking about the heaven, or encouraging any one to learn about geometrical lines for correction of morals?   As to music we know that he understood it only by ear; but he was constantly telling them on every occasion what was noble, and what manliness was, and c justice, and other virtues : he used in fact to call the interests of mankind absolute good; and all things else, he used to say, were either impossible to be achieved by men, or were akin to fables, playthings of Sophists in their supercilious discussions.   And he did not merely say these things without practising them.   But to write of his doings to you who know them, although not likely to be unpleasing, takes time, and I have recorded them elsewhere.   When refuted therefore let them cease, or betake themselves to what is reasonable, these men who were not pleased with Socrates, to whose wisdom the god bare witness while he

---

was yet alive, and they who put him to death found no expiation XENOPHON
in repentance. And so—what a noble thing—they fell in love d
with Egypt, and the prodigious wisdom of Pythagoras, men whose
excess and inconstancy towards Socrates was proved by their love
of tyranny, and exchange of frugal living for a table of Sicilian
luxury to serve their boundless appetite.'

So speaks Xenophon, with a hint at Plato. But Plato
in the *Republic* relates that concerning gymnastics and
music Socrates spake as follows:

CHAPTER XIII

'WHAT then, O Glaucon, would be a learning likely to draw **p. 746**
the soul from the transient to the real?   But while I am speaking PLATO
there comes into my mind this point: did we not say surely that
these guardians while yet young must be athletes in war?   Yes,
we said so. The learning then which we are seeking must have
this quality in addition to the former. What quality? It must
be of some use to men of war. It certainly must, if possible. b
They were to be educated, we said before, in gymnastic and music.
It was so, said he. And gymnastic, I suppose, since it presides
over growth and decay of the body, is concerned with generation
and corruption. That is evident. This then cannot be the study
for which we are seeking. It cannot. Can then music, so far as
we previously discussed it? Nay, said he, that, if you remember, c
was the counterpart of gymnastic, as training our guardians by
the influences of habit, by harmony imparting not science but
a kind of harmoniousness, and by rhythm a rhythmical movement, and as having in its words certain other moral tendencies
akin to these, whether the subjects of its discourse were fabulous
or partly true; but it contained no instruction tending to such
an end as you are now seeking.

'You remind me very correctly, said I; for music certainly
contained nothing of the kind. But what can there be of this d
character, my excellent Glaucon? For, I think, we regarded all
the arts as mechanical. Of course.'

Then further on he adds:

'We must never let those whom we are to educate attempt any

---

d 4 See Plato, *Republic*, 404 C   746 a 1 ibid. 521 D   d 5 ibid. 530 E

PLATO imperfect form of science that has not reached the point that all ought to attain, as we were saying just now about astronomy. Or do you not know that they treat harmony also in this way? For while they measure and compare with each other the notes and concords that are merely heard, they labour, like the astronomers, on a useless task.

'Yes, by heaven! said he, and it is ludicrous to see how they p. 747 name certain condensed intervals, and lay their ears on one side, as if trying to catch a note from their neighbours; and some of them say that they can still hear an intermediate sound, and that this is the very smallest interval which should be used in measuring, while others doubt this and say that they now sound alike, and both set their ears before their mind.

'You mean, said I, those good men who are always teasing and torturing the strings, and screwing them up on the pegs. But that the metaphor may not be extended too far about the beats b given by the plectrum, and the assent, and dissent, and petulance of the strings, I drop the metaphor, and say that I do not mean these men, but those others whom we said just now that we would consult about harmony. For they do the same as the astronomers; they investigate the numerical relations in the harmonies which fall upon the ears, but they do not rise to problems, to examine what numbers are harmonious, and what not, and the reason in either case.'

But now let this suffice in the way of preface to our defence that we have not without right judgement c neglected the useless learning of such subjects as these. Let us then make at once a new beginning and examine the mutual contradictions in doctrine of the aforesaid physical philosophers. Now Plutarch has collected together the opinions of all the Platonists and Pythagoreans alike, and of the still earlier physical philosophers as they were called, and again of the more recent Peripatetics, and Stoics, and Epicureans, and written them in a work which he entitled *Of the Physical Doctrines approved by Philosophers*, from which I shall make the d following quotations:

Chapter XIV

'Thales of Miletus, one of the seven sages, declared water to Plutarch be the first principle of all things. This man is thought to have been the founder of philosophy, and from him the Ionic sect **p. 748** derived its name; for it had many successions. After studying philosophy in Egypt he came as an elderly man to Miletus. He says that all things come from water, and are all resolved into water. And he forms his conjecture first from the fact that seed, which is watery, is the first principle of all animal life; thus it is probable that all things have their origin from moisture. His second argument is that all plants derive nourishment and fruitfulness from moisture, and when deprived of it wither away. And the third, that the very fire of the sun, and of the stars, and the world itself are nourished by the evaporations of the waters. For this reason Homer also suggests this notion **b** concerning water,

" Ocean, which is the origin of all."

This is what Thales says.

'But Anaximander of Miletus says that the first principle of all things is the infinite, for from this all are produced, and into this all pass away; for which reason also infinite worlds are generated, and pass away again into that from which they spring. So he says the reason why the infinite exists is that the subsisting creation may not be deficient in any point. But he also is at **c** fault in not saying what the infinite is, whether it is air, or water, or earth, or any other corporeal elements; he is wrong therefore in declaring the matter while excluding the efficient cause. For the infinite is nothing else than matter, and matter cannot have an actual existence, unless the efficient cause underlie it.

'Anaximenes of Miletus declared that the air is the first principle of all things, for from this all are produced, and into it they are resolved again. For example, our soul, he says, is air, for it holds us together; and the whole world too is encompassed **d** by air and breath, and air and breath are used as synonyms.

---

747 d 2 Plutarch, *De Placitis Philosophorum*, p. 875   748 b 3 Hom.
Il. xiv. 246

PLUTARCH But he too is wrong in thinking that living beings consist of
simple homogeneous air and breath; for it is impossible that
the matter can exist as sole principle of things, but we must
assume the efficient cause also. As for instance silver suffices
not for the production of the drinking-cup, unless there be the
efficient cause, that is the silversmith; the case is similar with
copper and various kinds of wood, and all other matter.

'Heracleitus and Hippasus of Metapontum say that fire is the
principle of all things: for from fire, they say, all things are
p. 749 produced and all end in fire: and all things in the world are
created as it gradually cools down. For first the coarsest
part of it is pressed together and becomes earth; then the earth
being resolved by the natural force of the fire is turned into water,
and being vaporised becomes air. And again the world and all
the bodies in it are consumed in a conflagration by fire. Fire
therefore is the first principle, because all things come from it,
and the end, inasmuch as they are all resolved into it.

'Democritus, who was followed long after by Epicurus, said
b that the first principles of all things are bodies indivisible, but
conceivable by reason, with no admixture of vacuum, uncreated,
imperishable, not capable of being broken, nor of receiving
shape from their parts, nor of being altered in quality, but
perceptible by reason only; that they move, however, in the
vacuum, and through the vacuum, and that both the vacuum
itself is infinite and the bodies infinite. And the bodies possess
c these three properties, shape, magnitude, and weight. Democritus,
however, said two, magnitude and shape; but Epicurus added
to them a third, namely weight. For he said the bodies must
be moved by the impulse of the weight, since otherwise they will
not be moved at all. The shapes of the atoms are limitable,
not infinite: for there are none either hook-shaped, nor trident-
shaped, nor ring-shaped. For these shapes are easily broken,
whereas the atoms are impassive and cannot be broken; but
they have their proper shapes, which are conceivable by
d reason. And the "atom" is so called, not because it is extremely small, but because it cannot be divided, being impassive,
and free from admixture of vacuum: so that if a man says
"atom" he means unbreakable, impassive, unmixed with vacuum.
And that the atom exists is manifest: for there are also

elements (στοιχεῖα), and living beings that are empty, and there is PLUTARCH the Monad.

‘ Empedocles, son of Meton, of Agrigentum, says that there are four elements, fire, air, water, earth, and two original forces, love and hate, of which the one tends to unite, and the other to separate. And this is how he speaks :

> “ Learn first four roots of all things that exist :
>   Bright Zeus, life-giving Hera, and the god
>   Of realms unseen, and Nestis, who with tears
>   Bedews the fountain-head of mortal life.”

For by “ Zeus ” he means the seething heat and the ether ; and by “ life-giving Hera,” the air ; the earth by Aïdoneus, and by Nestis **p. 750** and “ the fountain-head of mortal life,” the seed, as it were, and the water.’

So great is the dissonance of the first physical philosophers : such too is their opinion concerning first principles, assuming, as they did, no god, no maker, no artificer, nor any cause of the universe, nor yet gods, nor incorporeal powers, no intelligent natures, no rational essences, nor anything at all beyond the reach of the senses, in their first principles.

In fact Anaxagoras alone is mentioned as the first of b the Greeks who declared in his discourses about first principles that mind is the cause of all things.   They say at least that this philosopher had a great admiration for natural science beyond all who were before him: for the sake of it certainly he left his own district a mere sheepwalk, and was the first of the Greeks who stated clearly the doctrine of first principles.   For he not only pronounced, like those before him, on the essence of all things, but also on the cause which set it in motion.

‘ “ For in the beginning,” he said, “ all things were mingled together in confusion : but mind came in, and brought them out of confusion into order.” ’

One cannot but wonder how this man, having been c

---

749 d 12 Empedocles, *On Nature*, l. 59 (Mullach, i. p. 2)

the first among Greeks who taught concerning God in this fashion, was thought by the Athenians to be an atheist, because he regarded not the sun but the Maker of the sun as God, and barely escaped being stoned to death.

But it is said that even he did not keep the doctrine safe and sound: for though he made mind preside over all things, he did not go on to render his physical system concerning the existing world accordant with mind and reason. Hear in fact how in Plato's dialogue *Of the Soul* Socrates blames him in the following passage:

Chapter XV

PLATO **d** 'But once when I heard a man reading out of a book, as he said, of Anaxagoras, and saying that it is mind that sets all in order, and is the cause of all, I was delighted with this cause, and it seemed to me in a certain manner right that mind should **p. 751** be the cause of all things, and I thought, if this is so, mind in its ordering all things must arrange each in such a way that all may be best.

'If therefore any one should wish to find the cause of each thing, how it comes into being or perishes or exists, what he must find out about it is this, how it is best for it either to be, or to do or suffer anything else. According to this theory then a man ought to consider nothing else, whether in regard to himself or others, except what is best and most perfect: then the same man must necessarily know also the worse; for the knowledge concerning them is the same.

b 'Reasoning thus then I rejoiced to think that I had found in Anaxagoras a teacher of the cause of existing things after my own mind, and that he would tell me in the first place whether the earth is flat or round, and, after he had told me, would further explain the cause and the necessity, stating which is the better, and that it is better for it to be of such shape: and if he should say that it is in the centre, I thought that he would go on to

---

750 d 1 Plato, *Phaedo*, p. 97 B

explain that it is better for it to be in the centre: and if he c PLATO should prove all this to me, I was prepared to desire no other kind of cause beyond that.

'Moreover I was prepared to make the like inquiries concerning sun and moon and the other heavenly bodies as to their relative swiftness, and turning-points and other conditions, how it is better for each of them thus to act and be acted upon as they are. For I could never have thought that when he asserted that they were ordered by mind he would ascribe any other cause to them, except that it was best for them to be just as they are.

'I thought therefore that in assigning its cause to each of them severally, and to all in common, he would further explain what d was best for each and what was the common good of all. And I would not have sold my expectations for a great deal, but I seized the books very eagerly, and began to read as fast as I could, in order that I might know as soon as possible what was best and what worse. How glorious then the hope, my friend, from which I was driven away, when, as I went on reading, I saw a man making no use of mind, nor alleging any (real) causes for the ordering of things, but treating as causes a parcel of airs and ethers and waters, and many other absurdities.

'And he seemed to me to be very much in the same case as if one were to say that whatever Socrates does he does by mind, and **p. 752** then, on attempting to state the causes of each of my actions, should say first of all that the reasons of my sitting here now are these, that my body is composed of bones and muscles, and the bones are hard and have joints separate one from another, while the muscles are capable of contraction and relaxation, surrounding the bones as do also the flesh and skin which hold them together. When therefore the bones are lifted in their sockets, the muscles by their relaxation and contraction make me able, I suppose, now to bend my limbs, and this is the cause why I am sitting here with my knees bent. **b**

Again, with regard to my conversing with you, it is as if he were to state other causes, such as these, a set of sounds, and airs, and hearings, and ten thousand other things of this kind, but should neglect to mention the true causes, namely, that since the Athenians thought it better to condemn me, for that reason I too in my turn have thought it better to sit here, and

PLATO **c** more just to remain and undergo my sentence, whatever they may have ordered.

'For, by the Dog! I think these muscles and these bones would long ago have been near Megara or Boeotia, carried thither by their opinion of what is best, did I not think it more just and more noble to undergo any sentence which the state may appoint, instead of taking to flight like a runaway.

'But to call such things as these causes is extremely absurd: if however any one were to say that without having such things, bones and muscles and all else that I have, I should not be able to do what I thought right, he would speak truly; but to say that these are the causes of my doing what I do, and that I do so **d** by mind, but not by choice of what is best, would be a great and extreme carelessness of speech.'

Then he adds:

'And for this reason one man by surrounding the earth with a vortex makes it to be kept steady forsooth by the heaven, while another sets the air as a support to the earth as if it were a broad kneading-trough. But the power by which things are now set in the best possible way for them to have been placed, this they neither investigate, nor think that there is any superhuman force in it, but imagine that they might at some time discover an Atlas stronger and more immortal than this, and more capable of holding all things together, and suppose that "the good and *binding*" does in reality bind and hold together nothing at all.'

So much says Socrates of the opinion of Anaxagoras.
P. 753 Now Anaxagoras was succeeded by Archelaus both in the school and in opinion, and Socrates is said to have been a disciple of Archelaus. Other physical philosophers, however, as Xenophanes and Pythagoras, who flourished at the same time with Anaxagoras, discussed the imperishable nature of God and the immortality of the soul. And from these afterwards arose the sects of Greek philosophy, some of whom followed these, and some followed others, and certain of them also invented

---

752 d 4 Plato, *Phaedo*, 99 B

opinions of their own. Again then Plutarch writes of their suppositions concerning gods in this same manner: b

Chapter XVI

'Some of the philosophers, as Diagoras of Melos, and Theodorus Plutarch of Cyrene, and Euemerus of Tegea, altogether deny that there are any gods. There is an allusion also to Euemerus in the Iambic poems of Callimachus of Cyrene. Euripides also, the tragic poet, c though he was loth to withdraw the veil through fear of the Areopagus, yet gave a glimpse of this. For he brought Sisyphus forward as the patron of this opinion, and advocated his judgement.'

After these he brings in Anaxagoras again, stating that he was the first who formed right thoughts about God. And this is how he speaks:

'But Anaxagoras says that in the beginning the bodies were motionless, but the mind of God distributed them in order, and produced the generations of the universe. Plato, however, supposed that the primordial bodies were not motionless, but were d moving in a disorderly way: wherefore, says he, God having ordained that order is better than disorder, made an orderly distribution of them.'

To which he adds:

'They therefore are both in error, because they represented God as having regard to human affairs, and arranging the world for this purpose : for the living Being which is blessed and immortal, supplied with all good things, and incapable of any misfortune, being wholly occupied with the maintenance of its own happiness and immortality, has no regard for human affairs. But he would be a miserable being if he carried burdens like a labourer or artisan, and was full of cares about the constitution of the world.

'And again the god of whom they speak either was not p. 754 existing throughout that former age when the primary bodies were motionless, or when they were moving in disorderly fashion,

---

753 b 2 Plutarch, *De Placitis Philosophorum*, p. 880   c 9 ibid. p. 881

PLUTARCH or else he was either asleep, or awake, or neither of these. We can neither admit the first, for every god is eternal; nor the second, for if God was sleeping from eternity He was dead; for an eternal sleep is death. But surely God is incapable of sleep; for the immortality of God and that which is akin to death are far apart.

b   'If then God was awake, either He was in want of something to complete His happiness, or He was complete in blessedness. And neither according to the first case is God blessed, for that which is wanting in happiness is not blessed: nor according to the second case; for being deficient in nothing, any actions He might attempt must be void of purpose. And if God exists, and if human affairs are administered by His care, how comes it that the counterfeit is prosperous, and the worthy suffers adversity?

'For Agamemnon, who was both

c   "A valiant warrior and a virtuous king,"

was overpowered and treacherously murdered by an adulterer and adulteress. Also his kinsman Hercules, after purging away many of the plagues by which human life is infested, was treacherously murdered with a poisoned robe by Deianira.

'Thales held that god is the mind of the world; Anaximander that the stars are celestial gods; Democritus that god is like a sphere amid fire, which is the soul of the world.

d   'Pythagoras held that of first principles the monad is god: and the good, which is the nature of the One, is the mind itself. But the unlimited duad is a daemon and the evil, and it is surrounded by the multitude of matter and the visible world.'

Now after these, hear what were the opinions held by those of more recent time:

'Socrates and Plato held that (God is) the One, the single self-existent nature, the monadic, the real Being, the good: and all this variety of names points immediately to mind. God therefore is mind, a separate species, that is to say what is purely immaterial and unconnected with anything passible.

'Aristotle held that the Most High God is a separate species, and rides upon the sphere of the universe, which is an etherial

---

body, the fifth essence so-called by him. And when this had been **p. 755**
divided into spheres, which though connected in their nature are P<small>LUTARCH</small>
separated by reason, he thinks that each of the spheres is a living
being compounded of body and soul, of which the body is
etherial, and moves in a circular orbit, while the soul, being itself
motionless reason, is actually the cause of the motion.

' The Stoics set forth an intelligent god, an artistic fire, proceeding methodically to generate a world, which comprises all
the seminal laws, in accordance with which things are severally
produced according to fate : also a spirit, which pervades the **b**
whole world, but receives different names according to the
changes of the matter through which it has passed.

' They regard as a god the world, and the stars, and the earth,
but mind which is highest of all they place in the ether.

' Epicurus held that the gods are of human shape, but all to
be discerned by reason because of the fineness of the particles in
the nature of their forms.   The same philosopher added four
other natures generically imperishable, namely the atoms, the
vacuum, the infinite, the similarities, which are called homoeo-
meriae and elements.'

Such are the dissensions and blasphemies concerning God of the physical philosophers, among whom, **c**
as is proved by this narrative, Pythagoras, and Anaxagoras, and Plato, and Socrates were the first who made
mind and God preside over the world.   These then are
shown to have been in their times very children, as compared with the times at which the remotest events in
Hebrew antiquity are fixed by history.

Accordingly among all the Greeks, and those who long
ago introduced the polytheistic superstition among both
the Phoenicians and Egyptians, the knowledge of the
God of the universe was not very ancient, but the first of
the Greeks to publish it were Anaxagoras and his school. **d**
Moreover the doctrines of the polytheistic superstition
prevailed over all nations ; but they contained, as it
seems, not the true theology, but that which the
Egyptians and Phoenicians, as was testified, were the
very first to establish.

And this was a theology which by no means treated of gods, nor of any divine powers, but of men who had already been long lying among the dead, as was shown long since by our word of truth. Come then, let us take up our argument again. Since among the physical **p. 756** philosophers some were for bringing all things down to the senses, while others drew all in the contrary direction, as Xenophanes of Colophon, and Parmenides the Eleatic, who made nought of the senses, asserting that there could be no comprehension of things sensible, and that we must therefore trust to reason alone, let us examine the objections which have been urged against them.

Chapter XVII

b   'But there came others uttering language opposed to these.
Aristo- For they think we ought to put down the senses and their
cles   presentations, and trust only to reason. For such were formerly
the statements of Xenophanes and Parmenides and Zenon and
c Melissus, and afterwards of Stilpo and the Megarics. Whence
these maintain that "being" is one, and that the "other" does
not exist, and that nothing is generated, and nothing perishes,
nor is moved at all.

'The fuller argument then against these we shall learn in our course of philosophy ; at present, however, we must say as much as this. We should argue, that though reason is the most divine of our faculties, yet nevertheless we have need also of sense, just as we have of the body. And it is evidently the nature of sense also to be true: for it is not possible that the sentient subject should not be in some way affected, and being **d** affected he must know the affection : therefore sensation also is a kind of knowledge.

'Moreover if sensation is a kind of affection, and everything that is affected is affected by something, that which acts must certainly be other than that which is acted on. So that first there would be the so-called "other," as for instance, the colour

---

756 b 1 Aristocles, a Fragment preserved by Eusebius

and the sound; and then the existing thing will not be one: nor ARISTO-
moreover will it be motionless, for sensation is a motion.   CLES

'And in this way every one wishes to have his senses in a
natural state, inasmuch as he trusts, I suppose, to sound senses
rather than to diseased. With good reason therefore a strong
love of our senses is infused in us. No one certainly, unless mad,
would choose ever to lose a single sense, that so he might gain
all other good things.

'Those then who found fault with the senses, if at least they p. **757**
were persuaded that it was useless to have them, ought to have
said just what Pandarus says in Homer about his own bow,

> "Then may a stranger's sword cut off my head,
> If with these hands I shatter not and burn
> The bow that thus hath failed me at my need,"

and immediately after to have destroyed all their senses: for b
thus one would have believed them as teaching by deed that they
had no need of them.

'But now this is the very greatest absurdity; for though in
their words they declare their senses to be useless, in their deeds
they continue to make the fullest use of them.

'Melissus in fact wishing to show why none of these things
which are apparent and visible really exists, demonstrates it by
the phenomena themselves. He says in fact : "For if earth exists,
and water, and air, and fire, and iron, and gold, and the living and the
dead, and black and white, and all the other things which men say are c
real, and if we see and hear rightly, then 'being' also ought to be such
as it at first seemed to us to be, and not to change, nor become other,
but each thing ought always to be just such as it is. But now we say
that we see, and hear, and understand aright : yet it seems to us that
the hot becomes cold, and the cold hot, and the hard soft, and the soft hard."

'But when he used to say these and many other such things one d
might very reasonably have asked him, Well then, was it not by
sensation you learned that what is hot now becomes cold afterwards? And in like manner concerning the other instances.
For just as I said, it would be found that he abolishes and
convicts the senses because he most fully believes them.

'But in fact the arguments of this kind have already been
subjected to nearly sufficient correction : they have certainly
become obsolete, as if they had never been uttered at all. Now

757 a 4 Hom. *Il.* v. 214–216 (Lord Derby)

ARISTO-
CLES
indeed we may say boldly that those philosophers take the right course who adopt both the senses and the reason for acquiring the knowledge of things.'

Such then were the followers of Xenophanes, who is said to have flourished at the same time with Pythagoras **p. 758** and Anaxagoras. Now a hearer of Xenophanes was Parmenides, and of Parmenides Melissus, of him Zeno, of him Leucippus, of him Democritus, of him Protagoras and Nessas, and of Nessas Metrodorus, of him Diogenes, of him Anaxarchus, and a disciple of Anaxarchus was Pyrrho, from whom arose the school of those who were surnamed Sceptics. And as these also laid it down that no conception of anything was possible either by sense or by reason, but suspended their judgement in all cases, we may learn how they were refuted by those who held an opposite opinion, from the book before mentioned, **b** speaking word for word as follows:

Chapter XVIII

c   "Before all things it is necessary to make a thorough exami-
ARISTO-
CLES
nation of our own knowledge; for if it is our nature to know nothing there is no further need to inquire about other things.

'Some then there were even of the ancients who spoke this language, and who have been opposed by Aristotle. Pyrrho indeed, of Elis, spoke strongly in this sense, but has not himself left anything in writing. But his disciple Timon says that the man who means to be happy must look to these three things: first, what are the natural qualities of things; secondly, in what **d** way we should be disposed towards them; and lastly, what advantage there will be to those who are so disposed.

'The things themselves then, he professes to show, are equally indifferent, and unstable, and indeterminate, and therefore neither our senses nor our opinions are either true or false. For this reason then we must not trust them, but be without opinions, and without bias, and without wavering, saying of every single thing that it no more is than is not, or both is and is not, or neither is nor is not.

'To those indeed who are thus disposed the result, Timon says, will be first speechlessness, and then imperturbability, but Aene- sidemus says pleasure.

'These then are the chief points of their arguments : and now let us consider whether they are right in what they say. Since **p. 759** therefore they say that all things are equally indifferent, and bid us for this reason attach ourselves to none, nor hold any opinion, I think one may reasonably ask them, whether those who think things differ are in error or not. For if they are in error, surely they cannot be right in their supposition. So they will be compelled to say that there are some who have false opinions about things, and they themselves therefore must be those who speak the truth : and so there must be truth and falsehood. But if we **b** the many are not in error in thinking that things differ, what do they mean by rebuking us ? For they must be in error themselves in maintaining that they do not differ.

'Moreover if we should even grant to them that all things are equally indifferent, it is evident that even they themselves would not differ from the multitude. What then would their wisdom be ? And why does Timon abuse all other persons, and sing the praises of Pyrrho only?

'Yet, further, if all things are equally indifferent and we ought therefore to have no opinion, there would be no difference even **c** in these cases, I mean in the differing or not differing, and the having or not having an opinion. For why should things of this kind be rather than not be ? Or, as Timon says, why "yes," and why "no," and why the very "Why?" itself? It is manifest therefore that inquiry is done away : so let them cease from troubling. For at present there is no method in their madness, while, in the very act of admonishing us to have no opinion, they at the same time bid us to form an opinion, and in saying that men ought to make no statement they make a statement them- **d** selves : and though they require you to agree with no one, they command you to believe themselves : and then though they say they know nothing, they reprove us all, as if they knew very well.

'And those who assert that all things are uncertain must do one of two things, either be silent, or speak and state something. If then they should hold their peace, it is evident that against such there would be no argument. But if they should make a

statement, anyhow and by all means they must say that something either is or is not, just as they certainly now say that all
things are to all men matters not of knowledge but of customary
opinion, and that nothing can be known.

'The man therefore who maintains this either makes the matter
clear, and it is possible to understand it as spoken, or it is impossible. But if he does not make it clear, there can be absolutely
p. 760 no arguing in this case either with such a man. But if he
should make his meaning clear, he must certainly either state
what is indefinite or what is definite : and if indefinite, neither
in this case would there be any arguing with him, for of the
indefinite there can be no knowledge. But if the statements, or
any one of them whatever, be definite, the man who states this
defines something and decides. How then can all things be
unknowable and indeterminate ? But should he say that the
same thing both is and is not, in the first place the same thing
will be both true and false, and next he will both say a thing
and not say it, and by use of speech will destroy speech, and
moreover, while acknowledging that he speaks falsely, says that
we ought to believe him.

'Now it is worth inquiring whence they learned what they say,
b that all things are uncertain. For they ought to know beforehand what certainty is : thus at all events they would be able
to say that things have not this quality of certainty. First they
ought to know affirmation, and then negation. But if they are
ignorant of the nature of certainty, neither can they know what
uncertainty is.

'When indeed Aenesidemus in his *Outline* goes through the
nine moods (in all of which he has attempted to prove the uncertainty of things), which are we to say, that he speaks with
c knowledge of them or without knowledge ? For he says that
there is a difference in animals, and in ourselves, and in states,
and in the modes of life, and customs, and laws : he says also
that our senses are feeble, and that the external hindrances to
knwoledge are many, such as distances, magnitudes, and motions :
and further, the difference of condition in men young and old,
and waking and sleeping, and healthy and sick : and nothing
that we perceive is simple and unmixed ; for all things are
d confused, and spoken in a relative sense.

' But when he was making these and other such fine speeches, ARISTO-
one would have liked, I say, to ask him whether he was stating CLES
with full knowledge that this is the condition of things, or without
knowledge. For if he did not know, how could we believe him ?
But if he knew, he was vastly silly for declaring at the same time
that all things are uncertain, and yet saying that he knew so much.

' Moreover whenever they go through such details, they are only
making a sort of induction, showing what is the nature of the
phenomena and of the particulars : and a process of this kind
both is, and is called, a proof. If therefore they assent to it, it is
evident that they form an opinion : and if they disbelieve it,
neither should we choose to give heed to them.

' Timon moreover in the *Python* relates a story at great **p. 761**
length, how he met Pyrrho walking towards Delphi past the
temple of Amphiaraus, and what they talked about to each other.
Might not then any one who stood beside him while writing this
reasonably say, Why trouble yourself, poor fellow, in writing this,
and relating what you do not know ? For why rather did you meet
him than not meet him, and talk with him rather than not talk ?

' And this same wonderful Pyrrho, did he know the reason why
he was walking to see the Pythian games ? Or was he wandering,
like a madman, along the road ? And when he began to find **b**
fault with mankind and their ignorance, are we to say that he
spoke truth or not, and that Timon was affected in a certain way
and agreed with his sayings, or did not heed them ? For if he
was not persuaded, how did he pass from a choral dancer to a
philosopher, and continue to be an admirer of Pyrrho ? But if he
agreed with what was said, he must be an absurd person for
taking to philosophy himself but forbidding us to do so.

' And one must simply wonder what is the meaning to them
of Timon's lampoons and railings against all men, and the tedious
Rudiments of Aenesidemus and all the like multitude of words.
For if they have written these with an idea that they would render **c**
us better, and therefore think it right to confute us all, that so we
may cease to talk nonsense, it is evidently their wish that we
should know the truth, and assume that things are such as Pyrrho
maintains. So if we were to be persuaded by them we should
change from worse to better, by forming the more advantageous
judgements, and approving those who gave the better advice.

' How then could things possibly be equally indifferent and
indeterminate ?   And how could we avoid giving assent and
forming opinions ?   And if there is no use in arguments, why do
they trouble us ?   Or why does Timon say,

d   " No other mortal could with Pyrrho vie " ?

For one would not admire Pyrrho any more than the notorious
Coroebus or Meletides, who are thought to excel in stupidity.
     ' We ought, however, to take also the following matters into
consideration.   For what sort of citizen, or judge, or counsellor,
or friend, or, in a word, what sort of man would such an one
be ?   Or what evil deeds would not he dare, who held that
nothing is really evil, or disgraceful, or just or unjust ?   For one
could not say even this, that such men are afraid of the laws and
their penalties ; for how should they, seeing that, as they themselves say, they are incapable of feeling or of trouble ?
     ' Timon indeed even says this of Pyrrho :

          " O what a man I knew, void of conceit,
             Daunted by none, who whether known to fame
p. 762   Or nameless o'er the fickle nations rule,
             This way and that weighed down by passion's force,
             Opinion false, and legislation vain."

     ' When, however, they utter this wise saw, that one ought to live
in accordance with nature and with customs, and yet not to
assent to anything, they are too silly.   For they require one to
assent to this at least, if to nothing else, and to assume that it is
so.   But why ought one, rather than ought not, to follow nature
and customs, if forsooth we know nothing, and have no means
whereby to judge ?
     ' It is altogether a silly thing, when they say, that just as
b cathartic drugs purge out themselves together with the excre-
ments, in like manner the argument which maintains that all
things are uncertain together with everything else destroys itself
also.   For supposing it to refute itself, they who use it must
talk nonsense.   It were better therefore for them to hold their
peace, and not open their mouth at all.
     ' But in truth there is no similarity between the cathartic drug
and their argument.   For the drug is secreted and does not

---

remain in the body : the argument, however, must be there in ARISTO-
men's souls, as being always the same and gaining their belief, CLES
for it can be only this that makes them incapable of assent.

'But that it is not possible for a man to have no opinions, one
may learn in the following manner.   For it is impossible that he C
who perceives by sense does not perceive : now perception by
sense is a kind of knowledge.   And that he also believes his
sensation is evident to all : for when he wishes to see more
exactly, he wipes his eyes, and comes nearer, and shades them.

'Moreover we know that we feel pleasure and pain : for it is
not possible for one who is being burned or cut to be ignorant of
it.   And who would not say that acts of memory surely and of
recollection are accompanied by an assumption ?   But what need
one say about common concepts, that such a thing is a man, and
again concerning sciences and arts ?   For there would be none of d
these, were it not our nature to make assumptions.   But for my
part I pass over all other arguments.   Whether, however, we
believe, or whether we disbelieve the arguments used by them, in
every way it is an absolute necessity to form an opinion.

'It is manifest then that it is impossible to study philosophy in
this fashion ; and that it is also unnatural and contrary to the
laws, we may perceive as follows.   For if on the other hand
things were in reality of this kind, what would remain but that
we must live as if asleep, in a random and senseless fashion ?
So that our lawgivers, and generals, and educators must all be
talking nonsense.   To me, however, it seems that all the rest of
mankind are living in a natural way, but only those who talk
this nonsense are puffed up with conceit, or rather are gone stark
mad.

'Not least, however, one may learn this from the following case.
Antigonus, for instance, of Carystus, who lived about the same **p. 763**
times and wrote their biography, says that Pyrrho being pursued
by a dog escaped up a tree, and, when laughed at by those who
stood by, said that it was difficult to put off the man.   And when
his sister Philiste was to offer a sacrifice, and then one of her
friends promised what was necessary for the sacrifice and did not
provide it, but Pyrrho bought it, and was angry, upon his friend
saying that his acts were not in accord with his words nor worthy
of his impassivity, he replied, In the case of a woman certainly we

ought not to make proof of it. Nevertheless his friend might
b fairly have answered, If there is any good in these arguments of
yours, your impassivity is useless in the case even of a woman,
or a dog, and in all cases.

'But it is right to ascertain both who they were that admired
him, and whom he himself admired. Pyrrho then was a disciple
of one Anaxarchus, and was at first a painter, and not very successful at that; next, after reading the books of Democritus, he neither
found anything useful there nor wrote anything good himself, but
spake evil of all, both gods and men. But afterwards wrapping
himself up in this conceit, and calling himself free from conceit,
he left nothing in writing.

c 'A disciple of his was Timon of Phlius, who at first was a
dancer in the chorus at the theatres, but having afterwards fallen
in with Pyrrho he composed offensive and vulgar parodies, in
which he has reviled all who ever studied philosophy. For this
was the man who wrote the *Silli*, and said :

"Mankind how poor and base, born but to eat,
    Your life made up of shame, and strife, and woe."

And again :

"Men are but bags with vain opinions filled."

d 'When nobody took notice of them any more than if they had
never been born, a certain Aenesidemus began just yesterday to
stir up this nonsense again at Alexandria in Egypt. And these
are just the men who were thought to be the mightiest of those
who had trodden this path.

'It is evident then that no one in his right mind would approve
such a sect, or course of argument, or whatever and however any
one likes to call it. For I think for my part that we ought not to
call it philosophy at all, since it destroys the very first principles
of philosophy.'

These then are the arguments against those who are
supposed to follow Pyrrho in philosophy. And near akin
to them would be the answers to be urged against those
who follow Aristippus of Cyrene, in saying that only the
feelings are conceptional. Now Aristippus was a com-

panion of Socrates, and was the founder of the so-called
Cyrenaic sect, from which Epicurus has taken occasion
for his exposition of man's proper end.   Aristippus was p. 764
extremely luxurious in his mode of life, and fond of
pleasure ; he did not, however, openly discourse on the
end, but virtually used to say that the substance of
happiness lay in pleasures.   For by always making
pleasure the subject of his discourses he led those who
attended him to suspect him of meaning that to live
pleasantly was the end of man.

Among his other hearers was his own daughter Arete,
who having borne a son named him Aristippus,and he from
having been introduced by her to philosophical studies
was called his mother's pupil (μητροδίδακτος).   He quite
plainly defined the end to be the life of pleasure, ranking
as pleasure that which lies in motion.   For he said that b
there are three states affecting our temperament: one,
in which we feel pain, like a storm at sea ; another, in
which we feel pleasure, that may be likened to a gentle
undulation, for pleasure is a gentle movement, compar-
able to a favourable breeze; and the third is an intermediate state, in which we feel neither pain nor pleasure,
which is similar to a calm.   So of these feelings only, he
said, we have the sensation.   Now against this sect the
following objections have been urged (by Aristocles).

Chapter XIX

' NEXT in order will be those who say that the feelings alone c ARISTO-
are conceptional, and this was asserted by some of the Cyrenaics.   CLES
For they, as if oppressed by a kind of torpor, maintained that
they knew nothing at all unless some one standing by struck and
pricked them ; for when burned or cut, they said, they knew that
they felt something, but whether what burned them was fire, or
what cut them iron, they could not tell.

---

764 c 1 Aristocles, *Fragment* 4

' Men then who talk thus one might immediately ask, whether they at all events know this that they suffer and feel something. For if they do not know, neither could they say that they know only the feeling: if on the other hand they know, the feelings cannot be the only things conceptional. For "I am being burned" was a statement, and not a feeling.

' Moreover these three things must necessarily subsist together, the suffering itself, and that which causes it, and that which suffers. The man therefore who perceives the suffering must certainly by sensation feel the sufferer. For surely he will not know that some one is being warmed, it may be, without knowing whether it is himself or his neighbour; and whether now or last year, and whether at Athens or in Egypt, whether alive or dead, and moreover whether a man or a stone.

' Therefore he will also know by what he suffers: for men know one another, and roads, and cities, and their food. Artisans again know their own tools, and physicians and sailors prognosticate p. 765 what is going to happen, and dogs discover the tracks of wild beasts.

' Moreover the man who suffers anything certainly perceives it either as something affecting himself or as another's suffering. Whence therefore will he be able to say that this is pleasure, and that pain? Or that he felt something by taste, or sight, or hearing? And by tasting with his tongue, and seeing with his eyes, and hearing with his ears? Or how do they know that it is right to choose this, and avoid that? But supposing them to know none of these things, they will have no impulse nor desire; **b** and so would not be living beings. For they are ridiculous, whenever they say that these things have happened to them, but that they do not know how or in what manner. For such as these could not even say whether they are human beings, nor whether they are alive, nor, therefore, whether they say and declare anything.

' What discussion then can there be with such men as these? One may wonder, however, if they know not whether they are upon earth or in heaven; and wonder still more, if they do not know, though they profess to study this kind of philosophy, whether four are more than three, and how many one and two make. **c** For being what they are they cannot even say how many fingers they have on their hands, nor whether each of them is one or more.

'So they would not even know their own name, nor their ARISTO-
CLES
country, nor Aristippus : neither therefore whom they love or
hate, nor what things they desire. Nor, if they were to laugh
or cry, would they be able to say, that is laughable, and that
painful. It is evident therefore that we do not even know what
we are now saying. Such men therefore as these would be no
better than gnats or flies, though even those animals know what
is natural and unnatural.'

Although there are endless arguments that one might d
use against men in this state of mind, yet these are
sufficient. The next thing is to join them in examining
those who have taken the opposite road, and decided that
we ought to believe the bodily senses in everything,
among whom are Metrodorus of Chios, and Protagoras
of Abdera.

Metrodorus then was said to have been a hearer of
Democritus, and to have declared 'plenum' and 'vacuum'
to be first principles, of which the former was 'being,'
and the latter 'not-being.' So in writing about nature
he employed an introduction of this kind, 'None of us
knows anything, not even this, whether we know or do not know':
an introduction which gave a mischievous impulse to
Pyrrho who came afterwards. Then he went on to say p. 766
that 'all things are just what any one may think them.'

And as to Protagoras it is reported that he was called
an atheist. In fact he, too, in writing about the gods
used this sort of introduction:

'So as to gods I know not either that they exist, nor what
their nature is: for there are many things that hinder me from
knowing each of these points.'

This man the Athenians punished by banishment, and
burned his books publicly in the middle of the market-
place. Since then these men asserted that we must
believe our senses only, let us look at the arguments
urged against them (by Aristocles).

---

765 d 12 Diogenes Laertius, ix. 10   766 a 6 ibid. ix. 51

Chapter XX

ARISTO-**b**   'Now there have been men who maintained that we must
CLES   believe only sense and its presentations.   Some indeed say that
c even Homer intimates this kind of doctrine by declaring that
Ocean is the first principle, as though all things were in flux.
But of those known to us, Metrodorus of Chios seems to make
the same statement; Protagoras of Abdera not only seems, but
expressly states this.

'For he said that "the Man is the measure of all things, of
existing things, that they exist, of non-existent things, that they
do not exist : for as things appear to each person, such they also
are ; and of the rest we can affirm nothing positively."

'Now in answer to them one may say what Plato says in the
d *Theaetetus* : in the first place, why in the world, if such forsooth is
the nature of things, did he assert that "the Man" is the measure
of truth and not a pig or a dog-headed ape?   But next, how did
they mean that themselves were wise, if forsooth every one is the
measure of truth to himself?   Or how do they refute other men,
if that which appears to each is true?   And how is it that we are
ignorant of some things, though we often perceive them by sensation, just as when we hear barbarians speaking?

'Moreover the man who has seen anything, and then remembers
it, knows it, though he is no longer sensible of it.   And if he
should shut one eye and see with the other, he will evidently be
both knowing and not knowing the same thing.

p. 767   'And in addition to this, if that which appears to each is also
true, but what they say does not appear true to us, it must also
be true that the Man is not the measure of all things.

'Moreover artists are superior to the unskilled, and experts to
the inexperienced, and for this reason a pilot, or a physician, or
a general foresees better what is about to happen.

'These men too absolutely destroy the degrees of the more or
less, and the necessary and contingent, and the natural and
b unnatural.   And thus the same thing would both be and not be;
for nothing hinders the same thing from appearing to some to be,

---

and to others not to be. And the same thing would be both ARISTO-
a man and a block : for sometimes the same thing appears to   CLES
one a man and to another a block.

'Every speech too would be true, but also for this reason false :
and counsellors and judges would not have anything to do.
And what is most terrible, the same persons will be both good
and bad, and vice and virtue the same thing. Many other
instances also of this kind one might mention ; but in fact there
is no need of more arguments against those who think that they
have no mind nor reason.'   c

Then next he adds :

'But since there are even now some who say that every sensation and every presentation is true, let us say a few words about
them also. For these seem to be afraid lest, if they should say
that some sensations are false, they should not have their
criterion and their canon sure and trustworthy : but they fail to
see that, if this be so, they should lose no time in declaring that
all opinions also are true ; for it is natural to us to judge by
them also of many things : and nevertheless they maintain that
some opinions are true and some false.

'And then if one were to examine he would see that none even d
of the other criteria are always and thoroughly free from error, as
for instance I mean a balance, or a turning-lathe, or anything of
this kind : but each of them in one condition is sound and in
another bad ; and when men use it in this way, it tells true, but
in that way tells false. Moreover if every sensation were true, they
ought not to differ so much. For they are different when near
and far off, and in the sick and the strong, and in the skilled
and unskilled, and prudent and senseless. And of course it
would be altogether absurd to say that the sensations of the mad
are true, and of those who see amiss, and hear amiss. For the
statement that he who sees amiss either sees or does not see **p. 768**
would be silly : for one would answer, that he sees indeed, but
not aright.

'When, however, they say that sensation being devoid of
reason neither adds anything nor takes away, it is evident that
they fail to see the obstacles : for in the case of the oar in
the water, and in pictures, and numberless other things, it
is the sense that deceives. Wherefore in such cases we all lay

Aristo-
cles the blame not on our mind, but on the presentation : for the argument refutes itself when it maintains that every presentation is true. For at all events it declares the falsity of ours, which
b causes us to think that not every presentation is true. The result then for them is to say that every presentation is both true and false.

'And they are altogether wrong in maintaining that things really are just such as they may seem to us : for on the contrary they appear such as they are by nature, and we do not make them to be so, but are ourselves affected in a certain way by them. Since if we were to imagine puppies or young kids, as painters and sculptors do, it would be ridiculous to assert straightway that they existed, and therefore to represent them to ourselves as
c standing ready at hand.'

From what has been said then it is evident that they do not speak rightly who assert that every sensation and every presentation is true. But in fact, though this is so, Epicurus again, starting from the School of Aristippus, made all things depend on pleasure and sense, defining the feelings alone to be conceptional, and pleasure the end of all good.

Now some say that Epicurus had no teacher, but read the writings of the ancients ; others say that he was a hearer
d of Xenocrates, and afterwards of Nausiphanes also, who had been a disciple of Pyrrho. Let us see then what are the arguments which have been urged against him also.

Chapter XXI

Aristo-
cles   'Since knowledge is of two kinds, the one of things external, and the other of what we can choose or avoid, some say that as the principle and criterion of choosing and avoiding we have
p. 769 pleasure and pain : at least the Epicureans now still say something of this kind : it is necessary therefore to consider these points also.

---

768 d 4 Aristocles, *Fr.* 6

'For my part then I am so far from saying that feeling is the Aristo-
principle and canon of things good and evil, that I think cles
a criterion is needed for feeling itself. For though it proves its
own existence, something else is wanted to judge of its nature.
For though the sensation tells whether the feeling is our own or
another's, it is reason that tells whether it is to be chosen or
avoided.

'They say indeed that they do not themselves welcome every
pleasure, and shun every pain. And this is a very natural **b**
result. For the criteria prove both themselves and the things
which they judge : feeling, however, proves itself only. And
that this is so, they bear witness themselves. For although they
maintain that every pleasure is a good and every pain an evil,
nevertheless they do not say that we ought always to choose the
former and avoid the latter, for they are measured by quantity
and not by quality.

'It is evident therefore that nothing else than reason judges
the quantity : for it is reason that gives the judgement, "It is
better to endure this or that pain that so we may enjoy greater
pleasures," and this, "It is expedient to abstain from this or **c**
that pleasure, in order that we may not suffer more grievous
pains," and all cases of this kind.

'On the whole, sensations and presentations seem to be, as it
were, mirrors and images of things : but feelings and pleasures
and pains to be changes and alterations in ourselves. And thus
in sensation and in forming presentations we look to the external
objects, but in experiencing pleasure and pain we turn our
attention to ourselves only. For our sensations are caused by
the external objects, and as their character may be, such also are **d**
the presentations which they produce : but our feelings take this
or that character because of ourselves, and according to our state.

'Wherefore these appear sometimes pleasant and sometimes
unpleasant, and sometimes more and sometimes less. And this
being so, we shall find, if we should choose to examine, that the
best assumptions of the principles of knowledge are made by
those who take into consideration both the senses and the mind.

'While the senses are like the toils and nets and other
hunting implements of this kind, the mind and the reason are
like the hounds that track and pursue the prey. Better philoso- **p. 770**

ARISTO-
CLES

phers, however, than even these we must consider those to be who neither make use of their senses at random, nor associate their feelings in the discernment of truth. Else it would be a monstrous thing for beings endowed with man's nature to forsake the most divine judgement of the mind and entrust themselves to irrational pleasures and pains.'

CHAPTER XXII

So much from the writings of Aristocles.

PLATO **b** ' Let us then judge each of the three separately in relation to Pleasure and to Mind : for we must see to which of these two we are to assign each of them as more akin.

' You are speaking of Beauty, and Truth, and Moderation ?

' Yes : but take Truth first, Protarchus, and then look at three **c** things, Mind, and Truth, and Pleasure, and after taking long time for deliberation make answer to yourself whether Pleasure or Mind is more akin to Truth.

' But what need of time ? For I think they differ widely. Pleasure is of all things most full of false pretensions ; and in the pleasures of love, the greatest as they are thought, even perjury, as they say, is forgiven by the gods, its votaries being regarded, like children, as possessing not even the smallest share of Reason ; while Reason is either the same thing as Truth, or of all things most like it and most true.

d ' Will you not then next consider Moderation in the same way, whether Pleasure possesses more of it than Wisdom, or Wisdom more than Pleasure ?

' An easy question this again that you propose. For I think one would find nothing in the world of a more immoderate nature than Pleasure and delight, nor any single thing more full of moderation than Reason and Science.

' You say well ; yet go on to speak of the third point. Has Reason a larger share of Beauty than Pleasure has, so that Reason is more beautiful than Pleasure, or the contrary ?

---

770 b 1 Plato, *Philebus*, 65 B

'Is it not the fact, Socrates, that no one ever yet whether PLATO
waking or dreaming either saw or imagined Wisdom and Reason
to be unseemly in any way or in any case, either past, present, or
to come?

'Right.   p. 771

'But surely when we see any one indulging in Pleasures, and
those too the greatest, the sight either of the ridicule or of the
extreme disgrace that follows upon them makes us ashamed
ourselves, and we put them out of sight and conceal them as
much as possible, consigning all such things to night, as unfit for
the light to look upon.

'In every way then, Protarchus, you will assert, both by
messengers to the absent and by word of mouth to those present,
that Pleasure is not the first of possessions nor yet the second,
but the first is concerned with Measure, and Moderation, and
opportuneness, and whatever qualities of this kind must be **b**
regarded as having acquired the eternal nature.

'So it appears from what you now say.

'The second is concerned with Symmetry and Beauty and
Perfection and Sufficiency, and all qualities which are of this
family.

'It seems so, certainly.

'If then, as I foretell, you assume as the third class mind and
wisdom, you will not go far astray from the truth.

'Perhaps so.

'Shall we not say then that the fourth class, in addition to
these three, are what we assumed to belong to the soul itself,
sciences, and arts, and right opinions as they were called,
inasmuch as they are more akin to the good than to Pleasure?

'Very likely.   **c**

'In the fifth place then pleasures which we assumed in our
definition to be unmixed with pain, and called them pure cogni-
tions of the soul itself, but consequent on the sensations.

'Perhaps.

'And, as Orpheus says,

    " In the sixth age still the sweet voice of song."

But our discourse also seems to have been brought to an end at

---

771 c 7 Hermann, *Orphica, Fr.* xiii

PLATO the sixth trial. And nothing is left for us after this except to put the crown as it were upon what we have said.

'Yes, that is proper.

'Come then, as the third libation to Zeus Soter, let us with d solemn asseveration go over the same argument.

'What argument?

'Philebus proposed to us that the good is pleasure universally and absolutely.

'By the third libation, Socrates, it seems that you meant just now that we must take up again the argument from the beginning.

'Yes. But let us listen to what follows. On my part when I perceived what I have now been stating, and was indignant at the argument employed by Philebus, and not by him only but often by thousands of others, I said that Mind was far nobler than Pleasure, and better for human life.

'It was so.

'Yes, but, suspecting that there were many other good things, I said that if any of these should be found better than both the former, I would fight it out for the second prize on the side of Mind against Pleasure, and Pleasure would be deprived even of the second prize.

p. 772 'You did indeed say so.

'And presently it was most satisfactorily shown that neither of these was sufficient.

'Most true.

'So in this argument both Reason and Pleasure had been entirely set aside, as being neither of them the absolute good, since they lacked sufficiency, and the power of adequacy and perfection.

'Quite right.

'But something else having been found better than either of them, Mind has now again been shown to be ten thousand times closer and more akin than Pleasure to the nature of the conqueror.

'Of course.

'So then the power of Pleasure will be fifth in the award, as b our argument has now declared.

'It seems so.

832

'But not first, no, not even if all oxen and horses and other beasts PLATO together should assert it by their pursuit of enjoyment, though the multitude believing them, as soothsayers believe birds, judge pleasures to be most powerful to give us a happy life, and think that the lusts of animals are more valid witnesses than the words of those who from time to time have prophesied by inspiration of the philosophic Muse.

'Now at last, Socrates, we all say that you have spoken most truly.'

So writes Plato. But I am also going to set before c you a few passages of Dionysius, a bishop who professed the Christian philosophy, from his work *On Nature*, in answer to Epicurus. And do thou take and read his own words, which are as follows:

CHAPTER XXIII

DIONYSIUS
'Is the universe one connected whole, as it seems to us and to d ALEX. the wisest of the Greeks, such as Plato and Pythagoras and the Stoics and Heracleitus? Or two, as some one may have supposed, or even many and infinite in number, as it seemed to some others, who by many aberrations of thought and various applications of terms have attempted minutely to divide the substance of the universe, and suppose it to be infinite, and uncreated, and undesigned.

'For some who gave the name "atoms" to certain imperishable **p. 773** and most minute bodies infinite in number, and assumed a void space of boundless extent, say that these atoms being borne on at random in the void, and accidentally colliding with each other through an irregular drift, become entangled, because they are of many shapes and catch hold of each other, and thus produce the world and all things in it, or rather worlds infinite in number.

'Epicurus and Democritus were of this opinion: but they disagreed in so far as the former supposed all atoms to be b extremely small and therefore imperceptible, while Democritus

---

772 d 1 Dionysius of Alexandria, a Fragment preserved by Eusebius

D<small>IONYSIUS</small> supposed that there were also some very large atoms. Both,
A<small>LEX.</small> however, affirm that there are atoms, and that they are so
called because of their impenetrable hardness.

'But others change the name of the atoms, and say that they
are bodies which have no parts, but are themselves parts of the
universe, out of which in their indivisible state all things are
composed, and into which they are resolved. And they say that
it was Diodorus who invented the name (τὰ ἀμερῆ) of these bodies
without parts. But Heracleides, it is said, gave them a different
name, and called them " weights," and from him Asclepiades the
c physician inherited the name.'

After these statements he proceeds to overthrow the
doctrine by many arguments, but especially by those
which follow :

C<small>HAPTER</small> XXIV

d   'How are we to bear with them when they assert that the
wise and therefore beautiful works of creation are accidental
coincidences ? Works, of which each as it came into being by
itself, and likewise all of them taken together, were seen to be
good by Him who commanded them to be made. For the
Scripture says, " And God saw all things that He had made, and behold,
they were very good."

'Nay, they will not even be taught by the small and familiar
examples lying at their feet, from which they might learn that
no useful and beneficial work is made without a special purpose,
or by mere accident, but is perfected by handiwork for its proper
service : but when it begins to fall off and become useless and
p. 774 unserviceable, then it is dissolved and dispersed in an indefinite
and casual way, inasmuch as the wisdom by whose care it was
constructed no longer manages nor directs it.

'For a cloak is not woven by the warp being arranged without
a weaver, or the woof intertwined of its own accord ; but if it be
worn out, the tattered rags are cast away. A house too or a city
is built up not by receiving some stones self-deposited at the
foundations, and others jumping up to the higher courses, but the

---

773 d 1 Dionysius of Alexandria, a Fragment preserved by Eusebius, § 2
d 6 Gen. i. 31

builder brings the well-fitted stones and lays them in their place: DIONYSIUS
but when the building is overthrown, however it may occur, each   ALEX.
stone falls down and is lost.

'Also while a ship is being built, the keel does not lay itself, **b**
and the mast set itself up amidships, and each of the other
timbers of itself take any chance position ; nor do the so-called
hundred pieces of the wagon fit themselves together each in any
vacant place it finds : but the carpenter in either case brings
them together fitly.

'But should the ship go to pieces at sea, or the wagon in its course
on land, the timbers are scattered wherever it may chance, in the
one case by the waves, and in the other by the violent driving.
Thus it would befit them to say that their atoms, as remaining **c**
idle, and not made by hands, and of no use, are driven at
random. Be it for them to see the invisible atoms, and understand the unintelligible, unlike him who confesses that this
had been manifested to him by God saying to God Himself,
"Mine eyes did see Thy unperfected work."

'But when they say that even what they assert to be finely-
woven textures made out of atoms are wrought by them
spontaneously without wisdom and without perception, who can
endure to hear of the atoms as workmen, though they are inferior in wisdom even to the spider which spins its web out of **d**
itself?'

CHAPTER XXV

'OR who can endure to hear that this great house, which consists
of heaven and earth, and, because of the great and manifold
wisdom displayed upon it, is called the Cosmos, has been set in
order by atoms drifting with no order at all, and that disorder **p. 775**
has thus become order?

'Or how believe that movements and courses well regulated are
produced from an irregular drift? Or that the all-harmonious
quiring of the heavenly bodies derives its concord from tuneless
and inharmonious instruments?

'Also if there be but one and the same substance of all atoms,
and the same imperishable nature, excepting, as they say, their

---

774 b 3 Cf. Hesiod, *Works and Days*, 454   c 6 Ps. cxxxix. 16

DIONYSIUS magnitudes and shapes, how is it that some bodies are divine,
ALEX.   and incorruptible, and eternal, or at least, as they would say,
secular according to him who so named them, both visible and
b invisible, visible as the sun, and moon, and stars, and earth and
water, and invisible as gods, and daemons, and souls? For that
these exist, they cannot, even if they would, deny.

'And the most long-lived are animals and plants; animals, in
the class of birds, as they say, eagles, and ravens, and the
phoenix; and among land animals, stags, and elephants, and
serpents; but among aquatic animals, whales: and among
trees, palms, and oaks, and perseae; and of trees some are ever-
c green, of which some one who had counted them said there were
fourteen, and some flower for a season, and shed their leaves:
but the greatest part both of plants and animals die early and
are short-lived, and man among them, as a certain holy Scripture
said of him, " Man that is born of a woman hath but a short time to
live."

'But they will say that variations in the bonds which connect
the atoms are the causes of the difference in duration. For some
things are said to be packed close and fastened tightly together
by them, so that they have become close textures extremely
d difficult to unloose, while in others the combination of the atoms
has been weak and loose in a greater or less degree, so that
either quickly or after a long time they separate from their
orderly arrangement : and some things are made up of atoms of
a certain nature shaped in a certain way, and others of different
kinds of atoms differently arranged.

'Who is it then that distinguishes the classes, and collects
them, and spreads them abroad, and arranges some in this way
for a sun, and others in that way to produce the moon, and
brings together the several kinds according to their fitness for the
light of each separate star? For neither would the solar atoms,
of such a number and kind as they are, and in such wise united,
ever have condescended to the formation of a moon, nor would
the combinations of the lunar atoms ever have become a sun.
p. 776 Nay, nor would Arcturus, bright though he is, ever boast of
possessing the atoms of the morning star, nor the Pleiades those

---

775 c 5 Job xiv. 1

of Orion.   For it was a fine distinction drawn by Paul when he Dionysius
Alex. said, " There is one glory of the sun, and another glory of the moon, and another glory of the stars : for one star differeth from another star in glory."

'And if their combination, as of things without life, took place unconsciously, they required a skilful artificer : and if their con-junction was involuntary and of necessity, as in things without reason, then some wise leader of the flock presided over their gathering.   But if they have been willingly confined to the per- b formance of a voluntary work, some marvellous architect took the lead in apportioning their work ; or acted as a general who, loving order, does not leave his army in confusion and all mixed up together, but arranges the cavalry in one place, and the heavy-armed infantry separately, and the javelin-men by themselves, and the archers apart, and the slingers in the proper place, that those of like arms might fight side by side.

'But if they think this example a jest because I make a com-parison between large bodies and very small, we will turn to the very smallest.'   c

Then he adds next to this :

'But if there were neither word, nor choice, nor order of a ruler laid upon them, but they by themselves directing them-selves through the great throng of the stream, and passing out through the great tumult of their collisions, were brought together like to like not by the guidance of God, as the poet says, but ran together and gathered in groups recognizing their own kin, then wonderful surely would be this democracy of the atoms, friends welcoming and embracing one another, and hastening to settle in d one common home ; while some of them rounded themselves off of their own accord into that mighty luminary the sun, in order to make day, and others flamed up into many pyramids perhaps of stars, in order to crown the whole heaven ; while others are ranged around, perchance to make it firm, and throw an arch over the ether for the luminaries to ascend, and that the confederacies of the common atoms may choose their own abodes, and portion out the heaven into habitations and stations for themselves.'

---

776 a 4 1 Cor. xv. 41   c 7 Homer, *Od.* xvii. 218

Dionysius
Alex.

p. 777

Then after some other passages he says:

'But these improvident men, so far from discerning what is invisible, do not see even what is plainly visible. For they seem not even to observe the regular risings and settings either of the other bodies, or the most conspicuous, those of the sun, nor to make use of the aids bestowed through them upon mankind, the day lighted up for work, and the night overshadowing for rest. For "man," says the Scripture, " will go forth to his work and to his labour until the evening."

'Nay, they do not even observe that other revolution of the
b sun, in which he completes determinate times and convenient seasons and solstices recurring in undeviating order, being guided by the atoms of which he consists. But though these miserable men, the righteous, however, as they believe, be unwilling to admit it, yet "Great is the Lord that made him, and at His word he hasteneth his course."

'For do atoms, O ye blind, bring you winter and rains, that the earth may send up food for you and all the living creatures thereon? And do they lead on the summer, that ye may also receive the fruits of the trees for enjoyment? And why then do ye not worship the atoms, and offer sacrifice to the guardians of
c your fruits? Ungrateful surely, for not consecrating to them even small first-fruits of the abundant gifts which ye receive from them.'

And after a short interval he says:

'But the stars, that mixed democracy of many tribes, constituted by the wandering atoms ever scattering themselves abroad, marked off regions for themselves by agreement, just as if they had instituted a colony or a community, without any founder or master presiding over them; and the border-laws towards neighbouring nations they faithfully and peacefully observe, not
d encroaching beyond the boundaries which they have occupied from the beginning, just as if they had laws established by these royal atoms.

'Yet these do not rule over them: for how could they, that are non-existent? But listen to the oracles of God: "In the judgement of the Lord are His works from the beginning; and from

---

777 a 7 Ps. ciii. 23   b 5 Ecclesiasticus xliii. 5   d 5 ibid. xvi. 26, 27

the making of them He disposed the parts thereof. He garnished His DIONYSIUS
works for ever, and the beginnings of them unto their generations."'   ALEX.

And after a few sentences he says :

'Or what˙phalanx ever marched across the level ground in
such good order, none running on ahead, none falling out of
rank, none blocking the way, nor lagging behind his company,
as in even ranks and shield to shield the stars move ever onward,
that continuous, undivided, unconfused, unhindered host ?   **p. 778**

'Nevertheless, by inclinations and sidelong deviations, certain
obscure changes of their course occur. And yet those who have
given attention to these matters always watch for the right times
and foresee the places from which they each rise. Let then the
anatomists of the atoms, and dividers of the indivisible, and
compounders of the uncompounded, and definers of the infinite,
tell us whence comes the simultaneous circular revolution and
periodical return of the heavenly bodies, wherein it is not merely
one single conglomeration of atoms that has been thus casually
hurled out as from a sling, but all this great circular choir
moving evenly in rhythm, and whirling round together. And **b**
whence comes it, that this vast multitude of fellow travellers
without arrangement, without purpose, and without knowledge
of each other, have returned together ? Rightly did the
prophet class it among things impossible and unexampled that
even two strangers should run together : "Shall two," he says,
"walk together at all, except they have known each other ?"'

After speaking thus, and adding numberless other
remarks to these, he next discusses the question at length
by arguments drawn from the particular elements of the
universe, and from the living beings of all kinds included
in them, and moreover from the nature of man. And by
adding yet a few of these arguments to those which have **c**
been mentioned, I shall bring the present subject to
an end.

CHAPTER XXVI

'ALSO, they neither understand themselves nor their own circumstances. For if any of the founders of this impious doctrine

---

778 b 6 Amos iii. 3

<small>DIONY-</small> **d** reconsidered who and whence he is, he would come to his senses
<small>SIUS ALEX.</small> as feeling conscious of himself, and would say, not to the atoms,
but to his Father and Maker, "Thy hands fashioned me, and made
me," and like that writer he would have described still further
the wonderful manner of his formation : " Hast Thou not poured me
out as milk, and curdled me like cheese ? Clothed me with skin and
flesh, and knit me together with bones and sinews ? Thou hast granted
me life and favour, and Thy guardianship hath preserved my spirit."

'For how many and of what sort were the atoms which the
P. 779 father of Epicurus poured forth from himself, when he was begetting Epicurus ? And when deposited in his mother's womb,
how did they coalesce, and take shape, and form, and motion,
and growth ? And how did that small drop, after calling together
the atoms of Epicurus in abundance, make some of them into
skin and flesh for a covering, and how was it raised erect by
others turned into bone, and by others bound together with a
contexture of sinews ?

'And how did it adapt the many other limbs, and organs, and
entrails, and instruments of sense, some within and some without,
b by which the body was quickened into life ? For among these
no idle nor useless part was added, no, not even the meanest,
neither hair, nor nails, but all contribute, some to the benefit of
the constitution, and others to the beauty of the appearance.

'For Providence is careful not only of usefulness, but also of
beauty. For while the hair of the head is a protection and
a covering for all, the beard is a comely ornament for the philosopher. The nature also of the whole human body Providence
c composed of parts, all of which were necessary, and invested all
the members with their mutual connexion, and measured out
from the whole their due supply.

'As to the most important of these members, it is evident even
to the simple from their experience what force they have : there
is the supreme power of the head, and around the brain, as
enthroned in the citadel, is the attendant guard of the senses :
the eyes going on in advance, the ears bringing back reports, the
taste, as it were, collecting provisions, the smell tracing out and
d examining, and the touch arranging everything that is subject to
it. (For at present we shall only run over in a summary manner

------

778 d 3 Job x. 8, Ps. cxix. 73   d 5 Job x. 10

a few of the works of the all-wise Providence, intending soon, D<small>IONYSIUS</small>
if God permit, to complete the task more carefully, when we are   A<small>LEX.</small>
directing our efforts against him who is thought more learned.)

'Then there is the ministry of the hands, by which all kinds
of workmanship and inventive arts are perfected, separately
endowed with their particular facilities for co-operation in
one and the same work, the strength of the shoulders in
bearing burdens, the grasp of the fingers, the joints of the
elbows both turning inward towards the body and bending out-
wards, that they may be able both to draw things in and thrust
them off. The service of the feet, by which the whole terrestrial
creation comes under our power, the land to tread on, the sea to
sail, the rivers to cross, and communication of all things with all. **p. 780**
The belly, a store-room of food, meting out from itself in due
measure the provisions for all the members associated with it,
and ejecting what is superfluous : and all the other parts whereby
the administration of the human constitution has been manifestly
contrived, and of which the wise and foolish alike possess the
use but not the knowledge.

'For the wise refer the administration to whatever deity they
suppose to be most perfect in all knowledge and most beneficent **b**
towards themselves, being convinced that it is the work of
superior wisdom and power truly divine; while the others incon-
siderately refer the most marvellous work of beauty to a chance
meeting and coincidence of the atoms.

'Now though the still more effectual consideration of these
subjects, and the arrangement of the internal parts of the body,
have been accurately investigated by physicians, who in their
astonishment made a god of nature, yet let us hereafter make
a re-examination as well as we may be able, even though it be
superficial.

'Now in a general and summary way I ask who made this
whole tabernacle such as it is, lofty, erect, of fine proportion, **c**
keenly sensitive, graceful in motion, strong in action, fit for every
kind of work? The irrational multitude of atoms, say they.
Why, they could not come together and mould an image of clay,
nor polish a statue of marble, nor produce by casting an idol of
silver or gold; but men have been the inventors of arts and
manufactures of these materials for representing the body.

Dionysius
Alex.
'And if representations and pictures could not be made without intelligence, how can the real originals of the same have been
d spontaneous accidents?

'Whence too have soul, and mind, and reason been implanted
in the philosopher? Did he beg them from the atoms which have
no soul, nor mind, nor reason, and did each of them inspire him
with some thought and doctrine?

'And was the wisdom of man brought to perfection by the
atoms, in the same way as Hesiod's fable says that Pandora was
by the gods? Will the Greeks also cease to say that all poetry,
and all music, and astronomy, and geometry, and the other
sciences are inventions and instructions of the gods, and have the
Atomic Muses alone been skilful and wise in all things? For
p. 781 the race of gods constructed by Epicurus out of atoms is banished
from their infinite worlds of order, and driven out into the
infinite chaos.'

Chapter XXVII

'But to work, and to administer, to do good and to show
forethought, and all such actions are burdensome perhaps to the
b idle and foolish, and to the feeble and wicked, among whom
Epicurus enrolled himself by entertaining such thoughts of the
gods; but to the earnest, and able, and wise, and prudent, such
as philosophers ought to be (how much more the gods?), not only
are these things not unpleasant and arduous, but even most
delightful, and above all else most welcome; for to them care-
c lessness and delay in performing any good action is judged to be
a disgrace, as a poet admonishes them with his advice:

"Nor aught until the morrow to delay,"

and with the threat in addition:

"He who puts off his work
Must ever wrestle with malignant fates."

'We too are more solemnly instructed by a prophet, who says
that virtuous actions are truly worthy of God, and that he who
cares little for them is accursed: for he says, "Cursed be he that
doeth the works of the Lord carelessly."

---

780 d 7 Hesiod, *Works and Days*, 60 ff.   781 c 3 Hesiod, ibid. 408
c 5 Hesiod, ibid. 411   c 9 Jer. xlviii. 10

'Then too those who have not learned an art, and can only pursue it imperfectly because the effort is unusual and the work unpractised, find a weariness in their attempts: but those who are making progress, and still more those who are perfect, delight in the easy accomplishment of their pursuits, and would rather choose to complete what they usually practise, and to finish their work, than to possess all the things which men reckon good.

'For instance, Democritus himself, as the story goes, used to say that he would rather discover one single law of causation than receive the kingdom of Persia, and this, although he was vainly seeking causes where no cause was, as one who started from a false principle and an erroneous hypothesis, and did not discern the root and the necessity common to the nature of all things, but regarded the contemplation of senseless and random contingencies as the highest wisdom, and set up chance as the mistress and queen of things universal and things divine, and declared that all things took place in accordance therewith, but banished it from the life of man, and convicted those who worshipped it as senseless.   For example, in the beginning of his *Suggestions* he says : "Men formed an image of chance as an excuse for their own folly : for chance is by nature antagonistic to judgement : and this worst enemy of wisdom they said ruled over it; or rather they utterly overthrow and annihilate this latter, and set up the other in its place: for they praise not wisdom as fortunate, but fortune as most **b** wise."

'Whereas therefore the masters of those works which are beneficial to life take pride in the help which they render to their fellow men, and desire praise and fame for the works in which they labour for their good, some in providing food, others as pilots, some as physicians, and some as statesmen, philosophers proudly boast of their efforts to instruct mankind.

'Or will Epicurus or Democritus dare to say that they distress **c** themselves by their pursuit of philosophy? Nay, there is no other gladness of heart that they would prefer to this. For even though they think that good consists in pleasure, yet they will be ashamed to say that philosophy is not more pleasant to them.

'But as to the gods of whom their poets sing as "Givers of good things," these philosophers with mocking reverence say, The gods

---

782 a 6 Democritus, *Ethical Fragments*, l. 14 (Mullach, i. p. 340)
c 6 Homer, *Od.* viii. 325

DIONYSIUS
ALEX.
are neither givers nor partakers of any good things. In what way then do they show evidence of the existence of gods, if they neither see them present and doing something, as those who in admiration of the sun and moon and stars said that they were

d called gods (θεούς) because of their running (θέειν), nor assign to them any work of creation or arrangement, that they might call them gods from *setting* (θεῖναι), that is *making* (for in this respect in truth the Creator and Artificer of the universe alone is God), nor exhibit any administration, or judgement, or favour of theirs towards mankind, that we should owe them fear or honour, and therefore worship them?

‘Or did Epicurus peep out from the world, and pass beyond the compass of the heavens, or go out through some secret gates known

p. 783 only to himself, and behold the gods dwelling in the void, and deem them and their abundant luxury blessed? And did he thence become a devotee of pleasure, and an admirer of their life in the void, and so exhort all who are to be made like unto those gods to participate in this blessing, commending as a happy banqueting hall for them, not heaven or Olympus, as the poets did, but the void, and setting before them their ambrosia made out of the

b atoms, and pledging them in nectar from the same?

‘And moreover he inserts in his own books countless oaths and adjurations addressed to those who are nothing to us, swearing continually “No, by Zeus,” and “Yes, by Zeus,” and adjuring his readers and opponents in argument “in the name of the gods,” having, I suppose, no fear himself of perjury nor trying to frighten them, but uttering this as an empty, and false, and idle, and unmeaning appendage to his speeches, just as

c he might hawk and spit, and turn his face, and wave his hand. Such an unintelligible and empty piece of acting on his part was his mentioning the name of the gods.

‘This however was evident, that after the death of Socrates he was afraid of the Athenians, and that he might not seem to be what he really was, an atheist, he played the charlatan and painted for them some empty shadows of unsubstantial gods. For he neither looked up to heaven with eyes of intelligence, that he might hear the clear voice from above, which the attentive

d observer did hear, and testified that “The heavens declare the glory

---

783 d 1 Ps. xix. 1

of God, and the firmament showeth the work of His hands," nor did DIONYSIUS
ALEX. he with his understanding look upon the ground, for he would have learned that "The earth is full of the mercy of the Lord," and that "The earth is the Lord's, and the fullness thereof." For the Scripture says, "After this also the Lord looked upon the earth, and filled it with His blessings. With the soul of every living thing He covered the face thereof." '

' And if they are not utterly blind, let them survey the vast and varied multitude of living beings, land and water animals, and birds, and let them take note how true has been the testimony of the Lord in the judgement which He passed on all His works, " And all appeared good according to His command." '

These arguments I have culled from a large number **p. 784** framed against Epicurus by Dionysius, the bishop, our contemporary. But now it is time to pass on to Aristotle, and to the sect of the Stoic philosophers, and to review the remaining opinions of the wonderful sect of physicists, that so we may present to the censorious our defence for having withdrawn from them also.

---

d 4 Ps. xxxii. 5   d 5 Ps. xxiv. 1   d 6 Ecclesiasticus xvi. 29, 30
d 13 Cf. Gen. i. 31

BOOK XV

CONTENTS

p. 788   PREFACE CONCERNING THE WHOLE SUBJECT

I THOUGHT it important in the beginning of the *Preparation for the Gospel* to refute the polytheistic error of
all the nations, in order to commend and excuse our
b separation from them, which we have made with good
reason and judgement.

Therefore before all else in the first three Books,
I thoroughly examined not only the fables concerning
their gods which have been turned into ridicule by their
own theologians and poets, but also the solemn and secret
physical theories of these latter, which have been trans-
ported by their grand philosophy high up to heaven and
to the various parts of the world ; although their theologians themselves declared that there was no need at all
to talk gravely on these matters.

c   We must therefore carefully observe that the oldest
of their theologians were proved on the highest testimony
to have no special knowledge of the history, but to rely
solely on the fables. Hence naturally in all cities and
villages, according to the narratives of these ancient
authors, initiatory rites and mysteries of the gods
corresponding to the earlier mythical tales have been
handed down by tradition ; so that even to the present
time the marriages of their gods and their procreation

848

of children, their lamentations and their drunkenness, the wanderings of some, the amours of others, their anger, and their different disasters and adventures of all kinds, are traditionally received in accordance with the notices recorded by the most ancient authors, in their d initiatory rites, and in their hymns, and in the songs composed in honour of their gods.

But nevertheless, as a work of supererogation, I also brought out to light the refinements of these later authors themselves which they had pompously exhibited in physical explanations, and the subtleties of the sophists and philosophers. Moreover, as to the account of the renowned oracles, and the false opinion concerning fate so celebrated among the multitude, these I laid bare by evidence as clear as day in other three books following next after the **p.** 789 first three ; and for the proof against them I made use not only of my own dialectic efforts, but also especially of the sayings of the Greek philosophers themselves.

Passing on thence to the oracles of the Hebrews, I showed, in the same number of books again, by what reasonings we accepted the dogmatic theology contained in them, and the universal history taught by them and confirmed by the testimony of the Greeks themselves.

Next in order I refuted the method of the Greeks, and clearly showed how they had been helped in all things by Barbarians, and that they bring forward no serious learning of their own, making also a comparative table b of the times in which the celebrated Greeks and the Hebrew prophets lived. Again in the next three books I showed the agreement of the best-esteemed philosophers of the Greeks with the opinions of the Hebrews, and again made their own utterances my witnesses.

Moreover in the book preceding this I clearly detected those Greek philosophers who differ from our opinions as being at variance not with us only but also with their c own countrymen, and as having been overthrown by their own disciples. Throughout all these discussions

849

I show to my readers that the judgement of my own mind is impartial. and by the very facts and deeds, so to say, I have brought forward my proofs, that with no want of consideration, but with well-judged and sound reasoning, we have chosen the philosophy and religion of the Hebrews, which is both ancient and true, in preference d to that of the Greeks, which result was also confirmed by the comparison of the statements of the Greeks.

As we have been deferring up to the present time our final discourse hereon, which is the fifteenth Book of the treatise in hand, we will now make up what is lacking to the discussions which we have travelled through, by still further dragging into light the solemn doctrines of the fine philosophy of the Greeks, and laying bare before the eyes of all the useless learning therein. And before all things we shall show that not from ignorance of the things which they admire, but from contempt of the unprofitable study therein we have cared very little for them, and devoted our own souls to the practice of things far better.

When therefore by God's help this book shall have received the seal of truth, my work on the *Preparation* shall here be brought to a close ; and passing on to the p. 790 more complete argument of the *Demonstration of the Gospel*, I shall connect the commencement of my second treatise with the consideration of the remaining charge brought against us.

Now the fault alleged against us was this, that though we honoured the oracles of the Hebrews above those of our own country, we did not emulate and choose a life like that of the Jews. Against that charge I shall, with the help of God, endeavour to make answer after the completion of my present discourse. For in this way I think that the second part being connected in one bond, as it were, with the first, will unite and complete the general purpose of the whole discussion.

b   As to our present task, however, in the preceding Books

we have seen the philosophy of Plato sometimes agreeing
with the doctrines of the Hebrews, and sometimes at
variance with them, wherein it has been proved to disagree
even with its own favourite dogmas : while as to the
doctrines of the other philosophers, the physicists, as they
are called, and those of the Platonic succession, and of
Xenophanes and Parmenides, moreover of Pyrrho, and
those who introduce the 'suspension of judgement,' and
all the rest, whose opinions have been refuted in the
preceding discourse, we have seen that they stand in c
opposition alike to the doctrines of the Hebrews and
of Plato and to the truth itself, and moreover have
received their refutation by means of their own weapons.

It is time then to look down, as it were, from a raised
stage upon the other vain conceit of the Aristotelian and
Stoic philosophers, and also to survey all the remaining
physical systems of the supercilious tribe, that we may
learn the grand doctrines taught among them, and on
the other hand the objections urged against them by those
of their own side.

For in this way our decision to withdraw from these d
also will be freed from all reasonable blame, for that we
have preferred the truth and piety found among those
who have been regarded as Barbarians to all the wisdom
of the Greeks, not in ignorance of their fine doctrines,
but by a well examined and thoroughly tested judgement.

To begin with Aristotle. Other authors, and among
them philosophers not otherwise undistinguished, have
defamed his personal life. But for my part I cannot
willingly endure even to hear the man evil spoken of by
his own friends. Wherefore I shall the rather set forth
the defence urged on his behalf in the works of Aristocles
the Peripatetic, who in his seventh book *On Philosophy* p. 791
writes of him as follows :

Chapter II

' For how is it possible that, as Epicurus says in his *Epistle concerning moral habits,* when a young man he squandered his patrimony, and afterwards was forced into military service, and being unsuccessful in this had recourse to selling drugs, then, after Plato's walk had been thrown open to all, joined himself to him?

' Or how could any one accept what Timaeus of Tauromenium says in his *Histories,* that when advanced in years he kept the doors of an obscure surgery, or any others?

' Or who would believe what Aristoxenus the musician says in his *Life of Plato*? For he states that during his wandering and **c** long absence from home certain strangers rose up against him and built a Peripatos in opposition to him. Some therefore think that he says this in reference to Aristotle, whereas Aristoxenus always speaks of Aristotle with reverence.

' One may also say with reason that the memoirs by Alexinus the Eristic are ridiculous. For he makes Alexander when a boy **d** converse with his father Philip, and pour contempt upon Aristotle's doctrines, while approving Nicagoras, who was surnamed Hermes.

' Eubulides, also, in his book against Aristotle manifestly lies, first in bringing forward some frigid poems as written by others concerning his marriage and his intimacy with Hermias, and secondly in asserting that he offended Philip, and did not come to visit Plato when dying, and that he had corrupted his writings.

' As to the accusation of Demochares against the philosophers, why need we mention it? For he has reviled not Aristotle only, but all the rest as well. Moreover, any one glancing at the calumnies themselves would say that the man talks nonsense.

p. 792 For he says that there have been discovered letters of Aristotle against the Athenian state, and that he betrayed Stageira, his native city, to the Macedonians; and further, that, when Olynthus was destroyed, at the place where the booty was sold he pointed out to Philip the most wealthy of the Olynthians.

' Foolish also are the calumnies which have been brought against him by Cephisodorus, the disciple of Isocrates, saying that he was luxurious and a gourmand, and other things of this kind.

' But all are surpassed in folly by the statements of Lycon, who

---

791 b 1 Aristocles, a Fragment preserved by Eusebius

says that he is himself a Pythagorean. For he affirms that ARISTO-
Aristotle offered to his wife after death a sacrifice such as the **b** CLES
Athenians offer to Demeter, and that he used to bathe in warm oil,
and then sell it : and that when he was starting for Chalcis, the
custom-house officers found in the vessel seventy-five brass plates.

' These are nearly all the chief detractors of Aristotle : of whom
some lived at the same time with him, and others a little later,
but all were Sophists, and Eristics, and Rhetoricians, whose
very names and books are more dead than their bodies. As to **c**
those who came after them, and then repeated their statements,
we may put them aside altogether, and especially those who have
not even read their books, but invent for themselves, of which
kind are those who say that he had three hundred dishes : for
nobody could be found among his contemporaries, except Lycon,
who has said any such thing about him. He, however, has said,
as I mentioned before, that there were seventy-five plates found.

' But not only from the dates and from the persons who have
reviled him might one infer that all the things that have been **d**
stated are false, but also from the fact that they do not all bring
the same charges, but each says some things of his own : in
which if there was any one word of truth, he deserved surely to
have been put to death by his contemporaries not once only but
ten thousand times.

' It is manifest therefore that it has happened to Aristotle, as to
many others, to be envied by the Sophists of his time, both for
his friendships with kings, and for his superiority in argument.
But those who are right-minded must look not only to the
detractors, but also to those who praise and emulate him : for
these will be found much more in number and in worth.

' Now all the other stories are manifestly invented : but credit **p. 793**
seems to be given to these two things for which some blame him ;
one, that he married Pythias, who was by birth the sister, and by
adoption the daughter, of Hermias, to flatter him. For instance
Theocritus of Chios wrote an epigram of this kind :

> "To Hermias, eunuch and Eubulus' slave,
>   This empty tomb by empty sage was rais'd,
>   Who left the groves of Academe, and dwelt
>   By Borborus' streams, his ravenous maw to fill."   **b**

793 a 6 Theocritus of Chios, Bergk, *Poet. Lyr.* p. 676

' The other charge was that Aristotle was ungrateful to Plato.

' Now among many authors who have written of Hermias and Aristotle's friendship with him, the chief is Apellicon, and any one after reading his books will soon cease to speak evil of them.

' But with regard to his marriage to Pythias he has himself made sufficient defence in his *Epistles to Antipater*. For after the death of Hermias he married her because of his affection for him, she being also a modest and good woman, but in misfortune c by reason of the calamities which had overtaken her brother.'

Then afterwards he says :

' But after the death of Pythias, the daughter of Hermias, Aristotle married Herpyllis of Stageira, by whom a son Nicomachus was born to him. And he, it is said, was brought up as an orphan by Theophrastus, and when a very young man was killed in war.'

But enough of these extracts from the aforesaid book of Aristocles : for it is time now to consider the dogmatic philosophy of Aristotle.

CHAPTER III

d   WHEREAS Moses and the Hebrew prophets laid it down that the perfection of a happy life is the knowledge of the God of all the world and friendship with Him accomplished by piety, and taught that true piety is the pleasing God by every virtue (because this is the source p. 794 of blessings, for all things depend on God only, and all are procured from Him for the friends of God), and whereas Plato gives definitions agreeing with these, and declares virtue to be the perfection of happiness, Aristotle took the other path, and says that no one can be happy otherwise than through bodily pleasure and abundance of outward means, without which even virtue cannot profit. How the friends of Plato opposed him and refuted the falseness of his opinion, we may learn b from what follows :

Chapter IV

' For whereas by the common judgement of philosophers Philo- c Atticus
sophy as a whole makes promise of human happiness, and is
divided into three parts according to the distribution which makes
up the universe, the Peripatetic will be seen to be so far from
teaching herein any of the doctrines of Plato, that, though there
are many who differ from Plato, he will himself be shown to be
his strongest opponent.

' And in the first place he departed from Plato on the point of
universal and chief importance by failing to keep the measure of
happiness, and not admitting that for this virtue is sufficient; but **d**
having missed the power that is in virtue, he thought that it
needed the goods of fortune, in order to gain happiness with their
help ; but if it were to be left by itself, he complained that it
was a powerless thing incapable of attaining to happiness.

' Now this is not the time for showing how ignoble and mistaken
was his opinion both on this and on the other points : but I think
it is manifest, that whereas the object aimed at and the happiness
are not equal nor identical according to Plato and according to
Aristotle, but the one is ever crying aloud and proclaiming that
the most righteous is the most happy man, while the other does
not admit that happiness is a consequence of virtue, unless it be
fortunate also in birth and beauty and other things, and so

"To war he came, decked, like a girl, with gold,"   **p. 795**

according to the difference of the end the philosophy leading
thereto must also be different.

' For a man who walks only on one way which naturally leads
to something that is petty and low, cannot reach to greater things
that are set on high.

> " See'st thou where yonder hill stands up aloft
> Rugged with overhanging cliffs ? There sits
> The bird that lightly mocks thy feeble threat."

' Up to this lofty hill that shrewd and crafty beast is not able to **b**
ascend : but in order that the fox may come close to the eagle's
brood, either they must meet with some ill luck and fall to the

---

ATTICUS ground through the destruction of their own nest, or the fox herself must grow what it is not her nature to grow,

> "and circle on light wings,"

and so soaring from the earth fly up to the lofty hill. But as long as each remains on his own level, there can be no communion between things of earth and the offspring of heaven.'

c   After other statements he adds :

'Since then this is the case, and since Plato's endeavour is to draw the souls of the youths upward to the divine, and in this manner he makes them the friends of virtue and of honour, and persuades them to despise all else, tell us, O Peripatetic, how wilt thou teach these things? How wilt thou guide the lovers of Plato to them? Where in thy sect is so lofty a height of argument as to acquire the spirit of the Aloadae and seek the path to heaven, d which they thought might be made by piling up mountains, a thing which, as Plato says, is to be done by removing "the objects of human ambition."

'What help then canst thou give the young men towards this end? And whence find any argument as an active ally of virtue? From what letters of Aristotle? From whom of his followers? Out of what writings? I give thee leave even to forge, if thou wilt, only let it be something spirited. But in fact thou hast neither anything to say, nor would any of the leaders of thy sect permit thee.

'At all events the treatises of Aristotle on these subjects, entitled *Eudemian* and *Nicomachean* and the *Great Ethics*, have a petty, and low, and vulgar idea of virtue, and no better than an ordinary and uneducated man might have, or a lad, or a woman. For p. 796 the diadem, so to speak, and the kingly sceptre, which virtue received from Zeus, and holds inalienable,

> "For ne'er his promise shall deceive, or fail,
>   Or be recalled, if with a nod confirmed,"

this they dare to take away from her.

'For they do not allow her to make men happy, but set her on a level with wealth, and glory, and birth, and health, and beauty, and all the other possessions which are common to vice. For as

---

the presence of any whatsoever of these without virtue suffices not ATTICUS to render the possessor happy, so without these virtue, according to the same system, is not able to give happiness to its possessor. **b**

'Is not then the dignity of virtue dethroned and cast down ? Certainly : yet they say virtue is far superior to all the other good things. Of what avail is this? For they say also that health is better than wealth : but it is a fault common to all, that apart each from other they suffice not for happiness.

'If ever therefore any one, starting from these doctrines and this sect, should teach that he who seeks all that is good for man in the soul alone is happy, they say that he never mounts the wheel, nor could he who is oppressed by "misfortunes such as Priam's" **c** possibly be happy and blessed.

'But it is not unlikely that the possessor of virtue may fall into some such misfortunes.   Hereupon it follows, that happiness neither results from every condition to the possessors of virtue, nor remains always with them if it does come.

> "Of leaves one generation by the wind
>   Is scattered on the earth ; but others soon
>   The teeming forest clothe. . . .
>   So with our race, these flourish, those decay."

Thy similitude, O poet, is still narrow and timid :   **d**

> "The Spring-tide comes again."

It is a long time that intervenes, and in which nothing grows. If thou would'st give an exact similitude of the mortality and decay of the human race, compare it with Aristotle's happiness. This springs up and passes away more lightly than the leaves, not continuing through the circling year, nor within the year, nor within a month, but in the very day, the very hour, it both springs up and perishes.

'And many are the causes which destroy it, and all of them results of chance : for there are the body's "various dooms," and these are myriads, and there is poverty, and disgrace, and all **p. 797** things of this kind ; and against none of these are dear virtue's resources sufficient of themselves to give help ; for she is without strength to ward off misery or to preserve happiness.

'In what way then can any one who has been reared in these

---

c 1 Cf. Aristotle, *Nicom. Ethics*, **VII**. xiii. 3   c 7 Hom. *Il.* vi. 147-9
797 a 1 Cf. Hom. *Il.* xii. 326

ATTICUS doctrines and delighted with them either himself assent to the teaching of Plato, or ever confirm others in it? For it is not possible that any one starting from these principles should accept

b those other Herculean and divine dogmas, that virtue is a strong and noble thing, and never fails to give happiness, nor is ever deprived of it : but though poverty and disease and infamy and tortures and pitch and the cross, yea, though all the disasters of tragedy come in together like a flood, still the righteous man is happy and blessed.

'In fact, as with the tongue of the most loud-voiced herald, he proclaims the most righteous man, just as some victorious athlete,

c saying that he is the happiest of all men, who reaps the fruit of happiness from righteousness itself. Distinguish then, if you will, and variously distribute good things in threefold, fourfold, or manifold order; for this is nothing to the point before us; you will never by them bring us near to Plato.

'For what, if among good things, some, as you say, are worthy of honour, as the gods; and some worthy to be praised, as the virtues ; and some are powers, as riches and strength; and others are beneficial, as the healing arts? Or what, if you distribute them with less division, and say that of good things some are ends, and some are not ends, and call those ends, for the sake of

d which the others are taken, and not ends those which are taken for the sake of others ?

'Or what, if one were taught, that some are absolutely good, and others not good for all? Or that some are goods of the soul, and others of the body, and others external ? Or again, that of goods, some are powers, and others dispositions and habits, and others actions ; and some ends, and some matter, and some instruments ? And if one learn from thee to divide the good according to the ten categories, what are these lessons to the judgement of Plato ?

'For as long as you on the one hand, either equivocally or as you please, speak of the good things of virtue, and combine with it certain other things as essential to happiness, thus robbing

p. 798 virtue of its sufficiency, while Plato on the other hand gets from virtue itself what is complete for happiness and seeks for the other

---

797 b 3 Cf. Plato, *Republic*, ii. 361 ; x. 613 A

things only as a superfluity, there can be on this point nothing ATTICUS
common between you. You want one set of arguments, Plato's
friends want others.

' For as
> " Lions and men no safe alliance form,
> Nor wolves and lambs in friendly mind agree,"

so between Plato and Aristotle there is no friendship in regard to
the very chief and paramount doctrine of happiness. For if they b
have no evil thoughts one towards the other, yet it is evident
that their statements concerning what is important on this point
are diametrically opposite.'

CHAPTER V

AGAIN, whereas Moses and the Hebrew prophets, and c
Plato moreover in agreement with them on this point,
have very clearly treated the doctrine of the universal
providence, Aristotle stays the divine power at the moon,
and marks off the remaining portions of the world from
God's government: and on this ground also he is refuted
by the aforesaid author, who discusses the matter as
follows:

' Whereas, further, the most important and essential of the ATTICUS
things that contribute to happiness is the belief in providence,
which more than aught else guides human life aright, unless at d
least we are to remain ignorant
> " Whether by justice or by crooked wiles
> Mankind from earth may scale the lofty height,"

Plato makes all things connected with God, and dependent on
God, for he says that " He, holding the beginning and the middle
and the end of all things, passes onward in a straight course to the
accomplishment of His purpose." And again he says, that " He is
good, and goodness can never have any jealousy of anything. And
being free from jealousy, He makes all things as good as possible,
bringing them out of disorder into order." And while He cares
for all things, and orders all as well as possible, He has taken
thought for mankind also.'

---

798 a 7 Hom. *Il.* xxii. 262   c 9 Atticus, *Fr.* iii   d 3 Pindar, *Fr. Incert.*
129 (Boeckh)   d 6 Plato, *Laws,* iv. 715 E   d 8 ibid. *Timaeus,* 29 E

And after a few words:

p. 799
ATTICUS ' Thus speaks Plato. But he who puts aside this divine nature, and cuts off the soul's hope of hereafter, and destroys reverence before superior Beings in the present life, what communion has he with Plato ? Or how could he exhort men to what Plato desires, and confirm his sayings ? For on the contrary he surely would appear as the helper and ally of those who wish to do injustice. For
b every one who is human and constrained by human desires, if he despise the gods and think they are nothing to him, inasmuch as in life he dwells far away from them, and after death exists no more, will come prepared to gratify his lusts.

' For it is not impossible to feel assurance of being undetected in wrong-doing, if indeed it be necessary to avoid detection by men : it is not necessary, however, on every occasion even to seek to avoid detection, where a man has power to overmaster those who have discovered him. So the disbelief in providence is a ready way to wrong-doing.

' For a very worthy person indeed is he, who after holding out
c pleasure to us as a good, and granting us security from the gods, still thinks to provide a plan to prevent wrong-doing. He acts like a physician who, having neglected to give help while the sick man was yet alive, attempts after death to devise certain contrivances for curing the dead man.

' In a similar manner to him the Peripatetic acts. For it is not so much the eagerness for the pleasure, as the disbelief that the deity cares, that encourages wrong-doing. What then, some
d one may say, do you put Aristotle in the same class with Epicurus?

' Why certainly, at least in relation to the point before us. For what difference does it make to us, whether you banish deity from the world and leave us no communion therewith, or shut up the gods in the world and remove them from all share in the affairs of earth ? For in both cases the indifference of the gods towards men is equal, and equal also the security of wrong-doers from fear of the gods. And as to our deriving any benefit from them while they remain in heaven, in the first place this is common also to things without reason or life, and further, in this way, even according to Epicurus, men get help from the gods.

p. 800   ' They say, for instance, that the better emanations from them become the causes of great blessings to those who partake of them. But neither Epicurus nor Aristotle can rightly be reckoned Atticus on the side of providence.   For if according to Epicurus providence disappears, although the gods according to him employ the utmost solicitude for the preservation of their own goods, so must providence disappear according to Aristotle also, even if the heavenly motions are arranged in a certain order and array.

'For we seek a providence that has an interest for us, and in such that man has no share who has admitted that neither daemons, nor heroes, nor any souls at all can live on hereafter. **b**

'But therein Epicurus, in my judgement, seems to have acted more modestly : for as if he despaired of the gods being able to abstain from the care of mankind if they came in contact with them, he transferred them, as it were, to a foreign country, and settled them somewhere outside the world, excusing them from the charge of inhumanity by the removal, and by their separation from all things.

' But this our super-excellent discoverer of nature, and accurate judge of things divine, after putting human affairs under the **c** very eyes of the gods yet left them uncared for and unregarded, being administered by some force of nature, and not by divine reason.   Wherefore he himself cannot fairly escape that other charge which some imagine against Epicurus, that it was not according to his judgement, but through fear of men, that he allotted room in the universe to the gods, just like a spectator's place in a theatre.

' And they regard it as a proof of the man's opinion, that he deprived the gods of their activity towards us, from which alone a just confidence in their existence was likely to be derived.   For **d** this same thing is done by Aristotle also ; for by his both putting them far off and giving over the proof to sight only, an operation too feeble to judge of things at so great a distance, it may readily be thought that from shame he admits the existence of gods there.

' For as he neither left anything outside the world, nor gave his gods access to things on earth, he was compelled either to confess himself altogether an atheist, or to preserve the appearance of allowing gods to remain, by banishing his gods to some such place as that.   But Epicurus, by excusing the higher powers from diligent care because of the want of communication, seems to throw a decent veil over his disbelief in the gods.'

p. 801   Such are the remarks of Atticus against Aristotle's repudiation of the doctrine of providence. The same author further adds to what has been quoted the following remarks, aiming at the same philosopher's unwillingness to admit that the world was created.

CHAPTER VI

b   WHEREAS again Moses decided that the world was created, and set up God as Maker and Creator over the universe, and whereas Plato's philosophy taught the same doctrines as Moses, Aristotle, having travelled the contrary course on this point also, is refuted by the aforesaid author writing as follows word for word:

ATTICUS c   ‘ In the first place then Plato speculating upon the origin of the world, and considering that every one must necessarily seek after this great and very beneficial doctrine of Providence, and having reasoned out the conclusion that the uncreated has no need either of a maker or of a guardian for its well-being, in order that he might not deprive the world of providence, denied that it was uncreated.

‘ And we pray that we may not at this point be opposed by those of our own household, who choose to think that according to Plato also the world is uncreated. For they are bound in justice to pardon us, if in reference to Plato's opinions we believe

d what he himself, being a Greek, has discoursed to us Greeks in clear and distinct language.

“ For God,” says he, “ having found the whole visible world not at rest, but moving in an irregular and disorderly manner, brought it out of disorder into order, because He thought that this was altogether better than the other.” And still more plainly he shows that he did not adopt creation in an enigmatic way, nor yet for need of clearness, in the discourse which he has made the Father of all hold upon this point after the creation of the universe.

“ For,” says he, “ since ye have come into being, (and he is speaking

p. 802 to the gods) though ye are not altogether immortal nor indissoluble, nevertheless ye shall certainly not be dissolved, since ye have gained my will.”

‘ But, as I was saying, with those who talk to us at home, as

---

801 d 3 Plato, *Timaeus*, 30 A   d 10 ibid. 41 B

being our friends, we will discuss the matter in a friendly way ATTICUS
and quietly with gentle arguments. For Aristotle seems to have
brought them also over, as having been unable to resist his attack
upon the doctrine, and unwilling to impute to Plato what seemed
to have been detected as a fallacy.

'But according to our hearing, whereas Plato claims for the
world that it is the noblest work made by the noblest of Creators,
and invests the Maker of all with a power by which He made the
world which did not previously exist, and having made it, will if b
He please preserve it ever in safety, and whereas according to him
the world is in this way supposed to be created and imperishable,
who among the Peripatetics gives us any confirmation of these
doctrines?

'We must gently admonish their ally, that it is not absolutely
necessary that whatever has been created must also perish, nor
conversely that what will never perish must necessarily be uncreated. For we must neither admit that the sole cause of the
imperishable is derived from its being uncreated, nor must we leave
the passing of the created to destruction as admitting no remedy.

'Whence then are we to get any help on these points from the c
doctrines of Aristotle, a man who pursues the argument on these
subjects, not indirectly, nor merely as stating his own opinion,
but sets himself in direct opposition to Plato, and both brings the
created under a necessity of perishing, and says that what is imperishable maintains its imperishable condition only from the fact
of not having been created, nor even leaves any power in God, d
which He can use to do any good. For what has never existed
before now, this, he says, never can come into existence.

'And so far is he from supporting Plato's doctrine by these
statements, that he has ere now frightened some even of Plato's
zealous disciples by what he said, and led them to reject his
doctrine, because they were not able to perceive, that although,
according to the nature of things alone without the will and
power of God, neither the created is imperishable nor the imperishable created.

'Yet when one has established as the chief cause that which
proceeds from God, one must take this as guide in all things, and
show it to be a cause on no point inferior to any others. For it is p. 803
ridiculous that, because a thing has come into existence, it must

ATTICUS therefore perish, and yet not perish, if God so wills; ridiculous also that, because a thing is uncreated, it has strength to escape from perishing, and yet that the will of God is insufficient to keep any created thing from perishing.

'The builder is able to set up a house not yet existent, and a man can make a statue not previously existent, and another frames a ship out of unwrought timber and gives it over to those

b who want it, and all the other artificers, who pursue the constructive arts, have this power to bring some non-existent thing into existence; and shall the universal King and Chief Artificer not so much as share the power of a human artificer, but be left by us without any share in creation? Not so, if at least we be able in any small degree to form an estimate of a divine cause.

'But though competent to create and to will what is excellent, (for He is good, and the good feels no envy about anything), is He yet unable to preserve and guard what He has made? Yet surely even the other artificers are competent to do both. The builder,

c for instance, and the shipwright not only build new ships and houses, but are able also to repair those which are wearing away from time, substituting in them other parts in place of those which have been damaged.

'So that surely so much as this must be conceded to God also. For how can He who is able to make a whole thing be unable to make it in part? So then why need it be made new, if one who is a maker in general is also to preserve his beautiful work against every accident? For to be willing to undo what was well made is the part of an evil one.

d 'But there is no stronger bond for the preservation of things created than the will of God. Or, while many things which shared in the zeal and will of man, as nations and cities and works, after existing an enormous time still remain when he who willed them is no more, shall the things which have had a share in God's purpose, and have been made for Him and by Him,—shall these then pass away and no longer remain while their Maker is still present?

'What cause can have done violence to the purpose of God? Can it be the necessity proceeding from the things created themselves? But this by accepting the orderly arrangement confessed

803 b 7 Plato, *Timaeus*, 29 F

itself overcome by God. But can it be some cause from without ATTICUS
acting in antagonism to God? Yet neither does any such cause **p. 804**
exist, nor is it right to make God inferior to any in matters in
which He has before prevailed and made order, unless indeed we
altogether forget that we are discoursing about the greatest and
most divine power.

' But enough, for perhaps we are carried away by zeal into this
argument concerning the truth   One thing is plain which we set
forth, that they can be no teachers concerning the creation of the
world who do not allow it any creation at all.'

Further, concerning the fifth essence in bodies introduced by Aristotle we must quote the following state- **b**
ments :

CHAPTER VII

' FOR instance, with regard to the so-called elements, which are
the primary constituents of bodies, Plato, like those before him,
following the clear evidence concerning them, said that they were **c**
these four which are generally acknowledged, namely, fire, earth,
air, and water, and that all other things are produced from their
combinations and changes. But Aristotle, as it seems, hoped to
appear extraordinarily wise, if he could add another body, and
counted in with the four visible bodies the fifth essence : and he
thus made a very brilliant and bountiful use of nature, but failed
to observe that in physical inquiry one must not lay down laws,
but search out nature's own facts.

' To the proof then that the primary natures of bodies are four, **d**
which is what the Platonists want, the Peripatetic would not only
give no help, but would even be almost its only opponent. For
instance, when we say that every body is either hot or cold, or
moist or dry, or soft or hard, or light or heavy, or rare or dense,
and when we find that there can be nothing else to partake of
any of these conditions besides the four elements,—for if anything
is hot, it is either fire or air ; and if cold, either water or earth ;
and if dry, fire or earth ; and if moist, water or air ; and if soft,
air or fire ; and if hard, water or earth ; and light and rare, as for **p. 805**
instance, fire and air ; and heavy and dense, as water and earth ;
—and when from all the other simple forces we perceive that

ATTICUS there cannot be any other body besides these, this man alone opposes us, asserting that there can be a body which partakes not of these, a body, that is, neither heavy nor light, neither soft nor hard, neither moist nor dry, almost calling it a body that is not a body. For though he has left it the name, he has taken away all the forces by means of which it naturally becomes b a body.

'Either, therefore, he will withdraw us from Plato's opinion by persuading us of his own statements, or by confirming those of Plato he will himself withdraw from his own opinions. So that in no way is he of any use in regard to Plato's doctrines.

'Further, Plato will have it that all bodies, inasmuch as they are regarded as formed upon one similar kind of matter, turn and change one into another. But Aristotle claims absolutely an essence in all other things which is impassible, and imperishable, and unchangeable, lest forsooth he should seem to be the inventor of something contemptible: yet he says nothing at all extra-c ordinary and original, but transfers Plato's fine intuitions in other matters to such as are unsuitable, just like some of the more modern sculptors.

'For they too, when they have copied the head of one statue, and the breast of another, and the waist of another, sometimes put together things which do not suit each other, and persuade themselves that they have made something original: and indeed the whole, which any one would blame as being unsymmetrical, is their own; but the contributions which are brought together in d it, and have some beauty, are not theirs.

'In like manner also Aristotle hearing from Plato that there is a certain essence intelligible in itself abstractedly, and incorporeal colourless and intangible, neither coming into being, nor perishing, nor turning, nor changing, but always existing in the same conditions and manner, and hearing again at another time of the things in heaven that being divine and imperishable and im-passible they are yet bodies, he combined out of both and stuck together things not at all congruous: for from the one he took the property of body, and from the others the property of im-passibility, and so framed an impassible body.

'In the case then of the statues, even if the combination of the different parts was not beautiful, it was at least not impossible.

to be made.   For instance, even Homer shows us such combina- ATTICUS
tions, for he says,

> "In eyes and head   **p. 806**
> Like Zeus the Lord of thunder, with the girth
> Of Ares, and Poseidon's brawny chest."

But the body could never be impassible: for being combined with
a possible and changeable nature, it must necessarily suffer with
its yokefellow.   And if there were anything impassible, it must
be separated and free from that which suffers; so that it would
be without the matter, and when separated from that it must
necessarily be acknowledged to be incorporeal.'

Further, let us give our attention to these other points **b**
in which he proves that Aristotle is at variance with
Plato.

CHAPTER VIII

' THEN these are followed by many points in which they are at **c**
variance.   For the one says that the things in heaven have most
of their character from fire, while the other says that the heavenly
bodies have nothing to do with fire.   And Plato says that God
kindled light in the second circle from the earth in order that it
might as much as possible illumine the whole heaven, such being
his declaration concerning the sun.   But the other, not willing
that the sun should be fire, and knowing that light is pure fire,
or something of fire, does not allow that light is kindled round
the sun.

' Further, the one, attributing formal immortality to all the
heavenly bodies, says that there take place certain secretions from **d**
them and equivalent accessions; and he is compelled to say this,
in regard to the secretions, by the rays of the sun and the heat
produced in the efflux from him; and, in regard to the accessions,
by the equality in his apparent magnitude: for the bodies would
not appear equal if they received nothing in place of what they
emit: ' but Aristotle maintains that they continue altogether the
same in substance, without either any secretion from them or
any accretion.

---

806 a 1 Hom. *Il.* ii. 478   **c** 1 Atticus, *Fr.* vi   **c** 2 Cf. Plato,
Timaeus, 40 **A**   **c** 5 ibid. 39 **B**

Atticus   'Further, the one, in addition to the common motion of the heavenly bodies, in which all move in the spheres to which they are confined, both the fixed stars and the planets, gives them p. 807 another motion also, which indeed happens to be otherwise most admirable, and congenial to the nature of their body; for as they are spherical, naturally each would have a spherical motion of rotation : but the other deprives them of this motion also, which they perform as living beings, and leaves them only the motion which results from other bodies surrounding them, as if they were without life.

'Moreover he says that the appearance presented to us by the b stars as if they were in motion is an affection of the feebleness and quivering, as it were, of our sight, and is not a reality : as if Plato derived his belief in their motion from this appearance, and not from the reason which teaches that as each of these is a living being, and has both soul and body, it must necessarily have its own proper motion (for every body whose motion is from without is lifeless, but that which is moved from within and of itself is animated); and when moved, as being divine, it must move with the most beautiful motion, and since motion c in a circle is the most beautiful, it must move in this way.

'And the truth of the sensation would be in part confirmed by the testimony of reason ; it was not, however, this sensation that caused the belief in the motion.   With regard to the motion of the whole, he could not contradict Plato's assertion that it takes place in a circle, for he was overpowered by the clear evidence : yet here also this fine invention of the new body gave him room for dissent.

'For whereas Plato attributed the circular motion to the soul, d inasmuch as there were four bodies and all naturally moved in a simple and straight course, fire towards the outside, and earth towards the centre, and the others towards the intervening space, Aristotle, as assigning a different motion to each different body, so also assigned the circular as a sort of bodily motion to his fifth body, easily deceiving himself in all.

'For to bodies which move in a straight line their heaviness or lightness supplied a source of motion : but the fifth body, partaking neither of heaviness nor lightness, was rather a cause of immobility, and not of motion in a circle.

'For if to bodies that move in a straight line the cause of their

motion is not their shape, but the inclination of their weight, a ATTICUS
body, not only when placed in the centre of any like body, will
have no inclination in any direction, but, also, when set in a circle
round any kind of body whatever, will have no cause of inclination
towards anything,

> "Move they to right towards the rising sun,   **p. 808**
>   Or move to left,"

whether forward or backward.

'Further, when other bodies have been thrust out of their proper
places, the rebound towards these gives them a motion again of
themselves; but as that fifth body never departs from its own
localities, it ought to remain at rest.

. 'And with regard to the other bodies, when this fifth is put out
of the question, it is evident that Aristotle out of contentiousness
does not agree with Plato.   For Plato had inquired whether body
is heavy by nature or light by nature, and, since it was evident
that these terms are used according to the relation towards up **b**
and down, he had considered whether there is by nature any up and
down or not, and had exactly shown that according to the affinities of
the bodies to their places, the direction towards which they severally tended would be called " down," and the other direction from
which each would draw back be called " up."   And " heavy "
and " light " he disposed according to the same relation, and
further proved that neither their centre nor their circumference is
rightly called " up " or " down."   But Aristotle makes objection,
thinking that he must overthrow the other's doctrines on every
side, and urges us to call that which tends to the centre " heavy," **c**
and that which tends to the circumference " light," and the place
in the centre he calls " down," and the circumference " up." '

Thus widely do they differ from each other in regard
to the world, and its constituents, and the heavenly bodies.
Such are the opinions of these two.   But Moses and the
oracles of the Hebrews trouble themselves about none
of these things; and with good reason, because it was
thought that those who busied themselves about these
matters gained no benefit in regard to the right conduct
of life.

---

808 a ɪ Homer, *Il.* xii. 239

CHAPTER IX

d   'Now concerning the soul what need we say? For this is
ATTICUS evident not only to philosophers but also to nearly all ordinary
persons, that Plato allows the soul to be immortal, and has written
p. 809 many discourses concerning this, showing in many various ways
that the soul is immortal.

'Great also has been the emulation of the zealous followers of
Plato's teaching in defence both of Plato and of his doctrine; for
this is almost the one thing that holds his whole school together.

'For the hypothesis of his ethical doctrines was a consequence
of the immortality of the soul, since it was through the divine
nature of the soul that virtue was enabled to maintain its grandeur
and lustre and high spirit; in nature also it was in consequence
b of the soul's direction that all things gained the possibility of
being well ordered.

'"For soul," he says, "as a whole has the care of all soulless being, and
traverses all heaven, appearing at different times in different forms."
Moreover, science also and wisdom have been made by Plato
dependent on the immortality of the soul. For all kinds of learning are recollections, and he thinks that in no other way can
inquiry and learning, out of which science springs, be maintained.

'Now if the soul is not immortal, neither is recollection, and if
c not this, then neither learning. Whereas therefore all the doctrines
of Plato are absolutely attached to and dependent on the divine
nature of the soul and its immortality, he who does not admit
this overthrows Plato's whole philosophy.

'Who then first attempted to oppose the proofs, and rob the soul
of immortality and all its other power? Who else, I say, before
Aristotle? For of the rest some allowed that it has a continued
existence, and others, if not granting so much as this, yet assigned
to the soul a certain power and movement and works and actions
d in the body.

'But the more Plato tried to magnify the importance of the
soul, declaring it to be the beginning of creation, and the pupil
of God, and the power presiding over all things, so much the
more contentiously did Aristotle seek to destroy and to dishonour
it, and prove the soul to be almost nothing.

---

809 b 3 Plato, *Phaedrus*, 246 B   b 5 Plato, *Phaedo*, 72 E

' For he said that it was neither spirit, nor fire, nor body at all, Atticus nay, nor yet an incorporeal thing such as to be self-governed and to have motion, nor even so much as to be in the body without motion, and, so to say, soulless. For see how he ventured, or even was forced, so far as to rob the soul of its primary motions, deliberation, thought, expectation, remembrance, reasoning !

' For this secretary, as they say, of nature says that these **p. 810** are not movements of the soul. Surely this man may be quite trusted to have understood anything about the things outside him, who has made so great a mistake about his own soul, as not even to understand that it thinks ! For it is not the soul, he says, but the man that performs each of these acts, while the soul is motionless.

' Dicaearchus therefore following him, and being able to discern the consequence, took away the whole substance of the soul. It is manifest indeed that the soul is a thing invisible and concealed, **b** so that, through the clear evidence at least of our senses, we could not grant its existence : but though concealed, its motions seem to compel us to acknowledge that the soul is an existent thing.

' For almost every one seems to understand that the following are acts of the soul : to deliberate, to consider, and to think in any way whatever. For when we behold the body and its powers, and reflect that actions of this kind are not proper to the body, we grant the existence within us of something else which deliberates, **c** and that this is the soul. Since from what other source came our belief concerning soul ?

' If therefore any one take away these acts which are the chief evidences of the soul, and assign them to something else, he has neither left us any evidence of its existence, nor any purpose for which it would seem to be of use. What help therefore can he who would have the soul to be immortal derive from him that deals death to the soul ? And what is the explanation of the manner of its motion, according to which we call it self-moved, to be obtained from those who attribute to it no motion at all ?

' True ; but in regard to the immortality of the mind some **d** one may say that Aristotle agrees with Plato. For though he will not admit the whole soul to be immortal, yet he acknowledges the mind at least to be divine and imperishable. What therefore the mind is in its essence and its nature, whence it comes, and

ATTICUS from what source it separates itself and enters into man's nature, and whither it departs again, himself alone may know; if at least he understands anything that he says about the mind, and is not avoiding the proof by wrapping up the difficulty of the matter in the obscurity of his language, and, just like the cuttle-fish, making it difficult to catch him by means of the darkness he creates.

'But even in these matters he is altogether at variance with Plato. For the one says that mind cannot subsist without a soul, p. 811 while the other separates the mind from the soul. And immortality the one gives to it in partnership with the soul, as being otherwise impossible; but the other says that this survives in the mind alone when separated from the soul. And that the soul goes forth from the body he would not allow, because this thought pleased Plato: but he insisted that the mind is severed from the soul, because Plato judged such a thing as this impossible.'

These are the statements of Atticus: and I will add to them the views of Plotinus also, expressed in the following manner:

CHAPTER X

PLOTINUS **b**   'THE manner in which "entelecheia" is used in speaking of the soul may be considered in the following way. The soul, they say, holds in the combination the place of *form*, in relation to the body when alive as *matter*: but it is the *form* not of every body, nor **c** of body as such, but as physical, organic, and potentially alive.

'If therefore it is like that with which it has been compared, it is as the *form* of a statue to the bronze: and if the body is divided, the soul must be divided into parts with it, and if any part is cut off from the body, a portion of the soul is with the part cut off; and the supposed withdrawal of the soul in sleep does not take place, since the entelechy must be inseparable from that to which it belongs; but in reality there is no such thing as sleep.

'Moreover if there is an entelechy, there can be no opposition between reason and desires, but the whole must be affected throughout in one and the same way, without any self-discord. But sensations may possibly exist only contingently, while perceptions

---

811 b 1 Plotinus, *Ennead.* iv. lib. 2 : a Fragment preserved by Eusebius

cannot : wherefore they themselves also introduce the mind as PLOTINUS another soul, and suppose it immortal.

'The reasoning soul therefore must be an entelechy, if we must use this term, in some other way than this. Nor will the sensitive soul, since this also retains the impressions of the sensible objects when absent, retain them without the body's aid : otherwise, they will be in it just like forms and images : but if they **d** were therein in this manner, it would be impossible to receive them otherwise (than with the body's aid). Therefore, it is not an entelechy as being inseparable.

'Moreover that which desires not meats or drinks, but other **p. 812** than bodily things, is not itself an inseparable entelechy.

'Then there would remain the vegetative principle, which would seem to admit a doubt, whether it be in this way an inseparable entelechy. Yet even this seems not to be so. For if the beginning of every plant is at the root, and the rest of the body grows round the root and the lower parts in many plants, it is evident that the soul forsakes the other parts and is collected in some one : it is not then in the whole as an inseparable entelechy. For again, **b** before the plant grows the soul is in a little germ : if therefore it both comes from a larger plant into a small germ, and from a small germ into a whole plant, what is to hinder its being also wholly separated ? And how, being also indivisible can it become a divisible entelechy of a divisible body ?

'Also the same soul from one animal becomes another : how then could the soul of the former become the soul of the next, if it were the entelechy of one ? And this is evident from the animals which change into other animals. The soul then has not its existence from being the " form " of anything, but is an essence, not receiving its existence in consequence of its abode in a body, **c** but existing before it belonged to this, so that in an animal the body will not generate the soul.

'What then is its essence ? And if it is neither body, nor an affection of body, but action and production and many such things are both in it and from it, being an essence in addition to its bodies, what is its nature ? Must it not manifestly be what we call real essence ? For all that is bodily may be said to be generation but not substance, becoming and perishing, and never really being, but preserved by participation with being, so far as it may partake thereof.'

d   Now since we have related the opinions of Plotinus, it will not be out of place to observe what Porphyry also has said in his books against Boëthus *On the Soul.*

CHAPTER XI

PORPHYRY   ' IN answer to him who called the soul an entelechy, and supposed
p. 813 it, though utterly motionless, to be a cause of motion, we must ask what is the source of the strong excitements of the animal who understands nothing of what he sees and utters, though his soul discerns what is future and not yet present, and moves according to the same ? Whence also in the constitution of the animal come the acts of the soul as of a living thing, acts of deliberation, inquiry, and will, which are movements of the soul and not of the body ? '

Then presently he adds :

' To liken the soul to weight or bodily properties uniform and immovable, by which either the motion or the quality of the
b subject-matter is determined, was the part of a man who either willingly or unwillingly had utterly lost sight of the dignity of the soul, and had in no way discerned that by the presence of the soul the animal's body is made alive, as by the presence of fire the water placed close to it, though cold in itself, is made hot; and by the rising of the sun the air, which is dark without his shining, is made full of light.

' Yet neither was the heat of the water previously the fire nor the fire's heat; nor was the light of the atmosphere that light which is inherent in the sun : and in the same way the animation
c of the body, which seems like the weight or the quality in the body, is not that soul which was located in the body and through which also the body partook of a certain breath of life.'

Then afterwards he adds :

' So then all the other statements which others have made concerning the soul bring disgrace upon us. For must it not be a disgraceful doctrine which makes the soul the entelechy of the physical organic body? And is not that a shameful doctrine,

---

812 d 4 Porphyry against Boëthus *On the Soul,* a Fragment preserved by Eusebius

which represents it as having somehow a breath or intelligent fire, PORPHYRY
kindled or quenched by the cooling, and, as it were, dipping in the
air around it, and which makes it a collection of atoms, or represents it as wholly engendered of the body ? '   **d**

This is what in *The Laws* the author represented as
the impious doctrine of impious men. All such statements then are full of shame : but, says he, no one would
be ashamed for him who calls it a self-moved substance.

CHAPTER XII

' FURTHER, when Plato says that the soul pervading all parts **p. 814**
arranges all in order, and is that whereby the other philosophers ATTICUS
would admit that all things are so arranged, and that nature is
nothing else than soul, and evidently not an irrational soul, and
when from this Plato gathers that all things take place according
to providence, since they take place according to nature, in none
of these opinions does Aristotle agree with us.

' For he does not admit that nature is soul, and earthly things
ordered by one nature : for he says that for each several thing there **b**
are also different causes. For of the things in heaven which
always remain in the same relations and conditions he supposes
fate to be the cause : and of sublunary things, nature ; and of
human affairs, prudence, and forethought, and soul, showing
indeed nicety in such distinctions, but not discerning the necessary
truth.

' For if there were not some one animate power pervading the
whole, and binding and holding all things together, the whole
could not be either reasonably or beautifully arranged. It was
a proof then of the same blindness, to hope that a city could ever **c**
continue in well-being without unity, and to believe that one
could in argument preserve this universe in perfect beauty, such

it appears, without having bound and compacted it together
by participation in some one common principle.

' And something of this kind, he says, it is that arranges the
several parts, such as to be a principle of motion, but he will not
admit that this is soul; though Plato nevertheless shows that in

---

813 d 2 Cf. Plato, *Laws*, x. pp. 885, 900, 907

ATTICUS **d** all things that are moved the source and fountain of their motion is the soul.   And that which would be the work of a rational and wise soul, to make nothing without a purpose, this he attributes to nature, but gives nature no share in the name of soul; as if things were derived not from powers but from names.'

CHAPTER XIII

p. 815 ' BUT the chief point and power of Plato's system, his theory of ideas, has been discredited, and abused, and insulted in every way, as far as it was in Aristotle's power.   For as he was unable to conceive that things of a grand, divine, and transcendent nature require a certain kindred power for their recognition, and trusted to his own meagre and petty shrewdness, which was able to make its way through things terrestrial, and discern the truth in them, but was not capable of beholding the plain of absolute **b** truth, he made himself the rule and judge of things above him, and denied the existence of any peculiar natures such as Plato affirmed, but dared to call the highest of all realities triflings and chatterings and nonsense.

' Rather is the supreme and final speculation of Plato's philosophy that which treats of this intelligible and eternal being of the ideas, wherein verily the utmost toil and stress is set before the soul.   For a most happy man is he, who has shared in the effort and attained the end, while he who has failed from want **c** of power to obtain an insight is left without any share at all of happiness.

' And for this reason Plato too strives earnestly in every way to show the strength of these ideal natures.   For he says that it is not possible either rightly to assign a cause of anything whatsoever, except by participation in the ideas, or to have knowledge of any truth except by reference to these : nay not even a particle of reason would any have, unless they should acknowledge the existence of these ideas.

' They again who have decided to maintain the doctrines of Plato lay the chief stress of their arguments on this point, and quite necessarily.   For nothing is left of the Platonic system, if

---

815 b 1 Cf. Plato, *Phaedrus*, 248 B

one will not grant them on Plato's behalf these primary and **d** A<small>TTICUS</small>
principal natures. For it is in these that he is especially superior
to all other men.

'For as he conceived God in relation to these ideas as Father
of all, and Creator, and Lord, and Guardian; and as from men's
works he recognized that the artist formed a previous conception
of that which he was about to make, and then afterwards adapted
the likeness to the conception thus formed in the case of the things
made; in the same way therefore Plato comprehended at a glance
that God's conceptions, the patterns of the things made, are earlier
than the things themselves, being incorporeal and intelligible, ever
existing in the same conditions and modes, themselves the highest
and first beings, and in part the causes to all the rest of their being **p. 816**
just such as they severally are, according to their likeness to them;
and seeing that they are not easy to be discerned, nor yet able to be
clearly expressed in speech, Plato himself treated of these subjects
as far as it was possible to represent them in speech or thought,
and to prepare those who were to follow after him; and having
arranged his whole philosophy to this end, he asserts that with
these ideas and the perception of them are concerned the wisdom
and the science, whereby the proper end of man and the life of
blessedness are attained.'   **b**

So far speaks Atticus. I might have quoted yet more
than this from his book which I have mentioned: let
us be satisfied, however, with what has been set forth,
and pass on next to the sect of the Stoics. Among the
hearers then of Socrates was one Antisthenes, a man like
Heracleitus in spirit, who said that madness was better
than pleasure, and therefore used to advise his friends
never to stretch out a finger for the sake of pleasure.   **c**

And a disciple of his was Diogenes the 'dog,' who
seemed to entertain most brutelike ideas, and attracted
many followers. He was succeeded by Crates, and a
disciple of Crates was Zeno of Cittium, who was established as founder of the sect of the Stoic philosophers.

Zeno was succeeded by Cleanthes, and Cleanthes by
Chrysippus, and he by the second Zeno, and the rest in
order. All these are said to have been especially devoted

both to hard living and to dialectic.   The doctrines then
of their philosophy are somewhat as follows.

CHAPTER XIV

ARIS- **d**   'THEY say, like Heracleitus, that the element of the existing
TOCLES   world is fire, and that the original principles of fire are matter
and god, as Plato says.   But the former says that both principles,
the active and the passive, are corporeal, while the latter says
that the first active cause is incorporeal.

'Then, moreover, they say that at certain predestined and
p. 817 definite times the whole world is consumed by fire, and afterwards reorganized again.   The primordial fire, however, is as it
were just a seed, containing the reasons and the causes of all
things past, present, and future: and that the combination and
sequence of these constitute fate, and knowledge, and truth, and
law of all being, from which there is no escape or avoidance.
And in this way all things in the world are admirably arranged,
just as in any well-ordered state.'

CHAPTER XV

ARIUS **b**   'THE whole ordered world (κόσμος) with all its parts they call
DIDYMUS   god, and say that he is one alone, and finite, and living, and
eternal, and god: for all bodies are contained in him, and in him
there is no vacuum.   For the name order (κόσμος) is applied to
the quality of all substance as well as to that which has an
c arrangement of like kind consequent on the ordering (διακόσμησιν).

'Wherefore according to the former rendering they say that the
world is eternal, but as to its orderly arrangement created and
subject to change at infinite periods past and future.

'And the quality of all being is an eternal world and god;
d the name world (κόσμος) also means the system compounded of
heaven, and the air, and earth, and sea, and the natures contained in them; and again the name world means the dwelling-
place of gods and men, and of all things made for their sake.

'For in the same way as the name city has two meanings, the

---

816 d 1 Aristocles, a Fragment preserved by Eusebius: cf. Diels, *Doxo-
graphi Graeci*, p. 464, n. 9

dwelling-place, and the system resulting from the combination of   ARIUS
residents and citizens, so also the world is, as it were, a city   DIDYMUS
composed of gods and men, in which the gods hold the rule, and
the men are subject.

'There is, however, a community between them, because they
partake of reason, which is nature's law: and for their sakes all
other things have been made. From which things it follows that
we must suppose that the god who administers the whole takes
thought for mankind, being beneficent, and kind, and friendly to **p. 818**
man, and just, and possessed of all virtues.

'For this reason indeed the world is also called Zeus, since he
is the cause of our life ($\zeta\hat{\eta}\nu$): and inasmuch as from eternity
he administers all things unchangeably by connected ($\epsilon\iota\rho o\mu\acute{\epsilon}\nu\omega$)
reason, he is also called Fate ($\epsilon\iota\mu a\rho\mu\acute{\epsilon}\nu\eta\nu$): and Adrasteia, because
nothing can escape him ($\dot{a}\pi o\delta\iota\delta\rho\acute{a}\sigma\kappa\epsilon\iota\nu$); and Providence, because
he arranges things severally for good.

'Cleanthes would have the sun to be the ruling power of the
world, because it is the greatest of the heavenly bodies, and contributes most to the administration of the whole by making the **b**
day and the year and the other seasons.

'Some, however, of the sect thought that the earth was the
ruling power of the world. But Chrysippus thought it was
the ether, the clearest and purest as being most mobile of all
things, and carrying round the whole course of the world.'

Let this extract then suffice from the *Epitome* of
Arius Didymus. But with reference to the opinion of
the Stoics concerning God it is sufficient to quote the
words of Porphyry in the answer which he wrote to
Boëthus *On the Soul*, in the form following:

CHAPTER XVI

'THEY do not hesitate to call God an intelligent fire and **c** POR-
allow Him to be eternal, and to say that He destroys and devours   PHYRY
all things, being such a fire as that which is known to us, and
to contradict Aristotle who deprecates saying that the ether
consists of fire of this kind.

---

818 c 1 Porphyry, *On the Soul*, in answer to Boëthus

PORPHYRY   'But if they are asked how such a fire lasts so long, though they do not say that it is fire of another kind, yet after describing it as of such a nature, and claiming credence for their own assertion, they add on to this unreasonable belief that it is also an eternal fire, though they assume that even this etherial fire is partially quenched and rekindled. But why should one spend time in pursuing any further their blindness in regard to their own doctrines, and their indolence and contempt for the doctrines of the ancients?'

CHAPTER XVII

p. 819   'BUT what then is " being " ? Is it these four elements, earth and
NUMENIUS fire and the other two intermediate natures?   Are then these the real beings, either collectively, or any one of them singly?   But how can they be, since they are both created and destroyed again, for we may see them proceeding one out of another, and interchanging, and subsisting neither as elements nor as compounds?
b These cannot thus be a body with true being.

'But though not these, yet it is possible that matter may have true being?   But for matter also this is utterly impossible, through want of power to continue.   For matter is a running and swiftly changing stream, in depth, and breadth, and length undefined and endless.'

c   And presently he adds:

'So it is well stated in the argument that, if matter is infinite, it is undefined; and, if undefined, irrational; and, if irrational, it cannot be known.   But as it cannot be known it must necessarily be without order, as things arranged in order must certainly be easy to be known: and what is without order, is not stable: and whatever is not stable cannot have true being.

'Now this was the very point on which we agreed among ourselves before, that it is not permissible for all these things to be associated with true being. I should wish this to be the opinion of all men, be it at all events mine. I deny, therefore, that either matter in itself, or material bodies are true being.

d   'What then? Have we anything else besides these elements in the

---

819 a 1 Numenius, a Fragment preserved by Eusebius

nature of the universe? Yes, certainly. And this is not at all NUMENIUS
a subtle thing to express, if we would together try to discuss the
following point first in the case of ourselves.

'For since bodies are in their own nature inanimate and dead,
carried hither and thither, and not abiding in one stay, have they
not need of something to hold them together? Most certainly. And
if they should fail to find this, would they continue? Certainly
not. What is there then to hold them? If on the one hand
this also were a body, I think that being liable to be dissolved
and dispersed it would need a Zeus Soter to sustain it. If, **p. 820**
however, it must be freed from what bodies suffer, in order that
after they have been generated it may be able to avert their destruction, and hold them together, to me it seems that there is nothing
else left, except only the incorporeal. For of all natures this
alone is stable, and compact, and not at all corporeal. At all
events it is neither created, nor increased, nor subject to any
other kind of motion, and for these reasons the incorporeal was
rightly judged worthy to take precedence.'

CHAPTER XVIII

'BUT the oldest of this sect are of opinion that all things are **b** ARIUS
changed into ether, when at certain very long periods all are DIDYMUS
resolved into an ethereal fire.'

And afterwards he adds:

'But from this it is manifest that Chrysippus has not accepted
this confusion in reference to substance (for that was impossible),
but only that which was meant as equivalent to change. For the **c**
term destruction is not properly understood of the great destruction of the world which takes place in long periods by those who
hold the doctrine of the dissolution of the universe into fire, which
they call conflagration, but they use the term destruction ($\phi\theta o\rho\acute{a}\nu$)
as equivalent to change in the course of nature.

'For it is held by the Stoic philosophers that the universal substance changes into fire, as into a seed, and coming back again
from this completes its organization, such as it was before. And
this is the doctrine which was accepted by the first and oldest
leaders of the sect, Zeno, and Cleanthes, and Chrysippus. For the **d**

Zeno who was the disciple and successor of Chrysippus in the
School is said to have doubted about the conflagration of the
universe.'

CHAPTER XIX

'THE common reason having advanced so far, and a common
nature having become greater and fuller, and having at last
p. 821 dried up all things and absorbed them into itself, finds itself in
the universal substance, having gone back to the condition first
mentioned, and to that resurrection which makes the Great Year,
in which takes place the restitution from itself alone to itself
again.

'And when it has returned, because of an arrangement such as
that from which it began to make a similar organization, it according to reason follows the same course again, so that such periods
go on from eternity and never cease. For it is not possible for
all things to have a cause of their beginning, nor of that which
b administers them. For under things created there must lie a substance of a nature to receive all the changes, and the power that
out of it created them. For as there is in our case a certain kind
of creative nature, there must of necessity be something of the
same kind in the world also, something uncreated, for there cannot be a beginning of creation in the case of this nature: and
in the same way as it is uncreated, it is also impossible for it to
be destroyed, either by itself, or by anything external that would
destroy it.

CHAPTER XX

c   'THE seed, says Zeno, which man emits is breath combined with
moisture, a portion and fragment of soul, and a blending of the
parents' seed, and a concrete mixture of the various parts of the
soul. For this, having the same laws as the universe, when
emitted into the womb is caught up by another breath, and made
a portion of the female's soul and grows into one with it, and
d being there stirred and kindled by it grows in secret, continually
receiving additions to the moisture and increasing of itself.'

And a little further on he adds:

'With regard to the soul, Cleanthes, in setting forth the
doctrines of Zeno for comparison with the other physicists, says

that Zeno calls the soul an exhalation endowed with sensation, just
as Heracleitus does. For wishing to make it clear that there is
a perpetual production of intelligent souls by exhalation, he compared them to rivers, speaking as follows : "Though men step into
the same rivers, the waters that from time to time flow over them
are different " : and souls likewise are exhaled from moisture.

'So then Zeno, like Heracleitus, represents the soul as an
exhalation. And he says that it is sensitive for the reason that **p. 822**
the ruling part is capable of being impressed through the senses
from real and substantial objects, and receiving their impressions.
For these are special properties of soul.'

After other remarks he adds :

'And they say that there is a soul in the universe, which they
call ether, and air surrounding the land and sea, and exhalations
from them ; and that to this soul are attached all the other souls,
both those in animals, and those in the surrounding air ; for the
souls of the dead still continue.   **b**

'Some say that the soul of the universe is eternal, but that
the others at death are absorbed into union with it : and that
every soul has in it a certain ruling faculty, which is life, and
sensation, and appetite.'

And a little further on he proceeds:

'They say that the soul is created and perishable, but does not
perish immediately when freed from the body, but abides for
some time by itself; the soul of the good until the resolution of
all things into fire, but the soul of the foolish for certain periods
of time.

'But the continued existence of souls they thus describe, that **c**
we ourselves on becoming souls continue to exist, having been
separated from the body and changed into the smaller substance
of the soul. But the souls of the foolish and of irrational animals
perish together with their bodies.'

Such are the doctrines of the Stoic philosophy collected
out of the *Epitomae* of Arius Didymus. But in answer
to their absurd opinion about the soul, it is sufficient to
quote the refutations briefly stated in the following
words in Longinus, one of our own age :

Chapter XXI

d   'To speak briefly, it seems to me that all who repre-
LONGINUS sented the soul as a body have strayed, one after another, far
away from right reasoning. For how is it at all admissible to
assume that what is proper to the soul is similar to any of the
elements? Or how refer it to the compounds and mixtures,
which occurring in many ways are of a nature to generate forms
p. 823 of countless other bodies, in which, if not continuously, at all
events at intervals one may see the cause of the elements, and
the advance of the primary elements towards the secondary and
tertiary compounds? But of properties pertaining to the soul not
a trace nor a sign is found in bodies, not even if one should
strive, like Epicurus and Chrysippus, to turn every stone, and
examine every power of body for an origin of the functions of
the soul.

    'For what help would the subtilty of the breath give us for
b sensible presentations and reasonings? Or why has the shape of
the atoms so great power above all else and such facility of change,
as to beget wisdom, whenever it is mixed up in the moulding of
another body? I think indeed that not even if one chanced to be
one of Hephaestus' tripods and handmaidens, of whom the former,
Homer says, went self-moved to the assembly, and the latter
helped their master in his work, and lacked none of the advantages which living beings possess, much less those of the
fortuitous motes, . . . and on the other hand it is like the stones
c upon the sea-shore, in regard to being able to do anything remarkable towards producing sensation. For one might justly be
indignant with Zeno and Cleanthes for arguing so very con-
temptuously about the soul, and saying both alike that the soul is
an exhalation of the solid body. For what, in heaven's name,
is there at all in common between an exhalation and a soul?
And how is it possible for them, if they think that both our nature
and that of other animals is like this, to be able to preserve
either sensible presentations and remembrances permanently, or,
on the other hand, instincts and desires of things conducive to
d understanding? Shall we then indeed degrade the gods also, and

---

822 d 1 Longinus, *Fr.* vii   823 b 6 Hom. *Il.* xviii. 376

Him who pervades all things alike in earth and heaven, into an Longinus exhalation, and smoke, and such nonsense as this? And shall we not feel ashamed even towards the poets, who although they have not an exact understanding of the gods, nevertheless partly from the common conception of mankind, and partly from inspiration of the Muses, which is of a nature to stir them hereto, have spoken more honourably concerning them, and not called them exhalations, or airs, or breaths, and such nonsense?'

This is what Longinus tells you. But listen to Plotinus also, aiming against the same sect such remarks as follow:

CHAPTER XXII

'Now whether each of us is immortal, or wholly perishes, or Plotinus whether parts of him will pass into dissolution and destruction, p. 824 while parts remain for ever, which are the man himself, this one may learn as follows, by examining it in the natural way.

'In the first place, man cannot be a simple thing, but he has in him a soul, and has also a body whether as our instrument, or as b attached to us in any other way; at all events let them be thus distinguished, and let us examine closely the nature and essence of each.

'The body then, being itself compound, cannot, from the reason of the thing, be permanent; and our senses perceive it dissolving, and wasting, and suffering all kinds of decay, while each of the parts in it follows its own course, and one wastes another away, and changes into another, and destroys it; and this especially when the soul, which harmonizes them, is not present with the atoms.

'And even if each be isolated in coming into existence, it is not one, since it admits of separation into form and matter, of c which even simple bodies must be constituted; moreover having also magnitude, inasmuch as they are bodies, and can be divided and broken into small fragments, in this way also they would be liable to destruction.

'So if this is part of ourselves, we are not altogether immortal: but if it is an instrument, it must be of the nature described, as having been given only for a certain time. But the dominant

---

824 a 1 Plotinus, *Ennead.* iv. 7, p. 456 (Volkmann)

PLOTINUS part, even the man himself, would be either like the form in relation to the body as matter, or like the agent in relation to an instrument. And in either way the soul is the self.

'Of what nature then is this? Either it is body, and must cer-
d tainly be soluble, for every body is compound. Or if it were not body, but of some other nature, this also we must examine either in the same way or some other. And first we must consider into what this body, which they say is soul, must be resolved.

'For since life is an inseparable property of soul, this body which is the soul, if it consisted of two or more bodies, must either in each of the two or in every one have life innate, or one
p. 825 must have it and the other not, or neither have it. If then the life were attached to one of them only, this itself would be soul.

'What then would a body be, which derived life from itself? For fire, and air, and water, and earth, are without life from themselves: and to whichever of these soul is attached, the life which this one enjoys is adventitious. But besides these there are no other bodies. And by those who think that there are elements different from these, they were not said to be souls but bodies, and not to have life. But if, though none of them has life, the assemblage of them is said to have produced life, this is absurd.

b 'If, however, each has life, even one is sufficient: but rather it is impossible that a collection of bodies should produce life, and things unintelligent beget intelligence. Moreover they will not assert that these are produced by any and every mode of combination. There must then be the power that is to arrange, and the cause of the combination: so that this would hold the place of a soul.

'For there would not be even a simple body, to say nothing of a composite body, in the world of being, if there were not a soul in the universe; since it is the accession of reason to matter that makes body, and reason can come from no other source than soul.

c 'If any one should deny this, and say that a soul is made by a concurrence of atoms or indivisibles, he would be refuted by its oneness and community of feeling, and by analogy, since there can be no unity that does not extend throughout the whole, nor can a common feeling come from bodies which are without feeling and incapable of union; but the soul is conscious of feeling; also from things which have no parts there can come neither body nor magnitude.

'Moreover supposing the body to be simple, if they say that all Plotinus
that is material has no life of itself (for matter has no qualities), d
but that what is classed as the form (εἶδος) adds the life—then, if
they say that this form is the essence, only the one of these and
not the union of both will be the soul; and on the other hand,
there is no body, for even this is not produced from mere matter,
or else we must resolve it again in the same manner.

'But if they say that the form is an affection of the matter, but
not the essence, they will have to state the source from which
this affection and the life have come into the matter. For
certainly the matter does not give itself form, nor infuse into
itself a soul. There must, then, be something which provides life,
whether it be provided for the matter or for any of the bodies,
and this must be outside and beyond any bodily nature. Since p. 826
otherwise there would not even be any body, as there would be
no animal force.

'For its own nature is in flux and motion, and if all were
bodies they would perish very speedily, even though the name soul
should be given to one of them: for it would be affected in the
same way as the other bodies, they all having the same matter.
Or rather nothing would ever come into being, but all things
would remain as matter, if there were nothing to give it form.

'But perhaps even matter would not exist at all, but this
universe would be dissolved, if any one should entrust it to
a combination of body, giving it in mere name the rank of soul, b
though it is only air and breath that is most easily dispersed, and
has no unity of itself. For since all bodies are capable of division,
how can any one who makes this universe depend on any of
them, fail to make it unintelligent and moved at random?

'For what order, or reason, or mind can there be in breath
which needs a soul to give it order? But granted the existence
of a soul, all these are subservient to it for the constitution of
a world and of every living thing, a different power from each
contributing to the whole: whereas if there be no soul present in
the universals, they will not merely be without order, but will be c
nothing at all.

'These men are also themselves led by the truth to testify that
there must be something prior to bodies and superior to them,
a species of soul, since they suppose that breath is endowed with

887

d mind and that fire is intelligent, as without fire and breath the
Plotinus better part cannot exist in the actual world, but seeks a place
where it may be settled; whereas they ought to be seeking where
to settle the bodies, as it seems these must be settled in powers of
the soul.

'But if they assume that life and soul are nothing besides
breath, what becomes of their much boasted phrase "in a certain
state," in which they take refuge when compelled to assume some
active nature besides bodies? If then they say that not every
breath is soul, because countless breaths are inanimate, but the
p. 827 breath that is "in a certain state," they must say that this
"certain state," and this condition, is either something real or
nothing.

'But if they say it is nothing, there will be breath only, and
the "certain state" a mere name: and so it will result in their
saying that nothing else exists but matter, and that soul, and
god, and all things are a mere name, and that matter alone
exists. But if the "state" is something real and additional to
the substratum and the matter, existing in matter but itself
immaterial because it is not compounded again out of matter, it
must be not body, but a kind of reason, and a different nature.

b   'Moreover from the following considerations it is not less
evidently impossible that the soul should be a body of any kind
whatever. For then it must be either hot or cold, either hard or
soft, and liquid or solid, and black or white, with all other
bodily qualities differing in different bodies. And if it is hot,
it will only give heat, if cold it will only chill, and the additional
presence of lightness will make things light, and of heaviness
heavy, and blackness will make black, and whiteness white.

'For it is no property of fire to chill, nor of cold to make hot.
c But the soul both produces different effects in different animals,
and also contrary effects in the same animal; making some parts
solid and others liquid, and some thick and others thin, black and
white, light and heavy. Yet it ought to have produced only one
effect according to the quality of the body in colour and other
respects: but in fact it produces many.

'And how then will they explain the fact that the motions
d are diverse instead of one, since every body has one motion only?
If they allege choice as cause of some motions, natural laws of

others, so far they are right : but choice is not a property of Plotinus
body, nor laws, at least if they are different, while the body is
one and simple, and has no participation in any such law, except
what has been given to it by that which caused it to be hot or
cold.

' Also the power of causing growth in periods of time and up
to this or that measure—whence can the body itself get this ?
For it is natural to it to be increased, but to have no power in
itself of causing increase, except in as far as it may be taken into
service as a mass of matter by the power which by means of it
effects the increase. Even if the soul were a body and caused
increase, it must also be itself increased by an addition evidently
of similar body, if it is to advance equally with that which **p. 828**
receives increase from it. And the addition will either be soul, or
soulless body.

' And if soul, how and whence does it come in, and how is it
added ?   But if the addition is soulless, how is it to become
animated, and to agree with what was there before, and be one
with it, and share the same opinions with the first soul ?   Will
not rather this soul, as a stranger, be in ignorance of what the
other knows ; and just as with the other mass of our body, one
part will pass away from it, and another be added, and nothing **b**
will be the same ?

' How then are our remembrances formed ? And how our knowledge of our own selves, if we have never the same soul ?   Moreover if it is body, and the nature of body is that, when divided into
several parts, each of the parts is not the same as the whole, and if
a soul is of a certain size, then whatever is less than that will not
be soul, just as everything of a certain size by any subtraction
changes from being what it was.

' But if anything possessing magnitude should remain the
same in quality when diminished in bulk, it is altered as body
and as quantity, but may retain its sameness in quality as being **c**
different from quantity.

' What then will they say, who assert that the soul is body ?

' First as to each part of the soul that is in the same body, is
each a soul such as the whole is ?

' And so again the part of each part ? Magnitude then contributed
nothing to its essence ; yet it ought to have done so, as there was

PLOTINUS a certain fixed quantity; and it was whole in many different places, which cannot be the case with body, that the same should be whole in many places, and the part be the same as the whole.

d   'But if they say that each of the parts is not a soul, they will have a soul consisting of soulless parts. And further still, if the magnitude of each soul be limited in each direction, then if it become either less or greater it will not be a soul.

'Whenever therefore from one connexion and the same seed twin children are begotten, or even many, as in the case of the other animals, the seed being parted into several places, where each is a whole, does not this teach those who are willing to learn, that where the part is the same as the whole, this whole in its own essence transcends the quantitative existence, and

p. 829 must itself be without quantity? For thus it will remain the same when quantity is withdrawn, inasmuch as it is independent of quantity and bulk, as its essence is something different therefrom. The soul therefore and its laws are independent of quantity.

'But that, if the soul were body, there would be neither sensation nor thought, nor knowledge, nor virtues, nor anything noble, is evident from the following reasons. Whatever

b is to perceive anything by sensation must itself be one, and must apprehend everything by the same sentient power; even if there should be many impressions that enter through many organs of sensation, or many qualities of one thing, and even if through one sense there should enter a complex object, such as a face.

'For there are not different powers that perceive the nostril and the eye, but the same perceives all at once. And if one impression comes through the eyes, and another through hearing, there must be some one power which both reach: or how could one say that these are different, if the sensations did not reach the same sentient power at the same time? This, therefore, must be as it were a centre, and lines converging from the circumference of the circle must convey the sensations from all sides to it, and

c the percipient power of this kind must be really and truly one.

'For if this were to be extended, and the sensations were to strike upon both extremities, as it were, of a line, either they must run together again to one and the same point, as the centre, or to some other: and each different point will have a sensation of one of the two objects, just as if I were to perceive one object PLOTINUS and you another.

'And if the sensible object be one, as a face, it will be contracted into one, as is evidently the case; for contraction takes place in the very pupils of the eyes (otherwise how could very large objects be seen through them?): so that there is a still further contraction in passing on to the ruling faculty, in such d a way that indivisible notions are produced. And this faculty will be indivisible, or, if it were a magnitude, the perceptions would share its divisibility, so that one part (of the soul) would perceive one part (of the object), and another another, and nothing in us would perceive the sensible object as a whole.

'But in fact the whole sentient is one: for how could it be divided? For there can be no correspondence of equal to equal, because the ruling faculty cannot be equal to each and every sensible object. Into how many parts then shall the division be made? Or shall it be divided into as many parts as the number of varieties in the object of sense that enters? And so then each of **p. 830** those parts of the soul will also perceive by its subdivisions, or the parts of the subdivisions will have no perception; but that is impossible. And if any part perceive all the object, since magnitude by its nature is infinitely divisible, the result will be that each man will also have infinite sensations for each sensible object, infinite images, as it were, of the same thing in our ruling faculty.

'Moreover if the sentient be body, the sensation cannot take place otherwise than as seals impressed on wax from signet-rings, whether the sensations be impressed upon the blood or upon the **b** breath. If then the impressions are made as in liquid bodies, which is probable, they will become confused, just as if made on water, and there will be no remembrance of them.

'But if the impressions remain, either it is impossible for others to be imprinted while the former occupy the place, so that there will be no other sensations : or if others are made, the former will be obliterated, so that the remembrance will come to nothing. But if it is possible to remember, and to receive sensations one upon another, without hindrance from the earlier, it is impossible for the soul to be body.

'And the same may also be seen from the sensation of pain. **c**

PLOTINUS When a man is said to have a pain in his finger, the pain of course is about the finger, but the sensation of the pain, they must evidently admit, arises in the ruling faculty. While the suffering part therefore is different, the ruling faculty perceives the (animal) spirit, and the whole soul shares the same feeling.

'How then does this result? By transmission, they will say, the animal spirit about the finger having first suffered, and imparted the suffering to the next, and this to another, until it arrived at the ruling faculty.

d 'Necessarily, therefore, if the first had a sensation of pain, there must be another sensation for the second, if the sensation came by way of transmission, and another also for the third, and the sensation of one single pain must become many and infinite, and afterwards the ruling faculty must perceive all these sensations and its own in addition to them.

'But the truth is, that each of them is not a sensation of the pain in the finger, but that which is next to the finger is a feeling that the wrist is in pain, and the third is a feeling that another part farther up is in pain, and so there are many pains : and the ruling faculty does not perceive the pain in the finger,

p. 831 but the pain close to itself, and knows only this, and dismisses the others, not understanding that it is the finger which is in pain.

'If, therefore, it is not possible for the sensation of such a pain to be produced by transmission, nor possible that in the body as being a mass, when one part suffers, another part should be noticed (for in every magnitude one part and another part are different), we must suppose the sentient power to be of ˙such a nature as to be everywhere identical with itself. But to effect this is the property of a different kind of being from body.

b 'That it would not be possible even to think, if the soul were any kind of body, is to be shown from the following reasons. For if the meaning of sensation is, that the soul apprehends the objects of sense by making use of body, it cannot be that thought also means perception by means of body, or else it will be the same as sensation.

'If, therefore, thought is apprehension without the aid of body, much rather must the thinking faculty not be body, since sensation is of sensibles, but thought of intelligibles. But if they will

not admit this, at all events there must be both thoughts of some PLOTINUS
intelligibles, and apprehensions of things without magnitude.

'How, then, if it be magnitude will it conceive in thought that c
which is not magnitude, or by that which is divisible conceive
that which is not divisible ?   Will it be by some indivisible part
of itself?   But if so, the thinking faculty will not be body.   For
there is certainly no need of the whole in order to touch ; for any
one part is sufficient.

'If, therefore, they should admit, as is true, that the first
notions are those of the things which are most entirely free from
body, that is of absolutes, the intelligent faculty can form
notions only as being or becoming free from body.   But if they
should say that the notions are of forms embodied in matter,
yet they are only formed by abstraction from the bodies, the mind
making the abstraction.

' For certainly the abstraction of circle, and triangle, and line, d
and point has nothing to do with flesh, or matter at all.   In such
an operation, therefore, we must separate the soul itself also from
body : it must not therefore itself be body.   I suppose too that
beauty and justice are things without magnitude, and therefore
the conception of them also.   So that as they occur the soul will
receive them with its indivisible faculty, and they will abide in
it as indivisibles.

' Also if the soul be corporeal how can prudence, justice, fortitude, and other virtues belong to it ?   For then temperance, or
justice, or fortitude must be some kind of breath, or of blood ;
unless perhaps fortitude were the uneasiness of the breath, and **p. 832**
temperance its right temperature, and beauty a certain elegance
in forms, because of which, when we see them, we call men goodly
and beautiful in body.

' To be strong and beautiful in form might indeed be suitable
to breath ; but what does breath want of prudence ?   Nay ; but,
on the contrary, it wants to find enjoyment in embraces and
caresses, wherein it will either be warmed, or will desire a moderate coolness, or attach itself to things soft, and tender, and
smooth.   But for assigning to each thing its due worth, what
would it care ?   b

' And is it because they are eternal that the soul fastens upon
the conceptions of virtue, and the other objects of the intellect, or

PLOTINUS does virtue begin to exist in one, and must it perish again? But then who creates it, and whence? For thus there would again remain that former question. It must be, then, because they are eternal and abiding, such as are the conceptions of geometry: and, if eternal and abiding, not corporeal. Therefore also the soul in which they are to exist must be of this same nature; it must not then be corporeal; for everything of the nature of body is non-abiding and transient.

c   ' If, from seeing the operations of bodies, in imparting heat and cold, and thrusting, and weighing down, they put the soul in this class, as if seating it in a place of activity,—then in the first place they are ignorant that even these bodies work these effects by means of the incorporeal powers contained in them, and then that these are not the powers which we claim as belonging to the soul; but the powers of thought, sensation, reasoning, desiring, managing wisely and well, all require another kind of essence.

d   ' So by transferring the powers of the incorporeal to the corporeal, they leave none for the former. And that bodies can only produce their effects by means of incorporeal powers is evident from the following reasons. For it will be admitted that quality is one thing and quantity another, and that every body has quantity, and yet not every body has quality, as for example mere matter. But if they admit this, they must admit that quality, being different from quantity, is different from body.

' For if it have not quantity, how can it be body, since every body has quantity? Moreover, as was said somewhere above, if
p. 833 every body on being divided, and every mass, ceases to be what it was, but when the body is cut small the same quality remains entire in every part,—if for example, the sweetness of honey is none the less sweetness in every drop,—sweetness cannot be a body. The same is true of all the other qualities.

' Then further, if the powers were bodies, the strong powers must necessarily be great masses, and those which can effect but little, small masses. But if when the masses are great the powers are small, and a few very small masses have the greatest powers, their efficacy must be attributed to something else than magnitude, therefore to something without magnitude.

b   ' The fact too that matter, being as they say body, is itself the same, but produces different effects when it has qualities added to it,—does not this make it evident that the things added are PLOTINUS actually rational powers and incorporeal? And let them not reply that, when breath or blood has departed, the animals die. For it is impossible to exist without many other things besides these, and yet the soul can be none of them. Moreover neither breath nor blood extends through all parts, but soul does.

'Further, if the soul being body had pervaded every part, it would also have been mixed, in the same way as the mixture takes place in all other bodies. But if the mixture of the bodies c leaves none of the components in actual existence, neither will the soul retain an actual existence in the bodies, but only potential, having lost its existence as soul. Just as if sweet and bitter be mingled, the sweet no longer exists. And so we have no soul.

' And the fact that, being body, it is mingled with body, the whole throughout the whole, so that wherever either may be there the other is also, both having a mass equal to the whole, and that no increase has taken place by the addition of the other,—this will leave nothing that it does not divide. For the d mixture is not made in large portions alternately (for so they say it would be a juxta-position), but having passed through the whole, the addition being superimposed upon the less (a thing impossible, that the less should be found equal to the greater)—but nevertheless having so passed through, it divides the whole in every part.

' Therefore if this occurs at any point whatever, and there be no body between, which has not been cut, the body must have been divided into points, which is impossible ; and if the division be carried on to infinity (for whatever particle of body you take, it may be divided), the infinities will have not only a potential but an actual existence. Therefore it is not possible that body should wholly pervade the whole : but the soul does pervade the whole : therefore it is incorporeal.

' As to their saying that the same breath is an earlier nature, **p. 834** and when it has come into a cool place ($\psi v\chi\rho\hat{\omega}$) and been sharpened, it becomes soul ($\psi v\chi\acute{\eta}$), being made finer in the cool, —this certainly is absurd; for many animals are born in warm places, and have a soul that has not been cooled. But at all events they say that there is an earlier nature of the soul produced

PLOTINUS by external contingencies. The result, therefore, is that they make the inferior first, and before this another still less, which they call habit (ἕξις). And the mind comes last, as produced of course from the soul; or if mind is before all things, they ought to b make soul next, then vegetative nature; and the later always the worse, if it is a merely natural product.

' If, therefore, even God in respect of His mind is regarded by them as later, and as generated, His intelligence also being adscititious, it would be possible that neither soul, nor mind, nor God should exist. For if the potential could exist without the previous existence of the actual, and of mind, it would never attain to actuality. For what would there be to bring it on, if there exist not besides itself something prior? But if it is to bring itself into actuality (which is absurd), yet at least in so bringing itself forward it must have something to look to, which must exist not potentially but actually.

c ' And yet if the potential is to have the power of always remaining the same, it will of itself have attained to actuality, and this latter will be better than that which has only potentiality, as being a state desired by it. The better therefore will be the prior, both as having a different nature from body, and as always actually existent: mind, therefore, and soul are prior to mere nature; soul, therefore, does not exist as breath, nor yet as body. However, though other arguments might be stated, and have been stated by others, showing that it is not body, yet even what I have now said is sufficient.

' But since it is of a different nature, we must inquire what d this nature is. Is it then, though different from body, yet something belonging to body, as it were a harmony? For although the Pythagoreans used this word " harmony " in a different way, they supposed that it was something of the same kind as the harmony on the strings of the lyre.

' For as when the strings of the lyre have been stretched tight there comes a certain kind of effect upon them, which is called p. 835 harmony, in the same way also in our body, when a mixture is made of unlike elements, they thought that a mixture of a certain quality produces both life and soul, which is the effect upon the mixture. But many arguments have ere now been urged against this opinion to show that it is impossible.

'For it has been argued that the soul is the prior element, PLOTINUS
but the harmony subsequent: and that the former rules and
presides over the body, and in many ways contends with it,
but could not do so if it were a harmony: and that the one
is an essence, but the harmony is not an essence: and that the
mixture of the bodily elements, of which we consist, if it be
in due proportion, would mean health : also that in each part
differently compounded there would be a different soul, so that **b**
there would be many souls : and, as the chief argument, that
prior to this present soul there must be another soul to produce this harmony, as in the case of musical instruments there
is the musician, who puts the harmony into the strings, having
in himself the reasoning faculty in accordance with which he
will modulate it.

' For neither in that case will the strings of themselves, nor in
this case the bodily particles be able to bring themselves into
harmony. And speaking generally, these philosophers also make
animated things out of inanimate, and things casually brought
out of disorder into order, and instead of order from the soul
they make the soul itself to have received its subsistence from **c**
the self-made order. But this cannot possibly take place either
in the single parts or in the wholes. The soul, therefore, is not
a harmony.'

These extracts are taken from the work of Plotinus
against the opinion of the Stoics concerning the soul,
who say that it is corporeal. But since I have set forth
sufficiently for a summary statement the arguments
against Aristotle and the Peripatetics, and those against
the sect of the Stoics, it is time to go back again and **d**
survey the wonderful physical theories of all their noble
philosophers together, seeing especially that all the
Greeks in common believed in and worshipped as visible
gods the Sun, and Moon, and the rest of the luminaries,
and the other elements of the world, and have transferred
the fabulous and nonsensical tales about their polytheistic
error by more seemly physical explanations to the primary elements and the divisions of the whole world.

Wherefore I think it necessary for me also to collect

their opinions on these subjects, and to review their disputes and their vain conceit.

p. 836   These matters also I will quote from the work of Plutarch, in which he collected the opinions thereon of all the philosophers both ancient and modern, writing in the following manner:

CHAPTER XXIII
OF THE SUN.

PLUTARCH   'ANAXIMANDER: that there is a circle twenty-eight times as large as the Earth, having its circumference like a chariot-wheel, **b** hollow, and full of fire, and partly showing the fire through an opening, as through a bellows-pipe: and this is the Sun.

'Xenophanes: it is formed from the sparks which are seen to be collected from watery vapour, and which compose the Sun out of burning clouds.

'The Stoics: a flame out of the sea, endowed with intelligence.

'Plato: out of an immense fire.

'Anaxagoras, Democritus, Metrodorus: a fiery mass of metal or stone.

c   'Aristotle: a globe of the fifth corporeal element.

'Philolaus the Pythagorean: a disk as of glass, which receives the reflected radiance of the fire in the cosmos, and transmits the light to us; so that the Sun's fiery appearance in the heaven is like the light which comes to us dispersed by reflexion from the mirror: for this light also we call the Sun, being as it were an image of an image.

'Empedocles: there are two Suns; the one archetypal, a fire in the other hemisphere of the cosmos, which has filled that hemisphere, being always opposite to its own reflected light; and **d** the other which we see is the reflected light in this other hemisphere which is filled with air mixed with heat, formed by reflexion from the spherical surface of the Earth and falling upon the crystalline Sun, and carried round with the motion of the fiery Sun: but to express it more shortly, the Sun is the reflexion of the fire that surrounds the Earth.

'Epicurus: a compact mass of earth, resembling pumice or sponge in its pores, and kindled by the fire.'

---

836 a 6 Plutarch, *On the Opinions of Philosophers*, 889 F

Chapter XXIV

Of the Sun's Magnitude.

'Anaximander : the Sun itself is equal to the Earth, but the p. 837
orbit from which it breathes out its fire, and by which it is Plutarch
carried round, is twenty-seven times as large as the Earth.

'Anaxagoras : many times as large as Peloponnesus.

'Heracleitus : the breadth of a man's foot.

'Epicurus again says that the aforesaid descriptions are all
possible : or else that it is of the same size as it appears, or a little
greater or less.'   b

Chapter XXV

Of the Shape of the Sun.

'Anaximenes : the Sun is flat like a plate.

'Heracleitus : like a boat, concave.

'The Stoics : spherical, like the universe and the stars.   c

'Epicurus : the aforesaid descriptions are all possible.'

Such is their Sun, the mighty god of all things visible
in heaven. But Moses and the Hebrew oracles waste no
labour on any of these matters.

Chapter XXVI

Of the Moon.

'Anaximander : it is a circle nineteen times as large as the d
Earth, full of fire, as in the case of the Sun, and is eclipsed in
consequence of the rotation of its disk. And it is like a chariot
wheel, having its circumference hollow, and full of fire, with only
one vent.

'Xenophanes : a cloud condensed.

'The Stoics : a mixture of fire and air.

'Plato : of earth for the more part.

'Anaxagoras, Democritus : a fiery solid, having in itself plains,
and mountains, and ravines.

'Heracleitus : earth surrounded with mist.

'Pythagoras : a mirror-like body.'

Chapter XXVII

Of the Moon's Magnitude.

p. 838   ' The Stoics represent it as larger than the Earth, as they also Plutarch say of the Sun.

     ' Parmenides : equal to the Sun, for it is illumined from it.'

Chapter XXVIII

Of the Moon's Shape.

b   ' The Stoics : it is spherical, as the Sun.

    ' Heracleitus : like a boat.

    ' Empedocles : like a disk (or quoit).

    ' Others like a cylinder.'

Chapter XXIX

Of the Moon's Illumination.

    ' Anaximander : it has light of its own, but somewhat scanty.

c   ' Antiphon : the Moon shines by its own light; but the portion of it which is partially hidden is obscured by the Sun's light falling upon it, as it is the nature of the stronger fire to obscure the weaker : which happens also with the other heavenly bodies.

    ' Thales and his followers : the Moon is illumined from the Sun.

    ' Heracleitus : the Sun and Moon are affected in the same way : for the heavenly bodies being boat-like in shape, and receiving the products of the watery evaporation, become luminous in

d appearance; the Sun more brilliantly, because it moves in a purer atmosphere, but the Moon moving in a turbid atmosphere therefore also appears more dim.'

Chapter XXX

What is the Substance of the Planets and Fixed Stars ?

    ' Thales : the heavenly bodies are of earth, but on fire.

    ' Empedocles : of fire, from the fiery element, which the air contained in itself and thrust out at the first separation of the elements.

p. 839   ' Anaxagoras : the surrounding atmosphere is in its substance fire, but by the energy of its revolution catches up stones from the earth, and having set them on fire has made stars of them.

---

838 d 4 Plutarch, 888 D

'Diogenes : the heavenly bodies are porous like pumice, and are PLUTARCH the breathing-holes of the universe. But again the same author thinks that they are stones, which, though at first invisible, often fall upon the Earth and are extinguished, just as the stony meteor which fell in a fiery form at Aegospotamoi.

'Empedocles : the fixed stars are fastened to the crystalline sphere, but the planets are free.

'Plato : for the most part they are of fire, but partake also of the other elements as a cement.   **b**

'Xenophanes : they consist of clouds on fire, but are extinguished every day, and re-kindled in the night, just like live coals: for their risings and settings are their kindlings and quenchings.

'Heracleides and the Pythagoreans think that each of the stars is a world, including an Earth, and an atmosphere and an ether in the infinite space. These doctrines are introduced in the Orphic Hymns, for they make each star a world.

'Epicurus rejects none of these opinions, but adheres to his **c** "possible." '

CHAPTER XXXI

OF THE SHAPE OF THE STARS.

'THE Stoics : the stars are spherical, like the universe, Sun, and Moon.

'Cleanthes : conical.

'Anaximenes : like studs fastened in the crystalline sphere.

'But some say that they are plates of fire, as it were pictures.' **d**

Such are the discoveries of the wonderful philosophers concerning what they call visible gods. But learn also from the same Plutarch's voice, what decisions they have pronounced concerning the universe :

CHAPTER XXXII

HOW THE WORLD WAS CONSTRUCTED.

'THE world, therefore, has been fashioned in a rounded form, in the following manner. As the corporeal atoms have an

---

839 d 6 Plutarch, 878 C

p. 840 undesigned and fortuitous motion, and move continuously and
PLUTARCH very swiftly, many of them were collected together, and from
this cause had great variety of shapes and sizes.

'And when these were all gathered in the same place, all the
larger and heaviest settled down : but as many as were small,
and round, and smooth, and easily moved, were thrust out in the
collision of the bodies, and carried up on high.

'When, therefore, the propelling force ceased to carry them
upward, and the propulsion no longer tended towards the height,
b while on the other hand they were prevented from sinking downward, they were compressed into the places which were able to
admit them ; and these were the places around them.

'So the multitude of the bodies were turned round towards
these places, and becoming intermingled one with another in the
turning they generated the heaven. But the atoms retaining
the same natural tendency, and being of various kinds, as I have
said, were thrust out towards the upper region, and produced
the nature of the stars.

'But the multitude of the bodies which were exhaled kept
striking upon the air and thrusting it away ; and the air in its
motion being turned into wind and encompassing the stars
c carried them round with it, and maintained the revolution which
they now have on high. Afterwards out of the particles which
settled down the Earth was produced, and out of those which were
carried upward the heaven, and fire, and air.

'And as there was still much matter included in the Earth,
which became condensed in consequence of the blows from the
winds and the currents from the stars, all of its shape that
was formed by minute particles was further compressed, and
generated the watery element.

'And this having a fluid tendency was carried down into the
hollow places which were able to receive and hold it ; or the water
settled down of itself and gradually hollowed out the places
d below it.'

Such is their wonderful cosmogony ! And with this
is connected much other disputation, as they started
questions about problems of all kinds ; whether we ought
to regard the universe as one or many ; and the cosmos
as one or more ; and whether it has a soul, and is ad-

ministered by a divine providence, or the contrary : also
whether it is imperishable or perishable ; and from what
source it is sustained ; and from what kind of material
God began to make the world : also concerning the order
of the world ; and what is the cause of its inclination ;
also concerning what is outside the circumference of the
world ; and which is the right and which the left side of
the world ; also concerning the heaven, and, besides all **p. 841**
this, concerning daemons and heroes ; and about matter,
and about ideas : about the arrangement of the universe :
yet more, about the course and motion of the stars : and
besides this, from what source the stars derive their
light : also about the so-called Dioscuri, and the eclipses
of the Sun and Moon, and her aspect, and why she has
an earthlike appearance ; also concerning her distances ;
and moreover concerning the years.

Now all these questions have been treated in numberless ways by the philosophers of whom we speak, but since
Plutarch collected them in a few concise words, by bring- **b**
ing together the opinions of them all and their contradictions, I think it will not be unprofitable to us if they are
presented with a view to their rejection on reasonable
grounds. For since they stood in diametrical opposition
one to another, and stirred up battles and wars against
each other, and nothing better, each with jealous strife
of words confuting their neighbours' opinions, must not
every one admit that our hesitation on these subjects has
been reasonable and safe ?

Next in order to the aforesaid subjects I will add all
their disquisitions upon matters nearer to the Earth ;
concerning the figure of the Earth, and its position and **c**
inclination : also concerning the sea ; that so you may
know that the noble sages differed not only about things
high and lofty, but that they have disagreed also in
matters terrestrial. And to increase yet more your admiration of this wisdom of the wise, I will add also all the
controversies they waged about the soul and the ruling

faculty therein, unable as they were to discover what their own nature was. But now let us go back to the first of the aforesaid subjects.

Chapter XXXIII

d   WHETHER THE ALL IS ONE.

PLUTARCH   ' THE Stoics then represented the world as one, which they also affirmed to be the All, including the corporeal elements.

' But Empedocles said that, though the world was one, yet it was not the All, but only a small part of the All, and the rest useless matter.

' Plato derives his opinion that the world is one, and the All one, by inference from three arguments : from the notion that it will not be perfect, unless it comprehends all things ; that it will not be like its pattern, unless it be unique ; that it will not be indestructible, if there be anything outside it. But in answer to Plato it must be said, that the world is not perfect, for it does
p. 842 not include all things ; for man also is perfect, but does not include all things : and there are many examples, as in the case of statues, and houses, and pictures : and how can it be perfect, if it is possible for anything to revolve outside it ? And indestructible it is not, and cannot be, since it is created.

' But Metrodorus says it is as absurd that there should be but one world generated in infinite space, as that there should be but one head of corn in a great plain : and that the world is one of an infinite multitude is manifest from the infinity of causes. For
b if the world is finite, while the causes from which the world has come are all infinite, the number of worlds must be infinite. For where they all have been causes, there must also be effects : and causes they are, whether the atoms or the elements.'

Chapter XXXIV

WHETHER THE WORLD HAS A SOUL, AND IS ADMINISTERED BY PROVIDENCE.

' THE others all say that it has a soul, and is administered by providence.

---

841 d 2 Plutarch, 879 A   842 b 7 ibid 886 D

'But Democritus and Epicurus, and all who are for bringing c Plut-
in the atoms and vacuum, say that it neither has a soul, nor is   ARCH
administered by providence, but by some irrational kind of
nature.

'Aristotle says that, as a whole and throughout, it has neither
a soul, nor reason, nor intelligence, nor is it administered by
providence.   For while the heavenly regions partake of all
these properties, because they include spheres which are endowed
with a soul and life, the terrestrial regions have none of them,
but share in the orderly arrangement by accident and not
directly.'

Chapter XXXV

Whether the World is Imperishable.   d

'Pythagoras, and Plato, and the Stoics say that the world
was created by God; and that, so far as it depends on its nature,
it is perishable, because it is perceptible by sense through being
corporeal; nevertheless it will not be destroyed, through the
providence and support of God.

'Epicurus says that it is perishable, because created, like an
animal or a plant.

'Xenophanes: the world is uncreated, and eternal, and imperishable.

'Aristotle: the part of the world beneath the Moon may be
affected by change, and the things terrestrial therein are doomed
to perish.'

Chapter XXXVI

From what Source the World is Sustained.   p. 843

'Aristotle: if the world receives sustenance, it will also
perish; but in fact it needs no sustenance, and therefore is also
eternal.

'Plato: the world supplies its own sustenance out of its waste,
by a change.

'Philolaus: the decay is twofold, sometimes by fire fallen from b
heaven, and sometimes from the water of the Moon being thrown
off by the revolution of its atmosphere: and the exhalations from
these are the sustenance of the world.'

Chapter XXXVII

From what Material First God Began to Form the World.

PLUT-
ARCH **c** 'THE physicists say that the creation of the world began from Earth, as from a centre; and the centre is the beginning of a sphere.

'Pythagoras: from fire, and the fifth element.

'Empedocles: the ether was first separated, and next the fire, and after it the Earth, out of which, when very closely compressed by the rush of the sphere, the water gushed up, and the air was formed from it by evaporation. Then the heaven was produced from the ether, and the Sun from the fire: and the terrestrial parts were formed by condensation out of the other elements.

d 'Plato: the world was made visible according to the pattern of the intelligible world: and of the visible world first the soul, and after this the corporeal element, first the part produced from fire and earth, and secondly that from water and air.

'Pythagoras says that, whereas there are five solid figures which are also called mathematical, out of the cube the earth was produced; out of the pyramid the fire; out of the octahedron the air; out of the eicosahedron the water; and out of the dodeca-hedron the sphere of the universe.

'And herein again Plato follows Pythagoras.'

Chapter XXXVIII

Of the Arrangement of the World.

'PARMENIDES: there are wreaths twisted round one upon
p. 844 the other, one of the rare matter, and the other of the dense; and between them others of light and darkness mixed; and that which surrounds them all like a wall is solid.

'Leucippus and Democritus extend a tunic and a membrane in a circle round the world.

'Epicurus: the boundary of some worlds is thin, and of others dense: and of these part are in motion, and part immovable.

'Plato: fire first, then ether, after that air, next water, and earth last: but sometimes he combines the ether with the fire.

'Aristotle: first impassible ether, that is a fifth body; after that
passibles, fire, air, water, and earth last. Of these the celestial
portions have the circular motion assigned to them : and of the
portions ranged beneath them the light have the upward, and the
heavy the downward motion.

'Empedocles : the places of the elements are not entirely fixed
and limited, but they all in a certain way partake one of
another.'

Chapter XXXIX

What is the Cause of the Inclination of the World.

'Diogenes, Anaxagoras : after the world was established, and c
had brought forth the living beings out of the earth, the world
was somehow spontaneously inclined towards its southern side,
perhaps from design, in order that some parts of the world might
be uninhabitable and some habitable, in consequence of cold,
and torrid heat, and a temperate climate.

'Empedocles : when the air yielded to the impulse of the Sun,
the polar Bears became inclined, and the northern regions were
elevated, and the southern depressed, and the whole world accordingly.'

Chapter XL

Of the Outside of the World, Whether it is a Vacuum. d

'The Pythagoreans : outside the world there is a vacuum, into
and out of which the world breathes.

'The Stoics : infinite (vacuum), into which the world is also
dissolved by the conflagration.

'Poseidonius : not infinite, but sufficiently large for the dissolution.

'Plato, Aristotle : no vacuum either outside the world or
inside.'

Chapter XLI

Which are the Right and which the Left Sides of   p. 845
the World.

'Pythagoras, Plato, Aristotle : the right parts of the world
are the eastern, from which the motion begins, and the left are
the western.

PLUTARCH   'Empedocles : the right is the region of the summer solstice, and the left the region of the winter solstice.'

CHAPTER XLII

b   OF THE HEAVEN ; WHAT IS ITS SUBSTANCE.

'ANAXIMENES : it is the circumference of the outer zone.

'Empedocles : the heaven is solid, formed from air compressed by fire into a crystallized form, and encompassing the whole elements of fire and air in each of the hemispheres.

CHAPTER XLIII

c   OF DAEMONS AND HEROES.

'IN connexion with the discourse concerning gods we must inquire into that which concerns daemons and heroes.

'Thales, Pythagoras, Plato, the Stoics : daemons are beings of the nature of souls : heroes also are souls which have been separated from their bodies ; and the good souls are good daemons, and the bad souls evil daemons.

d   'But Epicurus admits none of these opinions.'

CHAPTER XLIV

OF MATTER.

'Matter is the substratum to generation and decay and the other changes.

'The Schools of Thales and Pythagoras, and the Stoics : matter is wholly and thoroughly subject to change and alteration and flux.

'The School of Democritus : the primary elements are impassible, namely, the atom, the vacuum, and the incorporeal.

'Aristotle and Plato say that matter is corporeal, without form, specific character, shape, or quality, so far as it depends on its own nature, but receptive of the specific forms, as it were p. 846 a nurse, and a mould, and a matrix. But those who say that matter is water, or fire, or air, or earth, no longer speak of it as

---

845 c 2 Plutarch, 882 B

without form, but as body : while those who say that it is the PLUTARCH
indivisible bodies and atoms, do regard it as without form.'

CHAPTER XLV

OF THE IDEA.

' AN " idea " is an incorporeal entity (οὐσία), subsisting itself,
and by itself, but giving its image to portions of formless matter,
and becoming the cause of their manifestation.   b

' Socrates and Plato suppose the ideas to be separable from the
matter, subsisting in the thoughts and in the presentations of
god, that is, of the mind.

' Aristotle allowed the specific forms and ideas to remain, not
however as separate from the matter, having freed himself from
the notion of its being done by god.

' The Stoic followers of Zeno said that the ideas are thoughts of
our own.'

CHAPTER XLVI

OF THE ORDER OF THE STARS.

' XENOCRATES thinks that the stars move on one superficies.   c

' The other Stoics that some are before others in height and depth.

' Democritus puts the fixed stars first, and next to these the
planets, after which the Sun, the Day-star, the Moon.

' Plato next to the position of the fixed stars sets first the
planet called Phaenon, that is Saturn : second Phaethon, that is
Jupiter ; third the Fiery, Mars ; fourth the Day-star, Venus ; fifth
Stilbon, Mercury ; sixth the Sun ; seventh the Moon.

' Of the Mathematicians some agree with Plato, but some put d
the Sun in the centre of all.

' Anaximander, and Metrodorus of Chios, and Crates think that
the Sun is placed highest of all, next to him the Moon, and
beneath them the fixed stars and planets.'

CHAPTER XLVII

OF THE COURSE AND MOTION OF THE STARS.

' ANAXAGORAS, Democritus, Cleanthes : all the fixed stars pass p. 847
from east to west.

---

846 c 2 Plutarch, 889 A

'Alcmaeon and the Mathematicians : the planets move in an opposite direction to the fixed stars ; for theirs is the contrary course from west to east.

'Anaximander : they are borne along by the circles and spheres on which they are each set.

'Anaximenes : the stars do not revolve beneath the Earth, but around it.

'Plato and the Mathematicians : the Sun, the Day-star, and Stilbon (Venus and Mercury) have equal orbits.'

CHAPTER XLVIII

b WHENCE THE STARS RECEIVE THEIR LIGHT.-

'METRODORUS : the fixed stars are all illumined by the Sun.

'Heracleitus and the Stoics : the stars are fed from the exhalation of the Earth.

'Aristotle : the heavenly bodies have no need of nourishment ; for they are not perishable but eternal.

'Plato : there is a common nourishment of the whole world
c and of the stars from themselves.'

CHAPTER XLIX

OF THE SO-CALLED DIOSCURI.

'XENOPHANES : what appear like stars upon the ships are little clouds which shine in consequence of a certain kind of motion.

'Metrodorus : they are flashes from the eyes which look at them with fear and amazement.'

CHAPTER L

d OF AN ECLIPSE OF THE SUN.

'THALES was the first who said that the Sun is eclipsed from the Moon (which is of an earthy nature) coming perpendicularly under it ; and that by reflexion in a mirror she is seen situated beneath the Sun's disk.

'Anaximander : from the closing of the orifice of the breathing-hole of the Sun's fire.

'Heracleitus: in consequence of the turning of the boat-like PLUTARCH figure, so that the concavity is above, and the convexity below facing our eyes.

'Xenophanes: by extinction, and then again there rises another Sun in the east. But he has incidentally mentioned an **p. 848** eclipse of the Sun lasting over the whole month, and again a total eclipse, so that the day seemed like night.

'Some say that it is a condensation of the invisible clouds coming over the Sun's disk.

'Aristarchus sets the Sun among the fixed stars, and makes the Moon move round the Sun's orbit, and the Sun's disk to be overshadowed in consequence of these inclinations.

'Xenophanes: there are many suns and moons, corresponding to the climes, and sections, and zones of the Earth: and at a certain season the Sun's disk falls into some section of the Earth which is not inhabited by us, and thus, as if stepping into a hole, **b** suffers eclipse. But the same author says that the Sun goes forward into infinity, but seems to revolve because of its distance.'

CHAPTER LI

OF AN ECLIPSE OF THE MOON.

'ANAXIMANDER: from the closing of the orifice of its circumference.

'Berossus: because of the turning of the dark side towards us. **c**

'Heracleitus: because of the turning of the boat-like figure.

'Of the Pythagoreans some say that it is an outshining and obstruction by our Earth or the counter-earth: but the more recent say that it is in consequence of the spreading of a flame which is gradually kindled in an orderly manner, until it produces the complete full moon, and decreases again in like manner until the conjunction, at which it is entirely extinguished.

'Plato, Aristotle, the Stoics, and the Mathematicians agree that it effects its monthly obscurations by travelling round with the Sun and sharing its illumination; but the eclipses by falling **d** into the shadow of the Earth when that comes between the two luminaries, or rather when it obstructs the light from the Moon.'

Chapter LII

Of the Moon's Aspect, and why it has an Earthlike Appearance.

PLUTARCH   'THE Pythagoreans say that the Moon has an earthlike appearance, because it is inhabited like our Earth, but by larger

p. 849 animals and more beautiful plants.   For the animals upon it are fifteen times as large, and emit no bodily secretion; and that the day is longer in the same proportion.

'Anaxagoras : on account of an unevenness in the mixture, because of its being both cold and earthy : for the misty part is mingled with the fiery, whence the Moon is also said to shine with false light.

'The Stoics : because of the admixture of air in its substance its composition is not pure.'

Chapter LIII

b   Of the Moon's Distances.

'EMPEDOCLES : the Moon is distant from the Sun twice as far as from the Earth.

'The Mathematical School : eighteen times as far.

'Eratosthenes : the Sun's distance from the Earth is four millions and eighty thousand stades : but the Moon's distance from the Earth seven hundred and eighty thousand stades.'

Chapter LIV

c   Of Years.

'A YEAR of Saturn is a period of thirty years: of Jupiter twelve; of Mars two; of the Sun twelve months; and the same for Mercury and Venus, for they run an equal course.   But the Moon's is thirty days: for this is the complete month from first appearance to conjunction.

'*The Great Year* some suppose to consist in a period of eight years, but others in nineteen years, and others in fifty-nine. Heracleitus makes it consist of eighteen thousand solar years : Diogenes of three hundred and sixty-five years, as many as the

year has days according to Heracleitus: but others of seven PLUTARCH
thousand, seven hundred, and seventy-seven years.'   d

So widely do the aforesaid persons differ from each
other in regard to things in the heavens above. But
now look also at their opinions about the Earth.

Chapter LV

Of the Earth.

' Thales and his followers say that the Earth is one.

' Hicetas the Pythagorean says that there are two, this and the
antipodal earth.

' The Stoics : the Earth is one, and finite.

' Xenophanes : from the lower part its roots reach into infinity,
and it is composed of air and fire.

' Metrodorus : the Earth is the deposit and sediment of the
water, and the Sun of the air.'   p. 850

Chapter LVI

Of the figure of the Earth.

' Thales and the Stoics : the Earth is spherical.

' Anaximander : it is like a stone pillar supporting the
surfaces.

' Anaximenes : like a table.

' Leucippus : like a kettle-drum.

' Democritus : like a disk in its extension, but hollow in the
middle.'

Chapter LVII

Of the position of the Earth.   b

' The followers of Thales say the Earth is the centre.

' Xenophanes : the Earth first, for its roots reach into infinity.

' Philolaus the Pythagorean : first, fire in the centre; for this
is the hearth of the universe : second, the antipodal Earth, and
third, the Earth which we inhabit, opposite to the antipodal both in
situation and revolution ; in consequence of which the inhabitants
of the antipodal Earth are not seen by those in this Earth.

' Parmenides was the first to mark off the inhabited parts of c
the Earth under the two tropical zones.'

Chapter LVIII
Of the Earth's Motion.

PLUTARCH ' ALL the others say that the Earth is at rest.

' But Philolaus the Pythagorean says that it revolves round the
d fire in an oblique circle, in like manner as the Sun and Moon.

' Heracleides of Pontus, and Ecphantus the Pythagorean make
the Earth move, not however by change of place, but by rotation,
turning like a wheel on an axle, from west to east, about its own
centre.

' Democritus : at first the Earth used to change its place,
owing to its smallness and lightness; but as in the course of
time it grew dense and heavy, it became stationary.'

After the utterance of these different opinions by the
noble philosophers concerning the Earth, hear now what
they say of the Sea.

Chapter LIX
p. 851 OF THE SEA, HOW IT WAS COMPOSED, AND WHY IT IS SALT.

' ANAXIMANDER says that the Sea is the remnant of the original
moisture, the greater part of which was dried up by the fire, and
the remainder changed through its burning heat.

' Anaxagoras : when the water, which in the beginning was
b a stagnant lake, was burnt up by the Sun's revolution, and the
greasy part evaporated, the remainder subsided into saltness and
bitterness.

' Empedocles : the Sea is the sweat of the Earth when scorched
by the Sun, because of the increased condensation.

' Antiphon : the sweat of the hot part, from which the included
moisture was separated, turned salt by being boiled down, which
happens always in the case of sweat.

' Metrodorus : from being drained through the earth it has par-
c taken of its density, just as liquids which are strained through ashes.

' Plato and his followers : of the elementary water the part
formed out of air, being condensed by cooling, became sweet; but
the part formed from earth, being evaporated by heat and
burning, became salt.'

So much, then, concerning the Sea. But as to those who professed to give physiological explanations about the whole world, and things celestial and ethereal, and the conception of the universe, how little they knew even of their own nature, you may learn from their discordant utterances on these points also, as follows.

Chapter LX

Of the parts of the Soul.   d

'Pythagoras, Plato: in the first analysis the Soul has two Plutarch parts; for it has one part rational and another irrational. But in close and exact consideration, its parts are three: for they distinguish the irrational into the irascible and the appetitive.

'The Stoics: it is composed of eight parts; five senses, sight, smell, hearing, taste, touch; and a sixth, speech; a seventh, generation; and an eighth, the actual ruling principle, from which proceeds the extension of all these through their proper p. 852 organs, in a similar manner to the tentacles of the polypus.

'Democritus, Epicurus: the Soul consists of two parts, its rational faculty being settled in the breast, and the irrational diffused over the whole complexity of the body.

'But Democritus thought that all things, even dead bodies, naturally partake of a certain kind of soul, because in an obscure way they have some warmth and sensation, though the greater part is dissipated.'

Chapter LXI

Of the ruling faculty.   b

'Plato, Democritus: it is in the head as a whole.

'Straton: between the eyebrows.

'Erasistratus: about the membrane of the brain, which he calls the epicranis.

'Herophilus: in the cavity of the brain, which is also its base.

'Parmenides: in the breast as a whole.

'Epicurus, and all the Stoics: in the heart as a whole.

'Diogenes: in the arterial cavity of the heart, which is full of c breath.

---

d 2 Plutarch, ibid. 898 E

PLUTARCH   ' Empedocles : in the composition of the blood.

'Others in the membrane of the pericardium: and others in the diaphragm. Some of the more recent philosophers say that it reaches through from the head to the diaphragm.

'Pythagoras: the vital power is around the heart; but the rational and intelligent faculty in the region of the head.'

So far, then, as to their opinions on these matters. Do you not think therefore that with judgement and reason we have justly kept aloof from the unprofitable and erroneous and vain labour of them all, and do not busy our-
d selves at all about the said subjects (for we do not see the utility of them, nor any tendency to benefit and gain good for mankind), but cling solely to piety towards God the creator of all things, and by a life of temperance, and all godly behaviour according to virtue, strive to live in a manner pleasing to Him who is God over all ?

But if even you from malice and envy hesitate to admit our true testimony, you shall be again anticipated by Socrates, the wisest of all Greeks, who has truthfully declared his votes in our favour. Those meteorological babblers, for instance, he used to expose in their folly, and say that they were no better than madmen, expressly
p. 853 convicting them not merely of striving after things unattainable, but also of wasting time about things useless and unprofitable to man's life. And this shall be testified to you by our former witness Xenophon, one of the best-known of the companions of Socrates, who writes as follows in his *Memorabilia* :

CHAPTER LXII

XENO-   c   ' No one ever yet saw Socrates do or heard him say anything
PHON   impious or unholy. For he did not discourse about the nature of the universe or the other subjects, like most of them, speculating upon the condition of the cosmos, as the Sophists call it, and by what forces of necessity the celestial phenomena severally are

---

853 c 1 Xenophon, *Memorabilia of Socrates,* I. i. 11

produced : rather he used to expose the foolishness of those who XENOPHON
troubled themselves about such things.

'And the first point he used to consider in regard to them was, d
whether they go on to study such matters, because they think
that they have already an adequate knowledge of human affairs,
or deem that they are doing their proper work in neglecting
human interests and speculating on the divine.

'And he used to wonder that they did not clearly see that it is
impossible for men to discover these things, since even those who
pride themselves most highly on the discussion of these matters
do not agree in opinion with each other, but are just like
madmen in their mutual feelings.

'For as among madmen some have no fear even of things
fearful, while others are afraid where no fear is; so some of
these think it no shame to say or do anything and everything even in a crowd, while others think it not right even
to go out among men : and some honour neither temple, **p. 854**
nor altar, nor anything else belonging to the gods, while
others worship any casual stocks and stones and wild beasts.
Also of those who study anxiously the nature of the universe some think that "being" is only one, others that
it is infinite in multitude : some too think that all things
are in perpetual motion, and others that nothing can ever be
moved : and some that all things are being generated and
perishing, but others that nothing could ever be generated or
perish.

'He also used to ask the following questions about them :
whereas those who study human affairs think that whatever they
have learned they will be able to practise both for themselves **b**
and for whomsoever they may wish, do those who search after
things divine think in like manner that when they know by what
forces of necessity phenomena are severally produced, they will
be able whenever they please to make winds and rains and
seasons, and whatever else of this kind they may need ?   Or,
without even hoping for anything of this sort, are they satisfied
merely to know how such phenomena are severally produced ?

'Such, then, was the nature of his remarks about those who
busied themselves with these matters : but he himself was always
discoursing of human interests, inquiring what was pious, what **c**

impious; what noble, what base; what just, what unjust; what sanity, what madness.'

These, then, were the opinions of Socrates. And next after him Aristippus of Cyrene, and then later Ariston of Chios, undertook to maintain that morals were the only proper subject of philosophy; for these inquiries were practicable and useful, but the discussions about nature were quite the contrary, neither being comprehensible, nor having any use, even if they were clearly understood.

For it would be no advantage to us, not even if soaring higher in the air than Perseus,

d   ' O'er ocean's wave, and o'er the Pleiades,'

we could with our very eyes survey the whole world, and the nature of all ' beings,' of whatever kind that is.

For we certainly shall not be on that account wiser, or more just or brave or temperate, nay, not even strong, or beautiful, or rich, without which advantages happiness is impossible.

Wherefore Socrates was right in saying that of existing things some are above us, and others nothing to us : for the secrets of nature are above us, and the conditions after death nothing to us, but the affairs of human life alone concern us.

p. 855   And thus, he said, he also dismissed the physical theories of Anaxagoras and Archelaus, and studied only

' Whate'er of good or ill our homes have known.'

And he thought besides that their physical discussions were not merely difficult and even impossible, but also impious and opposed to the laws. For some maintained that gods do not exist at all, and others, that the Infinite, or Being, or the One, are gods, and anything rather than those who are generally acknowledged.

Their dissension again, he said, was very great : for
b some represented the All as infinite, and others as finite ;

---

855 a 3 Homer, *Od.* iv. 392

and some maintained that all things are in motion, and others that nothing at all moves.

Moreover the following words of Timon of Phlius in his *Silli* seem to me the best of all on these very subjects:

> 'Say then, who urged them to the fatal strife?
> Echo's attendant rout: who filled with wrath.
> Against the silent, sent upon mankind
> A fell disease of talk, and many died.'

Do you see how at last these noble sages scoff at each c other? For instance, the same author, besides what I have quoted, describes their mutual jealousy and their battles and quarrels in the following style:

> 'There baneful Discord stalks with senseless shriek,
> Of murderous Strife the sister and ally,
> Who, blindly stumbling round, anon her head,   d
> With ponderous weight set firm, uplifts to hope.'

Since, however, we have now exhibited the dissension and fighting of these sages among themselves, and since the wholly superfluous, and unintelligible, and to us utterly unnecessary study and learning of all the other subjects in which the tribes of philosophers still take pride, have been refuted not by our demonstrations but by their own; nay more, since we have also plainly set forth the reason why we have rejected their doctrines and preferred the Hebrew oracles, let us at this point conclude our treatise on *The Preparation for the Gospel*; **p. 856** but the more complete treatise on *The Demonstration of the Gospel* it now remains for us to consider from a different basis of argument, which the question still needs for those who are to deal with its teaching.

It remains, therefore, to make answer to those of the circumcision who find fault with us, as to why we, being foreigners and aliens, make use of their books, which, as they would say, do not belong to us at all; or why, if we gladly accept their oracles, we do not also render our life conformable to their law.

---

b 6 Timon, *Fr.* 9 (Mullach I. p. 84); cf. Clem. Alex., *Strom.* **V.** 325 Sylb., Homer, *Il.* i. 8-10   o 5 Timon, *Fr.* 5; cf. Homer, *Il.* iv. 440-3

INDEX

Aaron 433 d, 434 c, 439 d.

Abae, temple burnt, *vid.* Phaÿllus 392 d.

Abaris, or Avaris, in Egypt 501 b.

Abel, 'sorrow' 518 b.

Abelbalus, king of Berytus 31 a, 485 b.

Abgarus, king of Osroëne 279 d.

Abraham, praised 309 c, d; receives circumcision 309, 310; mentioned by Berosus, Hecataeus, and Nicolaus Damascenus 417; taught Egyptians arithmetic and astrology 418 a, 419 a, 420 c; mentioned by Polyhistor and Eupolemus 418 c; taught Phoenicians 418 d; name, 'Father's Friend' 420 d; 505 years before Moses 484 d; derivation of name 518 c; mentioned by Orpheus 665 c.

Abydenus, mentions the flood 414 d; tower of Babel 416 b; Nebuchadnezzar 456 d; Nebuchadnezzar founder of Babylon 457 b; Babylon taken by Cyrus 457 c.

Abydos, 'the mystery' 198 a.

Academics, succession of 726 b; dissent from Plato 732 b.

Academy, first, Plato 726 a; division by Speusippus, Xenocrates, Polemo 726 b, c, 727 b.

Academy, second, Arcesilaus 727 c; third, Carneades and Cleitomachus 726 d; fourth, Philo, Charmidas 726 d; fifth, Antiochus 727 a.

Achelous, 'pure water' 111 d.

Acheron 670 a.

Acracanus, branch of Euphrates 457 c.

Acusilaus, mentioned 415 d, 488 b; founder of Greek history 478 b;

censures Hesiod 478 d; followed by Plato in Timaeus 497 d.

Adam and Enos, differ in meaning 307 c, 516 c.

Ἀδέσποτοι, books of unknown authors 420 b.

Adodus, king of Phoenician gods 38 c.

Adonis, allegorized by Porphyry 110 a.

Adrasteia, ' the Inevitable ' 818 a.

Adrastus, son of Talaus 238 c.

Adrian, *vid.* Hadrian.

Aeacus, his prayer 463 b, c; judge of the dead 579 d.

Aemilianus, son of Epithersis 206 c, 207 b.

Aenesidemus of Alexandria 758 d, 763 d; Ὑποτύπωσις 760 b; Στοιχειώσεις 761 b.

Aeon and Protogonos, Phoenician deities 34 b.

Aepytus 221 d.

Aeschines, orator 462 c.

Aeschines, Socratic philosopher 744 d.

Aeschylus, form and power of god 681 b, 689 b; verses criticized by Plato 643 c, 647 a.

Aesculapius, the sun (Porphyry) 112 c; not the sun 120 b, 121 a; killed by lightning 121 a; son of Apollo and Coronis 57 a; born at Tricca 124 a; Asclepiadae 121 a; son of Sydycus 37 d.

Aethiopians, *vid.* Ethiopians.

Africa, called from Afren, son of Abraham 422 a, b.

Africanus, his *Chronology* 487 d–491 d.

Agamemnon, Plato's derivation 518 a.

Agathocles of Syracuse, his sophism 733 c.

Euclus of Cyprus 495 c.
Eudoxus, mathematician 480 c,
482 b.
Euelpis of Carystus 155 d.
Euemerus of Messene, historian
and theologian 59 b, d ; mentions the Jews 458 b.
Euemerus of Tegea, atheist
753 b.
Eugamon of Cyrene, plagiarist of
Musaeus 462 d.
Evilmaluruchus, son of Nabuchodonosor 455 c ; slain by his
brother-in-law Neriglissar 455 c,
457 b.
Eumolpidae 66 b.
Eumolpus, ἐν Βακχικοῖς 27 d.
Eupolemus, wrote of Abraham
and the Jews 418 c ; of the prophecy of Elijah 447 a ; of Moses,
Joshua, Samuel, Saul 447 ; David,
Solomon 448, 449 ; of Solomon's
temple 449, 450, 451 ; of Jerusalem and the temple furniture
451 ; of Jeremiah 454 b ; see also
431 c, 452 a, 458 c.
Euripides, tragedian 157 c ; dismissed by Socrates 227 a ; commended by an oracle 227 c,
228 d, 229 a ; σκηνικὸς φιλόσοφος,
disciple of Anaxagoras 504 b.
Euripides, passages quoted, Fr.
of Syleus 242 c ; Phoenissae 19
258 c ; Phoen. 573 259 c ; Phoen.
549 259 c ; Medea 231 466 d ;
Melanippe 20 d, 466 d ; Antiope
679 d ; Pirithous 681 a ; Sisyphus
753 c.
Eurystheus 120 c.
Eusarthis 40 b.
Eusebius, on the first cause and
the second 320 c, 321 d ; Arian
tendency 321 d, 325 a ; peculiar
system of chronology 483 b,
502 d ; arrangement of his work
788, 789 ; on the many children
of the Patriarchs 310 d ; chronological canons 484 d ; Demonstration of the Gospel 789 d, 856 a.
Euthycles, a Locrian boxer 232 c.
Ezekiel, Iambic poem on Pharaoh
and the Jews 436 seqq. ; his
drama Ἐξαγωγή 439 d, 444 a.
Fables, i. e. Myths, referred to
natural phenomena 74 a ; how

far accepted by Romans 78 b,
79 d ; Greek, as explained by
Porphyry 97 d–115 ; allegorical
explanations refuted 119 c seq. ;
unworthy of wise men ; acknowledged and approved by gods
123 c ; fit for teaching children
575 d ; what they ought to be
576 b ; concerning gods to be
rejected 641–647, 649 a.
Faith, Christian, not groundless
3 d ; must be simple and docile
14 d ; needed in various arts 15 ;
approved by Plato especially in
the young 573 c ; their greatest
virtue 574 b ; in matters pertaining to the soul 575 b.
Fate, daughter of Uranus 37 c ;
more powerful than gods 238 c ;
seriously refuted by Eusebius
242–254 ; also by Oenomaus 255–
261 ; by Diogenianus 262–267 ;
by Alexander Aphrodisiensis
268–273 ; by Bardesanes 273–
281 ; by Origen 281–296 ; destroys philosophy, religion, retribution, carefulness, obedience
243, 244, 260 c, d, 281 c, d ;
annihilates liberty 244 a, 258 b,
266 c ; differs from natural law
246 c ; leaves no god 252 a ; inconsistent with Christian religion
253 a, 281 a ; makes punishment
unjust 260 b ; destroys all merit
260 d ; proved by Chrysippus
from Homer 262 a ; refuted by
Diogenianus 262 a ; why called
πεπρωμένον and εἱμαρμένη 263 c ;
made an efficient cause 268 d ;
identified with nature 270 b ;
disproved by differences of na-
tional customs 274 ; makes prayer
useless 282 fin.
Fire, preserved anciently in temples 28 d ; worshipped by Egyptians 94 a ; son of Genos (Phoenicians) 34 d ; connected with
man by Hebrews 517 b ; 'Fire
to fire,' proverb 510 c.
Flood, Noah's, mentioned by Chal-
dean Berosus 414 a ; by other
authors 414 b, c, d ; in the time
of King Sisithris 414 d ; foretold
by Cronos 414 d ; how far known
to Plato 587 d.

930

many visited Egypt and borrowed thence their ideas of the
infernal regions 480–482; taught
by Hebrew writers 460 d, 461 b,
663 d, 668 d.
Γυνή, Plato's derivation 517 b.

Hades, derivation 553 b.
Hadrian, abolished human sacrifice 156 b, 164 d.
Happiness, destroyed by eager
desires 387 a, 392 b; of the
wicked, what it is like 387 b;
true happiness, Hebrew idea
511 d; Aristotle's idea imperfect
794.
Harpagus 220 c.
Harpé, 'scimitar,' Thracian invention 475 d.
Hawk, sacred to the sun, in
Egypt 94 c, 116 d; compassion
on a dead man 94 c.
He, Hebrew letter 474 b.
Heaven, its nature 845 b; a
heavenly earth, Plato 564 d.
Heber, its meaning 520 b.
Hebrews, taught the Greek
philosophers 460, 461; according to Clement 663 d, 668 d;
mutually consistent 719 b, 720;
rightly preferred to Gentiles
301 b, 468 d; regarded the soul
more than the body 302 b;
religion older than Moses 304 b;
named from Heber 304 c, 309 b,
520 b; the Patriarchs 306 seq.;
best authority for their own
history 306 b; earliest Hebrews
not Jews 309 b; believe in providence and creation 317–319;
believe in angels 326 c, d, 327 a;
believe in daemons 328 d;
opinion of man's nature 330 c;
holiness of Moses' law, Philo
357 seq.; crimes punished by
death 357 d; respect for vows
358 d; humanity 358 d; obser-
vance of Sabbath 359 c; laws
known to all 360 b, 363 c;
sabbatical year 363 b; theocracy
361 d; tenacious of their own
laws 364 b, 368 d; priests their
judges 364 d; sublime ideas of
God 365 d; their sacrifices 365 d;
marriages 366 b; funerals 367 a;

filial duties 367 b; duties to
strangers 367 d; to brute
creatures 368 a, b; called by
Egyptians 'men of God' 372 a;
separate from other nations
371 d, 372 a; distinguish clean
and unclean birds 372 c;
animals with cloven hoof 373 b;
ruminants 373 c; bound to keep
God in remembrance 373 d,
374 a; mice and weasels unclean 374 d; sacrificed tame
animals 375 c; had twenty-two
letters, their names, &c. 474 b,
519 c; shepherds and kings in
Egypt 500 d; list of the judges
502 d; list of kings 503 a;
source of Plato's philosophy
509 seq.; their moral philosophy 511 d; dialectics 513 b;
poetry 514 a, b; names for
things 514 d, 516 a, 518 c; idea
of 'true man' 307 a, 507 c; why
God called 'Eloim' 517 c; Tetra-
grammaton, indicated by seven
vowels 519 d; their physical
philosophy 521 a; on true
'Being,' τὸ ὄν 523 d; acknowledged the Word of God 532–
534; commended by Orpheus
665 c.
Hecataeus, 415 d; On Abraham
417 b; book On Abraham and
Egyptians 680 d; younger than
Sophocles 680 d.
Hecataeus of Abdera, mentions
Jews 351 c, 408 a.
Hecataeus of Miletus (vid. Orig.
c. Cels I. 15, p. 334) 466 b.
Hecate, the Moon 113 c; her
apparel 113 c; queen of daemons
(vid. Serapis) 126 c; foul amours
126 c; oracle concerning herself 191 b; submits to incanta-
tion 193 c; prescribes forms for
her images 200 b, 201 c; her
symbols as Ceres 202 c, d.
Hector, Plato's derivation of
name 517 d.
Hegesarchus, boxer 266 a.
Hegesinus, succeeded by Carneades 737 a.
Heliopolis, Mnevis and Apis worshipped 117 c; infamous for
vice 162 d.